mpson

Ft. Rae Ft. Providence Artillery L.

Gr. Slave Ft.

Big I. & Ft. Ft. Resolution

wheldyahad

Slave R.

Hay R. Buffalo R. T North lined L.

Ft. Vermillion S Fts. Chipewyan Ft. Fond du Lac Black L.
Ft. du & Wedderburne
Old Ft. Tremble H L. Athabasca Black L.
ace R. Rouge R. or L. of the Hills

N O R

Pierre au Calumet Elk R. Athabasca or Wollaston L. L.
Loon L. Too-oot-awney

Bedfont Ho. S. Indian
White Fish L. Clear Wr. La Loche Portage Deer L. or Big L.
Lesser Slave L. & Ft. R. Methy L. & Ft. Carribeau
Buffalo L. or Deer L. Ho. Granville L.
N. W. Ho.
neboine La Crosse Ft. & L. Missinnippi Churchill or English R. Nelson
Red Deers L. Church Missionary Frog Port.
Athabasca R. Beaver L. L. La Ronge & Ft. Rapid Burntw.
Pembina R. Beaver R. Riv. Ft. Cold I. L. & Ho.

N. Saskatchawan Ft. George Green L. & Ft. Beaver L. Reed L.
Edmonton Ho. R. Pelican L. Cumberland Ho. Pine I. L. Playgreen L.
Beaver L. Manchester Ho. Finlays Basquia R. Moose L. & Ft.
Rocky Mt. Ho. Battle Ho. Cumberland St. Cedar L. Gt. Rap.
R. Ft. Pitt Nepowewin Christ Ch. Cross L.
Buffalo L. Carlton or A la Corne Red Sh. R.
Eaglehill Cr. S. Branch Ho. Ho. Deer R. Swan L.
Red Deers R. Capot R. Ft. & Ho. Fairfor
S. Saskatchawan Touchwood Hills Ho. Swan R.
Bow or Askow R. R. Elbow Ft. Hibernia Ft. Pelly
Chesterfield Ho. C Manitoba
Mochatsh Blackfoot Indians Quapelle Dauphin L. & Ho. L.
Bull Pound R. & Ft. Ellice Ft. Red Riv.
ne Ft. Birdstail Ft. Assiniboine R. White Hors.
head Ho. Boundary 1818 Brandon Ho. Portage
White Fish R. Turtle Mt. Ho. N.
Ma rias R. Porcupine R. Mouse R.
Medicine R. Milk R.
Union R.

The Curious Passage of Richard Blanshard

OTHER BOOKS BY BARRY GOUGH

Royal Navy and the Northwest Coast
To the Pacific and Arctic with Beechey
The Northwest Coast
Gunboat Frontier
First Across the Continent: Sir Alexander Mackenzie
Britannia's Navy on the West Coast
Fortune's a River
Historical Dictionary of Canada
From Classroom to Battlefield
Historical Dreadnoughts: Marder and Roskill
That Hamilton Woman
Churchill and Fisher: Titans at the Admiralty
Pax Britannica
The Elusive Mr. Pond
Juan de Fuca's Strait
Possessing Meares Island

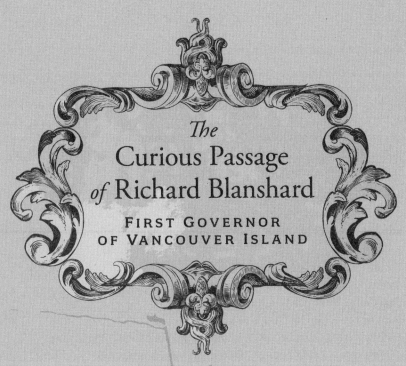

The
Curious Passage
of Richard Blanshard

FIRST GOVERNOR
OF VANCOUVER ISLAND

Barry Gough

HARBOUR
PUBLISHING

Harbour Publishing
P.O. Box 219, Madeira Park, BC, V0N 2H0
www.harbourpublishing.com

Edited by Audrey McClellan
Indexed by Colleen Bidner
Text design by Roger Handling / terrafda.com
Dust jacket design by Dwayne Dobson
Endsheet image: Detail from a historical map of North America by
    John Arrowsmith (1790-1873) courtesy John Motherwell
Printed and bound in Canada
Printed on 100% recycled paper

Harbour Publishing acknowledges the support of the Canada Council for the Arts, the Government of Canada, and the Province of British Columbia through the BC Arts Council.

Library and Archives Canada Cataloguing in Publication

Title: The curious passage of Richard Blanshard : first governor of Vancouver
    Island / Barry Gough.
Names: Gough, Barry M., author.
Description: Includes bibliographical references and index.
Identifiers: Canadiana (print) 20230532446 | Canadiana (ebook)
    20230532578 | ISBN 9781990776380 (hardcover) | ISBN 9781990776397
    (EPUB)
Subjects: LCSH: Blanshard, Richard, 1817-1894. | LCSH: Governors—British
    Columbia—Vancouver Island—Biography. | LCSH: Vancouver Island
    (B.C.)—Biography. | LCSH: Vancouver Island (B.C.)—History—
    19th century. | CSH: British Columbia—History—1849-1871. | LCGFT:
    Biographies.
Classification: LCC FC3822.1.B53 G68 2023 | DDC 971.1/02092—dc23

Dedicated to David Thornton McNab

So the world changes, so our feverish activities fill the spaces between the two silences; but to an old sailor, who recalls many men and things in the peace of his last days, it is difficult sometimes to distinguish phantom from reality, and easier to believe that the pines are still waving in their solitude, and the rivers running undisturbed to the great ocean.

—Admiral John Moresby, then lieutenant in HMS *Thetis*, recollecting Vancouver Island, 1852

The settlement of our colonies was never pursued upon any regular plan; but they were formed, grew, and flourished as accidents, the nature of the climate, or the dispositions of private men, happened to operate.

—Edmund Burke, *An Account of the European Settlements in America*

Queen Victoria's great seal of the Colony of
Vancouver Island and its Dependencies.
Courtesy of Wikimedia Commons

Abbreviations

Bart.   Baronet
C-in-C Commander-in-Chief, Royal Navy Pacific Station
HBC   Hudson's Bay Company
HMS   Her Majesty's Ship
PSAC   Puget's Sound Agricultural Company

Prologue

Our scene opens in dramatic fashion in the convulsive 1840s in North America. The United States quested westward. Texas, Mexico, California and Oregon were acquired, partitioned or otherwise reconfigured. In what seemed the twinkling of an eye, the United States added 1,366 miles to its Pacific coastline, from Baja California to Juan de Fuca's Strait. In the circumstances, Great Britain's claim to a transcontinental empire, the future Canada, was in jeopardy. These years in the history of the farthest west were compressed and complicated. Documentary evidence now available shows a tense time when all seemed uncertain. Indigenous America was about to be changed, overrun by imperial powers vying for control of the last wilderness of the continent in those latitudes. Technology was subverting old economies. Pestilence reduced Indigenous numbers. The processes were relentless and had lasting legacies, many of them those of regret, charged with cries for reconciliation and atonement. The march of History continues, bearing all before. The past cannot be cancelled.

The year 1849 ranks as of supreme importance in the history of the Pacific Northwest. That year stirring events took place: California's gold rush, proclamation of the Oregon Territory, and transfer of the depot of the Hudson's Bay Company from Fort Vancouver on the Columbia River to Fort Victoria on Camosun waterway at Vancouver Island. To complete the list, there was the creation of "the Colony of Vancouver's Island and its Dependencies" and, last but not least, the appointment of Richard Blanshard as the colony's governor and commander-in-chief.

In this book, our minds are called back to a decade before the epochal British Columbia gold rush of 1858. Britain led the world in industrial output, machinery and invention, spinning and weaving, shipbuilding and shipping, and insurance and seaborne trade. London was the world's banker. Britain was leader in naval and mercantile seamanship. Britannia ruled the waves—and, it might be said, waived the rules. The "surplus population" of the British Isles flowed overseas, forming colonies and dominions under the Union Jack—and, in so doing, reordering spaces occupied by Indigenous peoples. The sordid trade in slaves to the Americas, from which Britain had so shamefully profited in the past, had been stopped by British diplomatic pressure and naval coercion. Plantation slavery had been abolished in the British Empire. Plantation owners had been compensated under provisions defined by Parliament. Some persons believed the Empire to be an opportunity to pursue God's high and holy work: "at heaven's command" was their motif. But everywhere there were difficulties. Imperial obligations spelled bureaucratic quagmires for British ministries. Benjamin Disraeli, later the most eloquent of imperialists, contended that colonies were "millstones around our necks." Other statesmen thought similarly, believing that free trade would make empire obsolete. Trade, not dominion, counted most. Still, cutting colonies adrift was never considered.

In the United States, in these same ten years, different circumstances prevailed. Texas, Mexico and California came under the acquisitive view of proponents of "manifest destiny." Rhetoric of restless American statesmen matched settler ambitions to have farms and ranches in soil-rich Oregon. The incomers had been led to believe that the British and the Indigenous peoples would melt before them. Slavery and the expansion of slaveholding cast long shadows over the western frontier. Removal of Indigenous peoples and "Indian wars" were the order of the day. The US Army provided means of coercion. The American Empire marched westward to Pacific shores and threatened to turn north.

In 1849, as the decade closed, final scenes of the far-western drama were being played out. The Hudson's Bay Company (HBC or "the Company"), central to our story, was proxy empire. One man, Governor Richard Blanshard, Queen Victoria's representative, had been appointed the constituted guardian of the northern realm, headquartered in what he called Victoria. Though he bore the royal commission—and he had been recommended by the Hudson's Bay Company—it remained to be seen if he would be a misfit or would find a place among the field officers of the Company on the spot. In great matters, as Admiral Lord Nelson said, something had to be left to chance.

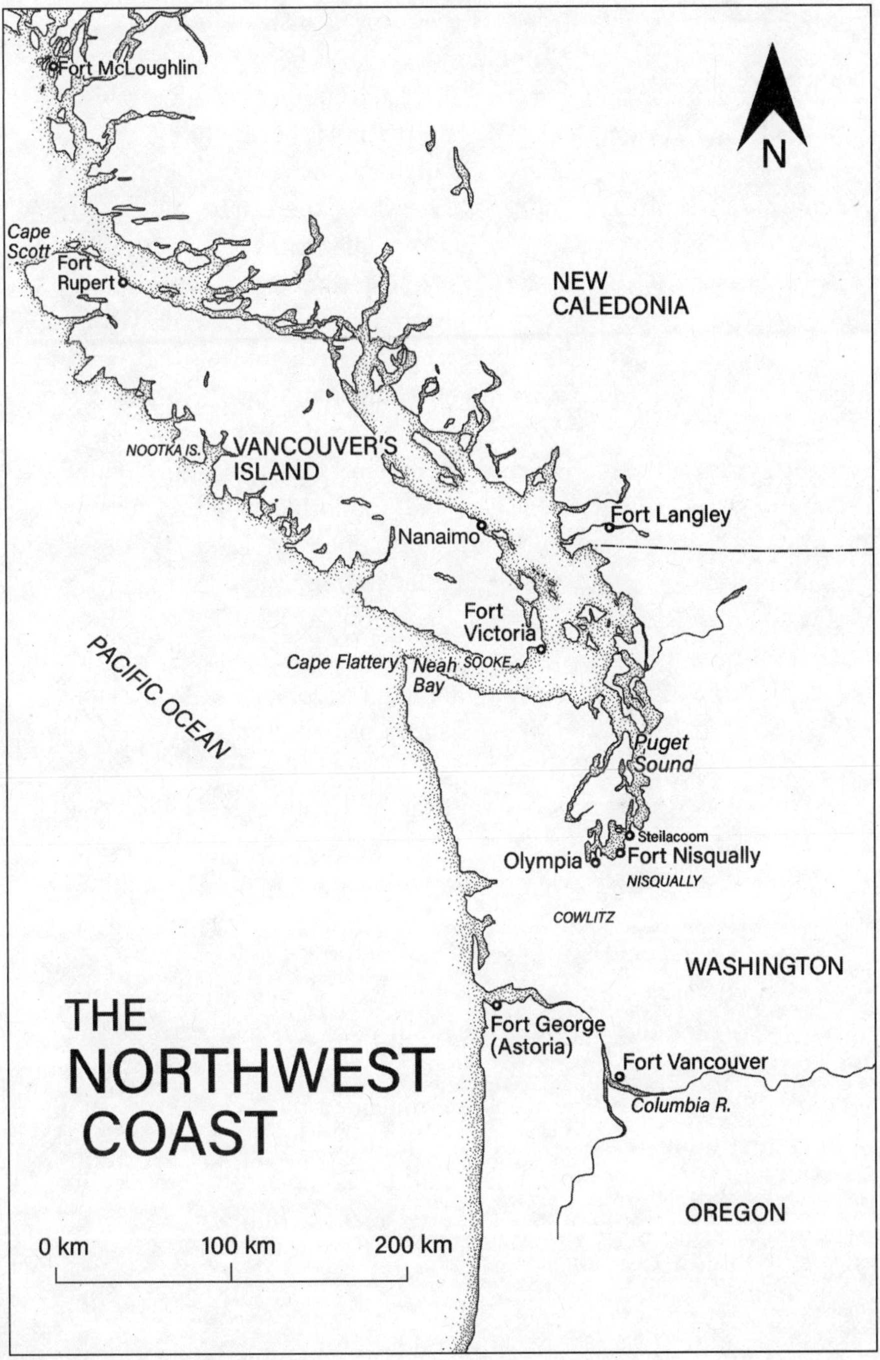

THE NORTHWEST COAST

Fort McLoughlin

Cape Scott

Fort Rupert

NEW CALEDONIA

NOOTKA IS.

VANCOUVER'S ISLAND

Fort Langley

Nanaimo

PACIFIC OCEAN

Fort Victoria

SOOKE

Cape Flattery

Neah Bay

Puget Sound

Steilacoom

Olympia

Fort Nisqually

NISQUALLY

COWLITZ

WASHINGTON

Fort George (Astoria)

Fort Vancouver

Columbia R.

OREGON

0 km   100 km   200 km

Map by Emma Biron

Part I:

In Fields Unknown

Chapter 1:
Faraway World

Early that wintry day in March 1850, seven weary weeks out of sight of land, the well-dressed London stranger, a bachelor aged thirty-two, stood at the ship's rail taking in the immensity of the unfolding scene. Snow flurries obscured the rising sun. Snow, heavy in places, blanketed unfamiliar shores.

From Her Britannic Majesty's paddlewheel sloop-of-war *Driver*, steadily thumping forth on imperial purpose, all that His Excellency Richard Blanshard could make out to port, in reflected purple light upon the northern side, was a densely forested, rock-clad island rising to considerable height. Vancouver's Island they called it in those far-off days. This was his destination.

To starboard, in contrast, the fourth corner of the United States rose to greet him, a dark rampart reaching upward four to seven thousand feet in ice-capped grandeur; this was called the Olympic Range. The rugged wall vanished to the eastern horizon, then seemed to run north along the Cascade Mountains, past a volcano known as Mount Baker, as far as the human eye could see.

The Strait of Juan de Fuca, the fabled waterway between Vancouver's Island and the United States, although thirteen miles broad where it enters the north Pacific Ocean, narrows to eleven at Race Rocks, off Vancouver Island. In all seasons, winds blow up or down this passageway. Some sixty miles east of the open Pacific, the strait becomes a basin of considerable size; it is now sometimes called the Salish Sea. This is a playground of tides and currents. Then it darts to the northwest through islands and devious passages before it rejoins the ocean, three hundred miles distant. North again lies the central British Columbia coast of islands and inlets. The Queen Charlotte Islands, now Haida Gwaii, are prominent. Beyond again are Alaska and the lands and seas of faraway Siberia, Japan, Korea and China. In all, the

Governor Blanshard's main conveyance, Her Britannic Majesty's paddlewheel Sloop *Driver*, shown here operating under steam, a technical innovation that allowed the vessel to make steady progress upwind, or in light airs. *Cormorant* and *Virago*, also to call at Esquimalt in early colonial years, were of the same versatile, powerfully gunned class of vessel. *Image PDP00286 courtesy of the Royal BC Museum*

majesty and grandeur of this watery, island-studded and mountainous maze bounded on the dreamily unimaginable. Here was splendour without ceasing.[1]

These were not empty seas and shores. Rather, they were favourable, food-rich locales of Indigenous peoples who lived in numerous villages, with individual languages and customs, rivals one to another, competitive and warlike. They were seaborne in their workaday and seasonal habits, dependent on the resources of sea and shore. As of 1846, diphtheria was reducing their numbers, and from 1847 to 1850, measles had spread via transportation systems and trading patterns. As geographer Robert Galois has written, "Disease was an integral and devastating component in the dialectic of contact."[2]

Before the advent of a reliable census, populations of these people on Vancouver Island were a matter of guesswork. One authority suggests all Songhees numbered 2,700 in 1780 but 488 in 1906. The same source gives the Nootka or Nuu-chah-nulth at 6,000 and 2,159 respectively, and the Kwakiutl or Kwakwaka'wakw (including mainland) at 4,500 and 1,100 respectively.[3] Blanshard himself estimated Vancouver Island's Indigenous population at 10,000—close to the mark.

In April 1792, surveyor Captain George Vancouver, Royal Navy, remarked on the beauty and fertility of the southern shore, the country around Discovery Bay and that great inland sea, Puget Sound: "To describe the beauties of this region will on some future occasion be a very grateful task to the pen of the skillful panegyrist. The serenity of the climate, the innumerable pleasing landscapes, and the abundant fertility that unassisted nature puts forth, require only to be enriched by the industry of man with villages, mansions, cottages, and other buildings, to render it the most lovely country that can be imagined, while the labour of the inhabitants must be rewarded in the bounties which Nature seems ready to bestow on civilization."[4]

Half a century passed before the process Captain Vancouver had imagined was alive and active, and an epic chapter of Vancouver Island and British Columbia history was about to open. Then, as now, the promise of this waterway as a gateway of commerce was boundless. The Strait of Juan de Fuca was a waterway linking two shores. Yet it was also a barrier. An invisible boundary line ran down its middle. The stark difference in the histories and character of these two countries would become clear to Blanshard, and he was among the earliest to realize this. The writing of history is the art of comparison, and so it is in the recounting of Blanshard's experience in relationship to his nemesis, Chief Factor James Douglas.

On the afternoon of 14 March 1843, the Hudson's Bay Company's paddlewheel steamer *Beaver*, from Nisqually, at the head of Puget Sound, anchored in Shoal (McNeill) Bay, southernmost Vancouver Island.[5] Next morning Douglas led an expedition ashore with the objective of building a stockaded post. From minuscule beginnings, Fort Victoria was designated to be the new and robust seat of corporate empire on the Pacific. It was to become the marine depot of the Hudson's Bay Company's coastal and Pacific trade. Few events in Canada's western history are of this significance. From this derived Victoria, future capital of the province of British Columbia.

Seven years after the founding of Fort Victoria, a scheme was being implemented under British authority for a colony proper, one with settlers, all under English law and Colonial Office surveillance. Critics of the Company thought the scheme an utter folly. They were not far off the mark, as will be seen. All the same, this was to be a corporate development with loose imperial protection. So it was that the *Driver* steamed forward on the journey that would bring Governor Richard Blanshard to his fragile seat of authority.

For the observer aboard the *Driver* that day, the splendour, even desolation, of the scene masked old international quarrels for possession. Blanshard knew the essentials of the story. The Nootka Sound controversy, which began in 1789, had been one of the dramatic diplomatic crises of the eighteenth century. It ended Spain's quest to guard the northern reaches of New Spain. Yuquot, on Nootka Island, situated to the west of Vancouver Island, had been the point of intersection of Spanish, British and Russian aspirations. By the Nootka Convention of 1790, Britain secured rights of navigation, whaling and trade with Indigenous peoples. Spain sold its claims to the United States in 1819, reinforcing the insurgent influence of Boston sea otter traders among Indigenous peoples. The North West Company of Canada gained an ascendancy in New Caledonia and in the Columbia Basin. In 1814, the Treaty of Ghent ended the bitter Anglo-American War of 1812. That conflict left bruised feelings on both sides of the Atlantic. At this juncture, and in keeping with the terms of peace, commissioners set to work. The resulting Convention of 1818 extended the boundary between the United States and the British territories in North America from the Lake of the Woods to the Stony (Rocky) Mountains along the forty-ninth parallel of latitude. By other treaties, imperial Russia's southward quest was contained at 54°40' N latitude, to the satisfaction of London and Washington, DC.[6] The remaining vast expanse of real estate was often called Old Oregon or, more correctly, the Oregon country. The Hudson's Bay Company, assuming the North West Company's extensive trade in 1821, reorganized all business in what it called the Columbia, later Western, Department. All the same, under the Convention of 1818, renewed indefinitely in 1827, this vast region was without sovereignty, and here Britain and the United States vied for ultimate control of the last quarter. Either party could cancel the arrangement on twelve months' notice, thereby threatening war.

The stumbling block, the bone of contention, was establishment of a final boundary to the Pacific Ocean. From the voyage to northwest America by Vitus Bering in 1741 until the arrival of American farmers on the Columbia River almost a century later, the territory was the unchallenged domain of the trapper and the fur trader carrying on business with the Indigenous peoples. On the coast and in the Pacific cordillera, British and American traders had been resenting each other's presence for decades. Bickering was the order of the day. With reduced expectations of success, Britain's Foreign Office recommended to the Company the wisdom of consolidating its commercial activities north of the lower Columbia River, thereby reinforcing British claims to sovereignty. Fort Vancouver was duly established in 1825. The Columbia River south of the forty-ninth parallel of latitude seemed to many a natural boundary. But events overtook expectations.

Meantime, expedition reports from William Slacum and Charles Wilkes stressed the future importance of Puget Sound to the United

States as a maritime nation. Secretary of State John Quincy Adams foresaw that this distant region would become part of the republic. Preventing further British territorial expansion in the New World became a national project in the press and in Congress. The "Oregon question" preoccupied party politics. Manifest destiny's blustery "Fifty-four forty or fight!" formed an incendiary ingredient in United States affairs. Possessing all Oregon would fulfill national destiny and complete a scheme of free development for settlement and growth that seemed, to the American mind, providential. War was a fearsome prospect. The diplomats held the day, to American advantage: war over Oregon was averted. The Americans did not get all: they settled for Adams's old line of the forty-ninth parallel.

The terms of the Oregon Treaty were ratified by the United States Senate on 15 June 1846 and agreed to by the government of the United Kingdom. The agreement called for a demarcation between territories of Britain and the United States west of the Rocky Mountains along "the forty-ninth parallel of north latitude to the middle of the channel which separates the continent from Vancouver's Island; and thence southerly through the middle of the said channel, and of Fuca's Straits to the Pacific Ocean."

The Hudson's Bay Company had pressed British negotiators for protection of its properties "south of the line" and for protection of free navigation and commerce. The influence of the firm was surprisingly small when dealing with the Foreign Office: it had had no part in the decision to propose the forty-ninth parallel, with Britain retaining all of Vancouver Island. Nor did the negotiators insist on free and open navigation of the Columbia River for the Company and all British subjects, as specified in the second article. However, emphasis on the obligation of the British government to guard the interests of the Hudson's Bay Company and the subsidiary Puget's Sound Agricultural Company was reflected in the third and fourth articles. I quote them here in full. These were the source of much trouble experienced by Company officers in Oregon:

Article III
In the future appropriation of the territory south of the forty-ninth

parallel of north latitude, as provided in the first article of this treaty, the possessory rights of the Hudson's Bay Company and of all British subjects who may be already in the occupation of land or other property, lawfully acquired within the said territory, shall be respected.
Article IV

The farms, lands, and other property of every description belonging to the Puget's Sound Agricultural Company on the north side of the Columbia River, shall be confirmed to the said company. In case, however, the situation of those farms and lands should be considered by the United States to be of public and political importance, and the United States' Government should signify a desire to obtain possession of the whole, or of any part thereof, the property so required shall be transferred to the said Government, at a proper valuation, to be agreed upon between the parties.

To recap, in 1846 the border had been pushed westward from the Rocky Mountains to the open Pacific Ocean via the Strait of Juan de Fuca, leaving all Vancouver Island in British hands. In a rush to demarcate this boundary, mistakes had been made. HBC interests north and south of the lower Columbia had been sacrificed. The British foreign secretary, Lord Aberdeen, was careless of details.[7] The San Juan archipelago lay at the eastern end of the Strait of Juan de Fuca, and no one knew exactly the main channel leading through this maze of rock and water northward into the Strait of Georgia. For the moment, there the matter rested. What counted was that the favoured isle that came to be named after Captain Vancouver lay in British hands. British diplomats had refused to budge on this issue.

Moreover, when the southern border of the future British Columbia was determined, all that remained was called Oregon. From Oregon was carved off Washington, from Washington was set off Idaho, and from Idaho, for the most part, was carved off Montana. The country south of the line was already seeing the setting down of a raw American frontier society, which in the main was distrustful of British authority under the Hudson's Bay Company and the Puget's Sound Agricultural Company.

Vancouver Island offered the place for consolidation of Company business, an anchor of commercial empire on the coast with tentacles to the cordilleran interior. Fort Vancouver had given way under corporate decision-making that if you could not stay, you must certainly go.[8] Still, there had been a contest, hotly waged, within British politics as to who should manage a new colony on Vancouver Island that could keep out American squatters. Mormons wanted it, as did a British whaling firm. A Scottish crofters' agency had eyed it as a sheep farm, and a British syndicate saw potential in its coal.

In the end, there could be no dislodging the Hudson's Bay Company. The corporation had a nascent settlement at Fort Victoria, posts far to the north, even a long experience trading with the Indigenous peoples. Peace with the Indigenous peoples was an article of faith—peace for the purpose of profit. However, apart from the costs of occasional visits by British warships to give reassurance to the HBC, the British government intended to spend not one penny on developing a settlement of Britons north of the line. Economy was the first article of the financial creed of British politicians. The Colonial Office, under the 3rd Earl Grey, had guided the process through rocky times. We will enlarge on these details below.

The stranger at the ship's rail knew these historical realities. The Strait of Juan de Fuca, a waterway of forgotten dreams and a gateway of trade and empire linking old and new worlds, formed the passageway for the final leg of the *Driver*'s passage. As of yet, no lighthouse or lightship guided mariners in this waterway, and sailing directions had not yet been published, though Admiralty charts based on 1846 surveys gave reliable advice to mariners. To the uninformed mariner, finding the entrance to serviceable ports or places of refuge was often a matter of good fortune or rested on information gathered from some previous vessel. Introduction of steam to the Royal Navy removed one element of chance. Steam-powered vessels were less dependent on wind and tides.

The *Driver* was a state-of-the-art wooden black-hulled paddle sloop (designated as such by the Navy).[9] In those days a big vessel, at 1,058 tons burthen, she carried a full ship's rig. Everything aboard exhibited spit and polish. She was designed to carry a heavy armament in wartime, less in these times of peace. She had a ship's complement of 165: 20 commissioned and non-commissioned officers, and 145 other ranks and Royal Marines. The height of the steam funnel of the *Driver* was disadvantageous, because on the Pacific Station it was necessary to make long hauls under sail. The problem had been presented to the mechanics, or artificers, at Valparaiso, Chile, the Royal Navy's Pacific Station headquarters, and they modified the funnel so it could be lowered or raised as required. Tests at sea were conducted; these revealed that the vessel could outsail the flagship, the ship-of-the-line *Asia*. As modified, the *Driver* was a high-performance vessel under sail or steam. It was the first steam vessel to circumnavigate the globe, and in 1861 came to grief on Mayaguana Island in the West Indies.

Captain of the *Driver*, Commander Charles Richardson Johnson, was a significant figure in the evolution of steam in the Navy.[10] He had entered the Service in 1826, served as lieutenant in line-of-battleships in the Mediterranean, and was commended by a senior officer for his ability, zeal and activity in the capture of an American slaver on the Guinea coast. He studied steam propulsion at the Navy's Woolwich engineering establishment, then commanded the first purpose-built steam vessel, the *Comet*. He was promoted commander in 1847. His prospects soared when he was appointed to the *Driver*, bound for the Pacific via Magellan Strait to join the squadron based on Valparaiso. Here was a sailor who had known "the life on the ocean wave," and he was about to discover the influence of a British gunboat in complicated circumstances. He was an agent of Pax Britannica, as was his passenger, Richard Blanshard.

How Blanshard reached the *Driver* demonstrates the tyrannies of distance and communications in those far-off days. Seven months previous, having been interviewed by the HBC's directors in London and nominated by the Company's chairman, Sir John Henry Pelly, Richard Blanshard had been duly approved by the Colonial Office as the new governor of what was designated as "the Colony of Vancouver's Island and its Dependencies." His orders called for him to bring into effect and administer Queen Victoria's rule in the colony. Colonial Secretary Earl Grey's agreement to having the Company nominate the governor rested on the assumption that "as the power of the Governor would be restrained by an Assembly representing the inhabitants, I can see no danger in allowing the Company to select him."[11]

On 14 October 1849, Blanshard, his manservant Thomas Robinson and their baggage embarked on the Royal Mail Steam Packet Company's *Medway* at Southampton. They were destined for the far side of the world. Perhaps loved ones in their finery were at quayside. Fond farewells would have been spoken—and promises made of an early return. Robinson, from Liverpool, and a world voyager himself, was a sailor turned warehouseman; on short notice, he accepted an engagement to Blanshard as manservant. A prior connection seems likely, and Blanshard was to look after his interests in the future. Robinson recounts in his journal a happy trans-Atlantic crossing via beautiful, warm and festive Madeira. Some passengers put on a play, with Richard Blanshard taking the part of Sir Anthony in Sheridan's *The Rivals*. Robinson sewed his dress for him. Perhaps, as one historian merrily suggests, the spoof was a foretaste of what was to come.[12] The packet called at Saint Thomas and San Juan. At Kingston, Jamaica, Blanshard and Robinson shifted to the *Avon*, and presently reached Cartagena, Colombia, on the Spanish Main. Next, on 22 November, they stepped ashore at Colón, a steamy port at the mouth of the Chagres River. It was then called Aspinwall, after one of the founders of the projected Panama Railway. Colón, a hotbed of lethal fevers, stood on Manzanillo Island, separated from the mainland by dismal swamps.

Blanshard faced a rude awakening in this fetid and detestable zone and was happy to leave Colón. Transiting the Isthmus of Panama in a "bongo," a large dugout made of a single mahogany log and poled by locals who wore little clothing, proved perilous. For four nights, passengers huddled together on the floor of the bongo, pestered by lice, fleas and, most dangerous of all, mosquitos. They passed through swamps, jungle, hanging vines and banana groves, the silence of the rainforest broken by screaming parrots and chattering monkeys.[13] Likely Blanshard contracted malaria at this time. At the way station Cruches, he and other travellers exchanged bongos for mules, then followed the rough mountain trail so familiar to California-bound forty-niners. Panama Port, on Pacific shores, was happily reached 28 November. "The first view of these waters in the bay of Panama is remarkable as reviving all the romantic associations which the tales of youth threw around that vast ocean—coral islands, golden strands, missionary adventures, Spanish galleons, British privateers, and Red Indians [sic]," remarked a man of the cloth bound for Vancouver Island not long after the governor's transit.[14]

Blanshard had been told that the point of rendezvous with the Navy would be the port of Panama. However, no British ship wearing a White Ensign lay in sight: Admiralty orders had failed to reach the commander-in-chief (C-in-C) at Valparaiso in time. Ships "on station" worked the vast Pacific and might be found visiting Tahiti or Honolulu, Mazatlán or Sitka, and the effectiveness of the overstretched squadron depended on water and provisions, the need for repairs, the proximity of secure anchorages and the total available manpower. Panama was only an occasional port of call. Blanshard found it crowded with Yankees awaiting passage to San Francisco, entryway to the California goldfields. Panama Port was a gathering place of fortune seekers. From there the Pacific Mail Steamship Company ran four ships to San Francisco, return. In 1849, six hundred merchant ships cleared American east coast ports for the Golden Gate, and these ships, jammed with men impatient to pan for gold in California's streams, were said to carry large loads of freight and equipment as well.

Blanshard awaited his ship in vain, but learned from a British merchant, Captain Smith, that he should catch the next Pacific Steam Navigation Company vessel south to Callao. There, he was told, one of Her Majesty's ships would surely be found, protecting British commercial interests. Blanshard took this advice. Pleasant days were spent in Lima, with its splendid president's palace and cathedral to visit. Well-dressed females attracted Robinson's comments. Ice cream was available in the lovely plaza so typical of Spanish colonial capitals. Blanshard met Rear Admiral Sir Phipps Hornby, C-in-C Pacific. The admiral, keen to back British interests at Vancouver Island, and under instructions to do so, explained that HMS *Driver* awaited them at Callao.

On the morning of 17 January 1850, Blanshard and Robinson found the *Driver* at Callao, the port for Lima. Commander Johnson was on the lookout for him. He had received orders to deliver the governor to Vancouver Island, to aid the colony as required and to return to Callao via San Francisco.[15] The guests were piped aboard. Blanshard and Robinson would have felt a sense of relief after their tedious and dangerous passage across the isthmus. Now their adventure to the northwest coast of North America could begin.

At three in the afternoon the man-of-war set sail. An impressive eight knots was made under canvas. But the wind dropped and the vessel was becalmed for a few hours. Blanshard and Robinson were amused by the sailors at cutlass exercise, practising cut and thrust with the Navy's short, curved sword to prepare for close combat. Boarding nets and pikes were still carried in those languid days of Pax Britannica to prevent hostile forces from boarding.

Once the ship was moving again, a course was shaped westward under sail so as to cross the equator (done 30 January), then catch the northeast trades to near the Tropic of Cancer. From there strong northerlies and westerlies drove them on the long run toward the North American coast, with landfall at Cape Flattery.

For Blanshard, fair days passed at sea, with agreeable companionship among officers and men. He would have enjoyed the wardroom or officers' mess, with convivial chatter and bonhomie. Water and provisions were always at a premium, especially on long passages in the Pacific, that desert of fresh water. Tales from this time tell of Her Majesty's ships facing water shortages. Moreover, meal allowances were reduced—provisions for four persons were allotted to six. The ship's surgeon, Thomas Summerville, watched for the appearance of scurvy, that grey peril of the seas. The promise of fresh food, rest and repair, and recuperative time ashore could be expected at Esquimalt, Vancouver Island. Reports from commanders of British warships had said so.[16] In fact, that fair haven was known to ship's companies of vessels on Pacific Station as an agreeable location, though socially isolated—a solitary forested port populated by Indigenous bands.

Nearing the North American continent, the *Driver* fought heavy squalls and rising seas. All of a sudden, fair westerlies sped the passage to thirty miles from Cape Flattery, guardian entrance to the Strait of Juan de Fuca. "It then fell calm," recounted Commander Johnson, "with every appearance of its continuing so, with thick snowy weather." Taking into consideration the fact that vessels were often delayed a fortnight or more at the entrance of the strait, and bearing in mind that not a moment was to be lost, Johnson ordered steam raised for the first time since Callao. Any expenditure of coal at sea had to be accounted for. Design speed, the maximum speed the ship was designed for, was 9¾ knots, but, in the circumstances, it is likely the boilers and mechanisms delivered a service speed of 8 knots to conserve fuel.

With Cape Flattery now near and nightfall approaching, the vessel made for Neah Bay, on the headland forming the south point of entrance into the Strait of Juan de Fuca. This was home of the intrepid whale hunters, the Makah. Before dark on 8 March, the vessel came to anchor. From Callao, an extraordinarily swift passage of fifty days had been made almost entirely under canvas. There was no time for rest. The drums rolled, announcing gun drill. One of the big (and new) 68-pounders was fired, "which startled the natives," Robinson noted.[17] The sailors amused themselves by trading over the ship's side with the Makah, one sailor acquiring a bear skin for a shirt.

Blanshard now had time to take in the dark and forbidding atmosphere of this faraway place; no Portsmouth, Callao or Panama this. The rugged, heavily treed Northwest Coast (and its waterways) provided a thick-textured physical backdrop, while the Indigenous world, with its varieties and complexities, was something incomprehensible, alien, even formidable. The physical world was not foreign to the British eye, for many an explorer, going back to Captain James Cook, had described Nootka, but the Indigenous peoples, with all their languages and dialects, only interacted with the outsiders in the nexus of trade. Here were two worlds in contact, a marine borderland. But such equality as had existed in the old age of the sea otter chiefs and Boston traders was about to be upset by the imposition of American and British trading power that came by sea or overland. The *Driver's* arrival was at this very marked edge of the new world order.

ᗡᗡᗡ

About a half-hour before noon on 9 March, a Saturday, after transit from Neah Bay, the *Driver* anchored off Ogden Point, Victoria's Outer

Harbour, on the east side of the tight entrance to the restless tidal waterway leading to Fort Victoria. The Admiralty chart of the port showed that a bar guarded the entrance. Accordingly, a pilot with local knowledge was essential. The *Driver* could not be hazarded in the narrow entrance, less than a mile wide.

Local Indigenous people call the passage Camosun, or Cmaamosack—"the rush of waters" or "running water."[18] Some Indigenous Knowledge Keepers say that the place name is a variant of the Lekwungen word *Camossung*, which is the name of a girl turned into stone by the spiritual being (or transformer) Haylas to watch over the resources in what is now called the Gorge waterway.[19] Since the 1780s, the local Indigenous people had seen ships come and go. They had taken up their own role, mainly as labourers, in the rise of this little enclave on the Empire's westernmost margin. The people brought fruit and roots to the HBC fort, not having furs to trade. They fished for food, and the rich soil provided them with roots and camas bulbs in abundance. Nearby Indigenous peoples, notably Klallam and Makah, the latter from as far away as the entrance of Juan de Fuca Strait, were glad to bring furs and exchange them for these natural products. Tensions existed in inter-tribal relations and wars occurred from time to time. Below Beacon Hill, local Nations manned foreshore defences against Klallam raiders. In all, Camosun was a vibrant intersection of cultures and languages, of histories and traditions—a meeting place, as it were, an Indigenous nexus.

Artist Paul Kane, in 1847, painted the scene of this animated port with its canoe traffic in the tidal waterway and the Songhees lodges on the far shore. Before dredging solved the problem of the bar at the entrance to Victoria Harbour, large vessels were obliged to anchor in the Outer Harbour, as the *Driver* had done. From there, nearly a mile into the arm, after a sharp dogleg to starboard, lay the Inner Harbour. Directly ahead, the fort would come into view. We can see it now, on the far, or eastern, shore: the Hudson's Bay Company's young post, Fort Victoria. Blanshard knew what to look for: an engraved view of the stockaded fort from this same vantage point had appeared in the *Illustrated London News* of 26 August 1848.

These were the traditional lands and waters of the Lekwungen or

Songhees (correctly, the Lekwammen), today's Esquimalt and Songhees Nations,[20] who speak a dialect of Straits Salish. Their traditional territories extend along the southern tip of Vancouver Island, from Sooke to Swartz Bay; they were, and still are, coastal people, and in the 1800s they lived in seafront villages, originally at what is now Cadboro Bay, but "seeing the advantage of being near the white men they removed from their old home to the vicinity of the fort."[21] The Lekwammen, as historian John Lutz explains, were the HBC's most important trading partner, supplying food, building materials, provisions and labour as required.

Fort Victoria stood on land sold by the Lekwammen to the Company in 1843. One unsupported account says of that sale that these people offered the Company the fort site in exchange for three blankets.[22] At the time, to those involved, this was apparently regarded as fair exchange. In the more formal arrangement of 1850, the Lekwammen were guaranteed ownership of their fields and places of occupation. The so-called Songhees reserve, opposite Fort Victoria, grew as a place of Indigenous occupation. It is said that by 1850 seven hundred people lived there, but who is to say precisely? The population was fluid. In keeping with the development of the fort and nearby agricultural lands and pastures, the arrangement of labour (and compensation for same) continued unabated. The Songhees and Esquimalt Nations provided abundant labour, essential to colonization and laying out the land for colonists.[23] Trade continued. Sexual interaction with the Europeans likely was common. Here was a partnership of necessity and advantage.

Much misunderstanding exists about land tenure. In the "Fort Victoria treaties" of 1850 to 1854 (there were fourteen in all, including two at Fort Rupert and one at Nanaimo), the Indigenous peoples relinquished possession of their lands to the Hudson's Bay Company. These documents are now known as the "Douglas treaties" or "Vancouver Island treaties," but James Douglas, agent for the HBC, never called them treaties. They hold a unique place in Canadian law. In reference to Sooke, Esquimalt, Victoria and Oak Bay, plus other locales designated in the documents, it is correct to call them, as they wish, "traditional lands of the Lekwammen" rather than "unceded lands." Mark this statement from the treaty documents: "the land itself...

becomes the property of the white people forever."[24] Long the subject of historical and legal discussion, these deeds of conveyance follow, fundamentally, the Crown's intention (and that of its agent, the HBC) to recognize traditional Indigenous rights in occupation and property.[25] Retained were reserves that included village sites and cultivated land. The right to hunt and fish on unoccupied land was specified. (When Indian reserves were established under Canadian authority after 1871, the reserve lands were set aside for Indigenous occupation; Indian reserves are Crown land in the right of the Government of Canada.)

In addition to the local Lekwammen people, the rapidly expanding commerce at Camosun attracted Indigenous peoples from near and far, including northern warrior peoples—Haida, Tsimshian and Tlingit. Year by year, in summer months, the number of visitors rose. It is estimated that in 1860 up to four thousand northern Indigenous people congregated at Camosun, numbering twice the colonial population.[26] Nearer to Blanshard's time, in fall 1852, smallpox hit the Makah at Neah Bay hard.[27] Could it be that the disease came to Victoria with devastating effect? The records are silent. In 1862 a terrible smallpox epidemic arrived from San Francisco—and with it the forced removal or deportation of non-local Indigenous peoples. In later years the visitor numbers rose again: in 1866, the Reverend A.C. Garrett, principal of the Indian Mission, Diocese of British Columbia, who was living on the Songhees reserve, commented on the drunkenness and consequent riot that was the rule of existence there. The bishop of Columbia wrote in support of the priest, "The camp of the Hydahs is a constant scene of drunken riot, and I counted a few days ago seven unburied corpses. Garrett's suggested antidote was to have a constable reside on the reserve, his duty to compel the abatement of all nuisances and promote sobriety and peace." That same year the Victoria superintendent of police, Philip Hankin, told Captain Arthur Kennedy, the third governor of the Colony of Vancouver Island, that "there are about 200 Indian prostitutes living in Cormorant, Fisgard, and Store streets, in a state of filth and dirt beyond all description." He went on to describe the Chinese-owned shanties in the "Gully" between Johnson and Cormorant streets, the dens of iniquity where whisky sellers, prostitutes and bad characters were to be found. "Unfortunate sailors coming on leave from their ships are allured here by the Indian women, and robbed."[28] We are getting ahead of ourselves, though, for we cannot say that this state of affairs existed during Richard Blanshard's time in Victoria.

On his arrival, Blanshard saw Camosun waterway alive with canoes. Lekwammen canoes, sleek as well as graceful, featured a long prow worked out in the form of a bird's head. Northern canoes, by contrast, were characterized by a very heavy bow and a large, high stern. Mats were used as sails, but canvas was being introduced.[29] When beached at Camosun, canoes were always kept well away from the grasping reaches of spring tides. The Skagit ran an express canoe service connecting Camosun with Nisqually, carrying mail and passengers. John Work Tolmie recalled that as a boy he made one or two trips from Nisqually to Victoria, a passage of one hundred miles or more, in a canoe, at which time they paddled round the islands rather than go out into the strait for fear of storms.[30] There existed a vital link of another sort: from Fort Langley (established 1827) on the lower Fraser River, brigade trails from the Interior met up with, and were linked by, canoes and smaller sailing vessels such as the veteran *Cadboro*. The whole, we can imagine, was a maritime world of restless human action, a vibrant Indigenous world into which the Company had entered with expectation of success. So much depended on cross-cultural co-operation.

On the morning that the *Driver* cast anchor off Ogden Point, a chill grey dawn greeted Fort Victoria's early risers. New Year's festivities, of happy if fading memory, had given way to bitter, frosty weather, with bracing breezes from the north. A sheet of ice had covered the harbour not long previous, and Blanshard saw snow on the ground. Smoke from the fires in Indigenous houses drifted in the wind. A dreary, customary overcast pervaded the scene. And, as usual, "operations in hand," as the Fort's journal states, were going on. This was just as they had been the day before and the one before that—workers and overseers building, thrashing, cutting and carting firewood, and readying the "outfits" for the Interior Districts.[31] The work was prosaic. And so it was for the many officers, servants and engagés—toilers for the Company—who

Celebrated pioneer of steam navigation on the Northwest Coast and emblematic of nineteenth-century marine engineering, the workhorse *Beaver* plied British Columbia waters until 1889, when wrecked on Siwash Rock, Burrard Inlet. Fort Victoria in the background. *Painting by Adam Sherriff Scott, courtesy of Author's Collection*

were founding and developing this fur, shipping and merchandising outpost of commercial empire.

The Company steamer *Beaver* lay at the fort wharf. "She had the appearance of a small man-of-war," wrote a contemporary observer, "had four brass cannon, muskets, and cutlasses in racks round the mainmast, and hand grenades in safe places. Along her sides were boarding nettings, and these could be triced up vertically or placed horizontally as the case required. She had an old-fashioned steering wheel, and her anchors and cables were always ready as no wharfs existed on the coast in those days; carried plenty of hands, not only for defence but to cut wood for the furnaces, there being no coal in her early career."[32]

"The discipline on board is as strict as on a man-of-war," noted another. "And the greatest caution is used to prevent being taken at any time by surprise."[33] On 9 March 1850, as Blanshard approached the harbour, this workhorse of steam propulsion was getting up steam for a run through the inside passage with provisions to the new establishment at Fort Rupert, where surface coal was being gathered for sale. That place stood near the northernmost tip of Vancouver Island, on its east coast, facing various islands and Queen Charlotte Strait. The mountainous terrain there was fringed by islands; it held a different, more rugged character than lands near Victoria.

On board the *Beaver* were several Company officers Blanshard would get to know, including veteran Chief Factor John Work, his Spokane wife Josette Legacé and their family;[34] also George Blenkinsop, a young clerk destined for duties at Fort Rupert. At ten that morning, to the shrill of its whistle, the *Beaver* steamed out through the serpentine channel. The fort saluted with five guns, "as it was a matter of policy to keep up the dignity of the Hudson's Bay Company not only at Victoria but at all the company's posts along the coast to impress the Indians."[35] The *Beaver* was headed for territorial lands and seas of the Kwakiutl, who were zealous in the acquisition of possessions, material and immaterial. They were, too, a warlike people and powerful raiders, known and feared as far away as the Fraser River and Puget Sound. We will learn more about the Kwakiutl later, when we see how Blanshard considered them while he was at Fort Rupert.

As the *Beaver* exited Camosun waterway, the *Driver* came into view at Ogden Point. There she was, riding easily at anchor, her bow pointing into the light breeze coming from the north. She wore a commissioning pennant, indicating that the governor was on board.

Blanshard awaited his turn to go ashore. He watched as the captain's gig was lowered and manned, its crew readying for the pull to the fort. Commander Johnson and the purser, Henry Gibson, took their places.

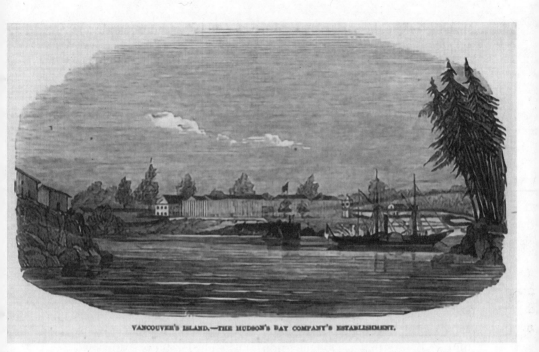

VANCOUVER'S ISLAND.—THE HUDSON'S BAY COMPANY'S ESTABLISHMENT.

If coming into port and approaching Fort Victoria, the inquisitive visitor would be presented with this animated scene—a palisaded fort of customary HBC architecture beneath which the famed steamship *Beaver* can be seen getting ready for its next coastal run. *Illustrated London News*, 26 August 1848

Then, to the bosun's pipe, the gig sped smartly away on its mission and disappeared from Blanshard's view. At that precise moment, from the fort, a Company officer spotted the craft round Shoal Point, then head toward the Inner Harbour. It wore an English flag, the Cross of St. George. The Navy had arrived.

When the ship's boat reached the post's landing stage, Johnson and Gibson stepped ashore. Johnson had come to advise on matters of protocol as to how His Excellency Governor Richard Blanshard must be received at the British Empire's newest colony. There was a money matter to settle too: the purser was obliged to register a charge on the HBC's accounts for the table charges of the governor while on board. The officers spent several hours ashore. Discussion that afternoon was with Chief Factor James Douglas and Chief Trader Roderick Finlayson. Douglas declined to pay, though it must be kept in mind that the Company was to bear all costs of colonial administration, including Blanshard's travel expense.[36] Getting the tight-fisted HBC to pay up was another matter, and its failure to pay the full bill caused Blanshard to suffer a financial loss. Johnson sent the account on to the Admiralty, where it disappears from view. The purser, under Admiralty regulations, was obliged to ask what fresh provisions (of vital importance) could be supplied to Her Majesty's man-of-war. Little could be provided.

Commander Johnson recounted his afternoon ashore: "I immediately visited Mr. Douglas the Chief Factor of the Hudson's Bay Company who expressed being taken by surprise at the Governor's arrival." According to Catholic priest Father Lempfrit, it was common for Douglas to manifest surprise.[37] Douglas informed Johnson and Gibson that a house for His Excellency was not ready but under construction. Blanshard had been informed by Company directors in London that he should find his residence completed at the time of his arrival.[38] But now Douglas said that Blanshard would have to lodge in his own house (that is, Douglas's house) when he left the warship.[39]

Turning to the key matter at hand, the naval officer made clear to Douglas that upon the governor's stepping on shore he would be greeted by a salute of seventeen guns from the ship, this to be answered by the same number from the fort. That was the protocol to be duly observed. The gig returned to the *Driver*. Blanshard was advised of the proceedings and was not pleased with the news about his residence.

Johnson ordered the vessel ready for steaming. The pilot came aboard. The final approach for Blanshard, now about ten thousand sea miles from London, was about to be made.

The *Driver* was piloted through contorted Camosun waterway by HBC senior mariner Charles Nevin. He had a reputation as a good-natured, active man—too fond of grog and women, some said.[40] He gingerly dodged menacing rocks, reefs and shoals (Shoal Point in particular, a place of recent calamity), fully aware that the *Driver* drew a prodigious fifteen feet. Nevin had awaited high tide before piloting the ship through the entrance and the marked doglegged channel.[41] Then, reaching James Bay, he pointed out a place to anchor, one with plenty of swing room, not far from the fort's wharf and waterfront entrance.

Here was sufficiently deep water, a factor already taken into account when selecting the site for the fort, intended to be, and fast becoming, as Blanshard could see, a depot for the Company's burgeoning marine department.

Later that same Saturday afternoon, Chief Factor Douglas (stiff and formal in bearing, wearing his customary mask of detachment and reserve) was rowed out to the ship to pay official respects to Governor Blanshard. In the wardroom, or captain's cabin, two agents of empire faced each other, flanked by the senior naval officer. They were entirely different characters with strong personalities. What was talked about? The silence of our documents is deafening. We can be certain of pleasantries exchanged, though taut and exact. The official proclamation, they decided, would occur on the Monday (the morrow being a Sunday). Blanshard may have been sensitive to the fact that Douglas had been the Company's first choice for the governorship. We know now that Douglas was relieved when notified by London headquarters that he had not been selected for the position, though if called upon he would have accepted, because submission to the will of his corporate superiors was with him a given. He likely said nothing to Blanshard on this disagreeable subject. As host and protocols officer, Commander Johnson would have gone over the details for the coming days, which Blanshard looked forward to with anticipation. His destiny was about to be revealed.

Next day, the weather was overcast and very cold. Biting winds swirled down from the north. Blanshard and several naval officers came ashore for eleven o'clock Divine Service. The bell summoned the fort's inhabitants to the Great Hall, rigged as the place of worship.

Douglas had set a high standard of qualifications for a clergyman on the frontier: "[He] must quit the closet & live a life of beneficent activity, devoted to the support of principles, rather than of forms; he must shun discord, avoid uncharitable feelings, temper zeal with discretion, illustrate precept by example."[42] Duly selected, the Reverend Robert John Staines, age twenty-seven, ordained in the Church of England, had reached the Island with his wife, Emma Frances Tahourdin, in 1849. This pioneer priest and political agitator, a flamboyant fellow and Trinity Hall Cambridge graduate, who tried some people's patience, was carried on the books of the Company in the dual office of chaplain to the Company and schoolmaster to the children of Company officers. "He was a man full of frills," grumbled Roderick Finlayson.[43] A visitor to Fort Victoria noted of the man of the cloth, "He does not get on very well with the occupants of Bachelors' Hall, but is I believe a very good schoolmaster."[44] The Company abhorred political progressives such as Staines. They were adjudged dangerous.

The energetic and animated Emma Staines was a teacher, well qualified in French and other languages. "I can see her now in my mind's eye," schoolboy James Robert Anderson recalled, "with a row of curls down each side of her angular face; by no means unprepossessing however, spare figure, clad in black, a lady undoubtedly, and when walking and holding out her skirts on each side and ordering the girls to follow her example."[45] As a white woman she was a unique person in that time and space. They were a remarkable couple, two of the eccentric and distinctive characters who made up the European population of early Fort Victoria.

It was on the day of Blanshard's first attendance at Sunday worship that he met the Reverend and Mrs. Staines, eventually loyal friends. A budding ally of the governor, Staines became one of the troublemakers, agitators we might call them, who stood against a powerful monopoly that controlled the affairs of this far and expansive frontier. Blanshard had no way of knowing that Staines not only would take a prominent position in supporting the governor in the difficult months ahead, but, a few years later, would lose his life in a bold yet tragic attempt to impress on the imperial government the tyranny of the Company's rule. But this comes later in our story.

All of this Blanshard would come to understand in due time. Yet, at the outset, that first day ashore on what his rival Douglas had described as "the perfect Eden," before he proclaimed the Queen's commission as governor of Vancouver's Island and its Dependencies, he was necessarily optimistic. Confidence had been placed in him by the Crown, the government and the Colonial Office that he would be able to establish civil government under the Crown at this newest formal addition to the British Empire. And the Empire was not known for failures on the spot. All the same, colonial governors of that age, by virtue of their office, were expected to please two worlds—the one close at hand and complicated, and the other remote but exacting. Governors were in a situation of jeopardy. However, what Blanshard was soon to find out was that along with the clamorous local circumstances, he also had two bosses to deal with: the Colonial Office (to which he answered officially) and the Company (to which he was obliged to communicate on certain matters). Further, the Company had its manager on the spot and its chairman and directors in London. Even before taking up formal office, the odds were stacked against him.

Blanshard returned to the ship and, as a dignitary, was piped aboard. He returned to the sustenance and camaraderie of the wardroom among his well-ordered naval companions—and awaited the morrow. All the confidence that had been placed in him to bring him to this locale at this special time was about to be transformed into a personal presence of gubernatorial power—and the realized birth of British institutional and constitutional authority in the farthest west and on north Pacific shores. A thousand thoughts must have passed through his mind. His past was soon to become prologue. And he must have wondered what he would make, or could make, of the opportunity that had been duly offered.

Chapter 2:
The Rivals

B lanshard, as said, knew the tortured genesis of this colony of which he was soon to be proclaimed governor. The future of Vancouver Island had been hotly debated in the British Parliament and extensively covered in the London press. Backroom deals between the Company and the Colonial Office were suspected. Could a business with a royal charter be given such a licence or charter of grant to colonize the Island and even all of far western British territories?

That called for investigation: legal opinion confirmed the Company's legitimacy to hold the grant, but details remained secret.[46] The Colonial Office had gained an ugly reputation for suppressing and garbling the documents. In August 1848, therefore, Parliament ordered the key "secret" correspondence printed. The details were now exposed to public scrutiny—and to ridicule.[47] In 1848, Robert Montgomery Martin published a book, a hack account, that effusively supported the Company's legitimate right to colonize the Island. This work countered the sharp attack, again in the form of a book, by James Edward Fitzgerald, which abhorred the prospect of a settlement colony under monopolistic power. In short, the Colony of Vancouver Island was founded under public suspicion at home in an age when indifference to colonial projects was the norm. This explains Colonial Office parsimony and goes a long way to explaining Company indifference to the whole and dubious project of colonization.

The Company's undoubted advantage in all the calculations of the

Colonial Office was that it already had establishments in place, a network of trade relations on the coast and in the interior, and experience in trading with the Indigenous peoples, who were considered to be warlike and predatory. Fort Langley, for instance, was founded in 1827 on the Fraser River. Fort Victoria, named for the young queen,[48] was the most recent of twenty-two posts of the Hudson's Bay Company. James Douglas, following orders, had chosen the site on what appeared to him as the most advantageous situation for the purpose within the Strait of Juan de Fuca. The harbour seemed adequate, he believed, and timber grew in abundance for construction and export. Fort Victoria's purpose was to facilitate the shipping and promote the security of the Company's interests in the Western Department, particularly its marine requirements. Provisions needed to be raised, and lands for livestock and dairy had to be developed. There was not a moment to lose. Parkland to the east of the Inner Harbour offered the best agricultural prospects anywhere on the southern island, he judged.

There were other reasons for the establishment of the new fort. The Columbia River was a danger to shipping. American settlers arriving in the Columbia and Willamette valleys of the Oregon country exhibited such lawlessness, jealous rancour and hostility to the HBC that a prudent removal to Vancouver Island would protect Company property from theft, pillage and destruction.[49]

Throughout the planning for the removal from the Columbia, Douglas carried out the plans that had been formulated with clarity and certainty by George Simpson, overseas governor of the Hudson's Bay Company from 1826 to 1860. These were of monumental proportions, and we look at them now, marvelling how "the Little Emperor," as he was called, set all in motion through cold business logic, evaluation and foresight.

We gain some insight into Simpson's trade strategy by reading what he advised the governor and committee in London in a letter from Honolulu dated 1 March 1842, after his survey of the coastal prospects from Sitka south to Juan de Fuca's Strait:

The southern end of Vancouvers Island, forming the northern side of the Straits of Fuca, appears to me the best situation for such an establishment as required…[T]here are several good harbours in that neighbourhood: no place, however, has yet been found combining all the advantages required, the most important of which are a safe and accessible harbour, well situated for defence, with waterpower for grist and saw mills; abundance of timber for house consumption and

Sir George Simpson, "the Little Emperor," was arguably the most powerful figure in Canadian business history in the nineteenth century. He charted the destinies of HBC field affairs in northern North America, from Ungava to Vancouver Island. Douglas owed much to his guidance. *Illustration by Stephen Pearce, 1857, courtesy of Wikimedia Commons*

exportation; and the adjacent country well adapted for tillage and pasture farms on an extensive scale...[From various reports] we have every reason to believe there will be no difficulty in finding an eligible situation in that quarter for the establishment in question.[50]

In retrospect, we see that Simpson, though opposed to colonization, had in 1842 devised the very scheme for the depot on southern Vancouver Island. He believed in strict economy and agricultural self-sufficiency for all forts and posts. Moreover, he knew exports or sales of foodstuffs would generate revenue. Whalers visiting the coast needed provisions and could pay for them. A naval ship in local waters was always good for business, too. Under these expectations the scheme was advanced. Quickly and dramatically, Fort Victoria emerged as the commercial emporium of the Northwest Coast in these latitudes, and also the marine depot and reprovisioning centre of the coastal and cordilleran trade. It became the watchtower of Company interests on the coast, fulfilling Simpson's expectations.

Simpson left the choice of location to Douglas, who thought the country in the immediate vicinity idyllic. It was equally attractive to visitors. As an example, the naturalist in HMS *Herald*, there in 1846, waxed eloquent:

In walking from Ogden Point round to Fort Victoria, a distance of little more than a mile, we thought we had never seen a more beautiful country; it quite exceeded our expectation; and yet [Captain] Vancouver's descriptions made us look for something beyond common scenery. It is a natural park; noble oaks and ferns are seen in the greatest luxuriance, thickets of the hazel and the willow, shrubberies of the poplar and the alder, are dotted about. One could hardly believe that this was not a work of art; more particularly when finding signs of cultivation in every direction—enclosed pasture-lands, fields of wheat, potatoes and turnips...We were astonished by all we saw.[51]

"From all accounts we heard of it," commented the Honourable Edward Ellice, MP, "it is a kind of England attached to the continent of America."[52] Fish and game were abundant. There was fine partridge and grouse shooting near the fort, and an elusive cougar was known to be preying on farm animals. The cat was hunted down by a visiting American party, to the delight of Company personnel.[53] Travellers found the location a hunting and fishing paradise.

Company dominance now reached Pacific shores, with a magnificent reach of trade and seaborne empire scarcely to be imagined in scope, a forerunner of Canada. Roots of Company power were as ancient as they were deep. On 2 May 1670, "The Governor and Company of Adventurers of England Trading into Hudson's Bay" received a royal charter, by writ of the privy seal under King Charles II, for incorporation. Prince Rupert of the Rhine, the first governor, along with seventeen associates became "true and absolute Lordes and Proprietors" of the territory under the name of Rupert's Land "in whatsoever latitude they shall bee that lye within the entrance of the Streights commonly called Hudson's Streights." The Company was awarded all lands drained by waters flowing to Hudson Bay, including soil, exclusive trade, rights of government and even rights to make war and peace. The charter gave them all mines of gold, silver and precious gems, and a trading monopoly throughout a region said to be ten times the size of the Holy Roman Empire. Rupert's Land proper consisted of some 1.4 million square miles of present-day Canada.

From our times, looking back on this real estate and trading arrangement, the munificence of the grant boggles the imagination. The HBC was to hold possession of it "in free and common socage, on the same terms as the Manor of East Greenwich," paying to the Crown two elk and two black beaver whenever the monarch should happen to enter Rupert's Land, which we might assume to be an unlikely event.[54] Terms also called for the Company to search for a northwest passage, but, truth to tell, only half-hearted measures were taken in that line. The Company's ships, forts, factories and places of trade were to be the responsibility of the firm, not a drain on the government. Trade and monopoly went hand in hand with these merchant adventurers (and they and their kind echo down through the history of the British Empire). The Company fought off many a competitor in the field, as well as challengers who claimed that the search for a northwest passage was not being pressed. It survived wars against the French. There were years of no dividends, but the Company persisted in its business, which was mainly to bring furs to the London and European markets and trade goods to North America. In commerce and in politics it became battle-hardened, ready for the fray. No wonder Parliament and the press looked on this empire within empire with unbridled suspicion.

Hudson's Bay Company House, built 1794, stood at nos. 3 and 4 Fenchurch Street, in the City of London's compact business district, where merchants had congregated for generations. Stone columns flanked the arched main entrance. This red-brick edifice, undistinguished in architecture, stood conveniently on the riverbank of the Thames. When Blanshard presented himself for his interview in 1849, he knew by reputation that from this four-storey establishment a fur and trading empire encompassing millions of square miles was managed with utmost economy and acute vision. As the Company proper was under royal charter, Parliament kept an eye on its proceedings. The governor (or chairman) and directors—sometimes called the London Committee—guided the firm's affairs and watched the balance sheets closely. A visitor to the Fenchurch Street headquarters called it one of the mainsprings of London's commercial life, the Tyre of modern times.[55]

There, Blanshard met Sir John Henry Pelly, Bart., one of the most striking figures of City of London life. He had been elected governor of the Company in 1822, and until his resignation and death in 1852 exercised enormous influence in the City, serving also as chairman of the Bank of England. The HBC's London-based administration was headed by the ever-efficient secretary Mr. Archibald Barclay, a lawyer. The Company wore many battle scars from a century and more of wars and deprivations. Although there were internal dissensions, its major challenges came from outside. It fought off rising competition from interlopers, notably the North West Company, based in Montreal. That crisis is now related.

In 1811, Thomas Douglas, 5th Earl of Selkirk, seized shareholding dominance in the HBC. This allowed him to finagle a grant of 116,000 square miles in what is now Manitoba, North Dakota, Saskatchewan and Minnesota. He named this land grant the Red River Colony and sent Scottish crofters to settle there. The Nor'Westers, aggressive in the fur, buffalo hide and pemmican trades, despised the "oatmeal-eaters," whom

31

they regarded as intruders. They determined to break up the colony. Stirring events followed. The skirmish in June 1816 at Seven Oaks, Red River, in which Governor Robert Semple, appointed to control all the factories of Rupert's Land, and twenty of his officers and men fell before the fire of a strong band of retainers of the North West Company, invited judicial inquiry. Further, murderous competition in Athabasca between the HBC traders and the Nor'Westers led to British governmental investigation. In 1821, after difficulties, the two firms amalgamated. From 1821 to 1869 the HBC was at the height of its expansion and ruled more than three million square miles, approximately one-quarter of the continent of North America.

In 1821 the terms of union placed upon the trade the responsibility of maintaining law and order. Parliament, by a statutory measure known as "An Act for Regulating the Fur Trade,"[56] authorized a licence, renewable in twenty-one years, for "the sole and exclusive privilege of trading with the Indians" over the whole of British North America "not being part of the lands or territories heretofore granted to the Governor and Company of Adventurers of England trading to Hudson's Bay, and not being part of any of our provinces in North America." That licence was issued 5 December 1821. A new requirement, reflecting then current thinking, had been included, which specified that the Company was obligated to provide for the moral improvement and religious instruction of the Indigenous peoples. The monopoly could now, with the blessing of the government, extend its control to the Pacific. The licence was extended indefinitely in 1827.

The Company was no philanthropic organization: it was a business run by the governor, deputy governor and seven managing directors, or committee, in London, and its object was to provide dividends to stockholders. There were one hundred shares, sixty of which "their Honours retain for themselves; and the remaining forty...divided among the chief traders and chief factors, who manage the affairs in the Indian country." A chief factor held two shares, a chief trader one. These commissioned officers received the proceeds of the shares allotted to them but were not to bear their share in the losses the Company might sustain.[57]

The Company resembled a collection and distribution agency: furs were collected, and manufactured goods (blankets, ironwork, firearms, cutlery, beads, trinkets, finery of various sorts and rum) were distributed. In keeping with government policy, and as a token measure of the improving instincts of the times, "the board expressed concern for the spiritual and material welfare of the Indian population, in particular for their conversion to Christianity and their protection from the scourge of alcohol."[58] That, at least at face value, was in keeping with what had been demanded by Parliament in 1821. In reality, Company men in the field sought peace with the Indigenous peoples. The Company's commissioned officers and their subordinates kept well clear of violence between Nations. They intervened only when Company property or servants were interfered with, as in a case of murder or piracy. The policy, strictly observed, was one of minimum intervention in Indigenous affairs. At the same time, the field traders worked to maintain peaceful relations with the Indigenous people by developing close trading partnerships. This they did by advancing them credit, supplying them with tools, traps, firearms and ammunition as required, and maintaining from year to year this same system without fail. Company men would rather overlook a debt than create hostility or envy. Herein lay their secret.

As to settlement, to ease Britain's surplus population, no systematic or specific plan was imagined. Except where it might be encouraged to supply agricultural products, as at, say, Red River, Nisqually and Cowlitz, or Fort Langley, settlement was discouraged as antithetical to the fur trade. In that view lay the reason for the delayed or latent contest for the control of lands and resources, one so remarkably different in quality and degree from that of the United States frontier.

An essential factor in the peace exhibited on the vast frontier of Company influence was the practice of HBC officers and servants taking Indigenous or mixed-blood wives. We know from superb research into the lives of commissioned officers in the field that marital connections were made with high-ranking females. So it was with James Douglas, Roderick Finlayson, William Henry McNeill and John Tod, as examples. These were relationships "in the custom of the country." Later such marriages were solemnized under Company rules (instituted in

1833), but the social continuum of these mixed-blood families continued. Many relationships in Fort Victoria's history are of this sort,
and, in effect, the women and their children lived "colonized lives."
How could it have been otherwise? The first "bride ship" did not arrive
in Victoria's harbour until 1861, and by then the power base of the
Company was being weakened by changing circumstances, not least
the 1858 gold rush, which altered the demographics considerably. Still,
the Indigenous and mixed-blood women lived influential lives, as did
their offspring.

Other servants had their unique places in the strict hierarchical
system. Clerks were in high demand. The Company recruited labourers
almost exclusively in the Orkneys, and they proved steady and useful.
"It is curious to note," observed a writer familiar with this trading world,
"how numerous Scotchmen are in the wilds of North America."[59] As a
rule, those in the employ of the Company in the field were a hard-
headed and weather-beaten lot, with strong survival instincts. They
were tough business practitioners who had worked their way up, by
seniority and capability, into managerial positions. As a rule, HBC ship
captains were also a tough, brawny, hard-drinking set. They faced
the perils of Cape Horn or the storm-tossed lee shores of Vancouver
Island or the north coast with courage, and they were ever on the alert
for pirates and Indigenous raiders. The deckhands were a hardened
breed but liable to desert when rumours of gold were heard. At any
one time the HBC had about six vessels. Some, like the *Cadboro*, plied
Puget Sound, the Strait of Georgia and Victoria, freighting furs, supplies and personnel. The *Mary Dare* frequently went to the Sandwich,
or Hawaiian, Islands with shingles and salted salmon. The *Una* sailed
to Haida Gwaii and to the Skeena River. Sea links were kept up with the
Columbia River, Yerba Buena, California, and Sitka, Alaska. The *Otter*
joined the *Beaver* in steam operations in 1853, making the northern
coastal services more efficient.

Pelly and Barclay managed the London operation and its communications with the distant margins. Closer to those margins was
the already mentioned George, later Sir George, Simpson, the governor of Rupert's Land, who was based at Hudson's Bay House at
Lachine, on the St. Lawrence River. From 1826 to 1860, Simpson was

governor-in-chief of all Hudson's Bay Company territories in America. He was the all-seeing, all-powerful field general, bringing economy and structure to the Columbia Department. "The Little Emperor," a stickler for appearances and balanced accounts, travelled extensively over this quasi-sovereign possession. He was an intriguing fellow, a master of strategies, a martinet. He took notes on how to make systems more efficient—or otherwise redundant. He kept a secret, inquisitorial character book, in which his pungent and visceral remarks on the Company's chief officers were jotted down in code. He could make or break an officer's career. On the eve of the Oregon Treaty, he had achieved mastery of far-western trade strategy. The likes of Dr. John McLoughlin (chief factor at Fort Vancouver), Peter Skene Ogden (McLoughlin's successor) and James Douglas felt the power of his despotism. Douglas, who kept up a correspondence with Simpson, benefited from it. In information-gathering, Simpson had no rival, and his demands of obedience, and partialities, brought deep resentments. Chief Trader John McLean, exiled to dreary Fort Chimo in Ungava, remarked in his 1849 book, "In no colony subject to the British Crown is there to be found an authority so despotic as is at this day exercised in the mercantile Colony of Rupert's Land; an authority combining the despotism of military rule with the strict surveillance and mean parsimony of the avaricious trader. From Labrador to Nootka Sound the unchecked, uncontrolled will of a single individual gives law to the land."[60]

The Columbia Department, to which Simpson gave special attention, was an imperial domain of impressive dimensions. On its borderlands it was maintained by outtrading American rivals on the south and Russians on the north. The monopoly undercut American free enterprise in the Snake River basin and elsewhere. American mountain men and companies fought among themselves, and unregulated relations developed with the Indigenous peoples. The HBC, by contrast, as the US superintendent of Indian Affairs observed, acted quickly when any trader showed improper conduct. As he said, the British maintained a stability and orderliness in their regulated commerce with Indigenous peoples in a rather "despotic yet salutary way."[61] The HBC's interest was profit, and profit could best be realized by keeping the peace in the frontier areas.

Simpson masterminded the redesign of the Company's far-western business strategy. This included the policy to hunt as bare as possible all the country south of the Columbia River and west of the Continental Divide—that is, the Snake River country. The purpose was to undercut all American rivals. This policy found fulfillment under Peter Skene Ogden. For years this fearless and experienced trader was in charge of the river brigades. As to the area to the north, Simpson put it this way in a letter to Ogden in 1825:

It appears to us that this side of the Mountains presents a fine field for extension of Trade particularly to the Northward and we conceive that important advantages would be gained by attaching New Caledonia to this Department; the Coasting Trade (which we have entirely neglected and which has realized fortunes to many Adventurers who could not have embarked in it without heavy outlays and expenses to which we should not be exposed from the facilities afforded us by uniting it with the inland business) we are decidedly of opinion should be entered into with spirit and without delay; we are likewise of opinion that the principal Depot should be situated at the entrance of Frasers River as being more central for the general business.[62]

Simpson wrote this at Fort George (also known as Astoria), and we see that he anticipates the construction of Fort Vancouver on the north bank of the Columbia and Fort Langley on the Fraser River.

Best remembered in HBC history were Company officers who encountered conflict, for, as Professor John S. Galbraith reminds us, "conflict is the stuff from which history is written."[63] The fur trade suffered when lumbermen or farmers arrived, and in Oregon settlers destroyed the fur business. Douglas was referring to the Willamette settlers when he wrote, "The interests of the Colony and Fur Trade will never harmonize…the fur trade must suffer by each innovation,"[64] but his words could be applied generally. Ogden expressed similar views to Simpson, and to his way of thinking, the old order would give way to the new only with disruptions in race relations.[65] Douglas and Ogden were energetic officers with high qualities of management. Their superior in the Columbia Department, the beneficent Dr. McLoughlin,

Grizzled Nor'wester of earlier days, Dr. John McLoughlin headed the HBC's Columbia Department, restructured its northern coast trade, and was beneficent toward American settlers in the Willamette Valley. He became a US citizen and is revered as "the father of Oregon." *Image E-02648 courtesy of the Royal BC Museum*

aided American settlers in the Willamette Valley. In 1846 he gave Simpson notice of retirement from the Hudson's Bay Company. As a merchant and miller, he prospered. He died in 1857. He is known as "the father of Oregon."

Many were the friendships among chief factors and chief traders. Their wilderness loneliness was broken by a steady exchange of correspondence, books, newspapers and gossip. They were inured to the wild country, seemingly unfazed by its storms, heat and cold, floods, locusts, food shortages and other hardships of the life of rock and field. These new westerners wore buckskin jackets and hats, leggings and boots suitable to wilderness travel, whether in canoe or on horseback. They moved fearlessly among Indigenous peoples, and not a few married "in the fashion of the country" and had large mixed-blood, or Métis, families. They thereby strengthened their connections with Indigenous peoples. For instance, Chief Trader Charles Ross (placed in charge of constructing the post at Camosack) and his Anishinaabe wife Isabella, the first known fur-trade family living in Fort Victoria, had nine children when they arrived; the tenth child was born at Fort Victoria in 1844. Charles Ross died that same year, of appendicitis. He was buried in the ravine at what is now Johnson Street. Isabella Mainville Ross—Widow Ross, she called herself—became the first independent female landowner in British Columbia, and her Ross Farm is now part of Ross Bay Cemetery.[66]

In the employ of the Company were other officers, mainly factors, traders and clerks, but also bakers, master mariners, pilots and marine engineers, carpenters and other artificers. Blacksmiths were in high demand, including dynamiters (for the blasting cap had arrived to irretrievably change the face of rock-bound Vancouver Island). There were many French Canadians (or *Canadiens*) among the labourers and couriers, and a hard-drinking, God-fearing set they were too. They were pleased to see at Fort Victoria the arrival of the Oblate priest Father Lempfrit in June 1849. Many Indigenous people sought baptism from Lempfrit, who held service in a makeshift shed at waterside. There were some "Kanakas"—Sandwich Islanders, or Hawaiians— among the fort's labourers. These muscular fellows stood the night watch at the fort's gates. And they were superb boatmen and sailors, readily employed.

The post was under charge of Trader Roderick Finlayson, expert in raising sheep and cattle. He had been there since 1 June 1843.[67] He was rough-looking with brusque manners. French Canadian and Métis males made up the fort's construction crews.[68] Experience these artisans gained elsewhere made them familiar with plans, methods and materials for just such a fort and buildings. A sawmill was being erected at upper Esquimalt Harbour. In late 1848 there were three hundred acres under tillage and a dairy of eighty cows.[69]

Fort Victoria formed the nexus of the new enterprise. On the south-west corner stood an octagonal three-storey bastion with six-pounder black-muzzled cannon protruding. (The foundation level served as a jail.) As elsewhere in the Company's realm, these guns were for ceremonial purposes. No Company servant ever expected to fire the cannon in anger. An observer writing about Red River could have been discussing the state of affairs at Fort Victoria: "It is highly probable that such an attempt would have been attended with consequences much more dreadful to those *behind* than to those who might chance to be in front of the guns. Nevertheless, they were imposing."[70] A northeast bastion was erected when the stockade was expanded to include two large warehouses and the powder house. The whole was stockaded with cedar posts, fifteen feet in length—some sources say eighteen feet—and brought from nearby Cedar Hill or Mount Douglas (P'kols). Another commentator wrote, "There were inside about a dozen large block story-and-a-half buildings, say 60 X 40 [feet], roofed with long and wide strips of cedar bark. The buildings were for the storage of goods, a trading shop, and a large shop of general trade." A belfry, with a roof, stood in the centre of the yard. Its bell tolled for rising, for meals, for work and, on Sundays, for church service; it also sounded for weddings, deaths, fires and, sometimes, for warning.[71] Every time the bell rang, dogs in the Indigenous village across from Fort Victoria put up a shrill howl. Prevailing paint colours of the fort buildings were Spanish brown and whitewash. On the flagstaff near the western gate, the Red Ensign with HBC in the field proudly proclaimed the commercial purpose—and showed the direction of the wind. Nearby there was a well some eighty feet deep. The mess room, or Great Hall, stood near the back gate, at the corner of what is now Fort and Government streets. As this was an outpost on the frontier, the interior walls of the Great Hall were festooned with the taxidermist's wares: heads of various wild creatures of the forest; horns, hides and pelts; as well as antique weapons of all sorts, Indigenous regalia and more. Off from it lived Douglas and his family. Trader Finlayson, by contrast, lived with his family in the "counting house."

The fort's western gate opened on the Inner Harbour and a landing stage (and what came in time to be called Wharf Street). The back gate

Fort Victoria as Governor Blanshard would have seen it in 1850, with tilled fields rising to parkland and Mount Douglas and Mount Tolmie in the distance. *Image D-00027 courtesy of the Royal BC Museum*

led to Fort Street, and to swamps, meadows, rising parkland and rocky outcrops. A track led through the grounds from Wharf to Fort Street. In order to avoid the mud while walking across the yard, one had to negotiate a walkway consisting of two or three poles laid side by side. Enclosed within the stockade stood a combined barracks and new-arrivals building (a temporary measure). There were also men's quarters, a building shared by the carpenter and smithy, and a residence for the doctor of the day. Last but not least was the post office. Not long before Blanshard's arrival, the palisade had been enlarged to 465 by 300 feet, enclosing thirteen buildings, including a powder house. Young Edgar Fawcett, who arrived there nine years after Governor Blanshard, gives us the street names of the stockade boundaries: the high palisade of the fort ran along Wharf Street from the corner of Bastion to Broughton Street, up thence to Government Street, along Government to Bastion Street.[72]

On the eve of Blanshard's arrival, no houses stood outside the fort's walls save a storehouse and Chief Factor Douglas's residence, then under construction. All the officers and men, about seventy in number, lived securely inside the palisade, with gates locked tight every night and watchmen set. During the day the whole resembled a human beehive.

With shiploads of "settlers" expected imminently, Finlayson and his constructors were building two large unheated dwellings outside the palisade. These were to house, temporarily, any immigrants or hired artificers, miners or labourers who survived the hateful Cape Horn passage from England of eighteen thousand miles and were cast down on Camosun inlet's rocky shores, there to face whatever nature or the Company could provide. Those who had the good fortune to reside within the palisade were either Company servants (and their families) or guests. Other arrivals had to fend for themselves beyond the pick-eted enclosure. If you were not under contract to the Company, you were on your own.

∽∽∽

Finally the day came, Monday, 11 March 1850—the essential day, for Blanshard was to personify by public presence, as empowered by his commission and seal of office, the beginning of constituted civil government and law in the British (later Canadian) far west. Of high significance, the day presaged a transcontinental dominion of the north.

As it unfolded, the ceremony exhibited as much formality as the rudeness of the surroundings would permit. It was a raw winter day— cold, blustery and rainy—and even the weather gods seemed to cast a gloom on the scene. A foot of snow covered the land. It was no civic holiday: "People employed as usual, see labour book," notes the post journal.[73]

The governor cut a solitary figure. A tall, trim man, he wore a newly made dark tunic arrayed with silver buttons and silver lace (as was the gubernatorial style) and a black stovepipe hat. A sword of office hung at his side. He had kitted himself out in London, at his own expense, before his departure. He awaited the Navy's instructions.

The governor took his seat in the ship's cutter, attended by officers of the *Driver* and an armed colour party of smartly dressed sailors. He landed at ten o'clock. Blanshard's arrival was accompanied by a seventeen-gun salute from Her Majesty's warship, customary in circumstances such as this. Immediately Blanshard put his foot on the ground, recounts Robinson, the same number was returned by the fort.

Douglas received him on landing, attended by the gentlemen of the establishment, and conducted him to the Great Hall. A rotten day such as this necessitated that the proceedings occur inside. All took up their respective positions. His Excellency read himself in, as they say, reading his commission before Commander Johnson, who, bearing the Queen's commission in the Royal Navy, ranked highest in royal authority at this outpost of empire. Protocols heretofore not observed in an HBC post lent a unique air to the occasion.

By the end of the ceremony, Governor Blanshard was the first duly commissioned representative of the Crown to assume control of British possessions on the Northwest Coast. Many governors and lieutenant-governors would follow. The common law of England became effective, including habeas corpus, although there was a peculiarity. Slavery and slave-taking existed among the Indigenous peoples of Vancouver Island and its Dependencies, and also on the continental shores, estimated generally at about ten percent—higher in some locations, lower in others.[74] Britain professed a moral obligation to eradicate slavery in its territories, but in the circumstances, on Vancouver Island, imperial administrators thought it best to let Indigenous slaveholding and slave-trading or raiding practices stand. Prosecutions were never attempted, and a legal loophole was introduced to let the authorities off the hook, so to speak. When the Royal Navy seized ships involved in the slave trade, these ships and their owners or operators were tried in Vice-Admiralty courts. Blanshard was commander-in-chief and vice admiral of Vancouver Island, as well as the governor, with the authority to administer Admiralty law in the colony, including laws of salvage, shipping and safety measures at sea. However, a United Kingdom Order in Council of 25 June 1851 removed slave trader prosecutions from the responsibilities of Vice-Admiralty courts, so Blanshard did not have to deal with Indigenous slavery or the slave trade. As a rule,

Douglas, as HBC chief factor, took no action but trusted in moral suasion to eradicate a system he regarded as iniquitous.

All in all, Blanshard's great day was a low-key affair. There had been no band to play appropriate airs. However, sailors and Company hands alike gave three cheers, and we can imagine that some mulled wine or spirits were passed. Company officers were noted for their hospitality to visitors. Blanshard may have expressed some excitement in private letters, but there is a matter-of-fact nature to the laconic report he sent to the 3rd Earl Grey, secretary of state for war and the colonies, who had authorized his appointment: "On the 11th I landed and read my commission in presence of Commander Johnson of the *Driver* and the officers and servants of the Hudson's Bay Company." He then went on to complain that no lodging was ready for him ashore, and that for the interim he would remain on board the warship. That worrisome letter bore the date 8 April.[75]

Blanshard needed little time to consider his situation. To him all was abundantly clear. He had been, by his own acceptance, cast upon a distant corporate shore dominated by rocks and trees. No house awaited him. When the *Driver* left the colony and returned to southern waters, it appeared that he would be obliged to stay with Douglas and his family, or in noisy Bachelors' Hall with the other officers. In fact, first an apartment was arranged for him in the Great Hall; then he and his manservant were given a vacant storehouse to inhabit—a bleak house, Charles Dickens would certify it, cold, dingy and damp. All was makeshift. That was not all: no office was available, and no secretary either. A brazen promise of land had been given him in London, but now even that prospect was vanishing fast, soon to disappear. He would have been able to borrow a horse from the post's stable: there was much wonderful country to explore, and streams to fish. But for him all seemed tentative and uncertain.

His opposite, Chief Factor James Douglas, cast a narrow eye over the governor. Blanshard carried himself well, Douglas thought. His Excellency, Douglas reported to Chief Trader A.C. Anderson, at Fort Colvile (later Colville, Washington), in favourable and typically cautions terms, "has neither secretary nor troops, being accompanied by a single body servant. I have not had time to become much acquainted, but I may say that his quiet, gentlemanly manner is prepossessing." Englishmen of his era were naturally reticent, but Blanshard also had the self-confidence expected of a well-bred and well-heeled male of his social standing, university and legal background. He exhibited a natural conservatism. Londoners such as Blanshard were renowned for their quick wit and sophisticated self-interest. Douglas recognized admirable characteristics in Blanshard.[76] All the same, Blanshard was the outsider. Douglas intended to keep it that way.

Douglas also told Anderson that the governor had "not yet entered upon his Executive duties, further than reading his commission to the assembled states of the colony" (by "states" he meant representative persons gathered in the Great Hall at the time of his reading himself in as governor). But that was a sleight of hand, for the governor was engaged in considering the urgent appeal from Douglas that he exercise his viceregal influence, his weight of office, to avoid a potential calamity. Douglas knew that two vessels of hungry labourers and settlers, on their way round Cape Horn from England, must soon arrive. Many new mouths would have to be fed. The environs of Victoria, though boasting promising parkland for grazing, fields for dairy herds, and prairie lands for the growing of crops, were still under early development. Food was not in abundance, though gardens were being planted, land tilled and new grazing fields opened—all requiring methods of drainage. Foodstuffs had to be imported for the crews constructing fort, palisades and buildings. Fort Langley, founded in 1827 on the Fraser River, supplied much food. Nisqually, in what is now Washington State, was a source of cattle, sheep, oxen and horses. Not only did the local agriculture have to serve Fort Victoria, its servants and their families (who were kept on the fort's books), but it also had to supply daily provisions of food and drink for the expanding marine department and, further, provisions for the "outfits" for the various distributing posts, chiefly Fort Langley and Fort Rupert. We come to the details of this urgent need presently. In all circumstances, in conformity with his instructions, Blanshard intended to give aid to the colony by his personal power and influence.

In his letter to Anderson, Douglas assessed how Blanshard regarded his new territory: "He is rather startled at the wild aspect of the country but will get used to it in time."[77] Forests, mountains, inlets and streams dominated the landscape. The industrial age had hardly arrived.

This letter, written in confidence to A.C. Anderson, is our best window through which to see how the Company characterized the recently arrived governor.

We have no written record of Blanshard's raw impressions of the stiff and formal Douglas. They probably squared with many a description of the already impressive man who was well aware of his own pre-eminence and displayed an irritating conceit. We turn to Douglas now, an essential figure in British Columbia's early history. At age forty-seven, Douglas presented a formidable figure, one even more prepossessing than Blanshard. Over six feet in height, thickset, powerful of frame, dark in complexion and brawny, he was the example of an individual of frontier bearing yet of unusual managerial mien. He was as large in mental capacities and outlook as he was powerful of physique and commanding in presence. Cold, calculating and tough in the clinch, also able to counter or deflect any criticism, he was artful and assiduous in the performance of Company or official duties. A private fellow, he held matters close to his chest. He was reserved and even distant in his manner. He lacked a sense of humour, though loved a sense of occasion, particularly to "hold court" at the mess hall dining table. This "Scotch West Indian," as he was known in the fur trade, was son of John Douglas, a merchant of Glasgow, whose family's business included sugar and tobacco plantations in Demerara, British Guiana, now Guyana. There John formed an attachment with a Miss Ritchie, a free woman of Barbadian-Creole ancestry (and not, as has sometimes been stated, a "mulatto").[78] James was born there 18 August 1803. He was educated in Lanark, Scotland, and is known to have fought his own way with all sorts of boys, doing so successfully.

Already, in March 1850, when Blanshard arrived, Douglas was a fabled character, known by this superiors to be a steady, trustworthy and active trader, "well qualified for any Service requiring bodily exertion, firmness of mind and the exercise of sound judgement," as Simpson noted in his character book.[79] He had entered the service of the North West Company in 1819, and upon the merger with the HBC in 1821 had continued in the HBC's employ. His superiors thought he had every reason to look forward to early promotion. He married Chief Factor William Connolly's sixteen-year-old daughter Amelia at Fort St. James, in New Caledonia (now known as the Central Interior of British Columbia), doing so in "the custom of the country" (confirmed in a Church of England ceremony at Fort Vancouver in 1837). In earlier years Douglas could be furiously violent when aroused, but this he managed to quell by self-discipline. Amelia saved his life when he had an altercation with the local Dakelh. Douglas survived a "tumult" with persons known as the Carrier and, it is said, had killed an Indigenous person. Other testy episodes occurred during these distant years. He was assaulted by Indigenous people; his post was invaded. Threats abounded. Douglas was bent on leaving the high country. "Douglas's life is much exposed among these Carriers," his father-in-law Connolly knowingly reported to Governor Simpson in 1829. "He would readily face a hundred of them, but he does not much like the idea of being assassinated, [and] with your permission he might next year be removed to the Columbia; wherever he might be placed he can not fail of being essentially useful."[80] On Connolly's recommendation he was transferred to Fort Vancouver, where, as a member of the powerful Board of Management of the Columbia Department, he made his mark. He had already displayed business acumen of a high order. At Fort Vancouver he was guided by Dr. John McLoughlin, superintendent of the department. Douglas seemed to have been born to business, the epitome of trade policy and expansion. In 1840 he extended the activities of the marine department, with links to Yerba Buena, California, and Sitka, Alaska. It is not too much to say that he was master of all he surveyed. But with the Oregon Treaty, he and McLoughlin parted ways.

In 1849 Douglas removed to Fort Victoria with his family, for he had already arranged the shifting of the Company's headquarters, shipping depot and provisioning centre from Fort Vancouver to Fort Victoria. As stated, he selected the site for Fort Victoria and ordered its construction.[81] In a way, this was his fiefdom. Of note, Amelia Connolly Douglas (later Lady Douglas) advised her husband on Indigenous matters, was the mother of thirteen children (seven died in infancy) and died in Victoria on 8 January 1890.

Most Americans thought Douglas autocratic. That he was. He is best described as decisive and energetic, masterful in temperament (which controlled a considerable anger, as mentioned). He exhibited a tinge of self-consciousness. General Joel Palmer, US superintendent of Indian Affairs, found Douglas very gentlemanly and dignified, also courteous, kind and informative. Palmer's associate Joseph Watt recalled, "Douglas was a man that would hold back on his dignity; he

Lady Amelia Douglas —née Amelia Connolly—married James Douglas when she was sixteen. It is said that she was sweet, shy and loveable, with the blood of Indigenous heroes in her veins. The Beaver, *September 1934*

would step around in a way as much as to say: 'You are not as good as I am. I don't belong to your class.'"[82] "He...does not know the tone of a high-minded gentleman," said George Hills, first bishop of Columbia, "owing to the fact that he has never lived in England."[83] "The moral habit of the man was justice," wrote Gilbert Malcolm Sproat, who knew him well, while another said, "The boys all thought a good deal of him."[84] Douglas, like Blanshard, was businesslike and methodical. He was guided by three abiding principles: obedience to his duties; courtesy, even if he felt wronged; and restraint (he had learned early that an angry man is always at a disadvantage in an argument).[85] At the time of Blanshard's arrival, Chief Factor Douglas was senior officer of the all-powerful Board of Management of the Western Department; he was HBC agent for the sale of lands, minerals and timber, and for its trade to California, Hawaii and Sitka; and he was agent of the Puget's Sound Agricultural Company. Few people in history have commanded such positions of commercial power. He guided the destiny of the HBC's Western Department, especially its shipping enterprises and northern trading.

As of 1850, when Blanshard met him, greatness of an uncommon kind and a knighthood (Knight Commander of the Order of the Bath) lay ahead for Douglas. He was astute and artful, one might say careful and politic, in all dealings with the recently arrived governor. He was on guard against the new arrival. Douglas disliked intruders. He had no intention of overplaying his position. He knew how the HBC was distrusted in certain circles in London; this was especially so in those expansive free-trading spheres. There they hated privilege, distrusted the old order. For his part he would, indeed must, play by the rules. But the rules were weighted in his favour.

The Company did business according to its own methods; it guarded its files and ledgers with utmost secrecy. To gain intelligence of the Company's proceedings and expectations, Blanshard would have to gather his own data and form his own conclusions. In short, an administrative wall stood between him and Douglas and all the other officers of the Company. This was the first reality. The Company was lord and master throughout its vast realms. Now there was an intruder. The Company management was unaccustomed to having a governor bearing the Queen's commission anywhere in its territories. Unsurprisingly, five months after Blanshard's arrival, Douglas referred to the governor disparagingly (but privately) as "a very liberal man," and by that he meant a radical.[86]

Whatever disappointment Douglas may have felt about not being confirmed as governor, for he had been designated governor pro tempore when that was in the offing, he did not show it. Nor was he jealous of Blanshard; there was no reason to be. Time was on his side.

In the circumstances, Blanshard asked Commander Johnson if he could remain aboard ship while the viceregal residence was being prepared. This was completely in order and arranged pursuant to Admiralty instructions (which Johnson produced for the governor's scrutiny). For the next several weeks Government House was to float in the waters where the *Driver* ventured by sail or steam. One might call this quarterdeck administration.

In due course, the *Driver* shifted to Esquimalt, the commodious harbour to the west of Camosun waterway. Esquimalt, or Is-whoy-malth, means "a place gradually shoaling"—a reference to the shallows at the mouth of Sawmill Creek. Here was a harbour of magnificent proportions, its shores heavily treed with tall timber, a place safe from all winds. Streams provided fresh water, and spars for the squadron could be readily felled, cut, trimmed and stowed aboard ship. Since 1846, and especially after the Navy surveyed it in 1847, Esquimalt had become the customary anchorage for British warships on the Northwest Coast—at the time of Blanshard's arrival, the smart new frigate *Inconstant* rode at anchor there—and in 1862 would become headquarters of British warships on Pacific Station.

Blanshard familiarized himself with the local geography, doing so mainly on horseback. Only a rough trail linked Esquimalt Harbour with Camosun waterway until 1853, when sailors from HMS *Thetis* built a linking road. "The road from Esquimalt to the town of Victoria is pretty enough," said Captain W.R. Kennedy, of HMS *Reindeer*, "but is sadly disfigured by the numerous pot-shops which line each side of it, offering irresistible temptations to poor Jack when he goes ashore."[87] The Crimean War against the Russians lay a few years in the future, and Blanshard could have no concept of how it would transform the affairs of Vancouver

Island.[88] This port, so promising to international commerce, soon became equally advantageous in terms of imperial strategy, an anchor of empire.

Standing on the fort's boardwalk gallery, taking in the extraordinary panorama opening before him, Blanshard cast his eye over the surrounding lands and waters. Fort Victoria and environs, he could see, was an infant but all-dominating seat of corporate influence. It was the new emporium of the Company on the coast, all hustle and bustle. On shore, in and adjacent to the post, artisans and labourers went about daily tasks, clearing land and preparing construction timbers. No settlers could be seen.

Camosun was Indigenous waterway, its shores Indigenous space. The Indigenous people generally kept to themselves. That had not always been the case, and in the early years of the fort (1843–1844) difficulties had arisen as they came in large numbers from near and far. The palisade provided necessary security.[89] In 1848 the Indigenous presence near Fort Victoria had led to the Royal Navy making a show of intimidating force on what became the parade ground, later soccer pitch, at Beacon Hill Park.[90] But by 1850 all was still. Many Indigenous people were in the employ of the Company, paid in blankets for work done. A sizable Indigenous settlement lay adjacent to the fort on the south side,

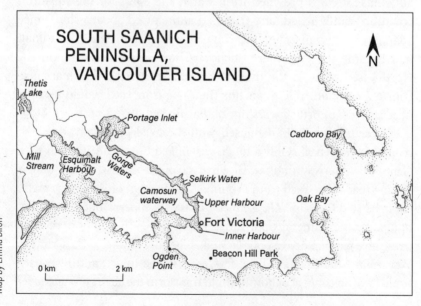

Map by Emma Biron

at what was then James Bay. Across the narrow harbour from the fort, on Songhees Point, and at other places, clusters of Indigenous lodges stood—rough, low, split-cedar buildings. On beaches lay handsomely crafted canoes, large and small; these disclosed the marine prowess of the people. There were many inveterate rivalries, notably with the Haida and Tsimshian, renowned for their seaborne prowess and raids as far south as Whidbey Island and Puget Sound. Expeditions of pillage and slave-taking enlarged the wealth of the victors. Indigenous visitors from far and wide were attracted to Camosun. Members of the Makah (Cape Flattery), Klallam, Skagit, Lummi, T'Sou-ke (Sooke) and Quw'utsun (Cowichan) Nations gathered to trade, work and play. Year by year, their numbers grew. Blanshard, if he saw them, did not comment on internecine contests for control. Nor did he regard the Indigenous presence as a danger. Indeed, what struck him as admirable was how easily the Company managed all affairs with the Indigenous bands. He had no quarrel with the Company on that score. Peace was the order of the day.

From his vantage point, Blanshard could see how Camosun waterway's Inner Harbour snaked northward to the Upper Harbour and through Selkirk Water, then disappeared from view westward through a narrowing and slender reach. There, all of a sudden, a rocky barrier called The Gorge presented itself, with a large reach of water beyond. And here a mill had been built for the milling of grains, essential to the settlement's survival. In good years, it was also a source of wheat that could be exported under contract to the ever-hungry Russians in Alaska (Russian America until 1867). Beyond the mill lay Portage Inlet, and beyond that an abundant freshwater supply in Thetis Lake and then the head of Esquimalt Harbour. Saw and grist mills were built, in 1848 and 1850 respectively, near the mouth of Mill Stream.

For the next few days, Blanshard messed with the officers and attempted to size up matters ashore. He began to ponder the possibility that the Company had chosen the wrong port for its fort and marine department depot. He could see that Esquimalt was spacious, well-treed and close to drinking water. Further, it was capable of developing marine industries, places of repair and shipbuilding. A couple of townsites could be laid out here, he reasoned. By contrast, Camosun was cramped. He was not alone in his view that Victoria Harbour should not have been the preferred choice.

When Blanshard began critiquing Douglas's choice of locale for Fort Victoria, he was bound to face Douglas's wrath. The selection of Camosun waterway for the Company's new marine depot had been Douglas's decision, approved by superiors. Blanshard's intervention was thus unwelcome. The matter was a contentious point with Douglas, who only considered the matter in relation to Company needs. While Blanshard envisioned Esquimalt as a place for two townsites, Douglas saw potential farms for the Puget's Sound Agricultural Company. Further, the London Committee had already instructed Douglas to reserve ten square miles of land at Esquimalt for agricultural purposes. In due course he set out plans for four farms—Viewfield, Colwood or Esquimalt, Constance Cove and Craigflower Farms, about twenty-five hundred acres in total—each with a bailiff in charge, with men from Britain to work the farms.

Blanshard was attentive to the colony's military needs, and for the small force of soldiers or marines that he thought necessary (about a hundred in number), he contended that a suitable piece of land should be set aside for the garrison. Likely he suggested a site near Macaulay Plains, with seaside access at a suitable bay. A Royal Engineer could lay out the cantonment on the most useful terrain. Blanshard thought in military terms. Such thoughts were alien to Douglas. His view was the less government interference the better.

The governor and chief factor held irreconcilable positions on colonial security. The former looked to the future; the latter focused on the existing state of affairs.

Chapter 3:
Frontier Frictions

For Douglas, the most pressing problem facing the infant set-tlement was that of feeding the Company's servants. The personnel expected to arrive from London had to be fed and looked after as well. The annual supply ship from London usually arrived at Fort Victoria in midsummer and commenced its return in October.

When Fort Vancouver was the main depot, the HBC always kept the equivalent of one cargo in store there so as to avoid any annoy-ance from the loss of a supply ship. The prudence of this measure was demonstrated in 1849, when the barque *Vancouver*, bearing the consignment from London, came to grief on the Columbia River bar: all supplies and trade goods were lost, but thankfully no lives. Fort Victoria in early years operated on equally slim margins, made more so by the need to ensure that when each vessel arrived with new arti-sans, coal miners in transit for Fort Rupert, agricultural labourers and even settlers, there would be food for all ashore and afloat. This rested on Douglas's shoulders.

In March 1850, two ships filled with newcomers were soon to arrive from London, the *Cowlitz* and the *Norman Morison*. This specific problem had already been brought to Governor Blanshard's atten-tion—and Douglas had also told Johnson the worrying details. The governor quickly decided to lend the weight of his office to a solution and request the Navy's assistance. On 15 March Blanshard penned this requisition to Commander Johnson:

In consequence of the scarcity of Provisions in the Colony, and a large number of arrivals being shortly expected, which may occasion the most serious results to the Colony from famine, I am compelled to request you, should your instructions from the Commander in Chief [of the Pacific Station] permit, to proceed with H.M.S[teame]r Driver to Nisqually and to bring thence to Fort Victoria such a number of Cattle and other Provisions as you conveniently can. The Hudson Bay Company will undertake to supply the quality of Coals necessary for consumption of the Service, but from the great number of desertions that have taken place among their Seamen, their own Vessels are not available for this Service.[91]

Here we observe, to our benefit, that Blanshard never wasted a word. Barrister's English was his preferred fashion: accurate, straight to the point. The matter under consideration was reasonable enough, and perhaps the governor wanted to have a look at a part of the Oregon country that had caused so much tension—and might continue to do so for some time. Johnson agreed to the proposition.

The issue Governor Blanshard referred to—would there be adequate supplies of food for soon-to-arrive immigrants?—was but one concern. Another was Douglas's fear that if Company ships were sent on this assignment, they would lose more men to desertion. The crew of the *Beaver* planned to desert en masse, but this was foiled. There was another consideration. Douglas failed to disclose the likelihood that HBC ships would be seized in US inshore waters. Indeed, we would like to know more about what Douglas had said to inform the governor and the naval commander of the turbulence that existed on the adjacent American frontier in Oregon Territory. Did he hold back information? Was it a trick intended to show the British naval presence in what were now American waters? Blanshard would have known about the militarization of the Oregon frontier and the recent arrival of US artillerymen at the head of Puget Sound. We do not question Douglas's motives; however, we are left guessing as to what intentions he had to send the governor in a British gunboat to Nisqually to embark livestock. US Customs dare not seize a British warship. So many issues were in the balance, as we will now see.

Douglas, adroit and prescient, had made a good case that famine might face the settlement. If that was not enough, desertions would further upset the shipping, and there were many reasons for desertion: the promise of cheap or free land in the United States, a female attachment or other sexual desire, gold to be found, hard shipboard life to be ended, poor pay, long indenture, officer brutality, freedom and adventure. Both British and US naval ships faced the same problem, though quantification of numbers is difficult if not impossible. California gold is cited as the main allure, but "the golden west" cast a spell over society, and the HBC's shipping department suffered. Three men deserted from the *Cadboro* at Nisqually the night of 26 September 1849.[92] The *Beaver* lost eight hands to desertion, and the *Mary Dare* some others. To keep the crew of this essential steamer, the Company paid a "gratuity" of £50 to engagés, persons under contract. Landsmen, who cut cordwood for the vessel, were not included: they were casual labour.

Blanshard learned of these desertions from HBC ships, which made it difficult to have the crews necessary for managing a vessel at sea. Douglas had told Commander Johnson that when the two incoming Company vessels arrived, more troubles of this sort were sure to present themselves. Indeed, when the *Cowlitz* and *Norman Morison* arrived, news spread that all the crew of the former had deserted at the Hawaiian Islands. The ship had been obliged to enter a crew of burly Hawaiians, or "Kanakas" as they were known on Vancouver Island, before sailing for Victoria.

Now yet another point of concern arose, as Johnson was worried that the "Kanakas" might settle their claim or right of possession from the Indigenous peoples. Here is an oddity. He reasoned as follows, giving a point of view not found elsewhere in the historical literature or its sources. "Kanakas" were a powerful presence at Camosun, and the prominent member of the Chekoneiin family of Songhees village was Chee-ah-thluk, known commonly as King Freezy on account of the frizzled hair that he inherited from his Hawaiian father.[93] Johnson provides no details, and surely he exaggerated the prospect of a takeover. However, he thought the fort's defences weak: there were only one hundred Company employees at Fort Victoria and another forty at Fort Rupert. And the sole British settler on Vancouver Island was

Captain Walter Colquhoun Grant, surveyor to the Company, who was attempting to establish a settlement at Sooke Basin (more on Captain Grant in Chapter 8).

The affairs of the Puget's Sound Agricultural Company, closely connected to the Hudson's Bay Company, now enter our story. The HBC experiment in using agriculture to halt the course of American settlement north of the Columbia River, a political expedient, was based on the assumption, largely developed by the Company's governor, and confirmed by the London Committee, that possession through occupation would strengthen the British diplomatic position when it came to finalizing the boundary with the United States. Fort Vancouver, Fort Colvile, Cowlitz and Nisqually Post are evidence of this policy. The Company's chairman, Pelly, shrewdly played his cards: he reminded the Colonial Office that the Hudson's Bay Company served a national as well as private interest in the Oregon country. The Company devised a defensive policy to ensure that its claims to the Oregon country north of the Columbia would be secured. Agriculture and settlement would be the means of exerting this policy, and the establishment of farms and the settlement of retired officers and servants as agriculturalists would be material evidence.

The Puget's Sound Agricultural Company (PSAC) was established to meet these objectives.[94] The management of this offshoot of the Hudson's Bay Company was entrusted to agents who were HBC shareholders. British settlers would farm and raise cattle at Willamette and Cowlitz. In 1839 the PSAC commenced operations near the southeastern head of Puget Sound, at a place near present-day Tacoma called Nisqually. Here, on the broad, gently rolling plains, the Company put up a stockaded post with bastions at each corner. Ships could come near to shore in safety. Potatoes, wheat and other crops were raised on a small scale in the sandy soil. On the wide and expansive prairie lying between Puget Sound and the Cascade Mountains to the east, the proprietors had pastures for immense herds of longhorn Spanish cattle, the greater number of which had been driven north from California. Bulls were also brought north. Sheep and swine were imported from England. In 1846 the farm at Nisqually was an extensive operation, with 8,312 sheep, 3,180 cattle and nearly 300 horses. Not only was it supplying Company posts, but it was also helping feed the Russians in Alaska, its main task. The Company sold fifteen thousand bushels of wheat to Alaska one year. Hides, horns, tallow and wool were shipped to England. American settlers purchased foodstuffs and stock. On occasion, surplus sheep were driven south to the Willamette Valley, as far as Eugene. In all, Nisqually was a paying proposition, and the availability of food and breeding stock was a boon to the companies. The rich soils of Cowlitz, tributary of the Columbia River, were better than Nisqually for pastoral pursuits and for the production of vegetables and grains. Nisqually was an ideal supply base, and a trade in furs became a subsidiary occupation.

Upon the demarcation of the boundary, however, the Puget's Sound Agricultural Company, like its parent, was hostage to fortune. History had decreed that its future lay north, in British territory. Shifting agricultural operations north of the border proved a protracted process. Shipping capacity was scarce, as vessels were often otherwise engaged. And moving agricultural operations from the broad plains near Nisqually to the rocky outcroppings, oak-covered uplands and boggy valleys near Victoria and Esquimalt harbours, or even to adjacent Cadboro Bay and Oak Bay, presented many problems for grazing, tilling, dairying and more. Blanshard could see it was a situation of making do. And from this time forward, he never wavered in his view that the HBC and PSAC were one and the same. As often as Chief Factor Douglas might tell the London Committee that insufficient lands existed for the objects in view, he was always overruled. His fear was that the settlement could not meet the needs of the day as they arose.

On 13 March, Douglas sent fair warning to Nisqually Post to get ready: the *Driver*, with Blanshard aboard, would soon arrive to board cattle and sheep. Commander Johnson proposed to carry to Vancouver Island a full cargo, say about two hundred cattle and four or five hundred sheep. Douglas asked that every exertion be made to get the cattle rounded up as soon as possible, as Johnson, facing many demands, could not spare more than seven days for this service.

Both Blanshard and Commander Johnson could expect a warm greeting from Dr. William Fraser Tolmie, chief trader at Nisqually. A kindly and good-hearted person, and a Glasgow University–trained surgeon, Tolmie had been in the Company's employ for decades, and in charge of Nisqually since 1843. Truly he ranks as one of the most picturesque figures in northwest history. Knowledgeable in matters botanical and avian, he was of scholarly inclination and philosophical mind. He had married Jane, a daughter of Chief Factor John Work. He was on intimate terms with James Douglas. His interest and competence as an agriculturalist turned the valley of the Nisqually River into the first home of scientific agriculture in that part of the world.[95] Nisqually's fields and ranges thrived under his administration.

However, in 1843 the first wave of American settlers arrived to ruin his quietude, squatting on the Company lands. Tolmie rose to the Company's defence, and his knowledge of law benefited him. Still, his world at Nisqually turned vexatious. It is said that he endured irritations with calmness and courage while defending a corporate empire's sagging monopoly. But underneath he seethed with anger at American high-handedness. Times were against him, though he knew the terms of the treaty and was bullish on maintaining international law.

When the Territory of Oregon was proclaimed in Oregon City on 3 March 1849, Puget Sound was still thinly populated by present-day terms: approximately 304 Americans lived north of the Columbia River, and this before gold was discovered in California. But already this was changing, as Blanshard would come to understand. By early March 1853, when the Territory of Washington was brought into existence, there were 3,965 American inhabitants, about half of whom lived around Puget Sound.[96] These sheltered waters saw a brisk seagoing trade in forest products. The sea became an important communication link for the small settlements. And as a result, Tolmie, ferocious guardian of the joint companies' interests at Nisqually, was facing harassment from US government officials as well as American squatters.

Vexations on Puget Sound began with the overzealous application of revenue laws to the goods of the Company. The first inspector of customs arrived at Astoria in 1849; he imposed punitive duty on HBC goods destined for Fort Vancouver. An irate Governor Simpson protested to Washington, DC; in consequence, goods were allowed to pass to territory north of the boundary duty-free, or in bond. Peace did not last. The US government tightened its grip, doing so on account of that energetic demagogue Samuel R. Thurston, Oregon's delegate to Congress, who was able to convince the secretary of the treasury to prohibit all direct intercourse between Victoria and Nisqually. The noose tightened quickly. In April 1850 the *Cadboro* was seized for carrying goods from Victoria direct to Nisqually. The Company's post at Fort Nisqually was seized for containing so-called smuggled goods. To cut down on cross-border voyaging—to seal the waterways to British ships and seafarers—all ships going to Nisqually were ludicrously required to go first to Astoria to clear customs.

The Customs District of Puget Sound was established 14 February 1851. Olympia, fifteen miles east of Steilacoom, was named port of entry, and later capital. The first inspector of customs at Olympia, the zealous and impulsive Simpson P. Moses, wanted the HBC out of Oregon and removed from the Indigenous trade. He demanded an assessment of HBC lands in Oregon Territory (the beginning of the "possessory rights" business). His attitude was "Pay them off and get them out." All this time, the agitation and antagonism of the settlers continued to increase.[97] We can only conclude that the Company and its agricultural affiliate were being driven out of American coastal waters by fair means or foul. The US Treasury Department agreed to move customs headquarters to Port Townsend, "the Key City of Puget Sound," at the northeastern tip of the Olympic Peninsula on Admiralty Inlet, which is the westernmost entrance to Puget Sound. Here was a watchtower from which US customs officers could keep an eagle eye on foreign—that is, British—shipping.[98] Governor Blanshard had to deal with this rising tide of zealous American protectionism.

The HBC faced a rash of ship seizures. In 1850, US artillery were being removed from Nisqually to Steilacoom, and the Company's vessel *Harpooner* was employed. However, because she carried some shingles and insignificant freight belonging to American settlers, she was seized as in violation of the revenue laws of the United States. HBC officers justifiably lived in fear of their shipping being shut down. Moses ordered the seizure of the steamer *Beaver*, with the brigantine *Mary Dare* in tow, for landing a passenger at Nisqually without first clearing at Olympia. These vessels then went to Olympia for customs inspection. Outraged, Tolmie at Fort Nisqually appealed to the courts.

In consequence, the *Mary Dare* was released under $13,000 bond. The *Beaver* was freed—and the Company awarded $1,000 for losses. An amusing detail is that Charles Stuart, captain of the *Beaver*, fled to British waters in a canoe to avoid arrest but in so doing lost his command. These petty but iniquitous persecutions and the resulting shipping crisis upset Company deliveries and loading of trading goods, export items and foodstuffs. Into the early winter of 1851 the HBC's shipping schedule suffered, became irregular.[99] Douglas realized it was time for the two companies to leave United States territory.[100]

Another source of anxiety preoccupied US officials and citizens and embroiled the British companies. "Indian wars" had not yet begun in Puget Sound, but by the time of Blanshard's arrival at Victoria there were warning signs. Indigenous peoples of the Columbia Valley had been depleted in number by the 1830–1833 influenza epidemics and further debilitated by other diseases and starvation. Now came a new threat. The Cayuse, near Walla Walla, showed hostility to missionaries.

Dr. Marcus and Narcissa Whitman headed up a mission at Waiilatpu, where Mill Creek joins the Walla Walla River, a tributary of the Columbia. Founded in 1838 by the American Board of Commissioners for Foreign Missions on good land, the settlement prospered. Then came the Great Migration of 1843 on the Oregon Trail. Immigrant trains bound for the Columbia found food and rest and medical care at the Whitman Mission. Dr. John McLoughlin, chief factor at Fort Vancouver, whom the local Indigenous people called the "White-headed Eagle," warned the mission that there would be trouble with the Cayuse. In 1847, dysentery, typhus and measles were introduced by immigrants heading for the fertile lands of the Willamette: a fearful mortality resulted among the Indigenous populations. Loss of land, inroads of disease, and unwelcome intruders made for a toxic brew.

The Cayuse and some of their allies unleashed their military power. In November 1847 the mission was attacked, Marcus and Narcissa Whitman were killed along with twelve more American men, and forty-seven women and children were taken captive. American historians call this event the Whitman Massacre (or Incident), and they call its retaliatory episode the Cayuse War.

When news of the killings reached Fort Vancouver, Chief Factor Ogden, who had great credit with interior First Nations (he was known among them as "Uncle Pete"), organized a party of two boats and sixteen canoe handlers and shipped a rich treasure upriver. He was bent on peace. The meeting place was Umatilla. Ogden made a bold speech: he blamed the young Cayuse leaders for sparking the affair. He warned that the Americans would begin war. He stressed the neutrality of the Company.[101] All consented to the surrender of the captives, and Ogden provided sixty-two blankets, along with cotton shirts, twelve Company guns, ammunition, tobacco and flints as ransom. The Company never presented a bill for services rendered.[102]

Simpson, invariably prescient, wrote to the London Committee and summarized the unfolding horrors: "There is no question…that the Americans will, in the end, glut their revenge upon the wretched Indians although from their want of discipline and means, it will require a length of time to effect the work of destruction."[103] The Company wisely determined to maintain a strict neutrality, though goaded by the provisional government of Oregon to afford assistance to punish those involved. Throughout, the Nez Perce also remained neutral, friendly to the whites at Lapwai, in order to maintain the goodwill of the Americans.

US Cavalry units east of the Rockies protected settler wagons heading west from Missouri against Indigenous reprisal. Beyond the Rockies, in Oregon, self-reliance was required of American citizens. A five-hundred-man force of volunteers of the provisional Oregon government was formed under Colonel Cornelius Gilliam. In January 1848, with warlike intent, it trudged eastward in search of the Cayuse. For three months skirmishes occurred—and then came closure. Five Cayuse leaders surrendered and stood trial for the murder of the Whitmans and other victims. On 5 June 1850 all five were hanged at Oregon City. The military power of the Cayuse Nation was snuffed out.

Already, another change had swept over the country. The Massacre, or Incident, was the key factor in breaking the deadlock in Congress over creation of the Oregon Territory. Congress passed the bill on

13 August 1848. President James Polk appointed General Joseph Lane from Indiana, a US Army veteran of the Mexican wars, as governor of the new territory. Joe Meek, who had carried the report of the Whitman murders to Washington, DC, was named US marshal of Oregon. In short, the episode ended with extension of federal control to Washington, Oregon, Idaho and parts of Montana; it was a turning point in western American history.

A year before Blanshard's appointment, Governor Joseph Lane had begun his term in Oregon Territory. He arrived at Oregon City on 2 March 1849 with a regiment of riflemen. Next day he proclaimed the existence of the Territory of Oregon. Federal money flowed in. The US Army was the shield of the republic. Arms and ammunition were distributed to settlers so they could guard against Indigenous encroachments and make reprisals against hostiles. The United States was sealing its northwestern frontier, arming its citizens. Extinguishment of Indigenous title was the essential point of policy. This was a rough and raw borderland of conflicting interests, Indigenous and white, where all was uncertain, in flux. For the previous three decades, the Hudson's Bay Company had given a sense of uniformity of management and trade. Now all had changed and the fight for land began, at the expense of the Indigenous population.

In accordance with the Oregon Donation Land Act, which Congress passed in 1850, 320 acres of land could be claimed by a single person and 640 acres by a married couple, though claimants could not receive final title to the land until they had lived on it for four years and made certain improvements. In consequence, Indigenous lands (relinquished by treaty or otherwise) and Hudson's Bay Company/Puget's Sound Agricultural Company lands, especially those at Cowlitz, were invaded, occupied and claimed by American settlers and squatters. It was a licence for violence. Reprisals could be expected, and fear spread among the settlers. What is known as the "blockhouse era" began, for government recommended settlers build stout wooden structures as places of refuge and defence. In all, twenty-two blockhouses or stockades were constructed to provide safe havens for settlers.[104]

The Indigenous peoples were not docile in the face of this new pioneer invasion and theft of lands. On 1 May 1849, ten months before Blanshard's visit, Patkanim, wily and combative chief of the Snoqualmie Nation, with one hundred of his people, all well-armed, stormed the gates of Nisqually Post. About this first organized and armed Indigenous confrontation with the whites of Puget Sound, authority Richard Kluger writes, "Doom awaited their race, Patkanim and his followers believed, if they let the Americans settle in multitudes around the Sound as they were now doing farther south."[105] A desultory skirmish occurred at the fort's gate. One American, Leander Wallace, was killed. Dr. Tolmie helped defuse the situation.

A war against settlers did not eventuate. However, the consequences were profound. Settlers, now armed by government, assumed an aggressive stance: they formed a militia company and took the offensive in a bloody reprisal. Those who recalled the incident were ashamed of their easy victory.[106] In the event, separating the guilty from the innocent was not the concern of the militia. The Snoqualmie took refuge in the mountains, dispossessed of their lands and homes and now well aware of settlers' retaliatory power. Tensions continued to rise: violence begat violence, but Governor Lane's measures during that volatile midsummer crushed an incipient "Indian war."[107] Soon settlements were established on lands belonging to the Nisqually, Puyallup and Duwamish and their neighbours.

Governor Lane's actions were backed by Washington, DC, in yet another way. In the spring of 1850, the *Massachusetts*, a propeller-driven steamer under contract of the US Navy, arrived in Puget Sound from San Francisco to make an examination of the shores with an eye to reserving land for military and naval uses and ensuring the security of commerce. Selection of sites to erect lighthouses or place lightships fell within its duties. On board the vessel were units of the US Artillery Regiment.

Lane directed Company M of the 1st US Artillery Regiment to set up a garrison and barracks near Nisqually Post,[108] using the lands and old farm buildings, frame huts and log cabins at Steilacoom, six miles from Nisqually Post across the plains. Steilacoom Barracks (the term adopted by historians so as not to confuse it with a post of the same name) was established 27 August 1849. It had no stockade. It lay on HBC lands rented to the United States Army for $600 a year. Tolmie was the rent collector. Here was a fist in the wilderness. So began the hostile militarization of "Indian Country,"[109] and the long and continuing militarization of Puget Sound.

When, a mere eight months later, Governor Blanshard reached Fort Nisqually, Company M was well set up at Steilacoom Barracks. He understood the realities of the situation. The establishment announced the intention of the US government to secure the frontier, guard the border, protect American settlers, and solve Indigenous problems with armed force. Settlers had received the attention they had so earnestly desired.

Captain Walter Colquhoun Grant, who had travelled to Steilacoom on his way to Fort Victoria and Sooke, assessed the situation: "This is the locale where the military are stationed, to whom the guardianship of the northern part of Washington territory is entrusted."[110] Having also judged the state of affairs, Blanshard may well have been alerted, if he was not already, to the need to have military force to protect the Colony of Vancouver Island. As we will see, he made recommendations to government to that effect.

Chapter 4:
Seagoing Governor

On 18 March the *Driver* steamed for Nisqually with Governor Blanshard aboard. Veteran mariner James Sangster, knowledgeable of the extensive arms of the sea that stretch toward the southernmost extremities of Puget Sound, stood at the bridge. He was lent by the Company as pilot and interpreter ("for the cost of victuals only," the ship's purser made clear). Sangster, sometime skipper of the *Cadboro* and pilot as required, was an ancient mariner.

A short and active fellow, he was slow in speech. He was known to have stood on Beacon Hill, headland at Victoria, and looked through his telescope, awaiting an approaching sail bringing supplies, miners, labourers and colleagues. Sangster knew all the safest passages and furious tidal rips. Assuming the *Driver* steamed at a conservative six knots, the distance from Esquimalt to Nisqually Reach, about eighty-five miles, would be covered in about fourteen hours' steaming time.

At seven in the morning of 19 March, in sunshine, the *Driver* cast anchor off Anderson Island, near pleasant Nisqually Post. Ice-capped Mount Rainier—Tahoma—loomed on the near horizon. The post stood on high, undulating prairie; it was situated some distance inland from Nisqually Flats. The cluster of small buildings sheltered within a customary Company palisade. In the forenoon Blanshard, accompanied by Johnson and Sangster, was rowed ashore. His requisition was presented to Dr. Tolmie, who acted immediately. He issued orders for cattle to be rounded up and sheep to be herded, all to be brought to corrals and pens near the beach, preparatory to being hoisted aboard the warship.

That evening, Blanshard, Johnson and Sangster were entertained at dinner by the charming and agreeable Tolmie. We can imagine conversations ranging over these burning topics—British politics of the day, American encroachments, Indigenous resistance, as well as Vancouver Island's future and Blanshard's role in it. Tolmie complained that he had lost all his workers to the goldfields; the Hawaiians had deserted. The local Indigenous people were very useful, he said, and all that he could trust. Blanshard listened attentively as his new acquaintance told of the complexities of the Company's prospects south of the boundary line. A sense of foreboding ruled HBC and PSAC affairs in the United States, the time of withdrawal coming nearer by the day. But the British companies were not easily moved, for they had been lords of the manor here for twenty years.

Dr. Tolmie observed Blanshard first-hand. He admired the stranger's appearance, habits and manners. Writing to George Simpson, he described the thirty-two-year-old Englishman as "a tall, thin person, with a pale, intellectual countenance—is a great smoker, a great sportsman—a protectionist in politics and a latitudinarian in religious matters. His manner is quiet, and rather abstracted, tho' free from hauteur, or pomposity, he does not converse much."[111]

Tolmie, a sober judge of character and a close observer, gives us two significant hints. As a Church of Scotland adherent himself, he was alive to Christian doctrines, and in referring to Blanshard as a latitudinarian in religious matters he was speaking, in admiration, of Blanshard's freedom from narrowness, seeing him as one who tolerated variety of action or opinion. In short, he possessed broad church sympathies. The High Anglican Church was not for him. As to being "a protectionist in politics," we take this to mean that he had been in favour of the retention of the Corn Laws (to protect British wheat producers against free importation of foreign or colonial wheat) and, quite likely, also opposed to the repeal of the shipping bill that had given preference to British shipping and shipowners. These had been contentious issues in British politics, but they had not gone the way Blanshard would have liked.

For all intents and purposes, Blanshard was an observer at Nisqually, a foreign official, though, as we shall see, later events drew him into prevailing problems. Blanshard learned that from Nisqually a route by land and water led southward to Cowlitz Farm and then on to Fort Vancouver. The HBC remained in commercial control here, and steady communication linked the affairs of the Columbia watershed with the burgeoning ones of the northern waters that commenced at Puget Sound.

Clouds were darkening over these lands and waters, however. Americans were squatting on Company lands at Nisqually and Cowlitz, claiming rights to soil by pre-emption. The HBC and its affiliate mounted stern resistance, but they faced a losing battle. One day Tolmie noted ominously in the fort journal that some Americans had come down to Nisqually via the Snohomish River, exploring for suitable lands to settle in considerable numbers.

The other fearful issue was the control of shipping, revenue and customs. The United States was sealing the frontier by enforcing trade laws against foreign shipping and collecting customs revenue. Blanshard was having a first look at two difficult matters: squatters on HBC land and seizure of British vessels in American waters, though British interests in the second matter were infinitely more legally defensible according to the precepts of the Law of the Sea.

Next day, 20 March, mounts were provided. Governor Blanshard, accompanied by Johnson and Sangster, rode across the gravelly prairie on their courtesy visit to Steilacoom Barracks, six miles distant. The Stars and Stripes (new in these parts) flew from the flagstaff. A pair of light 12-pounder howitzers were mounted in defence. A year older than Blanshard, Captain Bennett Hoskin Hill, a zealous officer, proudly commanded the company of artillery, numbering three officers and seventy-five men (most of them Irish and Scots). Approaching Steilacoom Barracks, Governor Blanshard received the recognition of a visiting foreign head of state and was saluted with fifteen guns, the echoes and reverberations passing through the river valley and around the sound.

Captain Hill knew a good deal about border tensions, having served in Maine during the "lumberjack war" over the boundary between Maine and New Brunswick in 1838 and 1839. Moreover, he was an old hand at fighting "Indian wars," pursuing the Seminole in the swamps of Florida and defending the Union position in Texas. He would serve in the Union Army during the Civil War and retire in 1865 as a brigadier general after thirty years of continuous service. He was known by his classmates of the US Military Academy at West Point for his gentlemanly manners and amiable deportment.[112]

That night Blanshard lodged ashore at Nisqually, a guest of Dr. Tolmie. Early next morning, the twenty-first, he went on a shooting excursion in the marshy wetlands, rich in wildfowl.[113] Later that day they rode down to the beach to watch the noisy spectacle of cattle and sheep being gathered before being taken on board the warship. All seemed in readiness. The party returned to the ship.

That evening it was the Navy's turn to entertain. Tolmie came on board for dinner and was joined by Captain Hill and the surgeon of Steilacoom Barracks, John M. Hayden. In the course of the evening, Hill and Blanshard talked closely about cross-border matters, continuing discussion about US Army deserters on British soil.

Captain Hill came to the foremost point. He informed the governor and Commander Johnson that he had the greatest difficulty keeping his men. Five had deserted a few days previous. He feared they had escaped to Fort Victoria, there to gain passage on a ship and sail for the Golden Gate. He cited the instance of two runaways who had slipped away in a canoe and stealthily boarded the HBC schooner *Cadboro*, secreting themselves deep in the fore hold. He complained that the two had been taken to Fort Victoria in the *Cadboro*. In his view, the HBC bore responsibility for aiding and abetting deserters. Sangster, who had been master of the *Cadboro* at the time, told Johnson that until he brought the vessel to Victoria, he had no suspicion that the stowaways were aboard. It had all been the carpenter's doing.

In pondering the matter of army desertions, Blanshard may have anticipated Captain Hill's allegation. Ten days earlier, on Sunday 10 March, the day before the governor read his commission at Fort Victoria, 2nd Lieutenant John Dement, US Artillery, acting as quartermaster, had arrived unannounced and brazenly searched through Fort Victoria with every expectation of finding the two deserters. He came away empty-handed.[114] Blanshard knew that Dement's action was a violation of British sovereignty, but Company officers did not resist his search. In consequence, when at Nisqually, Blanshard replied in the negative to Captain Hill's application to send an officer and a search party to Vancouver Island in future or to have the governor deliver up deserters.

Blanshard explained his actions to the Colonial Office:

An application was made to me by Captain Hill commandant of the U.S. military post at Chelakom [Steilacoom] to allow a force to proceed to Vancouver's Island to apprehend two men, military deserters from the United States Army who had, he stated, been taken from Chelakom by a schooner belonging to the Hudson Bay Company, incurring thereby a heavy penalty under the local laws of the state of Oregon. This I declined to allow, as I conceive that no reciprocal arrangement exists between Great Britain and the United States for the arrest of deserters for purely military offences.[115]

Blanshard was seeking to protect British territory from incursions by foreign armed nationals. He was correct in his actions, but his response had repercussions on US soil and in cross-border relations. Captain Hill told his military superiors and US Treasury Department officers of what he regarded as British failure to comply with US law. This was bound to invite further aggravations, penalties and disruption of trade.

Next day, the *Driver*, we note amusingly, resembled a cattle boat. The trick was to round up cattle and sheep, but the horses needed for this were in a wretched and weakened state, it being wintertime. Besides, the cattle were nearly wild and scattered across the range. In the end, all that could be collected at the beach were 86 horned cattle and 830 sheep. Tolmie says 85 longhorn (and scrawny) cattle and 800 ewes were boarded. Apparently, the warship could have carried more. At four o'clock in the afternoon the *Driver* steamed for Fort Victoria and landed the livestock there the next day before dark.

For the Navy, it was all in a day's work. As guardian of empire, the Navy undertook all sorts of tasks. Its ships could carry a governor, assist an archaeologist, take a bishop to a distant diocese, deliver antiquities to the British Museum or help a person of science. Freighting cattle, horses, pigs and sheep in large number was not the usual sort of work. A delighted Douglas was amused that a beautiful steam man-of-war would serve as a cattle boat. As for Governor Blanshard, he had accomplished his first task: the food stock of the settlement of Victoria had been boosted. Furthermore, he had made his point clear to Captain Hill: cross-border inspection by US troops would have no standing in British law.

For the moment, the *Cadboro* escaped the clutches of US authorities. However, shortly thereafter, on 22 April 1850, the ship *Albion*, from London, 480 tons, under Captain Richard Hinderwell, with former HBC shipmaster William Brotchie as supercargo, was not so fortunate. Under Admiralty contract to cut, stow and deliver spars to England, and with permission of the HBC (provided a ten percent royalty were paid if the items were taken from Vancouver Island), Brotchie determined that New Dungeness, on the American side of the strait, was the prime place to begin operations. On 15 January 1850 he had taken up a land claim under the laws of Oregon Territory. He hired Indigenous labour, felled and hauled forty-two great spars to water's edge, and stowed them in the *Albion*. Across the strait his activities were watched with amusement as an unprofitable speculation. At Astoria, US revenue officers heard of Brotchie's doings and set forth to investigate. They told Brotchie to cease, as he was on American soil, under the jurisdiction of the new territory, and he was in violation of US revenue laws. On 22 April 1850, US revenue officers seized, libelled, condemned, then sold the *Albion*. Hinderwell complained bitterly that he had the right to cut trees on American soil, for he had a contract with the British Admiralty to supply masts for the Royal Navy. He was incorrect in his assumptions. The matter was taken up with Governor Blanshard. He was unsympathetic and took the hard line. "Your supercargo Mr. Brotchie," wrote Blanshard in answer to Captain Hinderwell's appeal, "is I am informed well acquainted with the Northwest Coast of America, and consequently could not have been ignorant that you were trespassing on the United States territory nor that the U.S. Customs laws have been extended to Oregon territory."[116] Fact of the matter was that people previously in the employ of the Hudson's Bay Company were taking liberties in cross-border trade matters. Blanshard went by the book; it would be up to private interests to do battle in court. Blanshard would not support Captain Hinderwell or Brotchie. He refused aid on grounds that their business activities lay outside the jurisdiction of the colony and, more importantly, of the governor of Vancouver Island. Years later a US board of examination found in favour of Brotchie, and the US government compensated the *Albion*'s owners for the loss of ship and cargo.[117]

Brotchie, disheartened but unbroken, shifted his attention to Fort Rupert, on northeastern Vancouver Island. There he prepared spars for shipment. Indigenous labour was employed. Brotchie even got the reluctant Douglas interested in a joint enterprise, with the Company receiving its ten percent. Some spars were shipped to England in the HBC ship *Norman Morison*, on return passage to London. But time and circumstances would reveal how much easier it was to get spars at Sooke, on southern Vancouver Island. The enterprising and energetic Brotchie, foiled by customs on one side of the strait and by business complications on the other, wound up his affairs. Today he commands our sympathies as an entrepreneur caught in the maze of borders, monopolies, rules and regulations. Brotchie's later years were spent more profitably—shipping ice from Knight Inlet for sale in San Francisco, then serving as Victoria's harbourmaster.

Shortly after Blanshard returned from Nisqually, in April 1850, the schooner *Cadboro* was seized by the US Army near Nisqually, on grounds of smuggling. As Dr. Tolmie understood it, the 1846 Treaty, which established the forty-ninth parallel as the boundary between British and American territories, granted the British company the right to continue its trade south of the line. Americans ignored the fine print on this matter. American incomers, freshly arrived from Missouri and elsewhere, vehemently wanted the British gone. They were adamant in ousting the HBC. And in regards to the nicely worded fine print about navigation rights, these too should be swept aside. Tolmie was in no doubt as to HBC navigation rights in Puget Sound. He righteously attempted to hold the line, protesting on 17 April 1850, "I hereby hold the said Parties and all by whom they were employed liable and responsible for all loss to the said Companies from the detention of said Vessel, the Capture of such goods and the stoppage and derangement of business thereby."[118] us authorities, for their part, were sealing the frontier, enforcing customs regulations, exacting fines, seizing vessels.

It is not clear what actions Blanshard could take in the circumstances except to report the matter to London. The Colony of Vancouver Island had no revenue cutters and no marine police at its disposal, and it would have been foolish in the extreme to show the flag and take firm action in us waters. All the Foreign Office could do was send diplomatic complaints to Washington, DC, pointing out the right of the HBC to carry on business in these parts—which was an argument weakening by the day. The Americans were firm on the matter of border protection and of levying fees according to revenue laws.

This indeed was a turbulent frontier: the violence, destruction and displacement in the us territories have no parallel in British Columbia's history. From the Siskiyou Mountains north to the British Columbia border, a series of "Indian wars" occurred from the 1850s to the 1880s, until the zone of influence was pacified. The critical years were 1855 to 1860. us treaties with various First Nations were characterized by loss of Indigenous title, disarmament, removal to and consolidation of reservations, forbidding slavery and slave-taking, and enjoining against possession or use of spirituous liquor. Six treaties in Puget Sound began the process in 1850. Historian Roy Harvey Pearce, in his classic study of us Indigenous policy, tells compellingly of how, in 1851, the federal government began to protect settlers going west, acquiring western lands, assuring safe settlement of needed lands, and clearing the way for military roads and railways. The question, he says, was how to manage to control and civilize as peacefully as possible. He summarizes thus: "On the side of the civilizers there was little but dishonor; on the side of those to be civilized there was little but desperation; on both sides there was little but violence."[119]

Chapter 5:
Heart of Darkness

The running sore of Vancouver Island's affairs during Blanshard's governorship was in and near Fort Rupert, far from his seat of influence in Victoria—a different world really. Fort Rupert was at Beaver Harbour, which lies some 240 miles from Victoria by land or a little more via the "inside passage." In an era when voyaging under sail was the common practice of deep-sea mariners, it was at least half that again by sea via the treacherous, unlighted and unbuoyed west coast of Vancouver Island. Only a steam vessel would dare attempt the inside passage.

On the northeastern flank of Vancouver Island, where Fort Rupert and Beaver Harbour are situated, the transition from sea to shore seems imperceptible to the traveller. Inlets and sounds, bays and estuaries exist without number, and these are fringed by unforgiving rocky shores and backed by an evergreen tangle, the forbidding blue-grey forest and mountain terrain. Along this littoral, in sandy bays and coves, ledges of flat land afford space for clusters of dwellings, homes of members of the various Kwakiutl Nations, part of the Kwakwa̱ka̱'wakw or Kwak'wala-speaking peoples. As of mid-century, villages might have had a population of one or two hundred people, but at Beaver Harbour in 1850 the Company's recent economic activity had attracted many more. It was an animated scene, corporate and Indigenous seeming to mix together, but in fact existing side by side in contested and unsettled circumstances.

To the observer offshore, the shell-strewn waterfront at Beaver Harbour dominated the scene. High-prowed canoes, suitable for raiding, warfare or commerce, lay beached side by side. Between beach and housefronts lay a path, the main street of the community, so to speak, that followed the shoreline's gentle curve. The Admiralty chart of 1851 shows twenty-one "houses," five on one side of the fort and sixteen on the other. Regarding the latter, three rows of wooden structures ran parallel to the shore, eight nearest the shore, three in the middle row, and the rest in the inland row. Each Indigenous group had its own row.[120] Inhabitants of any one house were advertised to the wayfarer by startlingly bright-red and black heraldic emblems on the dwelling front. Beaver, thunderbird and whale were three such representations. In some cases these housefront designs covered the whole facade. Carved house posts conveyed messages—recounting the lineage of the chief within, announcing some famous event, containing a dead body or displaying the crest of a noble. These bright objects of pride also told wayfarers and, indeed, reminded the villagers themselves of the lineages and linkages, the parts and the whole, the myths and legends possessed by the dwellers. Their houses, as seen from offshore, resembled a fantastic conglomeration of cedar, all backing on the seemingly impenetrable forest. This beach near the edge of the world was bereft of defence emplacements; it lay open to attack. A footpath wound through the forest to the western inlets of Vancouver Island, where the proud Koskimo had their villages.

The Kwakiutl—"smoke of the world" in their own folk etymology—possessed, as they do today, a powerful sense of unity of culture and economy. The word *Kwakiutl* also means "fellow inhabitants of the same house." As of 1850 it became specifically associated with a confederation of closely related groups, or septs, living in near proximity to Fort Rupert. These four are the Kwakiutl, Kweeha, Komkiutis and Walas Kwakiutl. Their village, Kukultz, surrounded the post. They also referred to the location as Tsaxis, or Sakish, meaning "stream running on the beach." They closely traced their lineages and ancestry, and their hereditary privileges determined social ranking. Through an event known as the potlatch, they affirmed their social integration and, further, validated their ranking among themselves and in relation to their neighbours near and far. They were a people of public display, theatrical in their meaning and culture. To most peace-loving European visitors, they were a terror; but the HBC men, known for their trading acumen, had learned to exchange goods with them, though here as elsewhere they lived on Indigenous sufferance.

The Kwakiutl, and the Kwakwaka'wakw generally, lived in a world of rising expectations. The gathering of wealth, and the distribution of same at a potlatch, was designed to demonstrate undaunted power and was intended to shame all rivals. Perhaps no Northwest Coast society has attracted so much attention, or been the subject of such scholarly controversy, as the Kwakwaka'wakw.[121] It was the anthropologist Franz Boas who described a functioning civilization in its penultimate years, and his student Ruth Benedict who articulated her mentor's findings.[122] Helen Codere, not the last to comment on these investigators, described Kwakwaka'wakw society as one that in modern times had replaced military activity with "fighting with property."[123]

In Blanshard's time, this politically and militarily conscious cluster of villagers, the Kwakwaka'wakw, were a seaborne, raiding and slave-owning people. They formed no centralized nation. Their power was demonstrated village to village in a decentralized way. In the mid-nineteenth century, they exercised a wide-ranging influence in these latitudes. Geography and their own vigorous characteristics combined to make them the gatekeepers of the inside passage. They were constantly on guard against marauding warriors, having suffered terribly from the depredations of the Bella Bella (now Heiltsuk), a people consummate in their leadership organization and military strategies. From Nahwitti village south to Quadra Island's southernmost Cape Mudge, east to Malcolm and Cormorant islands, and across Johnstone Strait to mainland inlets, the Kwakwaka'wakw gathered their wealth at the expense of others. In the not too remote past, one group, the Laich-kwil-tach (Lekwiltok), numbering in 1846 about four thousand including slaves, had spread their power south to Quadra Island. The main village was Tsqulotn ("playing field") near Cape Mudge.

Farther north, on the shore of Queen Charlotte Strait, certain Kwak'wala speakers had villages in remote and exposed rocky places. These were the three groups known collectively as the Nahwitti (variously spelled). Their villages were at the northernmost end of Vancouver Island and on nearby islands. A main village prior to the mid-1800s was Nahwitti, Cape Sutil. Another, on large Hope Island, was at Bull Harbour, "one of the snuggest harbours on the coast."[124] Bull Harbour is likely named for the large and fierce sea lions that frequent the area. Today Hope Island is entirely a reserve of the T'łat'łasik'wala First Nation.

When British and American mariners came in search of the sea otter, the Nahwitti were well situated for trade and the acquisition of firearms. All the same, their position was exposed to raiders such as the Haida, Tsimshian and Tlingit, and so they, equally, became alert for attack and fearless in defence. It is the Nahwitti who feature in our particular story. But we return now to the story of Fort Rupert.

Founded in 1849, the year of Blanshard's appointment, Fort Rupert began its double role as station for the northern region of the Company's coastal trade and as a start-up centre for the mining of steamer coal. Simpson and Douglas had seen its potential. Steam vessels have voracious appetites, and the Navy was increasingly using steam as an auxiliary power. The commercial market showed promise also. The Company had no experience in mining and marketing coal, so Fort Rupert was a speculative undertaking driven by a web of circumstances predicated on the argument that steam was conquering the Pacific and the Company must engage in this pursuit. And so the faltering progress commenced.

A decade earlier, in 1835, while Dr. Tolmie was stationed at Fort McLoughlin (generally known as Bella Bella), some Kwakiutl men told him that "black stone" was burned near a village at Beaver Harbour on Vancouver Island. The next year Duncan Finlayson, under instructions, investigated. He found and reported coal beds at 50°30' N, "along the beach for some distance." He also noted a small creek affording fresh water and a very populous Kwakiutl village nearby. Finlayson said that the Kwakiutl would not allow the Company "to work the coals as they were valuable to them, but that they would labour in the mine themselves and sell to us the produce of their exertions."[125] So it was that officers of the Hudson's Bay Company learned from Indigenous people of the presence of coal at and near Beaver Harbour. The *Beaver* called there to examine the surface cropping, but the *Beaver* burned cordwood and made no use of the coal.

The Royal Navy, however, was beginning its slow conversion to coal. In the mid-1840s Rear Admiral Sir George Francis Seymour, commander-in-chief on Pacific Station, had one steam-powered paddlewheel sloop-of-war, the *Cormorant*, at his disposal.[126] Seymour realized that coal would increase the value of Vancouver Island to the strategic utility of Britain in the north Pacific. He sent the *Cormorant* to Beaver Harbour to investigate.

Commander G.T. Gordon of the *Cormorant* carried instructions to determine the quality of coal and its suitability for use by the Service. To this point, the Navy preferred Scottish, Welsh and Derbyshire coal— of highest quality, clean to burn and never in short supply. Perhaps Vancouver Island coal might serve New York–based shipping companies headed by the Aspinwall interest, which needed reliable, quality coal in abundant supply for the steam packets it was running from San Francisco to Panama and elsewhere. It seems now that Commander Gordon was overly bullish in his 1846 report about Fort Rupert coal. He thought the coal fields were of considerable size. True, when the coal was tested, the samples flared much in the furnaces, but it was of good quality, Gordon said, and was not injurious to the fire-bars or furnaces. It was good coal for forges too. Gordon turned to the critical matter of who owned the coal: "On first going ashore, the natives appeared tenacious of our examining the coals, and accused us of coming to steal them; but, having made a few presents to some of the chiefs, they entered into our views and became very active…The natives are a fine race of men, and appear industrious and friendly, but much addicted to thieving." He recommended to all deep-sea mariners that any shipping approaching Beaver Harbour do so by way of Cape Scott. The difficult and dangerous navigation of furious Seymour Narrows and windswept Johnstone Strait should be avoided at all costs.[127]

From this point on, the Navy and the Admiralty looked on Fort Rupert coal as a strategic commodity of national sea power, just as they regarded the handsome spars that came from the forests of Vancouver Island as essential for masts and yards of Her Majesty's ships. Incidentally, Gordon's report is significant in the history of geology of British Columbia as the first to evaluate mineral potential; it precedes reports on gold. As to Vancouver Island's other advantages to naval power, Seymour was pleased to learn that a ship of the line could enter Esquimalt under sail and find secure anchorage; in addition, trees could be felled for spars, and drinkable water was available. The squadron was much spread out in its supplies and logistics of support. Seymour was one of the first to trumpet Esquimalt's values, and did so on Gordon's information.

In the event, two years passed before any attempt was made to develop the location on a commercial basis. The driving force was William Henry Aspinwall, who in 1848 established the Pacific Mail Steamship Company to run steamers from Panama City to San Francisco. The firm hoped that the coal at Beaver Harbour would prove a less expensive and more convenient supply of fuel than Welsh coal. Samuel Cunard, founder of Cunard Steamships, also pressed the need: coal would conquer the Pacific. The HBC jumped at the chance of supplying all the coal Aspinwall needed and contracted with him to provide a thousand tons. However, the coal proved unsatisfactory, having but two-thirds the strength of Welsh coal. The disappointed Aspinwall bought no more Fort Rupert coal.[128]

Still, Simpson was keen to develop the mines on a more scientific basis. His knowledge and judgment as far as steamer coal was concerned left much to be desired.[129] Douglas, obedient to instructions, put the project in motion. Conscious of Kwakiutl opposition, Simpson wrote to Ogden, Douglas and John Work, who composed the Board of Management of the Western Department:

The subject of extinguishing the Indian title to the lands at the coal mine should receive early attention. I last year procured from Mr. Recorder [Adam] Thom [of Rupert's Land] a form of agreement to be entered into with the Indians which I submitted to the consideration of the Governor and Committee, who, in reply, stated that they would give attention to the matter and consult their legal adviser thereon... The report of the peaceable behaviour of the natives, their industry and anxiety to see us settle among them are very satisfactory; with good management we have no doubt they will be found very useful and in due time we hope to see them adopt the habits of civilized life and work as labour at the mines.[130]

Two deeds of conveyance of land to the Hudson's Bay Company were signed 8 February 1851 at Fort Rupert.[131]

Superintending construction of Fort Rupert fell to Captain William Henry McNeill, a storied figure in maritime history. His business acumen was second to none, and in earlier days, as a ship-owning rival of the Company in the maritime trade, he caused so much difficulty that Simpson ordered him to be bought out at any cost—and indeed this was done. He was made chief trader. McNeill, aged forty-nine, was noted for his kind-hearted nature, his courage and his enterprise. Children in Victoria loved him because he brought oranges, sugar and firecrackers from Hawaii in the 1850s. McNeill possessed a more severe side. He was tough as nails and noted, too, for strictness of discipline, a discipline in those days "as necessary as well ashore as afloat, altho' no one felt it, watchfulness having become a mere habit, or second nature, by reason of being constantly surrounded by real or supposed dangers."[132] As long as McNeill was there, the fort operated under rigid ship discipline.

Superintending the construction of Fort Rupert, from McNeill's point of view, was exhausting; indeed, at one point he threatened to retire unless given rest. So it was that his son-in-law George Blenkinsop was appointed in his stead under approval of Chief Factor Douglas.[133] Trouble lay ahead.

As the fort was being built, Indigenous labour gathered coal from the outcroppings and amassed it near the fort. It seems from accounts to have been brought from Suquash, nine miles to the south. From the mounds of coal at Beaver Harbour, it could be loaded into canoes and taken off to an awaiting ship. One at a time, an empty bucket or tub would be lowered from the ship, filled from the canoes, hoisted aboard and stowed—a dirty, heavy job.

The London Committee, hardly a specialist in the colliery business, imagined a lucrative opportunity. But a darker scenario presented itself. Peace had to be maintained with northern Indigenous groups. In this regard, for Fort Rupert, Governor Simpson pressed an active policy.

He anticipated Indigenous resistance. The fort's post journal of 13 April 1850 confirms his view:

> *This afternoon we were stopped by all the Chiefs for working in the Gardens on the lower part of the Fort. They told us we should enclose no more of their land as we had not paid them for it and that it blocked up their roads to the forest for wood &c. Knowing it to be had in contemplation by the authorities that the land was to be purchased of them, I thought it advisable to make each of them payment for the land necessary for gardening purposes &c. They willingly sold me all right to the land in the neighborhood of the Fort for a blanket and shirt each. I made them all put their marks to an agreement drawn on it to that effect so we may now consider ourselves the sole owners of the land or at least appropriate to our own use as much as we may require for gardens, mining purposes &c. They seemed highly pleased with the arrangement and said in putting their marks to the document "Loweelaa Secsaance" which being interpreted means we have no more to say and no further demands to make on you for our lands.[134]*

The Company was a seasoned hand at satisfying demands and easing tensions. But what would happen once trading ships began to arrive—intruders, so to speak—at this complex locus of internecine communications? Here are the essential details: Fort Rupert stood near the apex of rival Indigenous interests and on the sea route of these rival parties as they plied back and forth from places such as Haida Gwaii, the Stikine River and the Skeena south to Victoria and Puget Sound. If coal were to be mined and sold at Beaver Harbour, Peter Skene Ogden and James Douglas told the Navy, a constant supply would have to be kept there, guarded by sufficient force "to protect it against the natives, who are numerous, bold and treacherous; and to carry on the mining operations." Ogden and Douglas were imagining what was called in earlier days a factory, an armed fort garrisoned by irregular military personnel. Matters could not be left to chance.

As senior commissioned Company managers, Ogden and Douglas had no capacity or authority to initiate such a bastion of power. They made that clear. In the circumstances, they recommended to the Navy that, through the government in London, it request the Company to undertake such a project. Imperial "politics" steered in all channels.[135] Fort Rupert must become a protected depot of British power. Ogden and Douglas were prescient. This was a theme Blanshard would take up—and he would bring military analysis to the matter at hand.

Company officers could see that outcroppings and piles of coal were exposed to the elements. The stock was deteriorating in that wet, raw environment. Purchasers of steamer coal were choosy customers, disliking the poor quality on offer. A better grade of coal was needed: for this, shafts would need to be sunk by experienced hands. Other hazards existed. This was a new form of enterprise for the Company. No one was more dubious than Douglas. He was truly doubtful about the whole enterprise, as he told Captain John Shepherd of HMS *Inconstant*: "The result of this experiment is questionable in consequence of the peculiar circumstances of the Country, the savage and treacherous disposition of the natives, the expense and difficulty of procuring labourers, and the limited though increasing demand for coal in these seas, circumstances which present serious obstacles to the successful prosecution of this enterprise."[136] Douglas was as correct as he was forthright in his evaluation of the prospects of Fort Rupert. However, he too became swept up in the coal rage.

In 1848 the Company, through an agent, offered employment to the Muirs, a family of Scottish coal miners from Kilmarnock, Ayrshire. The arrangement was entered into this way. John Muir, eldest of the family, responded to a Company advertisement for land on Vancouver Island. Good land was available at £1 per acre, with a minimum allotment of one hundred acres. An alternate way of acquisition was to emigrate as "consignee" workers, with twenty-five acres being given in return for three years of work. Their passage would be in a Company ship round Cape Horn; their destination, Fort Rupert, seemingly at the ends of the earth. The prospects were nonetheless promising: a hope of a new life in a new land.

The party that sailed in the barque *Harpooner* from the River Thames was made up of John Muir and his wife, Annie; their four sons, John, Robert, Andrew and Michael; their widowed daughter, Marion, and her two children; a nephew, Archibald Muir; and two other men, John McGregor and John Smith, with Smith's wife. John Muir was the oversman, or foreman; among them was a blacksmith.[137] Six dreary months passed at sea. Arrived at Fort Victoria, the men were disagreeably employed as labourers until such time as the *Mary Dare* could convey the party to Fort Rupert, there to commence mining on an industrial scale. At Fort Victoria the Company engaged them in blasting rock to prepare the site for a dry dock, where in later years the Esquimalt and Nanaimo Railway station stood. They did not like the work. With relief they boarded the *Mary Dare* on 27 August, said goodbye to fair Fort Victoria, and set off for their new home in the northern wilds. A stormy month-long voyage via the Island's west coast, then around Cape Scott at the northern tip, brought them to their destination, Fort Rupert, Beaver Harbour. The date was 24 September 1849.[138]

The arrival of the miners and family was watched guardedly by thirty-five Company employees and about a thousand Indigenous people. The fort's occupants were wary of newcomers, hired hands. For the next six months, until Blanshard arrived at Fort Rupert, tensions ran high. Contractual problems were the order of the day. For the Muirs, the winter of 1849–1850 passed in toil, misery, discontent and seething anger. They seemingly had been led on a fool's errand.

Mining proceeded without result. All sorts of nearby locations were tried in quest for a rich underground seam. The Muirs, in their main attempt, dug a shaft at Fort Rupert, at the bottom of which they bored a further twenty fathoms (120 feet).[139] They gave up in despair of finding coal. Surely coal ought to exist somewhere, ran the rationale. Surface outcroppings indicated it. They turned to Suquash ("the place where seal meat was cut into strips"); this appeared most promising. The location, as said, was about nine miles south of the fort. It could be reached by canoe or scow or by overland trail. There, they knew, bull work in the dark and forbidding forest would be required. They set to the task, however. Depredations occurred at night, setting back progress. Another problem arose. The proud Scots, accustomed to skilled work "at the [coal] face," objected to doing field and pit work befitting only labourers.[140] This constituted a breach of contract. They also objected to being visited by armed Indigenous people threatening to shoot them. Several times, as Andrew Muir wrote in his diary, the fort was having "rows with the Indians"; further, the miners had to put up with "Indian annoyance by day and depredations by night."[141] The miners were poorly housed at Fort Rupert, another cause for complaint. Wintery weather, marked by freezing rain and heavy snowfalls, posed dangers to human health and well-being. In the desperate wintertime at Fort Rupert, three men perished for want of shelter.

On 24 March 1850, Blanshard set sail in the *Driver* from Esquimalt bound for Fort Rupert. The governor, in apparent good health, remained safely aboard for this winter excursion to northern waters. Colder, heavier and wetter weather could be expected. He intended to inspect the place of which so much was promised. He expected to meet the officers in charge and the miners, to observe the workings of the miners and to see Indigenous locations. Moreover, he wanted to make his own estimate of its acclaimed prospects. Unknown to everyone who sailed on this expedition, Blanshard knew a good deal about coal mining. His father had extensive business in the coal industry in County Durham. Blanshard, disclosing his streak of independence as governor, intended to reach his own conclusions—and not be taken in by the puffed-up reports of the hidden wealth yet to be dug from the rocky mounts of northern Vancouver Island.

His voyage north was through the inland passage between Vancouver Island and the mainland. As it does to this day, the journey held countless fascinations. James Sangster, competent in Chinook jargon, had been to Beaver Harbour in the *Cormorant* in 1846 and was a vital intermediary in communications with the local Indigenous peoples. And so here he was again, on board a British man-of-war steamer, to give advice on passages and anchorages. The *Driver* followed the track of the *Cormorant* via Rosario Strait, on the easternmost side of the San Juan Islands and hard by the mainland, then through the broad Strait of Georgia and north. In southern Discovery Passage, Commander Johnson remarked, they found the navigation very safe and easy for a steamer.

Suddenly, all changed and the tidal rapids commenced. At one point the current grew furiously strong and uncertain in its set; there you dare not steer by compass, Johnson wryly noted. In broiling Seymour Rapids, the ship could make no headway even though a surprising 9.8 knots was registered by the log hove in the wake. The ship was being set back. The *Driver* fought against the churning and contorted water. Four ratings staunchly manned the wheel as a check on misadventure. Blanshard, taking in the wild scene, may have brought to mind Dryden's translation from Virgil's *Georgics*: "So the boat's brawny crew the current stem, / And, slow advancing, struggle with the stream: / But if they slack their hands, or cease to strive, / Then down the flood with headlong haste they drive." The decision was made to anchor in nearby Menzies Bay, a sort of anteroom for northbound vessels approaching Seymour Narrows. There the vessel lay for two hours, awaiting slack water so it could transit the passage in safety. All proceeded according to plan. They steamed easily through.

Facing biting headwinds, they pressed ever northward, through long and lonely Johnstone Strait, then into Queen Charlotte Strait. In our mind's eye we can see a solitary, smoke-belching vessel churning through dark waters defined on either side by forbidding forested lower slopes rising to snow-capped peaks. Westerly gales could slow progress here. The weather was both cooler and wetter in these northern latitudes than in Victoria, and periodic storms from the Pacific brought heavy wind and rain.

About noon on March 27, the Company flag at Fort Rupert and the whitewashed, palisaded establishment came into view. The *Driver* dropped anchor in Beaver Harbour—a poor roadstead, for the tide came well out here, requiring a vessel to stand far offshore. The vessel was saluted with seven guns from the fort; the warship returned the same. Coal—about twelve hundred tons of it, collected by the Kwakwaka'wakw—lay heaped on the beach under watch of Captain McNeill or, in his frequent absences, George Blenkinsop. The *Driver* took on board eighty-seven tons, this given in exchange for that consumed in taking cattle from Nisqually to Cattle Point, Victoria. One hundred Indigenous people were employed in freighting coal, by canoe, to the ship.[142] Commander Johnson would not buy any coal, owing to the exorbitant price. As to Indigenous affairs, Johnson had this to say:

"Captain McNeill states that all the Tribes of Indians are exceedingly tractable, good tempered and peaceable. So we found them, and always ready and happy for any labour or employment, for about one farthing's worth of tobacco for a day's wages." This was a welcome report, and likely Governor Blanshard heard the same thing from Company officers. The sale of spirituous liquors had been for a considerable time prohibited, and the prohibition appeared to be strictly enforced. In his letter to the Colonial Office, Blanshard went further: he made clear that McNeill, considered to be better acquainted with the Indigenous population than any other person, estimated their number for Vancouver Island at ten thousand at the most but considered them to be steadily decreasing.[143]

Forty whites were housed snugly within Fort Rupert, serving the interests of the trading establishment. Eight of them were miners—the Muir party. At Suquash they had sunk a shaft in search of workable coal seams, but to little immediate benefit to the coal trade, which depended on many factors for success. A wharf was constructed. John Muir, the oversman, told the visitors that reports of surface coal were "absurdly overrated." Coal could be gathered from spots around and about but would only pay for the necessary Indigenous labour. Johnson and Blanshard had a look with Muir at some of the beds and test sites. These were stated to be eighteen inches thick, but only eight showed any coal, the rest nothing but slate. Johnson had samples tested in the *Driver*'s boilers and proved the point. Johnson also took on board enough coal to make up a number of casks, duly sealed, for testing at a later time in England.

Blanshard spent two hours with the miners. He heard all their complaints and listened patiently. As the governor could see, all was at sixes and sevens at Fort Rupert. McNeill had coal to sell. The Indigenous people worked the small economy, depending on seasons. Muir expressed unbounded hopes of finding immense quantities of coal. Early on he had foolishly proclaimed that he never saw a more promising or fairer prospect. Now all approached a standstill. He bitterly complained of the labour that he had to undertake. Indeed, until a forty-horsepower pumping engine arrived (it had been ordered out from England) to clear away water and lift and lower a cage and platform, no possibility existed of digging a shaft to a suitable depth.

Blanshard made inquiries of Muir. He then questioned some Company personnel and labourers. Conversant with the law of contract and of labour law, the governor recognized disaffection when he saw it. "The miners are unprovided with proper implements, discontented with their employers, and can scarcely be induced to work," he told Earl Grey, the colonial secretary.[144] Here was an accurate description of the situation, but as one authority puts it, "it was used against him by those in the colony who wished to see him gone."[145] As the *Driver* got up steam for departure and the governor prepared to leave the locale, Blanshard could see a confused and conflicted future for Fort Rupert. The Company made an uncompromising employer. The hands at Fort Rupert seemed an unhealthy and unsavoury lot: "Such a miserable set of devils I believe were never before congregated," the writer of the post journal had noted a few months earlier.[146] Moreover, the Ayrshire miners were a proud and fiercely independent set, quite capable of defending their labour rights even if they had to strike or leave.

Douglas sent veteran Chief Factor John Work to assess the situation. The Irishman, whose journals of various expeditions to the Snake River tell us so much about how the Company outtraded American opposition there, has been described as a man of strong rather than graceful physique. "His mind, like his frame, was constructed for practical use and endurance," wrote H.H. Bancroft, who added: "His strict integrity commanded universal respect, and his kindly disposition won all hearts."[147] But at Fort Rupert the Company officer misjudged the state of affairs. The soft-sell impressions he provided on his return to Victoria, that all was going well and that the miners were in high spirits, held no credibility with the astute Blanshard. Here, rather, was a place of dark complexities, seething problems and racial tensions.

HBC officers at Fort Rupert took kindly to Commander Johnson. We find this in the fort's journal (30 March 1850): "Captain Johnson is a nice man and uncommonly kind and rendered us a great deal of service by coming here. The appearance of a vessel of war has a good effect on the Indians."[148] Here is indication that the Company servants and the miners lived in some fear (hard to quantify, of course) of Indigenous populations, which were sizable. Blanshard gained the opinion, based mainly on McNeill's assessment, that the Fort Rupert and adjacent Indigenous groups were "numerous, savage and treacherous."[149] The only HBC defences were the stockade and bastion. Further, the only mode of coercion was the threat to stop trade: the Indigenous people were dependent on British goods.[150] Blanshard could see that the next Navy ship to visit these parts ought to remain longer for the security of the settlement and economic progress. He advised Rear Admiral Phipps Hornby, commander-in-chief of the Pacific Station, accordingly.[151] This is exactly what happened: his plea was acted upon.

For the present, his three-day visit to upstart Fort Rupert had been enough to reveal to the governor the difficulties ashore. The *Driver* had other pressing obligations. The ship's provisions were running low. The time had come to make for Esquimalt, via the west coast of Vancouver Island—invariably a difficult passage on a storm-tossed coast.

On 30 March, the vessel steamed for Esquimalt. A seventeen-gun salute echoed across Beaver Harbour as the governor departed the scene. A course was made to proceed north around Cape Scott. The channels, usually treacherous, appeared surprisingly calm, and the vessel steamed to an offing where sail was made. A brief time passed under canvas. The weather grew thick and dirty, with strong adverse winds. Steam was raised. The vessel made for safer waters offshore. Late in the evening of 3 April, and in heavy rain, the *Driver* entered Esquimalt Harbour and came to anchor in familiar Constance Cove.

All in all, and in review, the seagoing governor had experienced an eye-opening circumnavigation of Vancouver Island, one facilitated by steam power. The pulse of empire was quickening. "Showing the flag" had revealed several complex matters that the Company and the colony faced. Blanshard had seen them all. These were, notably, difficulties near Nisqually, where the Americans were flexing their muscles: British shipping was in peril of seizure by US authorities. Moreover, the militarization of the American frontier and settler unrest there foreshadowed wars with the Indigenous population. In addition, on British soil, to date there was a failure to mine saleable steamer coal at Fort Rupert. Tensions there ran high. Infractions of contracts and labour law had been presented. Now the governor, characteristically observant, as were his countrymen, could write home to the Colonial Office with a degree of authority that he otherwise would not have had. He had met all the principal personages, lions of the frontier. He had seen for himself. And he had more than an inkling of the complexities of the matters he was dealing with. The colony was in its earliest years, wanting settlers, devoid of capital investment—and all under monopoly capitalism. At Fort Rupert, as elsewhere, the Hudson's Bay Company was a law unto itself.

After reaching snug Esquimalt, Blanshard remained aboard the *Driver* for four days. He learned that Chief Factor Douglas had cleared a room in his own residence for him, as it would take some weeks before his own house, now under construction, could be finished. The weather and season had changed suddenly from winter and snow to clear, warm weather. Spring was in the air; planting of crops and gardens was fully under way.

Blanshard had ample time to reflect on the misery of the miners and the related complications ashore at Fort Rupert. He probably expected that before long he would be returning to that ill-starred place to deal with its various problems. It was time to draw up his report to Earl Grey at the Colonial Office.

On 8 April Blanshard completed his first letter, or despatch, to Grey. This reported his proceedings to date—the state of the colony, the visit to Nisqually, the complications with the US company of artillery, the closing American frontier, the visit to troubled Fort Rupert and the return to Esquimalt. He gave a disheartening opinion about arable land on the Island: it was so limited, he said, and consisted almost entirely of broken ranges of rocky hills intersected by ravines and valleys so narrow as to render these useless for cultivation. Blanshard's account of the natural capabilities of Vancouver Island gave no favourable appraisal of its so ardently proclaimed prospects. He entrusted his despatch to Commander Johnson or the ship's purser for mailing in San Francisco. And when his report reached Downing Street, it was not what they had expected or hoped for. It surprised and disappointed Colonial Office secretaries because it was much less enthusiastic than other exaggerated accounts from recent visitors or, for that matter, puffed-up assessments of agricultural opportunity.[152]

It was time to leave the security of the ship, which had been his floating home for ever so long. In the evening of 6 April, Blanshard and his domestic servant landed with their luggage. News soon spread to the fort that the governor intended to make his residence on shore. But he was disappointed when he saw the progress, or lack of same, on his residence. He complained to Douglas, who gave replies explaining how difficult it was to get tradesmen and materials. The governor's patience was running thin. From his perspective, Douglas and Finlayson were not giving his promised viceregal residence the attention it deserved.[153] This was to become a running theme with the governor and an irritant to Douglas.

Blanshard was not alone in his sharp critique of Vancouver Island's colonial affairs. Commander Johnson, preparing his report on proceedings for his commander-in-chief and the Admiralty in London, noted that the HBC ships *Cowlitz* and *Norman Morison* had arrived recently. Worryingly, the crew of the former had jumped ship in Hawaii, and those now manning the ship were Hawaiians. The *Norman Morison* had eighty immigrants on board; not one of them was unconnected with the HBC or its PSAC affiliate. Johnson was thinking solely in terms of the number of white colonists, or occupants, when he drew up this total: one hundred at and near Fort Victoria, forty at Fort Rupert, all Company servants. Then there was Captain Grant, surveyor to the Company, based precariously at exposed and defenceless Sooke. "No settlers had yet arrived, neither had the Company, it appears, settled their claim or right of possession from the Indians," warned Johnson. Would American adventurers make a try for empire here and run up the Stars and Stripes or some private flag of their own? Provisions on hand were scarce on account of the number of American ships putting in for supplies before heading to Puget Sound, there to cut spars and lumber for export to needy San Francisco. Douglas told Johnson that at Fort Victoria and environs they had 400 horned cattle, 1,200 sheep and a few horses, also 330 acres under cultivation. The Americans were good for business, and Douglas had no cause for complaint; however, Johnson worried that the ardent Captain Hill, at Steilacoom Barracks, would seize the *Cadboro*, thereby leaving the HBC unable to bring its furs from Fort Langley to Fort Victoria for forwarding to London auctions. Johnson was correct in his prediction, as we have seen: the *Cadboro* was seized within days.

The ship's purser, as required, had kept watch of the on-board cost of Blanshard for this imperial mission: £135 5s. 0d.—duly billed to the HBC.[154] Not presented for reimbursement were medical services and pharmaceutical supplies. But, as we shall learn, Blanshard's health was precarious, and he surely missed the attention that the ship's surgeon had supplied. Here was a tipping point for Blanshard, for the medical services ashore at Fort Victoria were uncertain. Company surgeons were assigned as Company needs demanded: piecing together scraps of information found in John Sebastian Helmcken's account, we know that Fort Victoria's medical establishment stood on no firm footing.

Aboard the *Driver* all was in readiness for the return voyage to southern waters, first port of call San Francisco. Water tanks had been filled, chopped wood for the fires stored. Magnificent fir spars, cut and trimmed by some hands at Esquimalt, had been hoisted aboard and secured. At first light on 6 April the *Driver* steamed from Esquimalt, finding just outside the *Norman Morison* inbound from London, drifting in light airs. Accordingly, Johnson ordered her towed to the entrance of Victoria Harbour. The Company could look after her from there. (In the event, the *Norman Morison* came into the serpentine passage and grounded on treacherous Shoal Point, though freed next day.)

The *Driver* steered to Sooke Basin to lend aid to Captain Grant. Off the narrow Sooke Harbour entrance they idled a few minutes in order to land some cows, sheep and wheat for seed to stock the farm. Grant's livestock had been brought from Nisqually. Once again, the Navy was coming to the colony's aid, "as no other conveyance could be looked for." The Company had no local steamer or tug to lend assistance; settlers were entirely on their own. As for Johnson and the *Driver*, no more noble work could be done, and other duties beckoned: time had come to say goodbye to fair but troubled Vancouver Island, leaving the governor to his own devices. Fifteen spars were on board for the use of ships on Pacific Station, and one ton of coal was stowed for testing in England.

∽∽∽

Early that evening, the *Driver* left Metchosin and Sooke to stern in the mist and gathering twilight. Beyond Duncan's Rock—that pinnacle said to have been seen by Juan de Fuca, the Cephalonia mariner in the service of Spain—the open Pacific beckoned past dangerous Cape Flattery. When it came on to light airs and foggy weather, steam was raised. Johnson ordered an offshore course for San Francisco, first passing Cape Mendocino, then entering the Golden Gate. The passage proved uneventful, and the ship anchored, as British warships did in those days, in Sausalito Bay. The date was 15 April—a mere five days from Sooke.

Commander Johnson now faced unimagined demands, and they merit notice, for they bear on the ill fortunes of the Colony of Vancouver Island. Looking across magnificent San Francisco Bay, he could see a forest of masts—of forlorn-looking ships. Gold fever had claimed many a crew. Ashore, lawlessness abounded. Every man carried his six-shooter; "drunken and disorderly" was a common charge. Vigilantes ruled. Here was the raw American frontier's gateway to the goldfields.

At that time San Francisco had no British consul, and no official to act for shipowners and besieged masters in distress.[155] There was no agent to deal with abandoned ships of British registry, and no one to adjudicate other disputes as they arose. Johnson sorted out many problems and was praised for his work by US customs officials. Another matter required his attention. Gold dust needed to be collected from British agents and sources and conveyed safely to the Bank of England. Johnson was happy to oblige. A shipment home would be profitable to him, his ship's company, the admiral on station, and Greenwich Hospital for Seamen. In those days the Royal Navy was the Securicor, or Wells Fargo, of the seas. Almost every British warship returning home to England from California, and especially Mexico, carried a shipment of bullion, or specie, all done under regulation.

San Francisco was all a-bustle, but what did that have to do with sleepy colonial Vancouver Island? Present in San Francisco was the inquisitive correspondent of the *Times* of London. He anxiously inquired of Johnson as to the state of affairs in the new British colony. Did it prosper? Johnson told the correspondent that, upon arrival, Governor Blanshard had been well received with a return salute of seventeen guns. Johnson turned to other matters and was frank in his answers. The reporter took note. "At Victoria," runs the newspaper account, "matters are not very thriving. There are no more than

100 whites at the settlement—all Hudson's Bay Company's people. The place is languishing from want of labour, the labourers and servants having most of them left for California. The natives are to a certain extent useful, however, and very docile, and a gratifying and marked improvement in their morals is perceptible which is attributed to the laudable exertions of a French missionary stationed with them. They have abandoned polygamy and other vices since he has sojourned among them." The news item recounted Governor Blanshard's visit to Nisqually, the transporting of livestock, the visit to Fort Rupert mines. Coal prospects were good, and a thousand tons of "surface coal" was available. "What a pity that this fine island, with a healthy climate, a great portion of which is capable of being converted into a garden, is not properly settled! Surely, with such a near and daily increasing market as ours [in San Francisco] is for corn, vegetables, and fruits, some effort should be made to settle Vancouver [Island], and take advantage of the splendid and easy opportunity of enriching its inhabitants by cultivating the soil and bringing its productions to California!"

The fact of the matter was that Vancouver Island was not a garden and could not feed its own population and also service markets near and far in foodstuffs. Indeed, its reliance on food imports would continue. The *Times* correspondent had it right when he reported on the faltering activities of the HBC at Vancouver Island. That truthful if damaging account, dated 1 May 1850, was published in London 4 July.[156] An ominous dark cloud settled over Hudson's Bay House in Fenchurch Street.

The *Driver* sailed for Valparaiso, reached 21 June, completing the prodigious cruise to northern waters—in all, about twenty thousand sea miles. Such were the days of "gunboat diplomacy." As for Johnson, he was promoted captain and retired as vice admiral. His contribution to empire-building had been on a small scale, but the aid given to the nascent Colony of Vancouver Island in delivering and assisting Governor Blanshard had been significant. In short, this had been a seaborne operation to a most remote quarter of the temperate world, where a faltering colonization project was being coaxed into existence, overseen by the fur barons and watched from afar by the Colonial Office.

As for the colonial governor, now ashore and temporarily housed in Fort Victoria, he had drawn his own conclusions, which he had sent in the London-bound mail packet carried by the *Driver*. "As no settlers have at present arrived, I have considered it is unnecessary as yet to nominate a Council, as my instructions direct; for a Council chosen at present must be composed entirely of the officers of the Hudson's Bay Company...And they would moreover be completely under the control of their superior officers."[157] Even at this early date, Blanshard had been thwarted by circumstances beyond his control. His was one-man rule over matters of civil and criminal law, and heavy is the head that wears the crown. Before long, allies would gather round him, though they were few and far between. It was the oddest of colonies, a business estate dominated by chief factors, factors, chief traders, traders, and other officers and servants of the Company of Gentlemen Adventurers of England Trading into Hudson's Bay and those who did their bidding. Years later, during the 1857 parliamentary inquiry, J.A. Roebuck, MP, asked Blanshard the obvious question: "Would any great mischief have happened if there had been no Governor at all?" To which Blanshard replied: "There would have been a great deal of quarrelling; it was necessary that someone should be at the head; that there should be some kind of law on the island, and to enforce it."[158]

Part II:

Spider's Web

Chapter 6:
English Gentleman

When, on first impression, Chief Factor Douglas sized up Richard Blanshard as "prepossessing," he did not err. For what he observed with a critical eye might be expected to be seen in an English male with all the breeding, wealth, education and circumstances of the governor's upbringing and disposition. The governor was a man who, you might say, was comfortable in his own skin. He had every right to be. Douglas's ability to evaluate a man's character was of high order, and it was not in doubt in regards to Blanshard. Douglas's further assessment that Blanshard, on first encounter, was astonished by the wilds of the country when he was set down on Vancouver Island's rocky shores in winter 1850 also rings true.

Blanshard was well travelled and had seen other frontiers of empire, but he was astonished because Vancouver Island and the Northwest Coast were indeed, at least by London standards, a wilderness, rockbound and heavily forested. The industrial age—steam power, milling machinery, paddlewheel steamers—was just starting to appear on this far shore. Admittedly, steam navigation had come this way in 1836 with the arrival of the steamer *Beaver*, but all of the material infrastructure of HBC empire on the coast was non-industrial. Not a nail was used in the construction of Fort Victoria's buildings. Trading goods were shipped from England on annual account, and furs, wool, tallow and spars went outward on sale and exchange. The HBC thrived in the pre-industrial age. No wonder Blanshard was astonished; only months before, he had left London, throbbing heart of the world's commerce.

Blanshard was cut from a different cloth than Douglas. He was born into a dramatically changing England. The middling classes, as they liked to call themselves, formed a wealthy new order: bands of enterprising individuals living in new urban societies. The powers of castles, manors and broad acres had given way to "the vast and solid riches of those middle classes, who are also the genuine depositaries of sober, rational, intelligent and honest English feeling."[159] Their swelling ranks ranged from wealthy merchants, industrialists and bankers to naval and military officers, professional men, clergymen and civil servants.

Fair to say, he exhibited the profound humourlessness exhibited by other young men of that era and class. They were representatives of Victorian earnestness, moral rectitude and probity—all the essentials of a proper Englishman of the time. He was not aloof or cold but steady and amiable in a quiet sort of way. Self-governed, one might say. Good at business, he was also careful in his matrimonial quest. Service in the interests of the nation and Empire he pursued as a noble duty. He was no John Bull patriot; he spoke from legal and constitutional positions, positions that would encourage progressive growth. The Victorians craved improvement under good management. Blanshard was one of their champions.

He is best described as a gentleman capitalist of legal mind. He was a man of property. His father had extensive landholdings and promoted agricultural economy. Richard Blanshard was well-heeled from the banking, coal mining, industrial and shipping enterprises that had made him, his sister and brother-in-law, his brother, his father and perhaps his uncle and their families wealthy. He was not of the first rank of society. As to social class, he was gentry, though never landed gentry with a title and coat of arms. None of that mattered to Richard. He was a modernist. He had no expectations of a seat in the House of Lords. He never stood for election to the House of Commons or any other elected office. That sort of thing was for the old guard or for new and coming aspirants. He favoured the liberalization of rules that protected special interest groups. An age of reform was under way and held his attention. What fascinated him, besides the law of contract, were the moving engines of commerce and industrial enterprise. He had powers of judgment and an air of authority that marked him as exceptional. By higher education and legal training, he stood above the rest in the nascent colony.

Richard Blanshard embodied attitudes and actions of the commercial classes of wealth and well-being that flourished in early and mid-Victorian Britain. If God was an Englishman, Blanshard met the criteria of commercial promise at least. And he was typical of his era, a model of a certain type of Englishman, or Briton. In a class-ridden society, he had his own firm niche, as did his father, sister and brother. His father, his uncle and his brother-in-law owned slave plantations in the West Indies and had been compensated for the loss of "property" in 1834, when slavery ended in the Empire. Richard Blanshard came from a line of shipowners, bankers and investors; they were also insurers or underwriters, capitalists, plantation owners, estate agents. They lived prudently and securely according to the state of their bank accounts and availability of merchant capital. Government regulations favoured their interests, though they operated under no special powers granted by government.

In other words, Blanshard was a free capitalist, an independent; he was not tied to corporate rules and regulations such as were laid forth for the HBC. Sir James Stephen at the Colonial Office was correct when he said that the HBC resembled in its charter and rights some of the old constitutions given to some early American colonies. In fact, when Blanshard encountered the HBC, it was about to enter its final phase, in which its investments in land and infrastructure would be compensated by its arrangements with both the United States government and the British government. This is known as "the possessory rights question," which was brought to a close in about 1869. Thereafter the HBC became a land company, and still later a merchandise operation. It was successful in new modes of operation, which differed completely from the last years of the fur barons that were being played out in the 1840s and early 1850s.

The Blanshard family history presents a tightly woven tapestry. In 1600 the Honourable East India Company sent its first ships to ports of the Asian subcontinent to bring back muslin, silks, tea and spices.

Later, the Company hired private vessels. These broad-beamed, loftily rigged Indiamen were purpose-built ships given the sailing distances required, and they were built on the River Thames. A cartel of shipbuilders began building Indiamen and leased them to the Company. A shipowner had the right to build a replacement ship. With one voyage out East every other year, commanders made fortunes in a matter of three successful voyages. Four expeditions to the Indies consumed a ship's life, and the replacement vessel would be built by the managing owner, called the "ship's husband."[160]

The Blanshard family's East India Company connections began with the governor's grandfather, John Atkinson Blanshard, captain of East Indiamen *York* and *Rockingham*, doing business mainly to Bengal. The Book of Common Prayer he carried to sea reveals a long history in shipping and enterprise.[161] His son Henry—that is, Richard Blanshard's father—like his father before him (and also his uncle, Commander John Blanshard, East India Company Marine), prospered in shipping. Henry became managing owner of the *Rockingham*. Times favoured this man and so did the pulsing aspirations of the British Empire.

East India Company trade offered Henry Blanshard boundless opportunities. This was the era of what is called the "Country trade," of independent shipowners and merchants trading under the banner of the East India Company but investing and risking their own ships and cargoes. In short, Henry Blanshard was a shipping magnate, and he had ships built for him at Blackwall, such as the *Catherine*; he also owned at one time or another the *Lord Lowther*, *Thames*, *James Sibbald* and *Countess of Harcourt*. The *Thames* sailed from China to England in only 115 days.[162] All through the Napoleonic Wars and afterward, we speculate, his interests in marine trades benefited his schemes. His ships sailed to India's main ports, and to China and to South Australia. He was not a soldier, though had suggested connections with the army, especially the Indian Army. The family fortune was first built on East India Company shipping. One of his ships, *Tephene*, sailing home from Bengal, shipped raw silk in bales, a very valuable cargo. The spirit of British merchant enterprise was unbounded, said Henry Dundas at the Board of Trade, and so it was with the Blanshards in the late eighteenth and early nineteenth centuries.

Meanwhile, Henry Blanshard was also in an inner circle of bankers, investors and moneylenders in the City of London. This was, perhaps, first and foremost among his occupations. Henry was in close co-operation with Richard Percival, whose bank, Willis, Percival & Co., conducted business in Lombard Street, City of London. In those days, individuals exercised importance in the world of finance. This was before the evolution of joint-stock banks with shareholders, such as today's National Westminster, Royal Bank of Scotland or Hongkong and Shanghai Bank (HSBC). It is highly likely that Richard Blanshard (apart from his time in Vancouver Island) was fully conversant with and active in the banking business—and more likely than not attending to his father's extensive financial and industrial empire. Henry Blanshard would be known to the influential financiers of England. They form a group that historians P.J. Cain and A.G. Hopkins have rightly called "gentlemanly capitalists."[163] Henry Blanshard knew the immensely powerful Sir John Henry Pelly, governor of the Bank of England, who was also governor of the Hudson's Bay Company. (Therein lies the essential clue to Richard Blanshard's nomination to be governor of the Colony of Vancouver Island.) Henry Blanshard was also a director of the London Assurance Corporation, established 1720, a premier marine and property insurer. British slavery records indicate that Henry was a trustee of two plantations in Barbados.[164] And a side note: individual bankers were intimately connected to Freemasonry. Willis, Percival & Co., in which he had an interest, was a firm synonymous with banking, one of the oldest (founded 1700) and most prestigious private banking partnerships. When it failed, in 1878, Lord Carnarvon, the pro grand marshal of the Grand Lodge, Grand Chapel and Masonic Chambers, proclaimed it a catastrophe.[165] The old order was giving way to the new service economy: the individual capitalists of yesteryear, such as Henry Blanshard and his sons, were yielding to new means of doing business.

But that was in the future. In the 1820s there was a new line of enterprise that the elder Henry Blanshard, capitalist and investor, was engaged in: the mining and marketing of coal. The United Kingdom was advancing through its industrial revolution, and this was the age of steamships and railways, and of canal and port development. Henry was at the leading edge. He could see the benefits of railway and port development, of iron- and steelmaking. He acquired the Coxhoe coal mine in County Durham, and in 1824 he developed a horse-drawn line, Clarence Railway, that ran twenty-six miles from Willington to Port Clarence, near the mouth of the River Tees. It had a branch to the Stockton and Darlington Railway, that famed early iron road for conveyance of goods and people. A contest ensued between Blanshard's group, of which he was chairman, and Stockton and Darlington, for the latter fought to maintain its primacy. Blanshard's idea was to promote the Tees Valley in County Durham, outflanking Tyneside interests of Newcastle, Northumberland, where much industry was developing. The Earls Grey of Howick Hall are prominent in the history of County Durham, another connection with the Blanshards.

At the dawn of the nineteenth century, landowners and tenants found themselves swept aside by the power of steam locomotion. Previously, it had been canals and toll roads; now it was iron rails. Landholders and conservative interests ardently resisted the Blanshard syndicate, but Henry Blanshard ultimately ran his Clarence Railway north into Hartlepool, a short distance from the lower Tees River, bringing coal to iron and steel industries via Port Clarence, benefiting Cleveland and Middlesbrough. Amalgamation with what had become the Stockton and Hartlepool Railway, the sharing of rail lines and the plans for a new protective pier, with graving docks, shipbuilding and bonded timber yards, were masterminded by 1851. The new organization was the Hartlepool West Harbour and Dock Company.[166] Henry, colliery owner and chairman of Clarence Railway, 1841–1853, willed his shares in the company to his sons Richard and Henry and daughter Margaret by deed; each received a portion of this valuable inheritance.[167]

Henry Blanshard was equally interested in agriculture, land use, land protection, crops, grazing and animal husbandry. Some of his earliest wealth may have been in land. The Napoleonic Wars favoured him, with demands and government contracts for grains, foodstuffs and delivery of same.

As a merchant banker, Richard's father was handsomely situated to promote agriculture and to build railways. He could extend credit and prudently invest. His will discloses a man very careful with his money, reminding this author of a comment made by a Canadian industrialist who said it had been his observation in life that those who had money were the ones who had looked after it—and all the Blanshards were careful with their money. At Henry's death, on 28 March 1854, he was a governor of the Royal Agricultural Society of England, of which he had at one time been chairman.

Henry Blanshard grew up in a prosperous and energetic family. His will shows that he was accustomed to affluence. It also shows that he was assured that the future would be looked after for his family and close friends, who were connected to him in business or the professions. His will stated that upon his death all his lands and property would come to his eldest son, Richard Blanshard. This was required by the laws of primogeniture.

Henry Blanshard married Sarah Ann Percival, daughter of his banking associate, on 24 March 1814, at St. Mary, Islington, giving his home parish as St. Andrew, Holborn. Their first offspring, and only daughter, Margaret Blanshard, was born 22 September 1815. In 1835 she married Richard Davis, a West India merchant with interests in plantations and slaves. Margaret's son, Richard Percival Davis (1840–1915), rose to be a colonel in Her Majesty's Indian Army. He retired and became a farmer and justice of the peace in Walton-on-Naze, Essex, and the esteemed high sheriff of Essex in 1903. Under the laws of primogeniture, he inherited all real estate of Governor Richard Blanshard. We return to him later.

Richard Blanshard was born 19 October 1817, first son of Henry and Sarah Ann Blanshard, then of Islington, North London. Like his siblings, Richard was raised in an atmosphere of finance and prosperity, nannies and governesses. Agricultural and industrial progress dominated the age. The family history shows an interest in collecting antiquities. The family were strong adherents to the Church of England. The world of the Blanshards over several generations rested in the power of the City of London and its global tentacles of influence in shipping, plantations and slavery. Londoners of their wealth lived in handsome townhouses. The family residence was 37 Great Ormond Street, Bloomsbury, and was four floors above stairs. That street then ran from the British Museum past the Coram Foundling Hospital for orphans to Gray's Inn Road.[168] Thirty-seven Great Ormond Street is now part of Great Ormond Street Hospital for Children. Like many of his station, Richard's father also had a country property—in his case, Kirby-le-Soken, Manningtree, Essex. He owned the island there, Horsey (purchased before 1840), and large acres of farmland and tenancies. This was a remote part of East Anglia, and Richard likely spent considerable time there. Indeed, Kirby was one of the consistencies of his life, and he knew it from childhood to his death.

There are many Richard Blanshards in the family genealogy, but perhaps the future Governor Blanshard was named for his illustrious uncle, Richard Blanshard of New Ormond Street, London, a fellow of the Royal Society and of the Society of Antiquaries. He was the eldest son of Captain John Atkinson Blanshard. His mother, Harriet Gale, was a granddaughter of the celebrated antiquary Roger Gale of Scruton, eldest son of Thomas Gale, Dean of York. *The Gentleman's Magazine*, 1836, gives this obituary of Uncle Richard: "This amiable gentleman acquired an independence as a merchant of London, in partnership with West India merchant Thomas Wilson, Esq. for many years MP for the City. Among other useful institutions in which his benevolent exertions were exercised, he was an active member of the Council of the Literary Fund Society." Wilson and Blanshard were shipowners. Keen on saving those in peril on the seas, Blanshard was also a founder of the Royal National Lifeboat Institution. He died in Paris, 21 February 1836, aged fifty-five. Wilson had interests in Grenada, "spice island of the West," and likely owned plantations and was therefore a slave owner. His partner was probably similarly engaged. When Governor Blanshard said that he had travelled in the West Indies, this likely meant he had visited Grenada.

Our Richard Blanshard's brother, Henry "the Younger," was three years Richard's junior. We know little of him. He was born 5 July 1819 and as an adult had his banking business in nearby Bedford Place, Russell Square. In short, the Henry Blanshards, father and son, were in the same line of banking, but the senior was a shipowner, marine insurer, and coal and railway proprietor as well.

As will be seen, this was a close-knit London-bred family. With their parents, the three children represented a nuclear cluster of wealth, privilege, station and enterprise.

Sadness came in April 1823 with the death of the mother, Sarah Ann Percival Blanshard. English death records for this year do not give cause of death. Richard was then a mere five and a half years of age. Although the loss of one's mother is difficult at any time, for a lad of his age it may have been especially so. His father never remarried. Richard's sister, Margaret, and their brother, Henry, faced a new world without a mother. Richard's streak of independence may have derived from these new circumstances. He may have acquired, too, a greater scope for action and adventure.

It is a matter of regret that no record survives of Richard Blanshard's early years. In any event, the following warning from old William Ewart Gladstone may pertain: "It is difficult to discern the true dimensions of objects in the mirage which covers the studies of one's youth." Perhaps Richard was sent to a public school, one where financiers of the City of London sent their sons, but of this I have no knowledge. He may have been privately educated. We do have the basics of his university years, and they reflect the greatness and the processes of self-selection that were the essence of the ruling class of England. George Canning, prime minister in 1827, opined that the public schools and universities of the age provided the discipline that prepared the youth of England for the duties of public life. There were naturally exceptions, he wrote, "but...I believe, that England would not be what she is without her system of public education, and that no other country can become what England is without the advantages of such a system."[169]

Richard was still a young lad, only fourteen, when he was sent up to Oxford in October 1831. As a university, Oxford (all-male in those days) was then slowly awakening from its lethargy, still dominated by old Tory postulations. It was largely a collection of seminaries and playgrounds for the aristocracy. From the dreaming spires and towers there still flowed the last enchantments of the Middle Ages. Gladstone, at Oxford just before Blanshard, and at the same college, found its quads, walls and staircases rich with traditions, nourishing and alive. As far as can be determined, Blanshard was accorded no special scholarship. Nor did he aspire to high academic attainments and a fellowship. His was the world of commerce. Blanshard's politics were always on the conservative side. He likely attended debates at the Union, where Catholic emancipation for voting privileges, land-holding, free trade and capital punishment were burning issues of the day. In 1832 came the Great Reform Act, which dislodged the landed aristocracy as the mainspring of political power. Change was in the air, and disquiet too.

Young Richard was admitted to the college of Christ Church, known to many as "the House." The college, then the most aristocratic of them all, is unique in that the dean, or head, is both the senior cleric and head of the college. At other colleges, a master or president was head of the college, though, as was required in those days, he would be a member of the Church of England who had taken holy orders and was a bachelor. Fellows—all bachelors in those days—often kept female companions in dwellings far from college, but that is another story. This was unquestionably a Church of England establishment, one of the wealthiest in the land.

Young Blanshard would have had his own tutor to read to him and guide his studies in Latin and mathematics through compulsory texts, essays on assigned themes, and more. Young men at the university developed the practice of speaking in small debating societies, impromptu, on any subject. We can imagine him there in his scholar's gown, dining regularly with others at oak trestle tables running the length of the hall from the elevated head table, where the dean, the venerable scholars and their guests ate and chatted in comfort. Oak-panelled walls gleamed in the candlelight. A festal magic permeated the air: tables set with ageless silver, crystal glasses glistening, grace said in Latin. Along the walls of Christ Church hall hung portraits of prime ministers and archbishops. It is said that the House could boast more of these sorts of worthies than any other college in the realm. Gladstone and Sir Robert Peel, prime ministers both, were students there, though not exactly during Richard's time. So were Earl Bathurst and Robert Hay, both in the Colonial Office, and the future statesman the 8th Earl of Elgin (famous for backing colonial self-government in Nova Scotia and the Canadas). Blanshard would have known them, and come to know them again in political matters concerning the Hudson's Bay Company.

Richard matriculated—that is, found himself admitted to the privileges of Oxford University—on 22 October 1835, but for reasons unknown he did not take a degree. He was eighteen years old.[170] All who matriculated in those days subscribed to the Thirty-nine Articles of Religion of the Church of England.

Then there is a three-year gap in the record of his life. These were likely years of travel and learning the ins and outs of his father's business interests in the corporate world of banking, insurance, shipping and industry. He avoided giving specifics about his travels in the West Indies and British Honduras. Could it be that he was in Barbados settling, for his father, trusteeship matters on two plantations owned by family business connections? After 1834, plantation owners there were being compensated as slavery ended and enslaved people were emancipated. Perhaps he visited his sister, Margaret, and her family in Grenada. He said once that he had been to British Honduras, but in what capacity we can only guess.

We find him next at Cambridge, where the colleges backed along the banks of the sleepy River Cam. The collegiate style replicated Oxford in every way. Blanshard was admitted to Queens' College, Cambridge, noteworthy on account of its association with Isaac Newton, the mathematician. The date of Blanshard's admission was 21 July 1838. We do not know what subjects he studied, but all students had Greek and Latin, mathematics and theology, and all those who were to matriculate were academically sound and tested. The secretary to the college president informed the author that the only record they possessed about Blanshard was Venn's *Alumni Cantabrigienses*, a record of scholars and students of the university. There we find an entry that tells us that Richard was son of Thomas Henry Blanshard, Esquire, Kirby, Essex. He matriculated at Easter the next year, 1839. He took a bachelor of arts degree, then styled "A.B.," in 1840 and, by application and payment of the requisite fee, an A.M., or master of arts, in 1844.

No grass grew under young Blanshard's feet. On 8 June 1839, on paying five guineas, he was admitted as a student to Lincoln's Inn, largest of the Inns of Court, London, to read for the law and qualify as a barrister-at-law. The rules specified that he must eat the requisite three dinners per term (twelve terms in all)—this is the way they took attendance so as to avoid absenteeism. Lest this be regarded as a swift and easy passage, be it known that as a student in good standing he was entitled to attend lectures given by the learned professors. He studied—and took examinations—in jurisprudence (including international law, public and private law), Roman civil law, constitutional law and legal history, common law, equity, law of real and personal property, and criminal law. After passing his public examinations, he was called to the bar in 1844 at the age of twenty-seven. He never argued a case in court, but he had chambers at 18 Gate Street, Lincoln's Inn Fields, which presumably was his London office while he attended to the extensive businesses, family and other. It was at this time that he voyaged to British Honduras, via Jamaica, and once again was involved in contractual matters relating to one sort of business or other. At that time, that colony was prospering in the logwood trade and in plantation products.

In 1847, according to *Boyle's Court Guide*, Richard Blanshard was a barrister at 64 Lincoln's Inn Fields. There he attended to family business matters: West India connections, import-export in the family's East India shipping, rural estates, banking and investment matters, and the coal and iron business related to railways in County Durham and Newcastle upon Tyne. Then there were the landed estates with their tenants and agricultural pursuits. Richard Blanshard needed no employer save his family.

Richard saw the changing world of London all around him. By the mid-1840s, London had grown and prospered to a degree that gave it the title "greatest city on earth." It was the centre of international trade, shipping, insurance and finance. It had its dark sides too, and many residents were poor, indigent and homeless. Streets were crowded with struggling life. Victorian London was a place of contrasts. While Kew, Hammersmith and Hackney lay on the outskirts, London proper was still a compact city. Richard, brother Henry and their father knew this, for their haunts were their banking establishments near Bloomsbury and in the City of London, all conveniently close to their residence at 37 Great Ormond Street, their shipping interests at Blackwall, and their legal work done at the Temple, secluded in old medieval London near the Law Courts.

The metropolis was growing by leaps and bounds; all the more reason to have a country estate easily accessible by railway from, say, Paddington Station, Liverpool Street Station or Waterloo. The old Georgian style of buildings was giving way to neo-Gothic, which became the consolation of antiquity placed on a city whose Houses of Parliament had gone up in smoke in the great fire of 1834. The Law Courts followed the pattern. But the stout buildings of Threadneedle Street, where the Bank of England stood, retained, as they do to this day, a resemblance to the old, stable order.

It was not a quiet era. Rather the opposite: change was everywhere. The Victorians thought of themselves as moving at breakneck speed. They exhibited tumultuous energy, and Alfred Lord Tennyson, the poet, thought of the people of his age as moving "down the ringing groves of change."

Richard Blanshard, when a young man, saw the transformation of the River Thames below Tower Bridge. Old docks and attendant dwellings for longshoremen were giving way to new basins and warehouses. Industry flourished here, while twice daily the tide ebbed and flowed. The waterway led to the ends of the earth. The river traffic of empire was well described in *Heart of Darkness* by mariner and writer Joseph Conrad, for it was on this stream that the knights errant of discovery and commerce had gone forth to make their commonwealths beyond the seas. "Hunters for gold and pursuers of fame, they had all gone out on that stream, bearing the sword, and often the torch, messengers of the might within the land, bearers of a spark from the sacred fire." Ships carried the dreams of men, the germs of empire. So it was with the Hudson's Bay Company, which sent ships annually to and from Gravesend in the Thames Estuary, where they loaded and unloaded at the customary wharves. The business had proceeded under royal charter since 1670, and like many another firm in London, or England, for that matter, had adjusted with the times.

In late 1848, just as the Colonial Office was devising the arrangement for the HBC to be imperial overlord of "Vancouver's Island and its Dependencies," we find thirty-year-old Blanshard in the northern, or upper, provinces of India. He must have taken passage to eastern seas in 1847. It was to this buffer state, in and near the Sutlej River, that

Blanshard was drawn. What, pray tell, was he doing there? Perhaps he had gone for tiger shooting or to conduct some banking transaction. Perhaps he was recruiting labour for West India plantations. More likely he was there on business in regards to the Ganges Canal works, the largest irrigation project undertaken by the government of India. In any event, he was in the Punjab, a region of five rivers of the upper Indus, a flat alluvial plain known for the hottest summers in India, and mild winters. We reconstruct his actions in India from various sources.[171] His uncle Thomas Blanshard, CB, was a major general in the Royal Engineers and an inventor of pontoon bridges. Richard's father had extensive shipping interests in these eastern seas, and probably banking interests ashore needing legal attention.

Blanshard arrived in India precisely when the British were completing the conquest of the subcontinent. Britain had long been the paramount power. The charter of the East India Company, subject to renewal in 1833, faced scrutiny by parliamentary committee (just as the Hudson's Bay Company came under fire in 1857, when Blanshard testified). "It is recognized as an indispensable principle," the committee asserted in a striking passage, "that the interests of the native subjects are to be consulted in preference to those of Europeans whenever the two come in conflict." Under Lord Dalhousie, Governor General of India, uniformity of laws throughout India was imposed by central government. Sectarian and communal violence was outlawed. Indians were not to be excluded from responsible office. Reforms included prohibition of *sati* (self-immolation of widows on the funeral pyres of their husbands as a religious duty) and a systematic campaign against *thagi*, an organized conspiracy of murder and robbery. Schools and colleges in which Western science was taught in the English language were funded; educational activities of missionaries were aided and encouraged. These were momentous changes and equally momentous times.

Blanshard's arrival in India coincided with constructive activity in great works of engineering begun by Dalhousie. This was the railway age in India. Railways as "public works" that would open up the country were an integral feature of the Victorian conception of civilization and improvement. The work was carried on by British companies using British capital, and railways contributed to welding India into a unity.[172]

Likely Blanshard arrived as a financial and legal agent, representing a London firm connected to his father. The conquest of the Punjab, completed in 1846, gave Dalhousie the opportunity to show how a model province should be organized. Henry and John Lawrence, deployed by the Governor General, reconstructed the province with extraordinary skill, suppressing anarchy, putting up a line of forts, opening up the whole with roads and bridges, and establishing impartial courts. Here was unbridled imperial power in action and in effect.

On the northwest frontier, problems of the Khyber Pass and Afghanistan, with its warring factions, continued. Beyond the mountainous defiles loomed imperial Russia, menacing the prospects of British India. The Great Game was being played out. The northwest frontier and the Russian danger preoccupied the minds of British military and political commanders. In 1841 the doomed army in Kabul had fought its way out in dreadful winter, a humiliating disaster to British arms.

Elsewhere, in Sind, the Sikh Army fought desperate battles against the British. Peace was imposed at Lahore in 1846, ending the First Sikh War. Sikh chieftains resented their subordination to the British. The Sikh Army, formidable in strength and artillery, sought to reverse the decision of 1846. In 1848 the Diwan of Multan split away from the Lahore government. British forces were sent to regain control. In 1848 came a rising of the Sikhs. They murdered emissaries of the Raj, Patrick Alexander Vans Agnew and Lieutenant W.A. Anderson, in Multan, the large fortress city of the plain. Agnew and Anderson were there to attend a ceremony for Sardar Kahan Singh Mann, selected by the East India Company to replace Diwan Mulraj Chopra as ruler of Multan. The Sikh Army overthrew the British protectorate and took the field. They had the best of a deliberately fought battle at Chillianwala. The British Army of India countered.

At this moment, Blanshard volunteered as a supernumerary in the 8th Regiment, Bengal Native Infantry. His services in support of the Raj are known through five testimonials to his character, war experience and valour. He acquired a martial bearing and a magnificent moustache. In Colonial Office minutes, Herman Merivale, who met him, refers to Blanshard as "Captain" and, in another instance, "Lieutenant";

indeed, he must have given Merivale the impression of being an officer in the Indian Army. However, it is widely acknowledged that he had joined the Indian Army as a volunteer and lent assistance throughout the Second Sikh War at and near Multan and Gujrat in the Punjab.

From these testimonials we piece together his military exploits, the stuff of *Boy's Own Annual*. Major Herbert B. Edwardes, formerly brevet major commanding the Irregulars at the two months' siege of Multan, produced a certificate stating that Blanshard was with the army during that arduous battle. He was "exposed to the same privations & dangers as anyone in the camp & took more than a Civilian's interest in the (very warm) military operations." Captain T.S. Price, 8th Regiment, Bengal Native Infantry, attested that Blanshard "shared in all our dangers." Blanshard had joined the camp in February 1848 and was regarded as one of their own. In short, he was a member of the officers' mess. He turned out on all occasions once the regiment got more arms. In October, Captain Price was ordered to go to Bahawalpur garrison to bring in a long column of ammunition. Blanshard accompanied him, as "an active and energetic assistant." In January 1849, twelve thousand troops assembled to conquer Multan. Bombarding the fortress, then breaching the walls, they formed the second siege against the stronghold, forcing the surrender. Captain Price, again, says that Blanshard found himself in the thick of things. He was present during the second siege, which brought the surrender of Multan fortress.

Then came a turn of events. Blanshard joined the regiment on its long route march to join the army of Commander-in Chief Lord Gough. Major General Sir W.S. Whish, in his testimonial, states that he received orders to join the main army with his force, and to do so by forced marches. The so-called Army of the Punjab went in search of the enemy. One regiment was left to bring in the guns, and this fell to the 8th Regiment, Bengal Native Infantry. This unfashionable job was likely to "cut us out of the army," says Price, who was obviously looking out for his friend Blanshard. Accordingly, under these circumstances, Blanshard found himself attached to Her Majesty's 10th Foot, under Lieutenant Colonel Thomas H. Franks. He was at Gujrat, the decisive battle of the Second Sikh War, on 21 February 1849. In this, he acted as a mounted orderly, or despatch rider, with the 1st Brigade,

1st Division, and "had a horse shot under him. I was close to and conversed with him, & certify to his having been with us in the first of the fight." Price concluded his testimonial: "It will be gratifying to all our officers to hear that he receives the honorary decorations; he shared in all our dangers."

Blanshard did indeed receive a medal for his military activities, probably the campaign medal, Second Sikh War. He also received an address presented to him after his embarkation from India, along with the above-noted six certificates to his credit. One of these testimonials of devotion to duty bore the signature of Lieutenant General Lord Gough, who noted that Blanshard's name ought to be included in the Medal Books for Multan and Gujrat. We can conclude that Blanshard's courage and initiative, his martial preparedness and horsemanship, were never in doubt. Nor was his patriotism or sense of honour. He had been at Multan and Gujrat at the critical hours, and witnessed brilliant successes in which he played his small parts. In the end, the Sikh Army was defeated and the area pacified, then annexed as the only means of assuring peace. So ended the Second Sikh War. The Punjab became part of the Dominion of India, and on partition in 1947, that area became Pakistan. The Sikhs migrated to India, and another chapter in their history began.

The Raj attracted all sorts of Britons. A commentator on these matters puts it this way: "Wherever they went to, these newcomers to India—known in Victorian times as 'griffins'—could expect to find themselves isolated and dependent for comfort and advice on Indian subordinates." They shouldered immediate responsibility, picking up the job as they went along. "In such situations young men matured quickly—and learned to follow precedent." The same authority says that newcomers learned they were members of the dominant race, but they also developed noblesse oblige.[173]

And then there were the social aspects of the Raj, in Blanshard's case the regimental mess. He had known this sort of thing at Oxbridge and the Inns of Court. The regimental mess was self-contained, familiar. Hunting and other sports, such as polo and pigsticking, cricket and croquet, billiards and cards, were the order of the day, to say nothing of mess dinners and special parades, all accompanied by martial strains and soldiers on parade. In the mess was welcome conviviality, shared stories, the ethos of empire. Devotion to regiment was a form of absolute brotherhood. Here among "Officers and Gentlemen," Blanshard would be classed with those invited to join the senior mess. Strangers were entertained. If he went to India to search for a wife, he did not find one, but then, he may have already had his chosen bride in mind. In India, said Viceroy Lord Curzon, "our work is righteous." Given the ethos, Blanshard had worked his own small share. He was "linked in the Chain of Empire," but he did not contribute to the staggeringly high death rate among Europeans in India. Newcomers were always vulnerable to typhoid and everyday irritants such as dysentery and malaria. These may have contributed to his ill state of health in Vancouver Island.

Blanshard declined a commission in the Army. He had no ambitions in that line. He had business in London, and family, loved ones and friends to be reunited with. Time had come to return home, and Blanshard set forth for England by fastest means. For £100, he would travel first-class on P&O steamships from Calcutta to Suez, taking the "Overland Route" across the land barrier to Alexandria on the Mediterranean. Then Marseilles to the English Channel, and a fast boat to Tilbury Docks would bring him home to London. The whole could be accomplished in less than three weeks. Here is an indication of imperial swiftness in communications: the Battle of Gujrat was 21 February 1849; Richard was back in London by 4 July. He had many tales to tell.

The prospect of becoming governor of Vancouver Island now appeared unexpectedly. Before long, Blanshard was caught up in a whirl of obligations and preparations for the journey to what seemed the other end of the earth.

One matter to attend to was an affair of the heart. For a number of years, and certainly before his departure for Vancouver Island, Blanshard had an attraction to Miss Emily Hyde, daughter of James and Anne Hyde of Aller, Somerset. No photograph of her exists. Sadly, too, we know nothing of her interests or occupations.

A well-respected professional family of the West Country, the Hydes ranked among the local gentry. Emily was born 23 August

1817, and she was baptized 6 November of the same year in the parish church, St. Andrew's. The Aller church, east of Taunton in a beautiful valley, is part Norman, having ancient connection to King Alfred and the Danes. Emily's father, James Hyde, born 1753, was a solicitor of the King's Bench. In 1793 he bought the title of Lord of the Manor of Aller. Thereafter he named his ten-bedroom home "Manor House." He is listed in registers as "Gentleman," which certainly he was. In 1795 he married Ann Burge in Wells, Somerset; they had seven sons and seven daughters. When James died, in 1832, he left £2,300 to Emily, then aged twenty-one.

On 8 August 1844, Emily's younger sister Miriam married Richard's brother, Henry Blanshard, at Aller. Henry Blanshard, we recall, was a banker in Bedford Place, Russell Square, London. The 1851 census lists Henry as "Banker in Private Firm." He worked in the same bank as his uncle Richard Percival of powerful Willis, Percival & Co. After his marriage to Miriam, they kept a residence in fashionable and lively Brighton, Sussex. Presumably, Henry commuted to London by rail as required.

It may be imagined that Richard and Emily (both aged twenty-seven) became acquainted when his brother and her sister married. Richard had only recently been called to the bar. He had business to attend to. Besides, he had a sporting instinct. Within the year he was outbound on adventures to the upper provinces of India, then into the face of battle in the Second Sikh War. We can imagine the dawning of romance, an exchange of affectionate letters, even suggestions as to what the future might hold. Even so, the process was slow, dogged by uncertainties unknown to us. And after Richard returned from India, any plans that he and Emily had to marry were upset by his being appointed governor of Vancouver Island. As Richard prepared to cross the Atlantic, Emily moved in with Henry and Miriam Blanshard at 76 Clarendon Mansions, Junction Road, Brighton. In the 1851 census for the parish of Brighton, Henry is shown as aged thirty-one, his wife, Miriam, twenty-nine, and Emily Hyde, his sister-in-law, thirty-two. Emily is listed as "Gentlewoman." She waited for Richard.

On the eve of departure for distant shores, Richard was given a gift bearing the stamp of antiquity, precious because of its rarity. He was made Freeman of the City of London on 4 July 1849. His father was one of the Honourable Company of Goldsmiths (now the Goldsmiths' Company), that venerable livery company of artisans, moneylenders and bankers dating from medieval times, and he was present at his son's admission in the same Company of Goldsmiths. Present also were Richard's brother, Henry, and his brother-in-law, Richard Davis. Here was another attestation to Richard Blanshard's considerable status in wealth, connections and character. It was, as they say, all in the family. They looked after their own.

Chapter 7:
Earl Grey Disposes

Mystery remains as to the reasons for Richard Blanshard's selection as governor of Vancouver's Island and its Dependencies. The full story is unlikely ever to be told. Still, there are hints to guide a sleuth, and the fun is in the chase. This much is clear: parliamentary and political opposition demanded an outsider. Moreover, a person who knew English law possessed an advantage. Chief Factor Douglas had been the Company's first choice as governor. However, as was explained to him, politics intervened, activated by "the jealousy of some parties, and the interested motives of others."[174] To avert criticism, the name of Blanshard was brought forward.

Our attention shifts to the nerve centre of the Empire. The Colonial Office was housed in decrepit nos. 13 and 14 Downing Street, backing on St. James's Park. The structure had been declared inadequate, unsafe and unworthy of substantial repairs. Ceilings had been shored up against impending disaster. A medieval sewer ditch flowed nearby, giving a building inspector cause to speculate on its long-term effects. The library, shared with the Foreign Office, had rooms where smells and draughts were enough to cause comment from visitors, who expressed astonishment that anyone could inhabit it. It had no maps fit to be consulted readily.[175] All papers were written longhand, and when some text needed printing, it was sent to the Foreign Office. Typists, telegraphists, telephones, cable and wireless would be employed at later dates. The Colonial Office had an all-important waiting room, where "disgruntled colonists," in one Colonial Reformer's famous caricature, nervously rehearsed tales for "Mr. Mothercountry," Sir James Stephen, the permanent under-secretary. Stephen ran the office, apportioned the work, advised on promotions, and drafted and reviewed colonial legislation. He, like Merivale (who eventually replaced him as permanent under-secretary), absorbed the Empire. As to their superior, Earl Grey, all details also had to come to him, usually with Stephen's advice. Grey complained that official business left him no time or energy for personal matters or politics, and thus he was reliant on good personnel to give advice.[176]

Charles Dickens in *Little Dorrit* dubbed the Colonial Office the "Circumlocution Office." He invented the Circumlocution Office as an epitome of slaving dedication to routine, and he portrayed it as remote from constructive accomplishment. It was all very well to blame the bureaucracy, but truth to tell, the persons who worked in rundown Downing Street were far removed from circumstances on imperial frontiers. The view from the centre differed from that of the dusty, windswept frontier post where a lonely servant of the Crown was endeavouring to carry out the Queen's writ and keep the settlement safe, secure, prosperous and growing.

Statesmen and politicians fretted about the multiplication of British responsibilities in distant lands. Agents of empire seemed to get the British into difficulties in every quarter of the globe. It was always one of the guiding principles of British colonial policy to preserve local law and customs as far as possible, and to do nothing that might break the continuity of the local government. Indigenous chiefs and organizations were not to be interfered with. The colonial administration concerned itself with protecting trade and settlement, developing trade, roads and public services and, in time, building up a cluster of such employees who could manage the colonial machinery with confidence and economy.

Downing Street had seen arrivals and departures of many secretaries of state in the years since the loss of the Thirteen Colonies. Several able persons had been appointed to the post, which had powerful influence in the ministry of the day. In July 1846 Lord John Russell formed a Whig administration. He chose the 3rd Earl Grey, a statesman of unusual ability and energy, as secretary of state for war and the colonies. Grey wore the mantle of the progressive: he had drafted the first bill for the abolition of slavery in the Empire. He professed free trade and ardently promoted colonial self-government. He contended that the system of parliamentary government that had long prevailed in the "Mother Country" could be immediately adopted in Nova Scotia, and he advanced "responsible government" in Nova Scotia, Quebec and Ontario, carried through by the adroit Lord Elgin, Governor General. Grey regarded the Empire as a solemn trust as well as a source of power and glory. He possessed an active and critical mind. He had studied colonial affairs long and earnestly. He was harassed by agencies proposing schemes of systematic colonization. He disliked Foreign Office adventurism as exhibited by Lord Palmerston, and unlike Palmerston he did not think Britons should be protected if they ranged beyond the reach of British power. South Africa was the grave of his reputation. Vancouver Island, a quagmire, provided little boost to his authority and prestige.[177] Once the British Empire became worldwide, the sun never set on its crises.

While Earl Grey sat in the House of Lords, Benjamin Hawes, MP, the parliamentary under-secretary, was his spokesman in the House of Commons. Hawes was Grey's voice, eyes and ears. He helped with the drafting of commissions, instructions and deeds of grant. He liaised with the Hudson's Bay Company. Nevertheless, Grey, as secretary of state, had the final say and asserted his authority. The secretary of state for the colonies also carried the title of secretary of state for war. (One office-holder remarked that the job he held, in truth, was "Secretary of State for War *with* the Colonies.")

Lord Grey had outstanding under-secretaries. Among these, as already mentioned, was Sir James Stephen. Stephen was a member of the Clapham Sect, a body of humanitarian reformers who opposed slavery and sought to guard Indigenous rights. He never worked happily with the so-called Colonial Reformers, who were radical imperialists, masters of the art of decrying all achievements but their own. He believed that Vancouver Island should be colonized because of its good harbours, and he thought a British naval station there would counter what the Americans possessed in San Francisco. He retired in October 1847. In succession to him was the equally bright and analytical Herman Merivale. Essential, too, was the legal head of the department, Arthur Blackwood, a senior clerk, and another twenty-three clerks. Incoming communications from governors or other departments were read and scrutinized by all in the office. Workloads were heavy, and the sorting and recording of information was of immense importance. All correspondence concerning the Colony of Vancouver Island survives in the National Archives, Kew—a tribute to the dedicated staff of the Colonial Office. In 1849 they were at the centre of a global empire of forty-three communities, comprising various races, languages, religions, laws and customs. Some were naval bases or garrisons, others convict stations, and still others emigrant outposts or places of refuge—colonies and dependencies all. Masses of official correspondence reveal their individual stories under Colonial Office guise. The Foreign Office, the Admiralty and other departments of state were consulted on pertinent points. Among the Vancouver Island papers are to be found correspondence to and from the Hudson's Bay Company. Looking at these documents today, we might conclude that nothing of the smallest importance had been thrown out.

Blanshard now enters the Colonial Office sphere. According to Blanshard, a friend told him that the governorship of Vancouver Island was open, and that he should apply. He did so. He was interviewed by the HBC directors. On 13 June 1849, the chairman and committee of the Company "resolved that Richard Blanshard Esq. be recommended to Earl Grey Her Majesty's Principal Secretary of State for the Colonies, to be appointed Gov[erno]r of Vancouver Island."[178] Grey had already held his first interview with the prospective governor. This is disclosed in Chairman Sir John Pelly's letter to Grey of 15 June, in which he refers to an interview held the previous Thursday at which he had introduced Blanshard. This would have been conducted in the Colonial Office. The recommendation was Pelly's. Grey accepted it without reservation. Historian Hubert Howe Bancroft says the suggestion to appoint Blanshard was Grey's, and Pelly agreed, but Bancroft provides no authority.[179]

Could it be that William Gladstone, a former secretary of state for the colonies, urged Blanshard to put his name forward? It is not beyond the realm of possibility, for it was Gladstone who, in the House of Commons, had raised many questions about the HBC's overweening power. He would have welcomed some counterweight. The Earl of Elgin may have tipped his hand, too. (Both Gladstone and Elgin were graduates of Christ Church, Oxford, as was Blanshard.) Another possibility is Sir John Pakington, who became secretary of state for war and the colonies in February 1852.[180] In any event, wheels were in motion to prepare the necessary legal papers under royal authority. The important point is that even before the last hot discussion in Parliament about the Hudson's Bay Company's unsuitability to be awarded the Charter of Grant for the colony—for monopolies were out of fashion and smacked of special privilege and corruption—the matter of Blanshard's nomination by the Company and approval by the Crown had been achieved.[181]

On 16 July 1849 the commission to Governor Richard Blanshard was issued in Queen Victoria's name and signed by writ of the privy seal.[182] On 16 July, also, his instructions were issued at court, at Osborne House, Isle of Wight, the royal residence.[183] On 21 July Earl Grey transmitted to Blanshard the commission as issued under the great seal of the United Kingdom, also letters patent under the seal of the High Court of Admiralty. The newly designed public seal of the Island of Vancouver and its Dependencies was transmitted to Blanshard by Grey. Accompanying the public seal was the warrant under the Queen's sign-manual for use of the seal; the warrant authorized the governor to use the public seal in the sealing of all public instruments made and passed in Her Majesty's name within that Island and its Dependencies.[184] Here were all the trappings of viceregal power, of executive authority, which in the pressing circumstances that awaited him on the distant rim of empire he was never shy of exercising. In those days, and until the union of the colony with the Crown colony of British Columbia in 1866, "Vancouver's Island and its Dependencies" appears as the official name, or "the Island of Vancouver and its Dependencies." "Vancouver Island" naturally became the short version.

We can be certain that Blanshard presented himself admirably at his interview with Grey, as with Pelly. The secretary of the Hudson's

Bay Company, Archibald Barclay, who met Blanshard at the time, characterized him, in correspondence with James Douglas, as "a gentleman of great intelligence and respectability."[185]

"With respect to the appointment of Mr. Blanshard to the Governorship of Vancouver's Island," Pelly explained in private correspondence to a dubious Sir George Simpson, "it was with my entire concurrence, indeed recommendation. It wrests from those adverse to the Company the charge of making the Colony subservient to their views alone, and retaining in their hands the power of tyrannizing over the settlers, which the ill-disposed are too ready to charge them with."[186] Not all senior HBC personnel saw it that way. Simpson would not have been pleased. And Eden Colvile, shortly to succeed Pelly, regretted that Douglas had not been confirmed in the position. Douglas could have conducted affairs of the colony just as well as a perfect stranger unconnected and unfamiliar with the Company, Colvile confided to Simpson. He added, with a touch of resignation, "Be that as it may I suppose there was no alternative left to you but to appoint a person unconnected with the Company, & we must try to make the best of it."[187] Colvile and Simpson had never encouraged settlement on Vancouver Island. Now, triumphantly, they had in their hands the Charter of Grant—a mighty bulwark guarding the fur trade of Vancouver Island and New Caledonia (the northern interior of British Columbia). Their motives in accepting the Charter of Grant are questionable and border on the duplicitous.

Richard Blanshard owed everything to Sir John Henry Pelly, Bart. Pelly ranked as a venerable and powerful figure in the City of London. He would have been an associate of Blanshard's father in banking circles, in business transactions and as a fellow member of the venerable Company of Goldsmiths. He was a veteran of the East India Company's marine operations, a sometime sea captain.

The Blanshard name was familiar as well as respectable in British banking and political circles. And Richard Blanshard, freshly arrived from India and conspicuous war campaigning, presented himself as a suitable candidate for colonial service. He was well-heeled and of excellent deportment, experienced in war and trade, well-educated and well-connected. In addition, adventure was not unknown to him, and even the immense distance from the Home Islands seemed no bar to his desires to make a mark in the colonial service on a faraway island. In fact, he hoped it would lead to greater things. His legal training was of no inconsequential merit; in fact, it was a decided advantage, beneficial to the Crown and to a new colony under the rule of English civil law for the first time. Frontier justice would be safe in his hands. Needless to say, Pelly, like Grey, saw in Blanshard the suitable candidate, with no marks against him, a traveller with a sense of adventure, and a private pocketbook agreeable to the circumstances of the far frontier.

As to previous colonial experience, Blanshard never revealed any details. Never one to give unnecessary information unless pressed to do so, he was always sharp and to the point, and his answers sometimes appear vague, even elusive, to the inquisitive historian. Brevity was his hallmark.

One matter attracted the most attention: work without pay. When Blanshard accepted the position, he was told that no salary would be paid to the governor until such time as the expense could be met by taxation and royalties on coal. He explained with candour to the select committee of Parliament inquiring into the affairs of the Hudson's Bay Company in 1857 that he expected, or had been led to believe by Sir John Pelly, that sums on the colony's account to pay his salary would soon be available. In the meantime, once taking up office he would receive a thousand acres of land. There were other allurements attractive to Blanshard, in particular that this first appointment might lead to other prospects in the colonial service.

In 1857 these extraordinary terms of employment attracted the searching attention of the parliamentary committee of inquiry. Two questions put to Blanshard—and his equally astonishing answers—tell the story:

Do you mean that you accepted the governorship of this colony, with the understanding that you were to get nothing whatever for your services in that respect?

—Nothing at the first beginning. I was certainly led to believe that colonial settlers would flock out there; that all facilities would be given to them; and that of course as the colony increased a civil

list would be formed; that the land sales and the royalties on the coal would produce a considerable colonial revenue.

And those expectations, with the grant of 1,000 acres of land, to be selected by yourself, were your inducements for going to the colony?

—Just so, and moreover I also hoped that my services would be considered by Her Majesty's Government afterwards.[188]

It is clear that Blanshard had no advance inkling of the irresponsible, uncongenial and disrespectful actions of the Hudson's Bay Company out on the margins of British influence. The Company exercised a habit of authority of deep-seated experience. Their servants might be described as a warrior class of traders, and they would brook no rivals.

The Company and the Crown shared one essential feature in policy-making: a deep-seated distrust of American values and aspirations characterized by land grabs and the forced removal of Indigenous peoples from their lands, begun under the 1830 Indian Removal Act. Grey must have explained to Blanshard that the big fear was American aggrandizement and squatter takeover. Only fourteen miles of seawater, across the Strait of Juan de Fuca, separated the restless tide of American squatters from the unsettled Vancouver Island. Keeping Americans out: that was the essential requirement, and the unequivocal plan to save Vancouver Island for the Crown. Here is what Earl Grey wrote about the Island's future: "Looking to the encroaching spirit of the U.S. I think it of importance to strengthen the B[riti]sh hold upon the territory now assigned to us by treaty, by encouraging the settlement on it of B[riti]sh subjects; and I am also of opinion that such settlement could only be effected under the auspices of the Hudson's Bay Co., w[hic]h I am therefore disposed to encourage."[189]

This confidential statement, marked "for Colonial Office eyes only," bears the date 16 September 1846, shortly after news of the Oregon Treaty reached London. It came also after Pelly had proposed that the best way to protect British interests would be to ensure that the HBC remain the dominant power north of the boundary line, and, further, that any colonizing project be under the auspices of the firm. Grey was a liberal imperialist, and when he came into office he had many problems to deal with—in southern Africa, New Zealand, the Australian colonies and now northwest America. He took to his job with energy and commitment. He did not seek to enlarge the imperial realm. Neither was he a "little Englander," desirous of reducing the pink spots on the worldwide map that connoted places of the British Empire. Grey said that even in the cabinet, some members were not free from the view that Britain had no interest in preserving the colonies and ought therefore to make no sacrifice for that purpose: "Cut the painter," ran the argument, and the colonies once cut adrift would look after themselves and save the British endless trouble and expense. The Empire grew in spite of such sentiments.[190] In the ten years beginning 1841, in addition to Vancouver Island, Britain occupied or annexed New Zealand, the Gold Coast, Labuan, Natal, the Punjab, Sind and Hong Kong. If this expansion occurred by "fits of absence of mind," we can say that despite the determination of imperial authorities, British rule was extended nonetheless. Vancouver Island was a colony of necessity, an orphan of empire.

At the time Grey took office, two theoretical considerations and an all-abiding financial one dominated colonial affairs. Under "theoretical," the first was the evolution of colonies of settlement and the encouragement of self-government and self-defence. During Grey's time in office, Nova Scotia obtained colonial self-government, with the legislative power dominating colonial prospects save in matters of defence and foreign policy. Lower Canada (Quebec) and Upper Canada (Ontario) quickly followed suit. The concept of a British North America, or Canada, from Atlantic to Pacific was being mooted. Encouraging emigration of Britons to these and other places of settlement was the object. "Shovelling out paupers" was one description of sending impoverished emigrants overseas. Relieving distress at home underscored many a scheme, finding wives for husbands (and vice versa) another, thereby peopling the Empire.

In Grey's time (1846–1852), and that of Stephen too (1836–1848), no one caused more problems in colony-making than the Colonial Reformer Edward Gibbon Wakefield. He was a statesman of immense though fragmented influence. He propounded a political theory of developing empire lands by settlement and purchase (after a certain number of years, at a "sufficient price"—what we might call nowadays "sweat equity"). All sorts of projects were proposed by Wakefield and other Colonial Reformers. Some came into existence. Wakefield's name will always be associated with South Australia and Christchurch, New Zealand. In the Wakefield view, a colonization society had ample scope for bringing to fruition the ideas of a governor and commissioners. These persons and their officers would supervise finance, control the distribution of land and make the choice of emigrants, the latter the strongest point of the undertaking. South Australia was established in 1836, with its capital at Adelaide. In the South Island, New Zealand, Scottish Presbyterians founded the province of Otago in 1848, its capital Dunedin. Another group, the Canterbury Association, founded the province of Canterbury in 1850. Gibbon Wakefield emigrated to Canterbury and died there in 1862. The "sufficient price" has vague reference to Vancouver Island. Lord Grey was an early convert to this concept: he set the purchase price of Vancouver Island land at £1 per acre. Only Britons need apply. The ideal colonist was a family man of small property who would find in the Island a place for improvement over life in England—in other words, a place for opportunity and hard work.

The second "theoretical" consideration was protection of Indigenous peoples in colonial areas. In 1837 a committee of the House of Commons had been struck to examine these matters. Interested politicians were reinforced by the powerful and high-profile activities of the Aborigines Protection Society (APS). The committee's report was a chivalrous defence of the oppressed, which declared that the contact of Europeans (except missionaries) was harmful to Indigenous peoples. Aware of abuses on the frontiers of empire, the APS, the Church Missionary Society and other agencies independent of government were quick to point out the errors of government: what they sought was the protection of Indigenous lives, land, property and ways of livelihood. They regarded empire under the Union Jack as a matter of trust. They were influential in the history of Vancouver Island, British Columbia and the Red River Settlement, to say nothing of their work elsewhere.[191] In large measure, Lord Grey, like Stephen and Merivale, stood on the side of the committee report. But, as Merivale would argue, colonists had rights too, and by the 1860s it was accepted that London's concerns were best managed on the spot, not from the centre.

As for the all-important financial consideration, the free trade and liberal-minded imperialists of the day preached economy and self-sufficiency, and this weighed mightily in British thinking. Parliament was dominated for the first time by free traders and persons suspicious of rising exchequer outlays and parliamentary estimates. Many in Parliament regarded colonies as a constant drain on public monies and believed colonies and other dependencies ought to be self-supporting or abandoned altogether. No more "limpet colonies," or hangers-on under protection of the Union Jack, were wanted. Britain had colonies all around the world—on any rock on which a cormorant could perch, as one critic, Canon Sydney Smith, amusingly put it. But against these views, Grey held firm in regards to the future of imperilled Vancouver Island. In his opinion, the essential thing was to bind the Company to establish a colony and then keep them to the mark. One of the myths of the "little England" era is that those in authority wanted to get rid of the colonies; however, close study shows that no part of the Empire was ever abandoned. As Queen Victoria put it, "What we have, we hold."

Much depended on asserting law and order in new colonial zones, and sometimes military force had to be employed. Some locations had intractable problems that are classified as Queen Victoria's little wars. South Africa was one; New Zealand another. The Colonial Office wanted no such repetition on Vancouver Island or, later, British Columbia. Secretaries of state and their under-secretaries, notably Stephen and especially Merivale, were eminently conscious of what was going on in adjacent American territories, where "Indian wars" were commonplace and theft of Indigenous lands on grounds of relocation to reservations the order of the day. Merivale, with his knowledge of American frontier violence, guided his superiors through many a pitfall. He opposed the militarization of Vancouver Island. Far better to rely on the occasional visits of Royal Navy ships to provide surveillance and give a sense of protection to the nascent colony than to have troops garrisoned there at expense to the British taxpayer. For that reason, he backed the HBC project as proposed by Pelly and encouraged by Grey.

The only check the Colonial Office put on the Company's proposal was to limit its desires specifically to Vancouver Island (therefore excluding the Queen Charlotte Islands, Haida Gwaii) and the mainland area then called New Caledonia. Added to this was the requirement that Indigenous peoples should retain their fishing, hunting and whaling rights, and that these would not fall under the control of the Company or be otherwise curtailed.

It took months in 1848 to work out the terms of the Charter of Grant by which the Company became the proprietor of the Colony of Vancouver Island. The Crown retained unhindered title, and the charter included a qualification that some matters might be reserved for future requirements for the Royal Navy, the colonial guardian. The Colonial Office under-secretaries laboured on the project. Stephen balked at the scheme, for it reminded him of the old-fashioned way American colonies were founded on proprietary grounds in the seventeenth century. The only merit, for him, was the naval advantage of having a British port on the north Pacific Ocean. Grey was insistent on pushing the project forward. Again, he made clear to the Company that the Crown would put not one penny into it. If the Company wanted to proceed, it must do so at its own cost. The cost of Blanshard's commission had to be defrayed either by himself or by the Company; the same was true for his legal textbooks and supplies. The Company was on the hook for his salary and for his passage allowance. Here lay the source of many difficulties. The question of costs and who would bear them began in London. Blanshard was kept largely in the dark, particularly in regards to the offering of land and promise of a residence. It may be charged that Blanshard was naive; more likely he was deceived. The Company saw him as an inconvenience and an intruder.

Foreign Secretary Palmerston, whose opinion was solicited, saw no reason why the Company should not colonize Vancouver Island. On the contrary, he thought it desirable that Britain should lay down a marker there as soon as possible so as to make crystal clear to the Americans that the British had taken possession.[192]

Reasons why the Hudson's Bay Company was given colonization powers over Vancouver Island are clear: it had establishments in place and was ambitious to expand trade. It had capital, which no other applicant had. It had experience with the local Indigenous peoples. Even the Company chairman, Pelly, advertised to Grey its high-minded aspirations in this regard. In October 1848, Pelly urged Grey and the government to consider whether "the object of colonization, embracing as I trust it will the conversion to Christianity and the civilization of the Native population, might not be most readily and effectively accomplished through the instrumentality of the Hudson's Bay Company."[193] This rang true to the times, complementing government policy. But in Parliament opposition ran hot. Under pressure, the Company was obliged to prove the validity of its 1670 charter and its legality in order to hold a grant to Vancouver Island from the Crown. Gladstone and other critics of monopoly called for a public inquiry to test and ascertain the validity of the rights of the Company. Grey took the matter right out of his hands: he required the Company to provide an incontrovertible legal opinion, obtained at its own expense. The Law Officers of the Crown raised not an eyebrow.[194] Grey was running true to his word: colonizing Vancouver Island and putting in place its administration would be completely at Company expense. Only naval protection would be supplied.

Whatever the true motives of the Company, and the possible charge of duplicity, Pelly's view coincided nicely with that of the Colonial Office and the British government. When the Charter of Grant appeared in final form in late 1848, it declared, with customary bravado, that the colonization of the Island by British subjects under Company auspices "would conduce greatly to the maintenance of peace, justice and good order, and the advancement of colonization and the promotion and encouragement of trade and commerce in and also the protection and welfare of the native Indians residing within that portion of our North American Territories called Vancouver's Island."[195]

Grey believed in the guiding impulse of the state in regards to Indigenous affairs in the colonies and dependencies of the Crown. The concept of trusteeship loomed large. Under-secretary Herman Merivale, fully conversant on matters of violence on the American frontier, cautioned against including any stipulation regarding "Indians" in the projected Charter of Grant. He wanted no repetition of "Indian wars" north of the forty-ninth parallel. "Little, in fact, is known of the natives of this island, by the Company or by anyone else," he advised in late 1848, in a confidential memo on the matter. "Whether they are numerous or few, strong or weak; whether or not they use the land for such purposes as would render the reservation of a large portion of it for their use important or not, are questions which we have not the full materials to answer. Under these circumstances, any provisions that could be made for a people so distant and so imperfectly known, might turn out impediments in the way of colonization." He thought it best to leave the matter to the Company, inasmuch as its dealings with the North American Indigenous peoples were extensive. This was the essential thing. Although aspersions had been cast on the Company by others, and many charges levelled, Merivale knew from his close following of frontier matters that "no distinct charges of cruelty or misconduct toward the Indian tribes under its control have been made out by reasonable evidence; while every year brings painful accounts of mutual wrongs and mutual revenge between Indians and whites from the neighboring regions not under their control." He cast a critical eye over United States history, born in violence.

As to the question of Indigenous rights in land, he acknowledged title in a specific way. He stressed that the stipulation must be made clear that "in parting with the land of the Island [to the Company] Her Majesty parts only with her own right therein, and that whatever measures she was bound to take in order to extinguish the Indian title are equally obligatory on the Company." Here is clear indication of the Crown's intention to extinguish Indigenous title; equally clear is that this intention was requisite on the Company's charge in equal measure.[196] This is a powerful statement that makes clear that the purchase of title under the so-called Douglas treaties was not a scheme cooked up by the Company but was a requirement set forth in British policy.

In London, among various offices of state, the terms of the Charter of Grant came under searching scrutiny. The Colonial Office passed it to the Privy Council, where by order-in-council it was referred to the Board of Trade. The Law Officers of the Crown reviewed it. The Company was involved at various stages. Fishing rights were reserved to Indigenous peoples by a change of the draft version. Royal advice needed to be acquired. The process was lengthy and methodical.[197]

Merivale's scheme carried the day. Grey duly crafted the final wording:

And, whereas it would conduce greatly to the maintenance of peace, justice, and good order, and the advancement of colonization, and the promotion and encouragement of trade and commerce in, and also to the protection and welfare of the native Indians residing within that portion of our territories in North America called Vancouver Island, if such were colonized by settlers from the British dominions...were vested...in the said governor and Company of Adventurers;...upon condition that the said governor and company should form...a settlement...for the purpose of colonization...and also, should defray the entire expense of any civil and military establishments which may be required for the protection and government of such settlements.[198]

The terms of the Charter of Grant are as follows. The Colony of Vancouver's Island and its Dependencies was created by Charter of Grant dated Westminster 13 January 1849. The royal instrument that conveyed to the Company "Our Island of Vancouver and its Dependencies" designated the Company of Adventurers the "true and absolute lords and proprietors" of the Island. The Company secured proprietary rights to Vancouver Island in return for a nominal rent of seven shillings a year. It promised to establish "a settlement or settlements of resident colonists, emigrants from Our United Kingdom." Within five years the Company must settle upon the land a colony of British subjects. The Company also agreed to defray civil and military costs from the sale of land and other natural resources. The Crown, that is, the government, retained residual control; it could revoke the Charter of Grant at the end of five years if the Company did not show results in colonization. Further, the already existing licence of exclusive trade with the Indigenous peoples could be withdrawn on expiry in May 1859 notwithstanding that the Company might fulfill its contract by establishing the required colony.[199]

The Charter of Grant stands as the foundation document of British Columbia's history. It forms the basis of constitutional government in the far west, on Vancouver's Island and its Dependencies, with overseeing responsibilities for the Queen Charlotte Islands (Haida Gwaii) and for the mainland, New Caledonia, the cordilleran area west of the Rocky Mountains. Its importance to a future transcontinental Canada is also manifest. In constituted structure it differed mightily from the Colony of British Columbia, created by Act of Parliament in 1858 and free from the trappings of corporate control.

One might say, in the narrow sense, that Vancouver's Island and its Dependencies was a Crown colony. In actuality, it was a *proprietary* colony, one under authority and surveillance of the secretary of state for the colonies. It resembled, as was observed at the time, some of the English colonies founded under syndicates in the seventeenth century.

The colony was born of expediency. On reflection, once British sovereignty was achieved in 1846, a system of government had to be instituted for the purposes of colonization in order to prevent American squatters and other unauthorized settlement and the possible subverting of British rule. This constituted the key question from the Colonial Office's viewpoint and the cabinet's too. How was colonization to be undertaken? The nod had gone to the HBC. Once the Charter of Grant was issued, the new scheme of law—civil and criminal—was mandatory. The British government put in place the new mode of government for the Colony of Vancouver Island. It must be understood that Parliament did not create Vancouver Island, nor did it approve the earlier 1846 border treaty: these were done by executive action under the royal prerogative. However, Parliament did have powers of discussion, critique and censure. And it did have powers to change existing statute law.

With the object of keeping Americans out, only Britons need apply for the purchase of land. That was the first qualification. The HBC was the real estate agent. Lord Grey set the price of £1 per acre, a preposterously high figure given cheap lands across the border. Further, purchasers of land had to proceed to the Island, a requirement designed to avoid absentee landownership (which was a problem in Prince Edward Island). This prohibited speculation in land. Land purchasers bound for Vancouver Island had to take labourers and settlers with them. No Briton could arrive in the colony and buy land; all must be pre-approved by the Company. These and other restrictions were a variant of British colonial development thinking of the day, and the price of a single acre owed something to the theorist Edward Gibbon Wakefield, the Colonial Reformer mentioned earlier.[200] In other words, as we can say with hindsight, the original system demonstrated idiocy in planning, guaranteeing failure in colonizing the Island. But it was entirely successful in excluding Americans. In this regard, it served the purposes of the Colonial Office and the Company in equal measure. It had the advantage, too (though this is never mentioned by historians), of delaying the impact of colonists on Indigenous lands and peoples. Here was a retarded and reluctant frontier. It suppressed development for all except the Hudson's Bay Company and its companion, the Puget's Sound Agricultural Company. Hence all the arable lands were occupied by these companies. We might say this was a corporate frontier, precisely the opposite of what was going on in the American far west. Blanshard thought the whole British scheme a folly. He had many allies in this regard.

In July 1849, as said, Richard Blanshard was duly appointed governor and commander-in-chief in and over the Island of Vancouver and its Dependencies. Those were the official designations of the office and of the jurisdiction. He was appointed by a commission under the great seal of the United Kingdom. Once the Queen's commission and proclamation were read in the colony, the common law of England came into effect. The transition would be complete—from British territory, as confirmed by the 1846 treaty, to colonial development authorized and regulated by the Charter of Grant, and thence to formal Crown executive powers being in place. For those on the spot, some shaking of heads must have taken place as they tried to fathom the nature of this change. It was the beginning of a new order, and it would take years for the influence of the Crown to expand its interests, while the Hudson's Bay Company would change the nature of its imperium, then retire from its formal possession of the Colony of Vancouver Island, which it held under the precious Charter of Grant. Change came reluctantly to the Company. The introduction of English civil law obliged the Company to change practices: now justices of the peace were to be introduced. And in criminal cases new rules had to be followed. Capital cases—murder and manslaughter—came within the governor's authority.

In further instructions to Governor Blanshard dated 15 September 1849, Earl Grey made clear how Vancouver Island was to differ in its law from that of mainland New Caledonia. In the House of Lords, 29 June, when the bill to provide for the administration of justice in Vancouver's Island was read for the second time, Grey explained that, under the old law, all serious offences committed on the northwestern coast of America had to be tried in the courts of Canada; the bill proposed to repeal that law so far as it related to Vancouver Island, and to establish local courts for the administration of justice.[201] The new measure was designed "to remove...the restrictive force of certain provisions" set out in the Canada Jurisdiction Act of 1803, whereby criminal cases could be tried by justices of the peace and magistrates empowered by the Company. In short, these amendments freed the colony from the fur traders' control. This legislation received royal assent 28 July 1849. (This is the first British legislation dealing specifically with the Colony of Vancouver's Island and its Dependencies, and the last.) This law, entitled the Vancouver Island Jurisdiction Act (12 & 13 Vic., c.48),[202] gave the governor unbounded powers.

By other measures, the governor was appointed vice admiral, with powers to deal with matters pertinent to admiralty law. These included marine salvage, wrecked or abandoned vessels, and registration of shipping. His responsibilities extended to verifying that a vessel was seaworthy—in condition to be able to set to sea—or otherwise to be condemned. British laws of navigation and shipping were subjects known to him on account of his study at the Inns of Court. Blanshard had authority to appoint a chief magistrate, magistrates, justices of the peace and sheriffs. The Colonial Office did not arrange for any of these; such persons would have to be drawn from qualified occupants of the colony. It was intended that the governor would meet the needs of the day as they arose, all costs being borne by the Company (which was not disposed to run up administrative costs on that score). He would appoint justices of the peace, taking into account nominations to these positions provided by the Company. Blanshard declined to appoint Company officers as magistrates; he was afraid they would abuse their judicial powers. The flare-up at Fort Rupert in 1850 and 1851 required a magistrate and justice of the peace; in consequence, Blanshard appointed recently arrived Dr. John Sebastian Helmcken, the only person he thought suitable for the job. Blanshard also turned his mind to appointing a chief magistrate. No result came of this; he would serve as such in the absence of a qualified male.

We now turn to how he was to get to Vancouver Island, half a world away from the Home Islands. With an eye to the future, Blanshard had indicated to Earl Grey and his secretaries that, given that emigration of qualified colonists was to be promoted, it would be of estimable value to know what travel routes and communications by sea and land were available to would-be settlers. In particular, he thought a transit of the Isthmus of Panama would be a faster way to populate the new colony than the usual journey around the tip of South America. Grey took up his suggestion: a request was sent to the Admiralty to the effect that if Blanshard could get to Panama by a certain date (1 January 1850), it was in the public service for one of Her Majesty's ships of war to meet him there and convey him as quickly as possible to his new seat of governance.

The idea was Blanshard's and it was brilliant in concept. However, he misjudged the difficulties of travel and the perils of tropical diseases. Nor did the HBC respond with alacrity, fearing it would have to bear the costs of Blanshard's transport from London to Panama, and then what the Admiralty would charge for provisioning the special passenger and manservant en route to Vancouver Island. That was true Company parsimony, ingrained by centuries of penny-pinching. We are reminded that this was a stockholding business, and shareholders had to be paid dividends. The Company never adopted a trans-Isthmian route for settlers; it stuck to the old and reliable sea channels of the long route round Cape Horn. And in the long run, Blanshard would have been better served by taking the customary route by Cape Horn. His anticipatory urge was to cost him dearly.

Chapter 8:
Vice-Regalities

When reading his commission at Fort Victoria on 11 March 1850, Blanshard began a colonial governorship unparalleled in the history of the British Empire. No government house awaited him, no hotel in which he could lodge, indeed nothing but fort buildings for himself and his manservant. He had no office. He had no secretary. At the outset he had no transportation of his own, borrowing from the fort's stable as required. He placed an order with Nisqually for a pair of nags, or small riding horses.

Eventually, in May 1851, Dr. Tolmie at Nisqually found him a gelding named Siskyo, a fine mount (at the cost to the governor of $30 plus shipping).[203] Further, he had no water transport of his own, and never was known to take passage on any HBC vessel. Presumably, he had brought his own fishing gear with him, doubtless for fly-fishing. He had brought his own big-game rifle and shotgun, perhaps a brace of pistols. He had brought out a set of silverware plate in expectation of being able to entertain. There was no place for him to entertain. He had no female company, as far as is known. He had no personal guard, no soldiers to form an armed escort. Postal services were via Company means. He drew his expense monies through the Company, which in turn dealt with his London bankers. He lived a life of exile. There was no social club, no up-to-date newspapers and no telegraph or railway.

As governor, Blanshard was all things in legal affairs. He would have to deal with criminal cases and all sorts of civil matters. The murder of whites seeking to escape to California and the goldfields came within his jurisdiction. All disputes between and among servants and others in the employ of the Hudson's Bay Company—tradesmen, miners, labourers, etc.—were matters that he had to adjudicate and settle. As justice of the peace and magistrate, he had to hear and settle cases, and his policy invariably was to settle matters so as not to impose a solution that would require jail time for persons found guilty. Most were released under warning and under their own recognizance. There being no jail and no jailer, this was the obvious course of action.[204]

The inquisitive parliamentary committee in 1857 wanted to know from Blanshard about these matters:

> *Would any great mischief have happened if there had been no governor at all?*
>
> *—There would have been a great deal of quarrelling; it was necessary that somebody should be at the head; that there should be some kind of law on the island, and to enforce it.*
>
> *Was not there a Company's servant there?*
>
> *—Yes [Chief Factor James Douglas]; but there were people there who were independent of the Company then, and they would not take the law from him.*
>
> *How was justice administered: was there a recorder, or anybody to administer justice?*
>
> *—I did it all myself; I had no means of paying a recorder a salary; there were no colonial funds. [Blanshard stated that he had been called to the bar.]*
>
> *And in that capacity, you administered justice there?*
>
> *—Yes.*
>
> *So that you were Governor and justice. Had you any constables?*
>
> *—Yes. When I wanted a constable, I swore one in.[205]*

This, then, was the way law and order was practised in the Colony of Vancouver Island in its earliest days. Blanshard was flexible and resilient in the way he acted to keep the peace.

Customarily, in most colonies, the governor set the social scene—held balls, entertained as lavishly as possible, extolled the happiness of British rule, led processions on special days, sat in a special pew in the colonial church, promoted goodwill and public decorum and, more generally, oversaw the colonial seat and its outskirts in a form befitting the personage of the Queen's Most Britannic Majesty. Not at Fort Victoria. Nothing like this was possible. A proto-British colony existed already. There was a social hierarchy. James Douglas "held court" at table; in consequence, Governor Blanshard was the guest. The governor did not need a flag detail to raise the flag at dawn and take it down at sunset. The Company did that already. In short, everything was upside down, nothing met expectations in the usual running of empire.

In his despatch to Earl Grey dated 15 June 1850, Blanshard reported dolefully that nothing of importance had occurred in the colony since his last report of 8 April. Day-to-day activities at Fort Victoria continued as before. Company activity ashore and afloat was brisk. As to colonial progress, nothing could be said: no settlers or immigrants had arrived; no land sales had been made. Coal, vainly expected, had not been discovered, though the miners had not yet, he was pleased to say, abandoned all hope.

He continued his report to London:

The Company has commenced a survey of the land reserved to themselves, which is bounded by a line drawn nearly due North from the head of Victoria harbour to a hill marked on the charts as Cedar Hill, or Mount Douglas, and thence running due east to the Canal de Arro [Haro Strait]. The extent is estimated at about ten miles (square). A tract adjoining, of similar extent, is reserved for the Puget Sound Agricultural Association [sic], the Hudson's Bay Company under another name…this last contains the harbour of Esquimalt, the only harbour in the southern part of the Island worthy of notice, as it is of large extent, has good anchorage, is easy of access at all times and in all weather, is well watered and in many places the water is of sufficient depth to allow ships anchoring offshore.[206]

By contrast, he regarded Victoria Harbour as very small, the entrance narrow, tortuous and shallow. No vessels could enter except at high tide and under favourable wind and weather. As there was no drinking water near to hand, such water required by the Company for its purposes had to be fetched from two miles away. So short was drinking water that during summer and autumn, the Company servants were kept on allowance as at sea.[207] Blanshard, astute in strategic matters, could see the merits of Esquimalt, and he planned a village or townsite there—though he never saw it come to fruition.

Douglas's choice of Camosun waterway and shores as the site for the fort and agricultural development suited the Company's immediate needs, but as far as settler prospects were concerned, Blanshard must have thought the decision ill-advised. He was correct as to the prospects of Esquimalt. It had a growing strategic value, which admirals and commanders of Navy ships quickly realized; not least, it could offer a place of rest and repair, and even a refuge for the wounded in a war pending against imperial Russia. In 1854, three hospital buildings—the "Crimea huts"—were constructed at Duntze Head, the beginning of the nascent naval base under British and later Canadian control.

The London headquarters of the Hudson's Bay Company took exception to Blanshard's folding the Puget's Sound Agricultural Company into the HBC.[208] Sure enough, the Colonial Office, clicking its heels in agreement, passed on the objection to Blanshard. This does not mean that Governor Blanshard accepted the differentiation. From his point of view, they were one and the same.

To Blanshard's continuing and sharp appraisals of colonial non-development and corporate dominance at Vancouver Island, the HBC countered with that self-assured character the firm exhibited in those days. Blame was placed on the California goldfields as a drain on manpower. Moreover, the Company was sending out another ship from London bearing agricultural workers and labourers, the barque *Tory*. Blanshard wanted armed protection for the colony. The HBC's response bears a disingenuous tone: "We have never found any serious difficulty in protecting the Servants and property of the Company from hostile attacks of Indians, and we have every confidence that a continuance of that temperate and prudent conduct towards them, which is the rule and practice of the Service, will be the means of restoring a good understanding with the tribes in Vancouver's Island with whom it may be necessary to maintain intercourse." Colonial Office staff noted with disbelief that the HBC statement "ill accords with the account sent home by the Gov'r...If the Company feel such confidence in their ability to restore order why ask for the frequent visits of a Ship of War?" And again, "It is certainly questionable: but Indian alarms often subside as suddenly as they arise."[209] The Colonial Office could do nothing, made no expression of support to Governor Blanshard, and let the matter drop.

Blanshard's report of 15 June included news of telling importance. This was the age of gold discoveries, and the governor alerted London of recent rich findings on the Spokane River. These were near the HBC's Fort Colvile, which lay just south of the forty-ninth parallel. These discoveries, Blanshard suggested, forecast gold seekers who would cross into creeks and streambeds north of the boundary. Consequences to British interests were clear. With a touch of exaggeration, Blanshard reported that the whole population of Oregon Territory was "flocking to the spot." He based his report on news he had received from Oregon, probably Fort Vancouver. Already the California mines were drawing off settlers and sailors; now the Spokane River would accentuate the drain of labourers from the colony: "Should the favourable accounts of these mines prove correct, I fear that it will draw away all the Hudson's Bay Company servants from Vancouver Island, and at present they form the entire population."[210] Blanshard gave fair warning. Obtaining truthful reports out of a mining country proved impossible. Real gold nuggets, so to speak, have a voice all their own. At Fort Victoria, meanwhile, peace and routine were the order of the day.

One spring day in 1849, a year before Blanshard's arrival, a strange vessel had dropped anchor off Fort Victoria. Chief Trader Roderick Finlayson recounts in his memoirs that the rough-hewn visitors wore red flannel shirts. When they landed, they were mistaken for pirates. "I ordered the men to the guns," he says, "manned the bastions, and made ready for defense." All the same, he was inquisitive. He cautiously went to the gate and issued a challenge. The men explained that they were peaceable traders, come from San Francisco with gold to trade for goods and provisions, as Fort Victoria was the only station on the northern coast where they could get the supplies they wanted. Finlayson writes:

Having satisfied myself that they were what they represented them-
selves to be, I let them in, and they then told me that gold had been
discovered in California in large quantities the previous fall, and
that they had gold nuggets, which they would gladly exchange for
goods. They produced several nuggets. The value of which I at first felt
doubtful of, but brought one of the nuggets to the blacksmith's shop,
and told him and his assistant to hammer it on the anvil, which they
did, and flattened it out satisfactorily.[211]

Finlayson paid $11 per ounce for all the gold they brought; Californian placer gold was worth $16.50 per ounce in those days. Other vessels came from California for the same purpose. The Company turned profits in supplying these ships.

A year later, Blanshard drew to the attention of the British government a surge of miners north toward the forty-ninth parallel west of the Continental Divide. We recite the restless progress of those who moiled for gold: Reading's Bar on the Trinity in 1849, Scott's Bar on the Klamath in 1850, and the Coquille River and Jackson Creek, both in Oregon soon thereafter.[212] The Company followed suit. In 1852, Chief Trader Angus MacDonald at Fort Colvile sent prospectors on northern discoveries. For thirty years, that post had been prominent on the Columbia, the chief inland post of the HBC, a rich agricultural flatland and nexus of horse and livestock breeding. Added to this now was a role as mining headquarters for the upper Columbia basin—or as it is known in Washington State history, the Inland Empire. Local Indigenous peoples, especially the Nez Perce, had no quarrel with the HBC, but the coming of miners (with miner rules), along with vigilantes and their committees, demonstrated the brutal characteristics of frontier law and order. "Indian wars" occurred in various places in eastern Washington, Idaho and Montana.

Blanshard witnessed the beginning of the American frontier turmoil in the farthest west. In his time, early warning signals had been made about the gathering storm. The horrific events at Waiilatpu in 1847 had a powerful influence on the settlers and provoked intervention from the government of the United States. The inaugural governor of Washington Territory, Isaac Ingalls Stevens, aged thirty-four, arrived at Olympia, the capital, in 1853. From Andover, Massachusetts, and a graduate of West Point, Stevens had given up his Army commission in order to take on the governorship. His powers resembled those of a Roman proconsul. He had the difficult task of making treaties with the tribes, thereby clearing the way for surveys for a transcontinental railway and the military Mullan Road (from Fort Benton, head of steam navigation on the Missouri River, to old Fort Walla Walla on the Columbia River). Stevens bore a War Department commission to find a transcontinental rail route from Lake Superior to Puget Sound. The US Army was brought in under General John Ellis Wool, who urged that the area be kept free of settlers so as to reduce conflict. Peace proved impossible. The restless tide of gold miners and land seekers brought Indigenous reprisals. This, in turn, brought the intervention of the US government in the form of lethal force, punishment and removal from Indigenous lands.

Under-Secretary Herman Merivale at the Colonial Office knew all about this vicious circle; he had warned others at the Colonial Office (and in his publications) that any Americanization north of the forty-ninth parallel would bring on war with the Indigenous peoples. What happened in Washington Territory and Oregon was no model for what the British ought to do north of the line, he warned. Anyone reading a general history of the Pacific Northwest concentrating on the late 1840s and 1850s cannot help but be astonished at the violence of the northwest American frontier, while by contrast, above the forty-ninth parallel, the rule of law persisted without the presence of an army.[213]

One factor that contributed to the northern peace was the lack of settlers due to the HBC's discouragement of Americans coming north and even Britons crossing the Atlantic. The first settler did not arrive until March 1849, in the person of Captain Walter Colquhoun Grant, late of the Scots Greys, 2nd Dragoon Guards. Blanshard had met him at Nisqually, when the Scot was making arrangements to have some cattle and sheep loaded into the *Driver* for delivery to Sooke, Vancouver Island. Grant was an original, long on charm and wit but short of farming experience. HBC Deputy Governor Eden Colvile

chuckled when he wrote to Simpson that the colony had only one settler, and this was Grant, aged twenty-seven.

Captain Grant was a chariot of fire, with a burning instinct to
establish a Scots colony on Vancouver Island. He was thwarted in his
expectations, as the following makes clear, but at the end of the day
he was to prove a worthy commentator and scholar on the prospects
of Vancouver Island as a seat of commercial enterprise. He looked on
Vancouver Island as "a grand field for fresh & vigorous enterprise."[214]
He naturally found an ally in Blanshard, who, like him, was the epitome
of the gentlemanly capitalist, emblematic of the age.

Like Blanshard, Grant had arrived with great expectations, lured by
HBC promises of land. Vancouver Island seemed attractive. It was, as
he recounted, a locale that he "pitched on as the fulcrum whereon my
future life is to rest."[215] His father had been intelligence officer to the
Duke of Wellington at Waterloo, but both father and mother had died
when Grant was a lad, and he was brought up by an avuncular relative.
He had been at the Royal Military Academy, Sandhurst, when financial
circumstances obliged him to leave the Army. He then learned of the
promise of Vancouver Island. In contact with the HBC in London, he
agreed to purchase two hundred acres of land and, in accordance with
the Company's provisions, establish settlers thereon. The Company
urgently needed maps of Vancouver Island to facilitate land sales, and
appointed Grant its surveyor at a yearly salary of £100. Grant recruited
eight fellow Scots, including a farm manager, labourers and house
builders, who sailed for the Island via Cape Horn, their way paid by
the good captain. He also arranged that the Church of Scotland would
supply a clergyman to be schoolmaster (and teach Gaelic); the poor
fellow, an ancient Highlander, died of cancer on the voyage out. Grant
brought out a piper. He also sent to the colony for his use carriage
harness, sawmill machinery, sporting rifles, tools, seeds, cricket equipment and surveying devices. He arrived independently of his party.
Landing near Clover Point, he mistook a Company milk cow for a buffalo and shot it, much to the consternation of the Company. Having
waited idly for two weeks, the disgruntled labourers were pleased to
see their master at last.

Grant had been told in London that he was to have free choice of his land. Expecting to find his two hundred acres of prairie land near Fort Victoria, he discovered that land masterfully in the Company's possession. This was his first disappointment. Douglas suggested he settle at Metchosin, but he found no source for a water mill there; instead, he chose a hundred-acre site on Sooke Basin, twenty-five miles northwest of Victoria, suitable for building a sawmill. He and his men built a house, Achaineach (Ravensfield), named for the family's Speyside mansion, at which a pair of cannon were mounted, and they soon had thirty-five acres under cultivation. In 1850 he had his water-powered mill cutting the abundant timber found nearby. Douglas had steered Grant to the margins, as the captain revealed in the *Royal Geographical Society Journal* in 1857: "On my arrival in the Island all the land in the neighbourhood of Victoria and Esquimalt, which comprised some forty square miles, and contained nearly all the available land then known, was reserved by the Hudson's Bay and Puget's Sound companies."[216] This squared perfectly with Blanshard's appraisal.

It is generally stated that Captain Grant's increasing involvement with his Sooke estate pushed his surveying duties to second place. Likely this is an exaggeration. The Company paid him for his work; he completed his obligations. Pressed by the Company to send sketches on tracing paper to London as soon as possible, Grant, in his role as Company surveyor of Victoria, completed the base lines for the proposed municipal area. He also established the perimeter for the hundred-acre property of HBC retiree John Tod, the only other colonist to have come to the island by September 1850. Grant made Tod's breathtakingly beautiful allotment 440 yards broad along the sea coast, with a depth of 1,000 yards. In actuality, Tod's Oak Bay acreage proved to be 109 acres, for which he paid the requisite pound-per-acre price of £109. Grant's several sheets, duly completed, survive in the Hudson's Bay Company Archives.[217] What Grant failed to do was complete his assignment of dividing the Victoria area into sections. Hampered by lack of assistance and time, Grant tendered his resignation in March 1850 and finally gave up the survey in September, leaving the Company awaiting arrival of a new surveyor (J.D. Pemberton). Grant voyaged to Hawaii for a winter vacation to, he averred, save himself from lunacy or suicide. "There are at present no settlers at all on the island;

Mr. Grant left for the Sandwich Islands some days ago," wrote Blanshard to the Colonial Office in a tone of despair. Colvile thought Grant's flightiness amounted to lunacy, but that was the opinion of a stolid manager and not that of a risk-taker.[218] We see Grant as an intrepid agent of empire. He certainly faced pioneer problems that Eden Colvile, master of corporate talk, could never have imagined facing. The latter was not accustomed to rolling up his sleeves.

Grant, like Blanshard, invites our sympathy: his challenges were complex, costs were exorbitant and nothing ran easily for him or his men. True, he did not endear himself to many in the New World: he took too much tobacco offered him (Cavendish, the favourite, scarce and in high demand); moreover, he borrowed a rare volume from Dr. Tolmie's library without promise of return. He was a misfit among the Company officers. By 1854 Grant had left Victoria. He re-entered his regiment, fought in the Crimean War as a colonel leading a cavalry regiment, and died in Saugor, India, in 1861, aged thirty-nine. Before his death, however, acclaim had come his way as an authority on the resources and prospects of Vancouver Island. In 1854 he completed the first independent account and analysis of the colony's circumstances, prospects and Indigenous peoples. In June 1857, as the parliamentary inquiry into the Hudson's Bay Company diligently continued its proceedings, his lengthy "Description of Vancouver Island, by its first Colonist, W. Colquhoun Grant, Esq., F.R.G.S.," was read at the Royal Geographical Society in London. Blanshard was present on the occasion. It was published that year in the society's prestigious *Journal* and became the authority from which the eminent writer William Carew Hazlitt crafted his widely read *British Columbia and Vancouver Island* (1858). In 1861 Grant's equally valuable article on Indigenous peoples was published in the same journal.

Grant became a natural associate of Blanshard and of others, such as James Cooper, former HBC sea captain and now an independent trader and landowner; James Yates, former HBC carpenter, now tavern keeper; and the Reverend Staines, whom we met in Chapter 1. From the Company's point of view, this was a syndicate of discontent. Grant blamed bad government oversight for the Island's problems. We last hear of him in a letter written from India in 1857 to the secretary of the Royal Geographical Society. Grant had an eye to the future: once the Indian Mutiny was settled, and if Vancouver Island were "not in the meantime provided with a better governor [than James Douglas]," he would certainly accept the post "provided government felt disposed to take the [colony's] affairs seriously in hand."[219] From personal observation he had come to definite conclusions: "It will be seen that Vancouver Island possesses in itself several resources, which, if developed by a free people, under free institutions, would tend to make it a flourishing colony."[220] The high price of land, when compared to that in Oregon at one-fifth the sum, barred settlers from considering Vancouver Island. What Vancouver Island needed, he said in summary, was the encouragement of individual enterprise, and then the country would progress and be peopled by independent freeholders accustomed to relying on themselves for support and with an interest in the general prosperity. Grant had many admirers, Helmcken, who described him as "a splendid fellow and every inch an officer and a gentleman," and Father Lempfrit among them.

The colonial survey continued under Joseph Despard Pemberton. An accomplished engineer and professor of practical surveying, this Dubliner had offered his services to the Company and was hired in December 1850. He reached Fort Victoria on 25 June 1851 and started work the next day. Blanshard would have been delighted to see him, for the townsite needed to be laid out, and agricultural lands and farms needed to be systematically defined. These tasks Pemberton accomplished with his assistant, Benjamin William Pearse. Having studied survey systems in eleven other colonies, he set the price on a town lot at £10 each, suburban lots £15, country lands at £1 per acre, with a minimum size of twenty acres. Only Britons need apply. Further, land was reserved for the governor, the clergy, a school, a church and a public park. By December 1853, when we leave him to continue his mammoth task of surveying the Island and British Columbia, Pemberton had surveyed six additional districts on southern Vancouver Island.

∽∽∽

An equally engaging figure in the Company's employ was recently arrived: Dr. John Sebastian Helmcken, a licentiate of the Society of

The engaging Dr. John Sebastian Helmcken, shown here about 1854, was medical officer in HBC service. A Londoner, he became one of the colony's most influential legislators. His *Reminiscences* give us powerful insight into the Fort Rupert "troubles" and what Douglas called "the Nahwitti War." *Image A-01351 courtesy of the Royal BC Museum*

Apothecaries and a member of the Royal College of Surgeons. Blanshard welcomed Helmcken's presence, not least because the previous Company surgeon had been reassigned to Fort Vancouver. Helmcken, tall, thin and cheery, and in Blanshard's presence self-conscious of his class, had been born and raised in racially charged Whitechapel, Brick Lane, in London's East End. He had sailed in the *Norman Morison* as medical officer, bound on a five-month voyage to the new colony. The point of departure was the wharf near Fenchurch Street headquarters. "A good deal of fuss was made about this first voyage to the colony," he recalled with mirth, as was his style, "and some grandees were on board drinking wine and speaking good wishes, etc. etc."

All told, eighty emigrants sailed in the *Norman Morison*—mostly English labourers and their wives and children. The labourers came under contract and travelled free in third class, or steerage. At the expiry of five years, at annual salaries of £17, they could, if they wished, return to England. A steam vessel towed the ship down to Gravesend, where it put to sea. Helmcken and all on board endured gales, thunder and lightning, quarrels and feuds, smallpox and a tedious passage. They reached the dreary shores of Vancouver Island wondering how this wooded, rocky and mountainous country could ever be culti- vated. Much to their relief, the ship cast anchor at snug Esquimalt on 24 March 1850. All the folk on board could do was look at the dark, treed shoreline, watch manned canoes as they passed, and gaze at smoke rising from the fires on the shoreline. So near and yet so far, they were denied access even to the rocky headland, for quarantine had been imposed on account of smallpox aboard.

Blanshard understandably wished to consult Helmcken about the condition of the emigrants. He also wanted to meet the man assigned to assist him as governor. Helmcken had been told by Company sec- retary Archibald Barclay that he would serve on a half-time basis as Blanshard's private secretary; the remaining half would be taken up with medical matters for the Company. He did not fancy the arrange- ment. In fact, Helmcken was a contrarian. He could always put up an opposing view, as the following relates. The *Driver* lay at anchor in Esquimalt, fresh from circumnavigating the Island. As a matter of courtesy as well as business, Blanshard decided to pay a call on

Helmcken on board the nearby *Norman Morison*. Helmcken takes up the story:

> *The Captain woke me, and said, "Governor Blanshard has come on board from the HMS Driver to see you." Well, I suppose, I grumbled, and the Governor sent word not to bother, as there would be plenty opportunities later. I did not see him. The fact is I should have got up with alacrity, but I suppose I was tired or lazy. Having a sort of hazy idea that I was to be his assistant [part-time secretary] should have made me at once meet him and show off my best qualities, if I had any.*

Helmcken remarks gratuitously that he and Blanshard "never became friends—he evidently did not care for me," which seems self-serving and petty.[221] Blanshard was forgiving of Helmcken's rudeness and lack of punctilio. Helmcken, by contrast, worried about his discourtesy. One afternoon, in company of jolly Dr. Alfred Robson Benson, the surgeon at Fort Victoria, he paid a call on the governor at his makeshift residence. The well-dressed Benson was affectionately known as "the Commodore." He was frequently seen striding around the fort's surroundings or farther afield in old sea boots, so as to avoid the mud and puddles. Helmcken writes:

> *We found Governor Blanshard smoking a very thick pipe with a very long stem. He was a comparatively young man, of medium height, with aquiline, aristocratic features, set off by a large, military moustache. He had arrived only a few days previously, and had been riding. He said, "Benson, you told me all the trails led to the fort, but you did not tell me they all led away from it. Now, I got off the trail, to wander about, and I lost it; but I found another, and it led away from it. I should not have been here now had I not turned my horse's head and tail—as it is, I have lost my dinner."*
>
> *He told me he had no salary, but that a tract of land had been put aside for the Governor, out of the rents of which he had to make an income!!....Although a very intelligent and affable man, he did not see his way to do it, and thought the "Wakefield system" a mere*

theory, sure to fail in practice. He proved to be right. We left him with his pipe-stem still in his mouth.[222]

Helmcken never became the governor's secretary. Not long after this visit, as we shall see, he was assigned to Fort Rupert. Certainly, Helmcken never joined the syndicate of discontent already forming at and near Victoria.

Much of this discontent arose among the new arrivals from the *Norman Morison*. When they finally came ashore, they faced heavy, wet weather, and at that time only two large, new barn-like structures awaited them on the north side of Fort Victoria's palisade, sorrowful and cavernous shelters indeed. These labourers and their families formed a forlorn and dejected group. They had been cast on a British shore but one quite alien to home, a rude place of grinding parsimony and little if any civic pride. They must make do, and they valued even more the friendships they had made aboard ship during the long and tedious doubling of Cape Horn. They enjoyed few liberties and complained of unjust treatment and exorbitant prices charged for necessities at the Company sales shop. Pelly, quite naturally, denied the charge of unfair treatment.

A second group of agricultural workers arrived a year later, on 14 May 1851, in the *Tory*, after a typically rough passage of six months. In the first-class cabin were twenty-one persons; in the second, thirty; and in the third, or steerage, ninety labourers and families. Among the arrivals were three bailiffs, each of whom had agreed to manage a farm for the Puget's Sound Agricultural Company. One of these was Captain Edward Edwards Langford, who arrived with his wife and their five daughters, along with a mastiff dog and a goat. Six hundred acres were allotted to Captain Langford to establish a sheep farm. Originally Esquimalt Farm, Langford renamed it Colwood after his home in Sussex. He was soon disenchanted with his lot, made charges against the Company for corrupt practices, and was perennially at odds with James Douglas. Langford had a distant family connection with Governor Blanshard, but in and of itself the filial connection is insufficient to lie at the root of any animus against Douglas.

The sole independent settler on the *Tory*—that is, independent of the HBC—was Thomas Blinkhorn, who came out from England with his wife and her niece. They took charge of a farm fifteen miles from Victoria at Metchosin, owned by James Cooper, a member of the syndicate of discontent. Blinkhorn had spent several years in Tasmania after being sentenced to transportation for stealing a horse, but the colonists on Vancouver Island did not hold this against him—or did not know about it. He was well liked and respected. In 1853 Douglas commissioned Blinkhorn as a magistrate and justice of the peace, as Douglas considered him "the only independent settler with a sufficient degree of education" to qualify for the office.[223] He cleared land for Cooper and established a dairy herd, and when William Fraser Tolmie left Nisqually for Vancouver Island, he had Blinkhorn manage his farm, which was fifteen miles away from Cooper's holdings in Metchosin. No wonder Blinkhorn was described as "the most energetic settler on the island," by a witness at the parliamentary inquiry into the affairs of the Hudson's Bay Company.[224] Mrs. Blinkhorn's niece, Martha Cheney, kept a diary, which is a valuable document describing life in the early years of the colony.

The predictions of critics that the Company could not promote free settlement seemed to be coming true. As Blanshard could see by running his gaze down the pages listing who owned what property, the figures for the sales of land were poor. The four farms of the Puget's Sound Agricultural Company (Craigflower, Constance Cove, Esquimalt/Colwood and Viewfield) accounted for twenty-five hundred acres in total. About five thousand acres had been sold or applied for. Governor Colvile used these figures to support his contention of 27 April 1852 that since the date of the Charter of Grant, progress had been made creditable to the companies. What he kept from view was that the majority of purchasers were HBC employees. Subsequent calculations, made between 1852 and 1855 (when the first census of servants—that is, Company employees—and settlers was taken), record that 312 "settlers" had been sent out. However, on closer inspection we find that they were either past or present officers and clerks of the Company. A church and three schools had been constructed, it is true, also two flour mills and five sawmills, all operational. As historian

John S. Galbraith makes clear, there had been some progress in colonization of Vancouver Island, but "it was scarcely enough to support Colvile's contention that the efforts of the Company had been 'tolerably successful.'" No emphasis was placed on free settlement; all was done to get miners for coal mines and bailiffs and labourers for Company farms. A puny amount was invested in advertising in Scottish, English and Irish newspapers. Galbraith concludes: "By their lack of emphasis on free settlement, the governor and committee demonstrated their conviction that independent settlers must necessarily clash with the Company, a viewpoint from which they already had impressive documentation in Oregon and at Red River settlement."[225] If writing history is the art of comparison,[226] then the following tells all: in the Territory of Washington as of 2 March 1853, a population of four thousand Americans, not quite seventeen hundred of whom were voters, inhabited the lands between the Columbia River and the forty-ninth parallel.[227]

Truth to tell, and unknown to the suspecting Blanshard, from the outset Governor Simpson, head of HBC operations in North America, blatantly discouraged colonization on any large scale. Simpson made clear to Douglas that the flow of settlers should be restricted. In 1849 Douglas had proposed one hundred a year, a reasonable number, one would suppose. Simpson took the opposite view: he considered this would upset the welfare of present and future settlers. He reasoned that the increase of the population should be proportioned to the capabilities of the soil and the ability to raise sustaining crops; otherwise, in a year of unfavourable crop yields, the scarcity occasioned "would inevitably lead to the immediate abandonment of the colony by the settlers who would seek more genial climes in Oregon or California."[228]

Douglas was obliged to agree with Simpson that a restrictive policy of emigration would best serve the Company. Simpson was prudent in his thinking; all the same, the accusation of duplicity might well be made that he wanted to restrict the influx of free farmers to the Island. He had the interests of the fur trade to consider: that was what holders of Company stock valued most. Simpson's strictures, written on the eve of Blanshard's arrival at Fort Victoria, were kept from the governor. As time passed, however, the governor fully grasped the machinations of the corporate bosses to constrict and constrain the growth of settlement.

That was still to come. In spring and summer 1850, a change had come over the waters. Blanshard's next report to Earl Grey tells of newly arisen dangers and difficulties besetting the colony.

Chapter 9:
Haida Gwaii Gold in the Balance

Out of the blue, a new threat faced Governor Blanshard. News of gold finds throughout the cordilleran west had fired many an imagination. This Blanshard knew from observation and rumour. Indeed, he had duly reported to London the warning of a recent finding on the Spokane River, hard by the forty-ninth parallel. Gold discoveries north of the border would upset British trade, encourage desertions from the Company and attract unwanted foreign gold seekers to British realms. The California pattern was familiar. But on lonely and remote Queen Charlotte Islands, Haida Gwaii—was a gold strike possible there?

Mountainous, densely forested Haida Gwaii, this magical archipelago "east of sundown," as they say, lies 50 miles from the nearest continental shore and some 550 miles north of Victoria. For British warships these were high latitudes, far from bases of supply. The islands were home of the Haida, "a fierce and wild race," as one observer wrote in the 1850s.[229] They were ingenious and inventive, wrote another, who further remarked that they were by far the best-looking, most intelligent and energetic people on the Northwest Coast.[230] Their seaborne prowess was legendary, and they raided near and far, fearing no rivals. Natural conditions had favoured them. The archipelago had gained international attention in the days of the sea otter trade, for it was rich in sea otter pelts. From about 1785, the scattered Haida seaside villages were lucrative haunts for hard-driving and heavy-handed merchant mariners; there was much interracial violence. That era passed in the 1820s, although some casual business with the outside world followed. But then, and suddenly, came explosive excitement!

"I have seen [at Fort Victoria] a very rich specimen of gold ore, said to have been brought by the Indians of Queen Charlotte's Islands, but I have at present no further account of it."[231] Governor Blanshard's warning letter to Earl Grey was dated 18 August 1850. Meanwhile, the principal field officers of the Hudson's Bay Company—Douglas, Work and McNeill—kept the matter secret while they crafted their own schemes. Seven months later, in March 1851, Blanshard reported to the Colonial Office that the Company intended to send expeditions to the islands that summer.

Those islands were British sovereign territory since the Oregon Treaty. But in an era known for unauthorized attempts by Americans to carve out private domains (as in William Walker's military expedition in Nicaragua), Blanshard realized that adventurers from south of the border might seize the moment and occupy Haida Gwaii. Friction could be expected, and shipping losses too. As well, the Haida had a long history of violent encounters with American shipping, going back to the days of the sea otter trade.[232] Not only were the Haida guardians of their resources; they were militant fighters, keen on revenge for past injustices at American hands. They were seafarers and were justly regarded as the Vikings of the north Pacific.[233]

Blanshard was prescient about what the Americans would do. He was equally correct about the Company's intentions. In all, the Company sent six expeditions to Haida Gwaii. The first two were undertaken in canoes, crossing the stormy sixty-mile width of Hecate Strait from Fort Simpson on the mainland. The third venture showed more promise. The fourth expedition, a robust undertaking by the brig *Una*, departed Fort Simpson on 16 July 1851. On board were Chief Trader McNeill, Chief Factor Work and eight men, besides the vessel's crew and several miners. They sailed to Mitchell (or Gold) Harbour and obtained about sixty ounces of gold by barter. At other locations they blasted for the precious metal. At Englefield Bay they found a handsome vein six inches thick. The *Una* made a second effort,

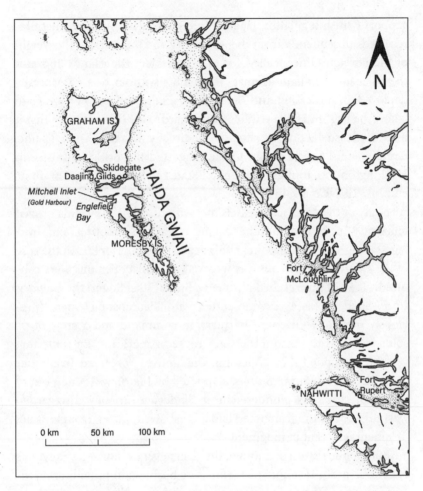

Map by Emma Biron

this time from Fort Victoria. At a later time, the Company sent the brig *Recovery*.[234]

It was foreign interference and a possible coup that the governor worried about. News of the discovery of gold could never be long concealed, and when this find was revealed, it caused great excitement in San Francisco. Before long, seven vessels, each bearing forty to fifty miners, headed for Mitchell Harbour: the *Susan Sturgis, Tepic, Palermo, Mexican, Eagle* and *Cecil* from San Francisco; and the *Georgiana*, from Olympia. Blanshard appealed to the Navy for aid. Rear Admiral Fairfax Moresby answered the call to guard British territory and support British regulations against foreigners. Moresby's instructions, received subsequently from the Admiralty and that carried the weight of the Foreign Office, called for him to protect the islands and also the adjacent mainland against "marauders without title."[235] Moresby deployed, in succession, the *Thetis*, *Trincomalee* and steamer *Virago* to "show the flag" in Haida Gwaii.[236] Blanshard's rule of thumb was that if he wished faster action, he should deal directly with the C-in-C Pacific. Simultaneously, the Foreign Office requested the British minister in Washington, DC, to press the United States government to restrain its citizens. This was a vain hope.

Many of the American vessels met with disaster. The Haida proved tenacious in controlling the bright metal, and looting and hostage-taking were common reprisals against the interlopers. In the case of the *Georgiana*, the ship was wrecked and thirty persons were captured. News of this reached Nisqually. From Puget Sound the *Demaris Cove*, fitted out as a revenue cutter, with Lieutenant Dement (previously met) of Steilacoom Barracks in command and a crew of US soldiers, sailed to ransom the shipwrecked Americans. En route that vessel was supplied at Fort Victoria. The captives were freed. In another case, the 150-ton *Susan Sturgis*, skippered by Matthew Rooney, out of San Francisco, was plundered near Skidegate. Rooney disregarded warnings about the fearsome Haida; he showed, James Douglas said, "a lamentable want of judgment."[237]

But for one reason or another, the rush never eventuated to anyone's benefit or profit save for the Company's business in providing provisions to ships. The Haida made their point as to their own resources and prevented these expeditions from carrying on any mining. Although the force on the American ships was considerable, and the men were well armed, they were beaten off and compelled to return empty-handed.[238] Blanshard's early warning to London, subsequently repeated, about what would likely transpire on Haida Gwaii, received the attention this serious matter so urgently required.

Turbulent frontiers are the "stuff" of British imperial expansion. The British government annexed the islands, and the governor of Vancouver Island became lieutenant-governor there effective 29 July 1853.[239] The Company's trading licence remained in effect, but the now-cautious Colonial Office made clear that the "dependencies" of the Colony of Vancouver Island under the Charter of Grant did not include Haida Gwaii. This limited HBC influence. Even so, freedom of navigation had to exist: thus, foreign shipping could not be excluded. So it was that the formal empire of Britain administered from Victoria grew strangely to include Haida Gwaii. This paradox existed: the Haida peoples occupied the lands, but the British held sovereignty. The expansion of the British Empire here, as elsewhere, was due more to circumstance than to imperial design.

This gold rush holds a vital place in coast history. It is significant in British Columbia history because it established the pattern of crisis and response by which British authority came to be exercised in a territory under nominal British sovereignty, as determined by international law and the 1846 treaty. Here was strange empire, full of drama, high hopes and terrible tragedies. It will come as no surprise to the reader that the Company anticipated a rich gold harvest. This proved a vain hope. Moreover, shipping losses were significant.

The HBC's *Una*, Captain Mitchell, bound for Fort Victoria from Haida Gwaii, was caught in a horrendous gale the night of 25 December 1852. She was driven on shore with two anchors down and was stranded on Cape Flattery. The Makah of Cape Flattery, according to the report received in Victoria, "behaved with great barbarity," maltreating the crew. Further details said that they pillaged the vessel, then burned it. Some crew members were robbed. The American sloop *Susanna*, providentially passing that location, rescued the castaways and also the cargo of furs and gold ore. The vessel carried them to Fort Victoria and safety. Sixty ounces of gold were landed at Fort Victoria. No lives were lost. The bill presented by the captain of the American vessel for time and work involved in the rescue operation was happily paid. The Company made an insurance claim for loss of the trusty *Una*. The disaster deprived the Company of a yeoman vessel at a time when the marine department faced many difficulties of ship losses and seizures by US officials.[240] A subtle show of force was called for. The *Cadboro* was sent from Fort Victoria with a strong-armed party to demand restitution and compensation from the Cape Flattery chiefs. Well aware that this was US territory, the officers on board the

Cadboro had strict instructions: violent measures were to take place only in self-defence.[241] As it transpired, peace was obtained. For a while the HBC became fixated on "moiling for gold" in Haida Gwaii. However, this proved a losing proposition. The islands returned to their general quietude.

But the Haida made many warlike expeditions south to the San Juan Islands, and at Whidbey Island engaged in murderous raids, killing one settler, Isaac N. Ebey, in 1857. US authorities were alarmed by these incursions, and they alerted British authorities in Victoria. Tensions on this maritime frontier as far south as Nisqually continued for some years. The militarization of the American territory and the presence of US Navy vessels ended that threat. Haida continued to come to Victoria, but went home on the arrival of smallpox there in 1862. The effects of the disease on the Haida villages were unimaginably terrible, and remnant peoples, refugees in their own islands, found their way to two "towns"—Skidegate and Naden, or Queen Charlotte City, both missionary locations. In these locations the Haida, though greatly diminished, survived this long and dark watch—and lived to see a glorious revival in the mid-twentieth century.

As for the collection of gold nuggets and flakes, the Company gathered at Victoria its various gains from Haida Gwaii and elsewhere—from Fort Kamloops and Tranquille Creek and Nicoamen River on the mainland. Secrecy was the byword. In February 1858 it shipped eight hundred ounces of coarse gold on board the propeller steamer *Otter*. That vessel steamed for San Francisco, the nearest mint. Volunteers at the local fire department there proclaimed that the next excitement would be on the Fraser River. The rush commenced in California. On 25 April 1858 the sidewheeler *Commodore* rounded the southern tip of Vancouver Island and anchored near Fort Victoria. On board were 450 miners from San Francisco, the true vanguard of a mass of thirty thousand that would arrive before summer's end. The *Commodore* carried sixty Britons and the remainder Americans, Germans, Italians and a variety of other nationalities, the collective bearing the general title of Californians. As one commentator unerringly put it, "The *Commodore* arrived just as Sunday church services were completed, and as the citizens watched the wooden vessel, they little realized that they were also watching the end of the fur trade era and the start of a rousing decade that would change the land and the people forever."[242]

Most British territorial acquisitions of the last half of the nineteenth century were for the purpose of stabilizing already held possessions. Where turbulence existed, boundaries expanded to contain it and stamp it out, for turbulence created vacuums into which the British feared other nations would rush. Blanshard saw the problem, and so did Douglas: Crown and Company acted together to keep foreign gold seekers out of Haida Gwaii. Here was a pattern of imperialism that was replicated when gold was discovered in the Fraser-Thompson area and in the Yukon.

But it was coal, not gold, that would cause Blanshard the most problems in his term as governor.

Chapter 10:
The Track of the Storm

We now return to Fort Rupert and environs. A miasma descends on the scene. Images become blurred. We saw in Chapter 4 that this was a northern Vancouver Island location of intense Indigenous activity. In this chapter and the next, we turn our attention to labour problems, the murder of Britons exposed to Indigenous attack, and government and Company reprisals. Blanshard's actions—and his policies—are at the heart of these affairs.

Since its founding in 1849, Fort Rupert was a place of stress and strain. The Company found the Indigenous peoples near the post numerous and troublesome. Thefts were common. Company servants feared attack. Visiting or transiting war parties added to the state of turmoil. This was because Beaver Harbour lay at the crossroads of Indigenous traffic and rivalries. Then there were labour problems relating to the mining of coal. Would the experienced field officers of the Company be able to set matters right, get the place on a firm footing?

We have already seen storm warnings. When Blanshard arrived at Fort Rupert in the *Driver* in March 1850, he had found the establishment in anything but a flourishing state. At that date the Ayrshire miners had not yet located a seam capable of yielding quality steamer coal suitable for sale. Blanshard found the miners hot with disaffection, unhappy with their housing, security and tools. Early in his governorship he had duly reported all this to London. He made his opinion known locally too. When he returned to Fort Victoria, he likely spoke about the awkward state of affairs to Chief Trader Captain William Henry McNeill, who was there, away from his Fort Rupert assignment.

In early April Captain McNeill returned to Fort Rupert in the *Beaver*. His formidable presence seemed to steady the society within the palisade. However, when he had to leave Fort Rupert on other business, he was obliged to pass the supervision to his son-in-law, the twenty-two-year-old clerk George Blenkinsop, who had a greenhorn assistant named Charley Beardmore. Blenkinsop may have been courageous, good-natured, active and intelligent, and Beardmore may have been active, fearless, energetic and a "little harum-scarum," for he always carried a sort of shillelagh and was prone to great exaggeration;[243] however, neither had much experience of life on the wild frontier. Their inexperience and lack of judgment told mightily in the coming struggles.

In McNeill's absence, tensions at the fort rose sharply. Frustrations increased among the miners. As described in Chapter 5, Blenkinsop, whose responsibilities made him officer in charge of mining operations, directed the Muirs to sink a mine shaft at Suquash, nine miles south of Fort Rupert. Preliminary results here since 1846 offered greater promise.[244] But the Kwakiutl demanded payment for land, and their thievery became serious; nighttime depredations were the rule. The miners resented having to redo the previous day's work and demanded that a stockade be built around their workings at Suquash.

On 10 April the miners demanded common labourers to help in the work. They further required safety from depredations by day and night, and, not unreasonably, adequate tools. They resented doing menial tasks, contending that labourers such as the "Kanakas" at the post should be so employed. The Muirs were correct in this, for there was a recognized division of labour in Scottish mines, one that Blenkinsop could not countenance or understand. In June a further quarrel ensued between the miners and Blenkinsop, and from time to time the Muirs downed tools. The common labourers in the Company's employ complained grievously of working conditions. They resented the poor food and the long hours, and the fact that they were ill-protected from theft and interference.

All had become more troublesome—a toxic brew. The miners

implemented a "go slow" policy, and it was this that most concerned Blenkinsop; accordingly, he sent a courier to Fort Victoria to get advice and help from Company officers.

Andrew Muir, eldest son of oversman John Muir, was clearly the chief dissenter. His journal entry for 27 April sends up a clarion call: "Revolution was approaching, the Company's day was gone by, and that men were beginning to hold their heads up &c. &c. and a lot of other rebellious language." Europe was aflame with revolution in 1848; the Chartists had raised the flag in England. Change was in the wind, even in these remote wilds of northern Vancouver Island.

In short, a mere two months after Governor Blanshard's visit of inspection at Fort Rupert and its mines, the situation had deteriorated dramatically. Social discord was the order of the day. The headstrong Blenkinsop flared in anger at the Scots. Andrew Muir and his cousin John McGregor refused to dig a drain. This was a breach of contract, said Blenkinsop, and he fined each of them £50, a full year's wages. He did not stop there: he charged Muir with being a rebel guilty of promoting dissent among the miners. Muir responded with a charge of defamation of character. On 26 April 1850 began the first Vancouver Island coal miners' strike. Blenkinsop had antagonized them repeatedly. Beardmore, meanwhile, was sizing up the "old hands," the Company officers, who little understood the passing of the age—the fur trade in the west was done, he said. Douglas dismissed him, "sent him about his business."[245]

Worse was to come. The heavy-handed Captain McNeill, known for his terrible temper, returned to the scene. To the subsequent disdain of his superiors, he vented his fury. Andrew Muir gives this testimony: "Capt. McNeill commenced like a madman, swearing and threatening, and ordered us to our work. We said not till we were fairly tried by English laws for what was charged against us. We were ordered to be put in irons and fed on bread and butter." For six days Andrew Muir and John McGregor were kept in leg irons in one of the fort's bastions, then released. Douglas thought putting the men in irons and on short rations a foolish mistake, but the deed had been done. When George Simpson heard of McNeill's rants and raves, he ordered the captain away from further duties ashore, reasoning that it were best if he remained in command of a ship. Chief Factor Douglas, heeding Simpson's wishes, sent McNeill to the Sandwich Islands for a time, far away from any difficulty that might draw him in.

Meanwhile, the miners had sent a petition to Governor Blanshard that outlined their grievances. Blanshard, sympathetic from the outset, thought the miners ill-used by the Company—"grossly mistreated" is the governor's term.[246]

As for the labourers, they too had reason to complain, as noted above. Blenkinsop took sharp action against them. On 9 May he sent a letter to Blanshard telling of repressive measures he had taken at Fort Rupert. The particulars inflamed the governor. "[I] regret to hear that you have found it necessary to resort to severe measures with some of the labourers under your orders," he wrote to Blenkinsop in reply on 22 June, "and still more so that the peace and security of the establishment should require such application. I have consequently appointed Dr. Helmcken to act as Magistrate and Justice of the Peace, which I trust will prove a check on all disorders for the future." He also requested that Blenkinsop report on the quantity of coal taken from that district, the names of the ships supplied and the quantity supplied to each.[247]

At this juncture, Dr. Helmcken was thrown reluctantly into the vortex. Steaming north on the *Beaver*, Helmcken, standing on the bridge, admired endless islands and inlets. But his grumbling and contrarian manner got the attention of the skipper, Captain Dodd. Helmcken tells the story:

We were passing along Johnstone Strait against the flood tide. As this island was approached, which stands in the middle of the channel, the tide rapidly increased in strength, owing to the island in the way, till the Beaver had extremely hard work to make any headway, the vessel sheering about in the swirling current. I asked the captain the name of the island near which we were struggling along. Captain Dodd replied, "It has no name, but I will call it after you, doctor, for it is like you, always in opposition." The island has since been known by my name.[248]

Douglas had assigned Helmcken to Fort Rupert as an officer of the

Company and the post's surgeon, in addition to his appointment by Blanshard as an officer of the law. Blanshard was exact in his instructions: "You are hereby appointed Magistrate and Justice of the Peace, for the protection and preservation of order amongst her Majesty's subjects in and about Fort Rupert, and in the adjoining district of Vancouver Island, subject always to her Majesty's approval of your appointment, when your Commission will be made out and forwarded to you, till which time this letter shall be an official warranty of your acting as Magistrate of the District, and exercising all powers that belong to that office."[249]

The self-admitted neophyte did his best to control the seething feelings within Fort Rupert. He found himself dealing with labour and management issues. In these he was out of his depth. Moreover, he was soon embroiled in Crown-Indigenous relations. None of this can in any way be regarded as his usual line of work, which was making up prescriptions and treating ailing patients. He found himself in a fiery situation where the Scots brought charges against McNeill, Blenkinsop and Beardmore for false imprisonment, against the Company for breaking contract and for bad treatment, and, in the case of Andrew Muir, against Blenkinsop for defamation of character. Helmcken took the only road possible. Pending further investigation by the civil authority (i.e., Blanshard), Helmcken bound them over on their own recognizance to keep the peace.[250]

As for Andrew Muir, in his diary he recorded his views that there was "talk of slavery being abolished, here it remains in full force." It was time for him to break for freedom. Muir realized the danger of desertion from the Company's service, which would be a breach of contract. Escape was dangerous as well as difficult. Blenkinsop used to give local Indigenous people ten blankets for the head of a deserter. Even so, Andrew Muir and a companion slipped away in a canoe. In Muir's words, they "determined to make for some Christian place." They found relief when a passing merchantman picked them up, and on 20 July they landed in San Francisco. (Muir, in one of history's strange twists, eventually returned to Victoria and became the settlement's first sheriff.) The rest of his family continued to work the mines.

∽∽∽

How did the mining misadventures at Fort Rupert bear on relations with the Indigenous peoples there? Liquor was the root of all evil. On 10 July 1850, Governor Blanshard alerted Earl Grey of riotous conduct by miners and labourers at Fort Rupert. The governor warned London that this might lead to serious consequences with the "numerous, savage, and treacherous" Indigenous population. The concern was spirituous liquor brought ashore from visiting ships. This wasn't an issue only in Fort Rupert. The availability of ardent spirits in Fort Victoria and Esquimalt, brought in ships or otherwise smuggled in, led him to observe the demoralized state of Indigenous people either living there or visiting there. These places could not be sealed off from the outside world. Further, the excitement at Fort Rupert in regards to trade and the search for coal seams brought various ships not connected to the HBC. Blanshard had no quarrel with the Company's "Indian policy." In fact, he thought it praiseworthy. The Company was not to be blamed on this account. As he explained to Earl Grey:

> *I may here mention that the accounts which have been published respecting the barbarous treatment of the Indian population by the Hudson's Bay Company, are, both from my own personal observation and from all I have been able to gather on the subject, entirely without foundation. They are always treated with the greatest consideration far greater than the white labourers and in many instances are allowed liberties and impunities in the Hudson's Bay Company's establishments that I regard as extremely unsafe. No liquor is given them by the Company on any pretense, but it is impossible to prevent them obtaining it from the merchant vessels that visit the coast.[251]*

In fact, liquor consumption beyond the palisade of Fort Victoria was extensive. Labourers, farmhands and colonists had unquenchable thirsts, and one of them, Robert Melrose, joked that it would take a steady line of ships arriving from California to satisfy the local need for booze. On one occasion men became riotously drunk. Blanshard swore in some special constables. He was observed, wrote Helmcken with his customary mirth and exaggeration, "walking his verandah with sword at his side, vowing that he would have peace and be very severe on those who broke it."[252]

"I would strongly recommend," Blanshard advised the Colonial Office, "a duty to be imposed on the importation and manufacture of ardent spirits, as their introduction tends to demoralize the Indians to a most dangerous degree, but I conceive I have not the power to impose such duty, free trade having been declared here, without further instructions which I would request on this point at your Lordship's earliest convenience."[253]

Blanshard correctly understood he could not impose a duty on "ardent spirits." The Colonial Office specified that only a colonial legislature could pass such legislation. Not unexpectedly, therefore, Blanshard received this reply from Grey: "With respect to imposing a tax on the importation and manufacture of ardent spirits I am of opinion that it would be very desirable whenever the time shall arrive for the creation of a Legislature, and the necessary authority for the imposition of duties can be thus obtained."[254] Blanshard must have laughed inwardly at the prospect: no possibility existed of a legislature being formed, not even an executive council of seven. Pure and simple, there were insufficient qualified settlers. But if he could not tax, he could enforce prohibition, stopping the trade and gift of tanglefoot, hooch, Old Tom and tarantula juice.[255]

The governor had already taken action on this issue. By executive authority vested in him as governor, Blanshard had drafted and signed the Act Regulating the Importation of Spirituous Liquors, 13 May 1850.[256] The document is written in his exquisite hand. The governor gives his rationale in the preamble: "The free and unrestricted traffic in Spirituous liquors has caused and does still cause great damage and inconvenience to the Inhabitants of Her Majesty's Colony of Vancouver's Island, by debauching and corrupting the population, both native and Immigrant." The measure applied equally to Indigenous persons and to non-Indigenous persons. It laid down regulations for specified volumes (minimum of two gallons in each cask or case) imported in any vessel. It specified that spirits could not be landed or sold without a permit signed by the local magistrate of the port of entry. It established penalties for unlawful offences ($100 for each offence), payable by the ship's master or a charge on the vessel. A vessel lying off the coast (that is, not in port) was similarly liable to these penalties. In all, Blanshard's intention was to prevent smuggling and lessen social evils attendant on such illegal importations. Here we see, for the first time, a measure of social reform, an attempt to curtail excessive drinking and illegal trading. Not least, it was intended to protect Indigenous persons from the evils of liquor. This was a call of the Victorian empire, representing the views of the Colonial Office, the Aborigines Protection Society and the Church Missionary Society. And it represented Blanshard's views.

Blanshard's law "had a salutary effect for a time," according to James Douglas, discouraging "the sale of intoxicating drinks, which are the bane of the settlement, and the great source of poverty & crime." But that was only "until the settlement of the American side of the Straits of De Fuca, where there is no restriction on the sale of Spirits, when the Law became a dead letter, in consequence of the facility with which it could be evaded and Spirits introduced clandestinely into the settlement. Drunkenness is now the crying and prevalent sin of this Colony."[257] Scandalous scenes of drunkenness and excess were again the disgrace of Victoria until the passage of the License Act of March 1853, which had the added advantage of generating colonial revenue.[258]

It wasn't liquor that brought matters to a head at Fort Rupert in June 1850 but rather the social disaffection at Fort Rupert, the growing enmity of the northern Indigenous peoples—their far-ranging raids into Puget Sound and its islands—and the evolution of a garrison mentality of anxiety and fear that never diminished but instead grew in intensity. Had murders not occurred, it might easily have been said that this anxiety was misplaced and exaggerated. But when murders did occur, English criminal law supplanted the old Company ways of law-making, which involved taking action into its own hands. ("It has been the uniform policy of the Hudson's Bay Company," Pelly reminded Grey in January 1852, "never to suffer the blood of a white man to be shed by a savage with impunity.")[259] With a governor present at Victoria, there could be no corporate response and reprisals. Now the governor must act in defence of English law and British persons.

Chapter 11:
The Nahwitti War

From miners' strikes and desertions we now shift attention to murders and reprisals. Here is an example of synchronicity in history, the coming together of variant forces. Helmcken was already thrown into events beyond his control. He was obliged to enforce English civil and criminal law. As a justice of the peace, one of his duties was to prevent conflict with the Indigenous peoples. Blanshard was in faraway Victoria. Helmcken, therefore, found himself at the centre of events, which began to swirl perilously around him.

On 7 May 1850, about a month after Governor Blanshard had seen Fort Rupert for the first time and assessed its problems with a critical eye, an American collier (coal carrier) named the *England*, on business for the Aspinwall interest, arrived at Esquimalt direct from San Francisco. The vessel then sailed by the customary outside route to Beaver Harbour to take in coal for San Francisco. The vessel arrived at Fort Rupert in early June. Loading was slow and tedious, there being no wharf. Boats and canoes shuttled back and forth from ship to shore. The days passed lazily.

In the circumstances, with time on their hands, the *England*'s crew spent much time ashore. Sailors of the *England* gossiped with Company servants. They spread news of the riches and pleasures of San Francisco and the California bonanza. A golden promise was easily raised in the minds of those listeners discontented with their lot.

The Company men, though not the officers, grew resentful and insubordinate. Contagion mounted as time drew near for the vessel to sail for the Golden Gate. Liquor was readily available in the ship, another attraction. On shore, quarrelling ensued among Company servants, and some men and women threatened to defect in canoes if they could not go in the *England*. But the officers talked to the Kwakwa̱ka'wakw chiefs and brokered a deal with them not to sell canoes to anyone defecting from the Company service and seeking escape. The fort's gates were locked tight.

"Dangers within; dangers outside; danger all round" was Helmcken's description of it. These were anxious days for him and for other Company officers, but fruitful days for those making plans of escape. Risk attended escapees in those days. Proof of the margin of safety, wrote a contemporary, was that a boat's crew of half a dozen white men, if well-armed, could travel unmolested on the east and north coast of Vancouver Island, except among the more dangerous K'ómoks (Comox) and Lekwiltok.[260]

Now the unexpected occurred. One day the *Beaver* steamed into Beaver Harbour on the hunt for three British sailors in the Company's employ. The three had deserted from the *Norman Morison* at Victoria;

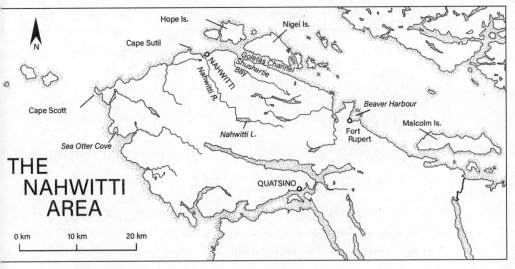

THE NAHWITTI AREA

Hope Is.
Nigei Is.
Cape Sutil
Goletas Channel
Shushartie Bay
NAHWITTI
Nahwitti R.
Cape Scott
Beaver Harbour
Malcolm Is.
Nahwitti L.
Fort Rupert
Sea Otter Cove
QUATSINO
N
0 km   10 km   20 km

Map by Emma Biron

they were now regarded by the firm as outlaws. The captain of the *Beaver* knew that the deserters had stowed away in the *England*, with hopes of reaching San Francisco. As soon as the *Beaver* hove in sight, the three men made a quick getaway. They slipped over the side of the *England* and fled in a canoe. They paddled northward, through narrow Goletas Channel, toward open waters. Their expectation (but surely their wildest hope) was that they would be picked up by the *England* as it sailed those same waters outward bound. So far, so good.

That night, they took refuge on Nigei Island, which lies halfway between Fort Rupert and Nahwitti. Nigei, according to good information, was the name of the hereditary chief of the Nahwitti. In 1851 it was shown on the chart as Galiano Island.[261] The Spanish explorers Galiano and Valdés, in the *goletas* (schooners) *Sutil* and *Mexicana*, had used the long and narrow passage (Goletas Channel) between Nigei and Vancouver Island in 1792. Small vessels had no difficulty, but it was tricky for large sailing vessels to navigate, particularly as fog often descended at the north end and near dangerous Nahwitti Bar, where the fairway splits as follows: Sutil Point (formerly Cape Commerell) on the Vancouver Island shore and Mexicana Point on the west of Hope Island.

The subsequent search was led by Old Wale, called such in the records. A high-ranking chief of the Quaeackar (Kweeha), Wale (or Whale) had been the first of twelve chiefs to agree to their treaty. Of middle age, he stood tall and dark, moustached and bearded. Collaborating with the colonial authorities, he took up the search to find the deserters. He returned to Fort Rupert empty-handed.

Subsequent information indicated that the runaways had left their Nigei Island resting place, but great misfortune befell them. They fell in with some Nahwitti near Shushartie Bay (on Vancouver Island across Goletas Channel from Nigei Island). According to Indigenous information, the three Britons were killed by three Nahwitti (whose names were Tackshiocoate, Tawankstalla and Killonecaulla) for refusing to submit to certain demands. Two of the victims were stripped and buried in hollow trees; the third was weighted down and sunk in the sea.[262] Old Wale found out these details and passed them on to a grateful

Blenkinsop, in charge at Fort Rupert. The exact date of the murders is not known but occurred in the month of June.

Now the terrible calamity of false news began to be perpetrated, and in due time it proved injurious to the governor. Before he knew they were dead, Blenkinsop had put up a reward: thirty blankets for the recovery of each of the three men. This information was conveyed to Old Wale through a French-speaking interpreter as thirty blankets *par tête*. This Blanshard interpreted as meaning "dead or alive." It was a large reward, but one that Blenkinsop hoped would bring back the escapee blacksmith, a valued tradesman essential for colonial progress. Confirmation of this offer exists, but the value of the award somehow changed. Andrew Muir, at Fort Rupert at the time, wrote: "Mr. Blenkinsop offered the Indians 10 blankets for each of their heads should they bring back only their heads. Was ever such barbarity heard of giving these blood hounds 10 blankets for one white man's head, these savages who care no more about taking a man's head than you should do of taking a meal of meat? Surely these things will not pass without punishment."[263]

In any event, Blanshard at Victoria followed the episode from a distance. "I have to inform your Lordship," Blanshard reported to Earl Grey on 18 August 1850,

...of the massacre of three British Subjects by the Newitty Indians, near Fort Rupert. Want of force has prevented me from making any attempt to secure the murderers; indeed, the only safeguard of the colony consists in occasional visits of the cruisers of the Pacific Squadron which only occur at rare intervals, and for short calls. The massacre of these men has produced a great effect on the White inhabitants, many of whom do not scruple to accuse the officers of the Hudson's Bay Company of having instigated the Indians to the deed by offers of reward for the recovery of the men (sailors who had absconded) dead or alive. I have not yet been able to inquire into the truth of this report, but it is very widely spread, and men say that they ground their belief on what the Hudson's Bay Company have done before. The establishment at Fort Rupert is in a very critical state.[264]

Based on what Helmcken had told him, Blanshard made clear to London that the people of Fort Rupert

...are so excited by the massacre, which they charge their employers with instigating, that they have in a body refused all obedience both to their employers and to him as magistrate, that he is utterly unable to maintain any authority as they universally refuse to serve as constables, and insist upon the settlement being abandoned; that to attempt such a step would lead to their entire destruction, as they are surrounded by Quacolts [Kwakwaka'wakw], one of the most warlike tribes on the coast, three thousand in number and well-armed. Mr. Helmcken has tendered his resignation as magistrate, as without proper support the office merely exposes him to contempt and insult, and he further states that being in the employment of the Hudson's Bay Company, he cannot conscientiously decide the cases which occur, which are almost invariably between that company and their servants. This is the very objection I stated to your Lordship against employing persons connected with the company in any public capacity in the colony.

He closed his report of woe with news that the miners had left the colony as a body, owing to their dispute with their employers. "The seam of coal is consequently undiscovered."

The governor sent orders from Victoria to Company officers at Fort Rupert that they must prohibit persons from leaving the post without special permission. "If the people attempt to abandon the settlement and straggle about the coast," he wrote, "they will infallibly be cut off by the Indians who are daily becoming more inclined to outrage, and are emboldened by impunity." In this, he was anticipating the Colonial Office's point of view.

The problems customarily lay on the remote margins of empire. Blanshard, like many another governor, could not ignore them: they fell within the duties of his office—to maintain law and order—and it is clear that Blanshard was exercising authority as best he could from Victoria. But Fort Rupert was inaccessible. It could have been on the other side of the moon. And even if he had been on the spot, he would have been helpless. Helmcken, who was there, had no constables to back him up. Neither did Blanshard have troops to serve as a guard or garrison. No military or police action could be mounted. His only option was to await the arrival of the next British man-of-war at Esquimalt. At that time, he would make an appeal and a request to the officer commanding to "come to the aid of the civil power." Who knew how long that would take and how long the murders would go uninvestigated? The Company had no intention of taking action.

The resourceful and determined Blanshard was facing his biggest challenges, and he did not come away from them unscathed in the historical record. At the time, British government legal policy on intervention in support of British subjects overseas was still being developed. In the case of Vancouver Island, the issue boiled down to how, and in what ways, British power should be used to protect British subjects ranging far from places of settlement and, equally important, what measures should be taken by way of reprisal if British subjects were indeed interfered with, even murdered. These policies were in limbo. For his part, Blanshard endeavoured to keep British subjects from ranging beyond the pale of British power. He found himself embroiled in the politics of intervention and faced the scrutiny of the Colonial Office.

We cannot blame Helmcken for how events unfolded or for retiring from the scene. He had played his role with tact and discretion, though hating the responsibility. In retrospect, we might argue that Helmcken resigned his civil office because of conflict of interest with the Hudson's Bay Company. He thereby left Blanshard, ships and officers of the Royal Navy (when present), Company officers and especially the Nahwitti to resolve "this miserable affair," as Helmcken rightly described it. The wild frontier was not his calling either. He returned to Fort Victoria, which he found more to his liking, and took a keen interest in the oldest of the Douglas daughters, Cecilia, to whom he proposed. Helmcken, we note amusingly, had to provide two testimonials of good character before James Douglas gave consent to the marriage. The all-powerful Douglas (the disposer of events) gave Helmcken an acre of land, on which was built a small log house.[265]

A painting of Dr. John Sebastian Helmcken standing before his house, now part of Royal British Columbia Museum, Victoria. The house, constructed of squared timbers and since clad in siding, is perhaps the oldest one in BC. It stands on land given to Helmcken and his wife Cecilia (née Douglas) as a wedding present from James Douglas, then chief factor of the Hudson's Bay Company. *Painting by John Gough*

Blanshard, demonstrating managerial instincts, was mindful of the fact that he had placed Helmcken on a "bed of thorns." He wrote him privately to say so, on 6 August:

> *I certainly did not suspect that the disaffection was so general, but I think the great cause of your trouble has been the* England *and Captain Brown. I should have come to your assistance [at Fort Rupert] before this had I been able to bring any means of enforcing my authority, but I know that though "the Queen's name is a tower of strength" it*

is only so when backed by the Queens bayonets, and as my visiting Fort Rupert is the only remaining threat that can be held out to the disaffected, I do not think it judicious to weaken its effect by coming alone, which could only end in bringing all authority into contempt... [He thought all that was said about desertion and mutiny "utter nonsense," and the Company employees knew that.] Above all, pray try and impress on the officers the necessity of using calm, temperate language at all times, the silly threats of shooting mutineers and hanging and flogging deserters form very plausible grounds for complaint and may lead to serious consequences...If the Quacotts want to avenge it it will be better to tell them (assemble a few chiefs for the purpose) that I am coming with a big ship to enquire who did it [and] that they need not trouble themselves about waiting, for a white man's blood never dies...Everybody here has got the Influenza.[266]

Blanshard put his finger on the problem: the HBC officers' heavy-handedness. He sought to keep the Indigenous peoples out of the quarrel at the fort and mines. How would he deal with the Nahwitti, he wondered, so far away and on the margins of Company influence? Douglas would, of necessity, have had to let the matter pass. Blanshard, as governor, could not do so. British subjects had been murdered. He must act. Otherwise, the Queen's law would be a dead letter. Moreover, if unchecked, Indigenous persons would continue assaults on innocent boat parties and small trading vessels.

At this juncture, a sense of relief came over Blanshard when in September the forty-two-gun frigate *Daedalus*, Captain George G. Wellesley, cast anchor in Esquimalt. That man-of-war had arrived, at Blanshard's urging to Rear Admiral Phipps Hornby, commander-in-chief on the Pacific Station, to provide security for British trade and settlement and to guard against Indigenous assault or disturbance threatening the settlements. Now, however, there were three murders to investigate. On 1 October, Blanshard sailed in the *Daedalus* for Fort Rupert via the west coast, Cape Scott and Queen Charlotte Strait. This coast was uncharted, and in the course of this cruise the master of the *Daedalus*, William W. Dillon, conducted surveys of Shushartie Bay and Beaver Harbour; these were published in 1851—an aid to all mariners.

Governor Blanshard and Captain Wellesley intended a show of force, a warning. The Queen's warrant was to be respected. The Empire's frontiers were expanding and with them imperial law. There was a specific consideration in mind. Although, on the face of it, this was a voyage of inspection and inquiry, it was designedly and specifically to investigate the death of three British seamen who were murdered a few months previous near Shushartie by some Nahwitti. The village Suchartie ("having cockles") was in a bay of the same name on the north end of Vancouver Island, facing Queen Charlotte Strait. In those days it was the main place of Nahwitti trade. Hope Island lies immediately north of Suchartie. Helmcken, on reconnaissance, had previously determined who the guilty persons were. Hope Island became the focus for investigation.

Before leaving Fort Victoria, Blanshard discussed matters with his opposite, the chief factor. There was an exchange of views. Douglas agreed on the intended action. Blanshard, Douglas learned, had forceful measures in mind—if necessary. Douglas confided to Blenkinsop at Fort Rupert that the Nahwitti would be "startled," particularly if the governor acted in the decisive way Douglas anticipated.[267] But the matter went deeper than that.

Douglas categorically supported the governor; as he put it famously, "Otherwise our position on Vancouver's Island will be insufferable and the civil government worse than a dead letter."[268] This indicates how serious Douglas believed the situation was and how necessary he thought it for the governor to take firm action against the Nahwitti in question. Douglas also believed that the ship's presence would have a good effect on the Company servants.[269]

When he arrived off Fort Rupert, Blanshard went ashore for consultations. He held a court of inquiry. He gathered evidence. He weighed the facts. He made his recommendations to Wellesley. A distant intervention was put in place. Helmcken had said the Nahwitti encampment was twelve miles from Fort Rupert. It could be expected that the quarry would be elusive and would take refuge in forested places or out-of-the-way locations. Blanshard left the details to the Navy. The plan, unexceptional in British imperial practice, was as follows. First, the murderers, if located and confirmed, would be seized. Second, if this failed, hostages would be taken. And third, if that too proved unsuccessful, an attack would be made on their camp, and their canoes and houses torched. On 12 October three well-manned and armed boats from the *Daedalus*—in all, sixty officers and men—under command of Lieutenant A.G. Burton pulled north via Goletas Channel to seek out the Nahwitti. They would likely be found on Nigei Island, on or near Loquillilla Cove (Whale Cove).

Lieutenant Burton steered for the long southern flank of Nigei Island. There he found one village deserted. Either here or nearby, some Nahwitti made their appearance. In his subsequent report to Captain Wellesley, Burton states that the defendants fired their muskets on a boat's crew, wounding an officer and two seamen. The Nahwitti made their getaway with the greater part of their property. The landing party conducted a fiery reprisal and burned the houses.[270]

On hearing the results, Blanshard understandably regretted that the matter had not been brought to a conclusion. He was not satisfied, for the guilty were still at large. He compiled his report to the Colonial Office from Fort Rupert on 22 October and entrusted it to the paymaster of the *Daedalus*, to be passed on to London. It was time to say goodbye to Captain Wellesley and the ship's company. Blanshard would have to await the next visit of a man-of-war. The *Daedalus*, short on provisions, sailed for southern climes and other obligations. So ended Act One.

Blanshard was left to find his way back to Victoria by canoe, and in this passage a near-fatal turn of events awaited him. (We return to this in Chapter 13.) As to Blanshard's table expenses, the claim was passed around, but in the end the governor grudgingly paid them himself, £47 15s. 0d.

The Navy in the Pacific, under successive C-in-Cs Phipps Hornby and Fairfax Moresby, had standing orders to guard Vancouver Island and British persons and shipping. Blanshard had alerted Phipps Hornby to the need in the first instance. On learning of the not fully realized efforts of Blanshard and the *Daedalus* when in pursuit of the Nahwitti, Hornby wrote to Blanshard, "Your Indians are…hard to get at or punish beyond the burning of their villages, but surely if the Company are serious in doing their best with the Island, they will speedily obtain the same hold over them that they exercise (if all I hear is true) so rigidly over the Tribes in their Dominion on the Continent."[271] The admiral told Blanshard that next summer, 1851, a warship would be sent in support for the length of the summer. He thanked Blanshard for sending Indigenous pipes and a waterproof coat. Furthermore, Hornby told Blanshard that he was collecting live specimens for the London Zoological Gardens and requested that should Blanshard have any such to contribute, he could do so by sending them for delivery to the Earl of Derby, a patron. Phipps Hornby, an amiable fellow, hoped Blanshard would meet up with him when next in London, and he proposed to dine with him at his club, The United Service Club.

Naval officers of Phipps Hornby and Wellesley's time were of a tough breed: they hated to see British authority flouted, and they acted with firmness and certitude. That was the age they inhabited. Admiral Fairfax Moresby, who took over the Pacific Station from Hornby, was another of the breed. He had won undying respect from the abolitionist William Wilberforce and the Admiralty in fighting against the East African slave trade and was eager to settle the Fort Rupert issue and bring security to the colony.

Fairfax Moresby had been well briefed by Phipps Hornby. The latter had learned from Captain John Shepherd of HMS *Inconstant* that naval support was a sine qua non of colonial progress and even survival. Phipps Hornby advised the Admiralty: "As regards the Colonization of the Island, *if such is the Co[mpany]'s object*, it is anticipated that much resistance would be offered by the Indians, the Tribes to the northward being described as numerous, well-armed, brave and warlike, & Captain Shepherd's opinion is, that no colony could be established upon it, without being in its infancy rendered safe against the Indians, by the presence of a strong detachment of Troops." Such senior naval officers' views mirrored those of Governor Blanshard, and Hornby's urgent recommendation was passed from the Admiralty to the Colonial Office—and then to the Company. However, in this as in every similar case, the Company doggedly denied the necessity of defence measures: in fact, no interference was wanted.[272] The Company would "manage" Indigenous affairs in the customary fashion—that is, defusing situations, forgiving depredations, ignoring outrages and giving presents.

Exemplar of Pax Britannica, and a veteran of catching slaving ships and freeing slaves, Rear Admiral Fairfax Moresby arrived in Vancouver Island waters to quieten Indigenous threats at Fort Rupert. His charges against HBC settlement subterfuge reverberated through London's corridors of power. *Image courtesy of Canada, Department of National Defence (DND)*

Accepting Blanshard's statement that the Company and the settlers seemed far from secure, Admiral Moresby decided on forceful measures designed to replace the sagging influence of the Company by the display of British force. Settlers and miners, traders and coastal traders should no longer live in fear of reprisals from northern Indigenous peoples (and, we are reminded, Fort Rupert was a locus of Indigenous visitors from as far south as Puget Sound to as far north as Alaska).

What follows is a sequel to the proceedings of the *Daedalus*. It forms the closing Act Two.

At eight in the morning of 27 June 1851 the *Portland*, wearing the flag of Rear Admiral Moresby, anchored in Esquimalt Harbour. This powerful vessel had sailed in company from Central America with the corvette *Daphne*, Captain Edward Gennys Fanshawe. They had come to bring security to colonial matters. Moresby spoke with Blanshard, who was pleased at the arrival of the naval force, and from information the governor supplied, Moresby concluded the HBC was ineffective in protecting its servants.

Moresby also interviewed Douglas and challenged him about colonial policies and law enforcement—as we will see in more detail in the next chapter, Moresby was disinclined to support the HBC's non-colonization policies. He also thought Douglas had some sort of executive power vested in him, as agent for the Company, to punish offences committed against British subjects by the Indigenous peoples. No, said Douglas, this was Blanshard's responsibility. The Company, within its own territories, when it had freedom of action, never failed to punish attempts against the lives of its servants. Douglas detailed to Moresby examples of the HBC's policies of retribution and "forest diplomacy," but his correspondence leaves no record of what these were. The Company was content to police matters affecting itself, and Douglas zealously sought to limit such Company operations, corrections and reprisals to those affecting its personnel, property and business.

This was the old HBC argument of only dealing in Indigenous matters of theft or murder of Company personnel. Here was limited empire. By contrast, Blanshard's mandate, as his commission and instructions detail, had much wider obligations for British law and order and safe navigation in the British sovereign territories of Vancouver's Island

and its Dependencies. Here, then, were two (perhaps irreconcilable) definitions of *empire*, the one corporate, the other Imperial. Hence the rivals' tug-of-war.

Moresby thought the HBC view tiring in progressive times. Douglas, privately quick to anger, took umbrage that an outside agent should pass opinion on the state of local affairs. Douglas disliked prying eyes; in self-defence, he reported his grievance to London headquarters.[273] The matter did not rest there, for Moresby continued his assault in official correspondence, all the while doing further damage to the Company's reputation.

The *Daphne* had arrived off Victoria Harbour the day before the C-in-C, and Captain Fanshawe, who would earn distinction and high command in the Navy, came ashore. Blanshard hosted him at the newly completed Government House, or, as it was known in Blanshard's time, the Governor's House. There was much coming and going when the Navy arrived. In the event, Moresby could stay only a few days, the reason being that the HBC could supply the flagship with only two days' provisions, and those at exorbitant prices.[274] Before Moresby headed for the Hawaiian Islands in the *Portland*, Fanshawe gave a picnic for Moresby, to which the chief residents were invited.

After the picnic, Fanshawe turned his attention to more serious matters. Peace if possible; war if necessary—these formed the essence of "punitive expeditions." In other words, if the Nahwitti did not co-operate, Blanshard would call for more disciplined measures. In that eventuality, he would request Captain Fanshawe to deploy a force to find and take the suspected murderers into custody—and, if this failed, to seize and destroy their encampment, canoes and other property. In other words, the work of the *Daedalus* of the previous summer was to be brought to a final effect. No Indigenous women or children are mentioned in the documents.

Company officers at Fort Rupert had instructions from Chief Factor Douglas to give every assistance. The critically important point for us to remember is that Douglas had backed Blanshard and did not have a contrary view. The governor believed that if the murderers were not given up, the entire group should be punished, a tactic the British believed the Indigenous peoples understood and used in their own warfare. But now Douglas began to have cold feet on the extent of any retributive justice, and this ultimately gave him a reason to blame Blanshard, though not the Navy, for the terrible events that closed "this miserable affair."

The midsummer date was 19 July 1851. Lieutenant Edward Lacy, following instructions, led the pinnace and other boats from the *Daphne*, rowed by sixty sailors. The object was to arrest the suspects. Clerk Blenkinsop volunteered for this expedition, his intent being to negotiate peace if the three guilty were given up—in other words, to gain "quiet possession of the murderers."[275] From information gathered by a spy, Lacy knew the camp to be at faraway Bull Harbour, Hope Island—and he took every precaution. The boats pulled toward the encampment in stealthy fashion. It fell dark.

An hour before midnight the boats anchored for the night and awaited the morrow. They were about a mile from their object. At first light they closed on the encampment. As it came into view, lookouts discerned it to be a strong position on what Lacy described as "a rock." He could see that this stronghold was linked by a wooden bridge with the forested shore. Lacy's strict orders from Fanshawe were to arrest the murderers.[276]

Blenkinsop takes up the story. He wished for freedom of action. Blanshard, however, had laid down the rules of intervention. Blenkinsop was miffed at Blanshard's stricture *not to fire first*. This is the way he tells it: "On the morning of the 20th we came on the Neweetees and completely surprised them but unfortunately, I think, Governor Blanshard ordered that the party were not to fire unless fired upon by the Neweetees." He continues, "We attempted to parley but in return a severe fire was opened which had it been well must have killed one third of our numbers. No one was hit." Blenkinsop gives us a view of the storming of the strongly picketed camp: "Nothing could withstand the gallant charge that was made." He says two Nahwitti were killed and four wounded.[277]

By contrast, Lieutenant Lacy's report to Captain Fanshawe makes for sobering reading: "On approaching, a fire of musketry was opened on the boats by the Indians, which was returned by the Pinnace's gun, and having nearly silenced their fire, we landed to take possession of the encampment, on which the Indians instantly abandoned it, and took to the bush, from whence they kept up an occasional fire, wounding two of the seamen, and where, from the nature of the ground, I did not consider it prudent to pursue them. I therefore, in compliance with your orders, burnt the houses, together with the property contained in them, and destroyed the canoes."[278]

The Nahwitti warriors had withdrawn to the bush beyond the reach of the landing party and naval fire. Their retreat was successful, for the landing party dare not go in pursuit. (The standing rule laid down by the Admiralty was that no shore parties were to be sent from a ship unless they could make their withdrawal unhindered and undamaged. In short, expeditions ashore were discouraged.) Eventually, Blanshard received news of the operation: the Nahwitti reported that one of their chiefs, Lookingglass, had been killed; three men of the village had been wounded.[279]

The Nahwitti now determined to give up those who had caused the trouble. They solved the matter in their own fashion: they killed the three who had murdered the sailors, desecrated the bodies and brought the mangled remains to Fort Rupert. There they were buried outside the stockade. There was an acceptance of guilt and a solution to justice in the old-fashioned way. A trial was not held. The Nahwitti had forestalled that, solved the matter their own way. The grim business had been brought to an end. It is believed that the Nahwitti found refuge to the west in Sea Otter Cove, San Josef Bay.

Blanshard was relieved, as were all the officers of the Company, particularly those at Fort Rupert. In Blanshard's estimation, "a most beneficial effect" had been produced on the neighbouring tribes. Fort Rupert remained in safety. Blanshard was clear, however, that the Indigenous peoples of the coast must learn, as he put it, that "a white man's blood never dies." Word must go out to the coastal communities that this was the way the colonial law would be duly enforced: violence and death would be treated with reprisal and penalty.

This view was entirely in keeping with that of Douglas and the Hudson's Bay Company. When he became governor, Douglas made clear to Earl Grey that the criminals "met the fate they so justly deserved."[280] Furthermore, he did not think the action against the

Nahwitti, for which Blanshard seems to have been held unjustly to blame, either ill-founded or excessive. He also wrote to George Blenkinsop at Fort Rupert, who knew the heart of the matter and was close on the scene of events: "It is to be regretted that the Indians were not more severely punished but I trust they have had a lesson they will not soon forget."[281] That was Douglas's view. Blanshard's error, Douglas held, was to hold the whole tribe responsible, and not individuals of that tribe, but it is unclear how Douglas would have handled this situation differently. Certainly, the *Daedalus* and the *Daphne* did not engage in a war against the Nahwitti. How events unfolded determined the response of the boat crews. Douglas erred in his appreciation of events. His intent was likely to embarrass Blanshard and hold him to blame. History has been kind to Douglas; he has never lacked supporters. As for Blanshard, he was the victim of Douglas's machinations and fervent desires to defend HBC policy against any Colonial Office investigation or critique.

Another episode, two years later, shows the indomitable Douglas in action. A well-armed expedition of investigation and reprisal was taken against the Cowichan peoples in consequence of the murder of a shepherd, the Scot Peter Brown, at Christmas Hill, north of Victoria. Douglas, on board the *Beaver*, took command of the expedition, with the auxiliary vessel *Recovery* carrying a naval detachment in company. Landing parties of naval ratings and Royal Marines were deployed. Douglas had discouraged missions and colonization in the Cowichan Valley on account of the extreme warlike nature of these people. Now he was obliged to intervene. He obtained results.

Eyewitness Lieutenant John Moresby, son of Fairfax Moresby, recounts what Douglas, then governor, said to the Cowichan in the Chinook jargon: "Hearken, O chiefs. I am sent by King George, who is your friend, and who desires right only between your tribes and his men. If his men kill an Indian, they are punished. If your young men do likewise, they must also suffer. Give up the murderer, and there will be peace between the peoples, or I will burn your lodges and trample out your tribes!" The murderer was delivered, presents were distributed, war songs changed into shouts of joy, and the canoes passed quietly upriver bound for the lodges. A second murderer was captured after a difficult chase near Nanaimo. Trial was held on board the *Beaver*. Evidence was heard and a decision reached: guilty! Gallows were erected on Execution Point, later Gallows Point, named by the officers of the Hudson's Bay Company. This was the south point on what was then known as Douglas Island, now Protection Island. "And here they met their death with steady fortitude," writes Moresby, "in the fashion of brave men all the world over—a fashion varying with neither race nor time."[282]

To return to the murders committed by the Nahwitti during Governor Blanshard's term of office, and the reprisal as directed by Blanshard, we note that in the end it was the Nahwitti who exacted justice in their customary way. In London, the Company was pleased at the Navy's actions that brought the matter to a close. The Company had received Douglas's report on the Navy's vigorous measures, and because they had "impressed the natives with a salutary terror," as a clerk at the Admiralty put it, there was every expectation that a permanent peace had been established. The Company was satisfied and told the Colonial Office so.[283]

At the Colonial Office, it was a different matter. Earl Grey, desperately attempting to limit official obligation, took issue with Blanshard's direction of policy. He did not believe that Her Majesty's government should protect British subjects who risked their lives by exposing themselves "to the violence or treachery of the Native Tribes at a distance from the settlements." He did not seem to care that these were Britons in colonial lands and colonial seas, part of the Empire. Frontiers of empire were becoming the graveyard of Grey's reputation; he wanted no addition of responsibility on a wild and remote frontier. On the basis of information received from Blanshard, and from other quarters (which he does not specify), he had no reason to believe that the settlements (he could only be referring to Fort Victoria and Fort Rupert) were in actual danger. Grey also specified that punishment should not be attempted for injuries committed upon such irresponsible wanderers.[284] In short, it was the wanderers who were to blame! Grey's stricture shows how completely out of touch the Colonial Office was with on-the-spot Vancouver Island affairs and colonial security. Was a British subject not entitled to the protection of the Crown and its ministers of state?

Blanshard considered His Lordship's stricture. London lay half a world away from Victoria. Grey did not understand the circumstances. The governor replied with spirit, as we would expect from him. He noted that his suggestion that a military force be positioned on the Island still remained one vital to colonial security. In regards to protecting persons outside the settlements, he begged to point out that it was "scarcely applicable to the unfortunate Seamen who were murdered at [actually thirty miles from] Fort Rupert, as the murder was committed at a considerably shorter distance from that point than is frequently visited by the servants of the Hudson's Bay Company on their shooting excursions." Turning to the peril of the settlement in question, "That the Settlement was in danger I was fully persuaded, both by what I saw myself, and by the apprehensions expressed by the Hudson's Bay Company's servants who were on the spot: and I still firmly believe that the visit of HMS *Daedalus* prevented a massacre."[285] Blanshard rested his case.

At Downing Street, Grey and his staff feared that such episodes as involved the *Daedalus* and *Daphne* would be replicated by the future course of events; they were correct to worry. These men wanted peace on every colonial frontier; that was their mandate, and a worthy one too, if impossible and even idealistic. The laws of war grew from the irregular boundaries of influence. The expanding zone of colonial interest and Company trade was bound to lead to more difficulties, even conflicts, in settler-Indigenous relations. The rules of intervention—and of crime and punishment—were time-honoured: the colonial governor exercised wide discretion; the Navy, as requested, came to the aid of the civil power. However, the British government was endeavouring to restrict its obligations. A new question had been raised. Could (and should) a Briton be protected everywhere he or she went? The forceful Lord Palmerston thought so in the famed Don Pacifico affair, when the Royal Navy blockaded Greek ports in response to attacks on a

British subject in Greece, but would this policy extend to the far-off Pacific, where Britons could get themselves into trouble and demand redress where no man-of-war or constable could exercise the law? The Foreign Office requested an opinion, and so the matter passed to the Law Officers of the Crown. In their report, the Law Officers recognized the extreme difficulty to point out the proper line of conduct to be pursued. They urged caution on the spot in demanding redress and punishment of offenders; furthermore, punitive measures should only be taken where and when the atrocities had been actually witnessed and reported (hearsay evidence was to be taken into account with utmost caution).[286] This guidance of mid-1853 was not confined to Vancouver Island; it was of global import.

We must consider Douglas's position in all of this. The events at and near Fort Rupert and the actions against the Nahwitti have been regarded as the great crisis of Blanshard's governorship. On Blanshard is heaped the blame. This is less than half the story. It is a little-known fact—and is only disclosed by deep digging in HBC files—that the London Committee complained twice to Douglas that he had not reported the measures he intended to take in future encounters with Indigenous peoples. They wanted no repetition of "such a melancholy event." They knew the actions taken by the officers and boat crews of the *Daedalus* may have caused harmful relations with the Indigenous peoples involved in this case. Now, however, they demanded to know what measures Douglas should adopt in the future to prevent what they called "a very inconvenient feud"—in short, one that had caused them a great deal of difficulty with the Colonial Office. They suggested that Douglas not sell any more arms and ammunition until the Indigenous peoples became more reconciled to the white people.[287] The Company sought to avoid having the Colonial Office breathing down its neck, watching its every move. Reports sent from the Admiralty cast light on Company misdoings. Many in the Hudson's Bay Company, in London and in the field, must have regretted that a new master—the British government—had to be accounted to in these wretched cases of crime and punishment; the old ways were vanishing quickly under government scrutiny.

Douglas, by dint of experience, had an uncommonly expansive knowledge of Indigenous affairs and Company policies. He was not likely to change his ways. He would continue to rule with a firm hand. His secret was that he was a better communicator than Blanshard and was, besides, a Company man. When he became governor of Vancouver Island, Douglas was always fulsome though cagey in his reports, more so than his predecessor, who kept words to a minimum.

Douglas was appointed governor and vice admiral of Vancouver's Island and its Dependencies on 16 May 1851, though five months passed before he received the news. As a matter of course, the Colonial Office, suspicious of Blanshard's motives and actions, wanted the new governor's views on the actions at Fort Rupert. Governor Douglas responded to Grey on 15 April 1852, noting that he had already sent His Lordship by letter of 21 October 1851 his views on "the proceedings taken by Mr. Blanshard for the apprehension of the Natives concerned in the murders of the British seamen at Neweete in the month of July 1850." Douglas had written:

> *The three natives concerned in the murder had been executed by their own countrymen, and...we had in consequence renewed peaceful relations with the Neweete Tribe, who have since then been remarkably quiet and orderly in their deportment, from whence I infer that the retaliatory measures adapted by Mr Blanshard, and so vigorously sustained by Lieut. Lacy, of Her Majesty's Ship Daphne have had a most salutary effect in impressing the minds of the Newette Tribe, as well as other Indian tribes who inhabit the north end of Vancouver's Island, with a proper degree of respect for the persons and property of Her Majesty's subjects, who may through accident fall into their power.[288]*

Douglas called it the Nahwitti war.

Douglas never lost an opportunity to request that the Navy deploy a ship to the colony on a regular as opposed to an occasional basis, and the dispatch of warships to Haida Gwaii already showed the implementation of that means of defence. As to Douglas's views on Blanshard's actions and the Navy's enforcement, he made indubitably clear to Earl Grey that Blanshard was correct in his policy decisions and the Navy's actions. The results had been salutary; peaceful relations had been restored; respect for British persons and property had been impressed on the minds of Indigenous peoples at the north end of Vancouver Island. Therefore, we conclude, they would be wrong who seek to pillory Blanshard and place on a high altar of acclaim his successor, for their policies were the same. They might have disagreed on matters of technique, but they were of the same mind as to the use of seaborne power. This marks a continuity of Vancouver Island history and that of "the mainland." The use of force and firepower was customary and continued to mid-1869, at which time the admiral on station and all officers were advised of the new rule, as stated in the Admiralty minute of 30 July 1870: "Their Lordships cannot approve of the wholesale destruction of the villages and boats of these savages."[289] The Colonial Office was advised of the new policy. Rules of intervention required new techniques.[290]

To review, the Company at headquarters had no difficulty with the policy as carried out. Douglas had no difficulty with it. Nor did Helmcken or Blenkinsop or other Company officers. The view from London's Colonial Office differed from that of people living on Vancouver Island. As Gladstone, "that old crocodile," was wont to say, the problems of empire always derived on the frontier.

At the Admiralty, discussions ensued about policies of intervention: sending a gunboat on a potentially punitive expedition was to be carried out with utmost caution, and forbearance was needed before exercise of force. Fair enough: this already was Blanshard's rule of thumb.

Before closing this subject (and this episode), we note that the punitive expedition against the Nahwitti for the murder of those unfortunate seamen was the first case of "gunboat diplomacy" in British Columbia waters. Numerous events of a similar nature followed.[291] What were the Indigenous roots of this? The Nahwitti were ill-disposed to the whites; they were in the habit of attacking traders, and killing whites was a subject they boasted of. They said they intended to kill more. The Nahwitti were not alone. The photographer aboard HMS *Scout*, on a tour of Indigenous villages by Governor Arthur Edward Kennedy in 1866, commented on the well-armed and troublesome nearby people called the Iklstart: "This tribe was the dread of travellers in the Queen Charlotte Sound, as so many had been murdered without the slightest notice being taken of the circumstance as everything conduced to hushing up the matter, the distance from Victoria and no whiteman's settlement near to, and the numerous islands in the vicinity."[292] In 1868 the sloop *Thornton*, Captain Warren, was threatened with piracy by these people, who he said were dubbed "the terror of the coast." Some of them mocked the traders. One of them went so far as to tell Warren to go and get a man-of-war and they would deal with that too. That was mere braggadocio. In his written account, Warren detailed several such attacks and murders.[293]

As an episode in frontier relations, the matters described in these chapters ring down through the years. As a subject of historical investigation, misinterpretations linger still. It began with Hubert Howe Bancroft, who, in his *History of British Columbia*, published in 1887, heavily criticized the Company, which he regarded as the main source of the problem in offering blood money for the capture of the murderers. And, he wrote, "officers of the imperial government" directed "the full force of their vengeance against the natives." This is as unjust as it is untrue. Bancroft was highly partisan against the Company. Helmcken, who read his book, decided to counter it with a lengthy Victoria newspaper article entitled "Fort Rupert"—all about the events of 1850.[294] Helmcken, true to the last, never wavered from his view that hunting down the deserters from the Company's ship *Norman Morison*, the cause of all the bother, was of signal importance to the fortunes of Fort Rupert at the time: "for if more had deserted the place would have been without defenders against the three thousand Indians outside."[295] Reading between the lines, we speculate that a war conducted by the Indigenous peoples against the Company had been averted.

It is true, as Blanshard admitted to Earl Grey, that he had been misinformed by Company officers at Fort Rupert that they had offered blood money for the bringing in of the deserters dead or alive; he subsequently reported the "true facts" of the case. However, this had no effect on the outcome. Helmcken puts it this way: "Even if Blenkinsop had offered rewards for the arrest of the deserters, he would have done no more than followed the practice of the naval ships here—a practice here to this day. These [the ships] were of great importance at Fort Rupert at the time."[296] As for Earl Grey, his view that people should not wander where they had no business going bears a hint of irresponsibility. Did not a British subject have the protection of English law?

So closed the affairs of Fort Rupert, the place Blanshard styled "this bed of thorns."[297] Long will "this miserable affair"—so labelled by Helmcken—go down in the annals of history as an example of how murders of whites did not go uninvestigated by legal authority, and how naval power, at Blanshard's request, brought summary punishment. But that is an age now long past. *Lex talionis*—an eye for an eye and a tooth for a tooth—has passed from Canada's criminal law.

Indigenous marauding and far-ranging predatory expeditions of killing and slave-taking disappeared under withering British sea power and legal sanction. Coercion and diplomacy marched hand in hand. Successive governors had dutiful naval commanders as partners. Blood feuds dried up. Old hostilities that lingered were reduced to name-calling. Pax Britannica came to this most violent of coasts over the course of four decades. It began with Blanshard. Given immense challenges of distance, seasons, storm-tossed coasts and shifting subjects of interest and concern, the work necessarily advanced slowly but never flagged. The power of a single gunboat or steam-powered man-of-war had a mighty influence.

And a postscript, now, on later events at Fort Rupert. In the summer of 1851 another party of five coal miners and their families arrived in Victoria en route to the northern Island mines. They could not have been more different in character than the troublesome Muir cohort. They were headed by Boyd Gilmour and his nephew Robert Dunsmuir. The former was a respectable, calm-tempered man; the latter, an astute geologist who had an extensive knowledge of mining in Scotland. "They are a different class, and require a different management, from that of the ordinary servants," cautioned Secretary Barclay in his message to Company officers that was designed to avoid any further troubles, "but are not difficult to deal with if treated kindly, and reasoned with on any matter that they do not at first understand."[298]

The arrival of Robert Dunsmuir was momentous in the history of Vancouver Island, and it wrought great changes in rapid succession. The beginning was unremarkable, however. The voyage from Gravesend was typical of the age, and on 3 July 1851 the Company's hired ship *Pekin* arrived in the Columbia River but grounded on a sandbar. The ship's crew deserted and headed for the goldfields. By boat, Gilmour and Dunsmuir, Dunsmuir's wife, Joan, and their two girls, Elizabeth and Agnes, made it upriver to Fort Vancouver and safety. Robert and Joan had been educated at Kilmarnock Academy and after a brief courtship had been married. They hoped by joining Boyd Gilmour to find prosperity in the new colony of Vancouver Island. Little did they imagine what fortune awaited them. Within days of arriving at Fort Vancouver, on 8 July, Joan gave birth to a son, James Dunsmuir (who ultimately became premier and lieutenant-governor of British Columbia). Fort Vancouver was by then occupied by the US Army. The site made for a strong military establishment, with good vegetable gardens, orchards and grazing fields. The HBC still claimed the country around, under protection of a clause of the Oregon Treaty, but only a shadow remained of the Company's previous anchor of the profitable Columbia, or Western, Department, now headquartered at Fort Victoria.

In September, Gilmour and the Dunsmuir family boarded the *Mary Dare*, bound from the Columbia River for Fort Victoria. From there they sailed to Fort Rupert, where Gilmour and Robert Dunsmuir took over from John Muir and set to work to see if they could advance the project. The search for a seam of coal continued below the surface. Today one can trace the tailings of the debris that was taken out of the shaft or shafts. Then, or later, one of the more promising shafts ran out to sea below high-water mark. The miners continued to suffer depredations and feared exposure to malefactors. The state of general disorder continued. The Company determined to send a guard-ship, if and when they could locate one, shipping being in high demand. Eventually, the *Recovery* was deployed to Fort Rupert as a show of force and protection.

But the mining misadventures at Beaver Harbour were eventually overtaken by events elsewhere.[299] The several attempts at Suquash were halted by news of a glorious find of fabulously rich coal beds at Wentuhuysen Inlet (named by Spanish navigator Narváez), now known as Nanaimo Harbour.[300] This location is seventy-five miles north of Victoria, linked by the Strait of Georgia and Haro Strait as well as other passages. Robert Muir and Archibald Muir opened the Muir mine, a shaft seventy-five feet thick. Nearby was the Douglas seam, eight feet thick.

An exuberant Douglas made a canoe excursion along the east coast of Vancouver Island to examine coal in that quarter. On 18 August 1852 he wrote with a sense of relief to Secretary Barclay in London: "I rejoice to say that our journey has been productive of very satisfactory results as we have abundant evidence to prove that the mineral wealth of Vancouver's Island has not been overstated."

"This discovery," concluded Douglas, "has afforded me more sat-isfaction than I can express, and I trust the Company will derive advantages from it equal to the important influence it must necessarily exercise on the fortunes of this Colony."[301] He described his feelings to the Colonial Office: "It was impossible to repress a feeling of exultation in beholding so huge a mass of mineral wealth, so singularly brought to light by the hand of nature, as if for the purpose of inviting human enterprise, at a time when coal is a great desideratum in the Pacific; and the discovery can hardly fail to be of signal advantage to the colony."[302] The purchase agreement stated that the Indigenous people at Nanaimo were "at liberty to hunt over the unoccupied lands—as formerly."[303]

All of a sudden coal became king on Vancouver Island. Douglas sent Trader Joseph William McKay to take possession.[304] Operations commenced on a large scale. John Muir was given a free hand. Miners' pay was increased. At Douglas's order, Gilmour and Dunsmuir shifted south. Suquash was dead. But, we note in passing, it would be pur-sued in later years by other firms. The Company engaged married men to colonize Nanaimo, and from England the barque *Princess Royal* brought twenty-one married men with their wives and forty-two children. A bastion and extensive wharves were under construction. Nanaimo witnessed rapid growth and industrial progress. It was an instant company town.

As for the Muirs, they took up farming, acquiring Captain Grant's property at Sooke and turning it into a successful farming operation. The Muirs' sawmill at Sooke was a paying concern of great promise. The family's lumbering and shipping business proved a success, serving local and export markets. The Muirs also built four ships at Sooke, including the brig *Robert Cowan*, using lumber from their mill. One of them, the *Robert Cowan*, was promptly sold to South American interests and never returned to these waters.

Chapter 12:
Blighted Prospects

We now return to April 1850, shortly after Blanshard's initial visit to Fort Rupert. On 6 April, when the governor stepped ashore from the *Driver* after circumnavigating Vancouver Island, he had every expectation that his official residence would be ready for occupation. After all, months before, Barclay at HBC headquarters had written to Douglas to say that a house would have to be provided.

On a pretty rise, at a distance not farther than sixty yards from the northeast corner of the fort, lay an adequate plot of land. It was well-drained, not subject to flooding in torrential rains. The site was on what were locally dubbed "fur trade lands"—that is, Company property. It lay, as indeed it must, outside the fort's walls. The house would face the waterfront. About 20 March, just over a week after Blanshard read his commission as governor, a fellow named Thomas and two Indigenous persons began construction. By fits and starts, weather and materials permitting, advances were made. Although additional workers were engaged on the project, including three "Kanakas," progress was painfully slow.

Until his residence was fit for habitation, Governor Blanshard lived in a wretched one-room storehouse, unheated and windowless, within the fort's palisade, taking meals with the officers of the establishment. From this gloomy abode, from time to time, His Excellency ventured forth to see what progress had been made on his house. Each time, he returned in despair. Spring passed into summer. Only one tradesman was at work now. In late June Blanshard testily questioned Douglas about the delay. Ten days later, and now on the point of exasperation, he sent a sharply worded letter to the chief factor, saying that he might as well withdraw the only tradesman from the job, "leaving one solitary man to carry on work that has already been loitered over for more than five months." He continued, with venomous irony: "I beg to state that you are at liberty to withdraw him also, as the labour of a single man is a mere mockery and I will consider such withdrawal as proof of the inability or unwillingness of the Hudson's Bay Company to furnish me with lodging."[305] Douglas forwarded the correspondence to Barclay, claiming that all possible had been done for the governor's housing. He did not want to hire workmen from the Columbia Department to do the construction; their labour costs were too high. Moreover, in the circumstances, he did not feel that he could neglect the Company's business requirements: to get the most for the least expense.

Douglas was unaccustomed to having someone bark at him. He was invariably measured in his responses, though it was known that he could become furious if riled. He wrote Barclay: "The Governor's complaints were excessively mortifying and have given me more pain than I can describe." He told Barclay that ten men, not one, were working on the house. "I have no wish however to indulge in complaints at the expense of Mr. Blanshard, for that would be unjust as with the exceptions of his letters, I never heard him make an unpleasant remark."[306] By mid-September the governor's house neared readiness for occupancy, a sigh of relief to Douglas, who thought it would be an end of trouble with the out-of-temper governor. Six months had passed, and at last Governor Blanshard was able to move into what he disparagingly called his "Cottage."[307]

Once completed, Government House, the official and elevated term, boasted a verandah across the front, facing Government Street. The outside was clad in planed shingles. Inside, the rooms had ceilings (rare in these western wilds) and painted interior walls. The house proper measured forty by twenty feet, with a kitchen eighteen by twelve attached, and also a structure twenty-four by eighteen for his servants (his domestic servant, cook, gardener and housekeeper or cleaner). Douglas boasted the governor's house had a very neat appearance, and he thought it, on the whole, the best finished building in what he still called Oregon. Still, it displayed a rustic hue, and Douglas stated that if other public buildings were to be built, then qualified journeymen carpenters and finish carpenters ought to be sent out to Victoria. He claimed he had not a single house carpenter or joiner at his disposal at Fort Victoria, and in his opinion the self-taught carpenters of the country were not capable of turning out a neat job. The house and premises cost $1,548.55 in materials and labour.[308] Blanshard, needing more space, built an addition to the house and sent Douglas a bill for $634.90 for the improvements. There was a well. There were gardens. It is not known if he had a stable for his horse. The location, Helmcken recollected (for he and his wife lived in the residence after Blanshard), was at the corner of Government Street and Yates Street on about

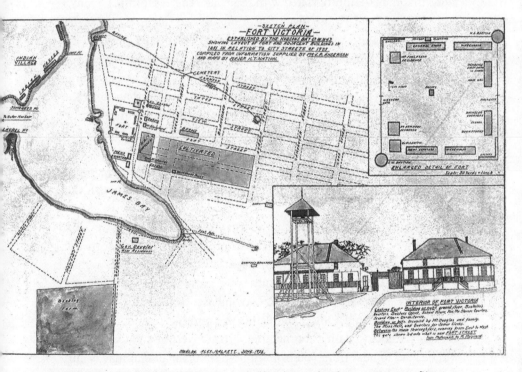

This plan and elevation of the HBC's Fort Victoria, placed in relation to the subsequent street map of Victoria, discloses key features of this self-contained compression of corporate power that James Douglas had placed hard by coastal waters to exploit limitless business opportunities. The Beaver, *September 1934*

four lots. He thought it a comfortable but not commodious house for the times.

It may be observed that Douglas was far ahead of the confused London Committee in arranging a site for and construction of Government House. It is a telling fact that it was not until 1 January 1851—nine months after Blanshard's arrival at Fort Victoria and a year and a half after he was named governor—that Mr. Secretary Barclay from Hudson's Bay House informed Blanshard that £4,000 would be advanced to him through the auspices of Douglas for erecting buildings most urgently required. These were public buildings—perhaps a jail or a courthouse, and certainly a public school. "These buildings will have to be made under the direction of yourself as Governor, and of your Council. You and your Council will hold the same, and the lands that may be appropriated with them, as Trustees for the Colony." As to Government House (again we are reminded that this is after the fact), Barclay specified, "The Governor and Committee would recommend that a moderate sized but respectable house and premises should be erected as the official residence for yourself as Governor, calculated for the commencement of the Colony rather than for what you may anticipate it may come to in time, as the funds that can be relied upon are limited and small at present." This was fair warning against overexpenditure. Then again, the house had already been built or was nearing completion. Public buildings, remarked Barclay, ought to be constructed of stone, preferable to wood, so as to diminish the risk of fire.

Normally, Barclay continued, the trust fund used for construction and maintenance of buildings needed London's approval but, in the circumstances, they granted Blanshard latitude to sanction public works, provided plans and estimates were presented. This move may have been intended to minimize Douglas's overbearing scrutiny. Countering Colonial Office complaints was another reason.

This letter closed on a cordial note: "The Governor and Committee will be glad to hear from you from time to time, on all that may occur, and on all subjects that may concern the advancement of the Colony."[309] We read between the lines. Rather than hearing the hostile or desperate news from Blanshard as relayed through the Colonial Office, the London Committee would rather hear directly from the governor. The Company tried to upset the usual triangle of communications that seemed always to end up with an inquiring demand from the Colonial Office as to peculiarities in the colony.

Blanshard was not lured by this offer: he held to the official line of communications, via the secretary of state for the colonies, Earl Grey. Hudson's Bay House did not always know what was happening on Vancouver Island. The whole saga of the authorization, building and completion of the first Government House testifies to the tyranny of distance, the complications of Company communications with Douglas, the local autonomy of the latter in the pressing circumstances and, perhaps above all, the unavailability of tradesmen and labourers.

In fact, Blanshard inhabited Government House only briefly, and most of that time in a sorry and sad state of debilitating illness and worrying bankruptcy. After Blanshard, Dr. and Mrs. Helmcken resided there for a time, as said, and there were other occupants. Douglas used it as an office. True, it was built on "fur trade reserve," but Douglas gingerly countered this in 1860 in a statement to the colonial secretary of the day, the Duke of Newcastle, that the land appropriated to Government House "was always regarded by me as a Government Reserve, and the colonial Surveyor had strict orders from me not to dispose of any part thereof." There were no deeds of conveyance, said Douglas, but they were not viewed as a matter of any moment at the time, "the intentions of the Hudson's Bay Company being so unmistakable."[310] In May 1859 the house and buildings plus lands appropriated to it were sold to private interests.[311]

Here it is necessary to describe how Blanshard's Government House became a subject of real estate wrangling. By the end of the 1850s, the property in question, and, indeed, all HBC property on Vancouver Island, had become, so to speak, a political football. The old order was passing. The Company insisted that when it surrendered its Charter of Grant and the licence of trade (due to lapse in 1859), it must be reimbursed by the Crown for all its improvements, buildings and coal mines dating from the time of the boundary treaty, 1846. To this was added their improvements made since the 1846 treaty. Various classifications of landownership—Company lands; lands sold to individuals;

government lands set aside for Government House, jail, courthouse, public school and other—all had to be accounted for. Large farms and dairy properties were all noted in the records. Not an acre was missed. Although one would assume that the Company would release all of this as a form of what we would now call decolonization, in fact it trenchantly defended its rights of possession and due compensation. Standing on the front line of defence was Douglas.

Alive to these proceedings, Blanshard sensed the jobbery in which the Company was engaged. He warned Lord Grey of this. When Douglas presented the governor with an account of HBC expenses for "improvements" in the colony, the matter reached a crisis. This required Blanshard's signature. He examined the columns carefully. He noticed that the account included amounts paid for surrender of Indigenous title. He had no objection to purchasing Indigenous title. To his astonishment, however, he discovered that the Company had grossed up the cost of the goods paid to the Indigenous bands for title to their lands around Victoria and Sooke; it had done so by a factor of three. This was three times as much as the Company was in the habit of paying for Indigenous labour. Having detected this, Blanshard wrote to Douglas on the subject. Douglas corrected the errors; he made no alteration to the prices. Blanshard signed the revision, but inscribed on the document that the cost was to be paid by the Company and not included in the colonial account. Blanshard knew the Company was "fudging the books."

Next, Blanshard and Douglas discussed this matter. Douglas brazenly and dismissively told Blanshard that the Company did not expect the Charter of Grant to be renewed at the expiration of the five years (that is, in January 1854) and that, in any case, the HBC would be entitled to a reimbursement of its expenditure. Blanshard sensed the underlying motive of running up the account. "At this rate," he told Earl Grey, "they may continue for the next three years paying away a few goods to the Indians to extinguish their claim to the soil, and by attaching an ideal value to their goods they will at the end of that time appear as creditor of the colony to an overwhelming amount, so that the foundation will be laid of a colonial debt, which will for ever prove a burden."[312] Blanshard was correct in this. But Douglas had time on his side. As gatekeeper he could allocate lands to corporate friends, fellow officers of the Company, family and associates as he pleased.

The matter did not stop there, and long and complicated is the correspondence that passed between Douglas, when made governor, and both the Colonial Office and Hudson's Bay House. The wrangling persisted over possessory rights, a "surrender price" and a deed of reconveyance to the Crown. In matters of property, as in issues of free trade, the statesmen and agents of the Victorian age were adamant in pursuing their rights. The student of history and land conveyancing will find much of interest in the papers on the "Crown Lands Question" of Vancouver Island. There was much bitterness, for it was a form of family quarrel. Almost ten years after the parliamentary recommendation that the title be surrendered, a deed of reconveyance was agreed. On 3 April 1867 the Hudson's Bay Company, by indenture of that date, reconveyed to the Crown all of Vancouver Island and premises, except such portions as may have been sold by the Company previous to 1 January 1862. In short, the Crown "repurchased" the island. The Company was reimbursed £57,500.[313] The old empire had passed unto the new.

Returning to 1850, Blanshard's promised thousand acres was another gnawing matter, one causing him endless grief and bottomless disappointment. It also caused rancour between the governor and Chief Factor Douglas. Blanshard was not shy in revealing how he had been tricked and misled. In 1857 he testified to the select committee on the Hudson's Bay Company that he had been given to understand, before leaving for Vancouver Island, that this property was intended for him personally. In London, at his 1849 interview, Sir John Pelly had promised one thousand acres. The directors confirmed this, remarked Blanshard. As he testified, "Sir John Pelly had told me that I might select such portions of land as I thought would turn out valuable, and that they would sell advantageously."[314] Blanshard was definite on this point. Sad to say, he had not gotten Pelly's promise in writing, and by the time of the parliamentary inquiry, Pelly was dead. The Company twisted and turned on this issue. While Blanshard was sailing the ocean blue en route to the colony, instructions sent from Hudson's Bay House to Douglas explicitly and adroitly denied Pelly's intent and broke the promise: "The Governor is to have a grant of land to the extent of 1000 acres, as he may require it. This grant is not made to him as an individual but in his public capacity and will always belong to the Governor for the time being. You and he together will select some eligible spot not included in what may have been set aside for the fur trade or Puget Sound Company."[315]

This was the unkindest cut of all. Blanshard's anger and disappointment upon his arrival, when he learned of the broken promise, may be imagined. Company duplicity ran deep. He testified in 1857: "Mr. Douglas, who was the agent for the land there, nominally evaded giving me any kind of title to it, and said that I should get it more easily settled in England. The Hudson's Bay Company declined to make it over to me, and said that those 1000 acres of land were merely intended for the Governor for the time being."[316] Blanshard's hopes of perhaps establishing a landed estate on Vancouver Island and bringing out his intended bride to develop an agricultural preserve with luxuriant gardens and glorious vistas died with the Company's scuttling of plans and discarding of promises. Blanshard had been tricked. Just before his departure from this land of sorrow, he did claim one hundred of the thousand acres for the benefit of his manservant Robinson, who wished to stay in the colony and live at Metchosin. Douglas referred the matter to London, where it rested and died. Robinson returned to England.

A third source of difficulties for Blanshard was the cost he had to pay for supplies. These proved ruinous to the governor, who was receiving no salary and had not only himself but also his servants to maintain. The Company was the only purchaser on the island; its sale shop at Fort Victoria was the only market where supplies might be bought or produce sold. Inasmuch as the officer in charge of the fort regulated or set the prices, the governor was obliged to pay on a price-scale as an individual. It turns out that he had to pay the highest tariff. These were called, ironically, "settler prices." The governor got no special rate along the same lines as, say, Douglas himself.

This source of irritation was much more directly Douglas's

responsibility. The tariff was set by the peak prices prevailing during the gold rush in California. Douglas and the Company might well have made a generous concession under the circumstances,[317] but Douglas would not budge.

The settlers, too, felt that their interests were subordinated to those of the Company. Here was another source of animosity and bickering. The colonists were dissatisfied with the Company. The Company's servants were perpetually at unrest. In short, life at the fort was scarcely in keeping with the beauties of its surroundings.[318]

In review, Blanshard faced three matters of immense disappointment to him and to his future life. First was the slow completion of his house, which meant he spent many months either without a fixed base or living in less than ideal conditions. Second was being denied the thousand acres of land, his personal fiefdom and source of imagined prosperity and livelihood on Vancouver Island. Third was the cost of living, having to pay full HBC prices out of his own pocket, even though he was governor of the Colony of Vancouver Island, to which the Company held tenure by the Charter of Grant. Being denied prospects promised by the Company made his position both impossible and disheartening. No wonder he was a disillusioned and dissatisfied viceregal head of the Company's ill-starred colonial venture.

Besides these more narrowly personal matters that made him bitter, policy considerations dogged him. Blanshard was thwarted by the Colonial Office and the Hudson's Bay Company in London. He had to serve two masters. Moreover, he faced the opposition of Douglas in the colony. He never wrote about Douglas. But we have Douglas's summary of his relationship with Blanshard, brought forth in consequence of the governor having exposed the fudging of colonial accounts in regards to payment for the surrender of Indigenous title. Douglas enlarged the scope of disagreements but dodged the matter Blanshard had raised. The chief factor wrote to the secretary of the Company, Barclay, dated 21 March 1851:

I have done everything in my power to meet Governor Blanshard's views and to support his authority in the Colony; but there are certain points on which we may be allowed to differ in opinion without necessarily involving a breach of harmony. The Governor for instance was always opposed on public grounds to the reserves of land held for the two Companys [sic] and in favour of having a military force in the colony for the protection of the inhabitants and in reference to these subjects he still maintains the same opinion, while I am bound as a servant of the company to follow the Committee's instructions and to study on every point to protect their interests.[319]

Blanshard, however, was prescient on matters of colonial security. He could see that the colony needed adequate defence to survive and prosper, and at a critical hour it found itself insufficiently defended when US armed forces occupied the San Juan Islands. Having a British colonial guard posted there would have deterred such an action.

As to the other matter, the two companies (HBC and PSAC) had indeed gathered up all the good agricultural lands to themselves, the biggest agricultural grab west of the Red River—and this ruined the prospects of a buoyant agricultural economy of industrious farmers and settlers. Corporate empire ruled on Vancouver Island.

This reality was clearly visible to the many Royal Navy visitors to Fort Victoria. Rear Admiral Fairfax Moresby's stopover in June 1851 was described in Chapter 11 in relation to the events at Fort Rupert.[320] The first British commander-in-chief, Pacific Station, to visit Vancouver Island, Moresby cast a sharp gaze over the unsettled scene. The welfare of a British colony in the north Pacific received Moresby's full attention. Here was a new agency of inquiry, one of an improving instinct; and the all-seeing Moresby was certain to be a thorn in the side of the Company. In addition to supporting and protecting imperial interests (and investigating relations with Indigenous peoples), he understandably wanted to know the state of agricultural produce and the availability of provisions and water, as well as wood and coal, for ships under his command that might call at Esquimalt. Unlike many admirals, he was an old hand at colonization projects. He had convoyed emigrant ships from the United Kingdom to plant the Albany settlement in South Africa, near Port Elizabeth. He was thus conversant with theories and practices of emigration policy. A progressive liberal, he was an energetic imperialist besides being a highly regarded flag officer. He was also not under direction of the Colonial Office. Far from it. He could send his own independent report to the Lords of the Admiralty in London, and they could do with it what they wished, and ruffle feathers at the Colonial Office if necessary. It did not take long for him to form strong opinions and put them to paper. An ally of Blanshard, he was a danger to the Company.

Moresby had no quarrel with Blanshard's administration. He saw that public expectations as presented to Parliament and administered by the Colonial Office were not being met on Vancouver Island. He objected to the unwillingness of the grant-holding Company to encourage colonization; the settler population was lamentably small. He protested that the Company charged its own servants twelve shillings per hundredweight for flour but required naval vessels to pay much higher prices. He charged that the Company had appropriated the most desirable land. No commercial competition could exist. Here was detestable raw monopoly at work. He reported to the Admiralty that the difficulties placed on colonists in obtaining land were "incompatible with the free and liberal reception of an Emigrant Community."[321] This blunt charge reinforced, with additions, those made by Blanshard. Moresby could acquire only seventy-eight pounds of vegetables, a sad disappointment to his ship's company that had been without fresh provisions for 183 days at sea since leaving Portsmouth, England. He thought Douglas's selection of a marine base faulty. "Victoria has been too hastily preferred to Esquimalt, it happily leaves this beautiful Harbour and its shores in their primitive state—I earnestly recommend the Government to reserve for Her Majesty, Her Heirs and Successors this Harbour of Esquimalt and its shores; the only place where a Naval Establishment can be formed, and admirably adapted for all its operations."[322] Moresby's was the first strong recommendation regarding a naval base here, and before many years passed a more thorough and cogent case would be put forward with the same object in view.

Moresby's critique on the sorry state of the colony proved to be one of several that exposed the domination of the Company and its unwillingness to encourage colonization. For instance, Captain Augustus Leopold Kuper of the *Thetis* reported to Moresby, 4 February 1853, that little or no improvement had been shown in regards to the colony since the admiral's visit. The fact of the matter was that much discontent existed in the settlement.[323]

Damaging reports from Moresby and his commanders were passed to the Colonial Office, which, in turn, requested the Company's response. The Company artfully replied that everything was being done "for the colonization and improvement of the Island, which it is no less their interest than their duty to promote."[324] That was how Pelly defended his Company to Grey's inquiry. The ever-nimble Pelly went so far as to say that the Company did not possess, and did not exercise, an exclusive right of trade in Vancouver Island: that was a sleight of hand. It is evident, however, that the Company was unwilling to invest in an unproductive colony. It further wanted to protect its fur trade and coal business, and guard its mainland trade; after all, in Company calculation, Vancouver Island was to be the bulwark against losing the trade of New Caledonia to interlopers.

It is true that there were desertions from merchant ships, loss of sea officers and men. The California gold rush drained labour from Fort Victoria and also from Nisqually and Cowlitz. In a moment of despair, looking back on these problems as of March 1854, Douglas wrote despairingly to Simpson, "God's will be done, I have done everything in my power to give it an existence in defiance of the adverse circumstances of the times, which have caused me so much trouble and anxiety."[325] That, it seems on reflection, was only half the story.

The independent-minded Captain Edward Fanshawe, who arrived in the *Daphne* a day before Moresby, and who went on to Fort Rupert, spent much time with Company servants and with the colonists at Victoria. He, like Moresby, was struck by the autocratic and domineering methods of the Company's officials. He was sympathetic to the destitute Walter Colquhoun Grant. He admired what those steady hands from Ayrshire, the Muirs, were developing at Sooke, the most promising lands he saw on Vancouver Island. Blanshard, we learn, entertained as best he could: one late August day he took Fanshawe and Edward Langford to shoot duck and geese out of a canoe on a lake near Langford's farm. Fanshawe, a fervid and accomplished watercolour artist, completed views of Esquimalt, Victoria, Beaver Harbour and his ship coasting under full canvas toward Woody Point (Nootka) en route to Fort Rupert. His scenes, now in portfolios in the National Maritime Museum, Greenwich, disclose the sylvan, primitive nature of the Island's landscape as of 1851, and the majesty and simplicity of the Island in the pre-industrial age. Here and there an Indigenous person's canoe animates the scene. Smoke from fires burning cleared brush floats across Victoria Harbour.

What, we may ask, did Fanshawe think about Blanshard as governor? He commented that local events had proved too strong for him, and when Blanshard sailed away in the *Daphne* on 1 September 1851, bound for San Francisco and Panama, Fanshawe writes solemnly in his memoirs that "the interests of all present and prospective settlers seemed hopelessly sacrificed to the company's absolute sway."[326] Fanshawe had been at Vancouver Island for two months, a vital observer and active participant in its affairs.

In the circumstances, Blanshard's duties in Victoria were confined to administrative and judicial matters of a constrained sort. There were no murders of whites locally during his time there, so no cases to investigate. On one occasion, foul play had to be ruled out: the governor assembled a twelve-man jury, headed by Roderick Finlayson, when one of the Company's labourers, William Gillespie, was found drowned. The verdict: "Accidental Death, owing to the deceased being in a state of intoxication."[327]

Matters relating to shipping and freedom of navigation fell within his jurisdiction. As noted above, when the British ship *Albion* was seized in US waters at New Dungeness, he advised the captain, Hinderwell, that the matter lay beyond his jurisdiction. Another case demonstrated the governor's alertness to problems and his powers of oversight. He empanelled three shipping masters and two shipwrights to report on the seaworthiness of the barque *Cowlitz*, which had grounded several times on passage from Fort Rupert to Fort Victoria. As the *Cowlitz* was destined for the Sandwich Islands for repairs, her seaworthiness was an important matter. The panel reported her fit and sound.

There was a more celebrated shipping case. As governor and vice admiral, Blanshard was obliged to enforce the United Kingdom

Navigation Act. It is tempting to imagine that perhaps he was looking for an opportunity to show Douglas that the governor had specific powers within his authority; this would be a misreading. In the event, he took Douglas to task for signing a clearance for the *Cadboro* when he had no right to do so. He hauled Douglas into court and tried him for disobeying the rules and regulations. Had there been a jail, Douglas would have been behind bars. As it was, Blanshard released Douglas on his own recognizance, and there the matter rested. Blanshard found the captain of the *Cadboro* guilty for taking the papers to the wrong authority for signing. It seems, on reflection, a petty matter, but every colonial governor in the British Empire exercised authoritative control in these shipping matters; we can expect no less of Blanshard. All the details were aired at the 1857 parliamentary inquiry.[328]

Douglas never befriended Blanshard. Rather, he snubbed him, gave him a cold shoulder. Douglas valued his power, and his vanity played to it, elevating his influence in his own eyes. He saw the governor as an intrusion, for the chief factor had to live with the bureaucratic fallout that routinely came from London. In return correspondence with the Colonial Office or the Company in London, Douglas adroitly shifted the subject under review to suit his purposes—and to serve his own ends and those of the Company that he had come to embody in the HBC's Western Department. His power was strongly entrenched well before the gold seekers arrived at Victoria in 1858 en route to their intended destination, the Fraser River.

Richard Blanshard was no fool. He had sent many in-depth, well-informed reports to the Colonial Office on the condition and prospects of the Colony of Vancouver Island. From the date of his installation, 11 March 1850, he had been treated scurvily by the Company. He was an outsider in his own jurisdiction. He had never received the promised thousand acres that would have given him a stake in the colony's future and led to a respectable and independent landed status in this promising commercial location. Land that was to have been his by promise was set aside for the Company or the fur trade trust interests. He had no prospect of a salary. He differed with Douglas on many material points, some irreconcilable. A man of considerable perceptivity, His Excellency could see the writing on the wall within a few months of his arrival. The Company never reimbursed him fully for his outbound travelling expenses, awarding him £175 on his claim of £300.

By contrast, Douglas fared well. The social affairs of the colony were tied up in those families close to James Douglas and Roderick Finlayson, and such appointments as were given by Douglas when he became governor went to members of his family or corporate associates. When a supreme court of justice was established, Douglas's brother-in-law, David Cameron, was appointed chief justice. With truth, observers of the colonial establishment such as Edward Langford called the regime the "Family-Company Compact." As governor, Douglas was allowed to retain his position with the Company as a chief factor and leading administrator of the Western Department, but he was also given by the Company £800 per annum as salary, a handsome sum for his troubles. Blanshard received no salary and no fee. The difference is startling; the Company always looked after its own.

Chapter 13:
At Death's Door

It is tempting to say that the origin of Blanshard's illness might date from travels in India, the West Indies or British Honduras. More likely, the cause stems from his December 1849 westbound transit across the mosquito-ridden Isthmus of Panama to fever-infested Panama City. The Isthmus of Panama, its fetid rivers and swamps, proved his undoing. The irony is inescapable, for it was he who had urged Colonial Secretary Lord Grey to consider this as a more promising route for settlers destined for Vancouver Island than that by way of time-consuming, distant and stormy Cape Horn. In those days, before the swamps were drained and the cause of mosquito-borne malaria and yellow fever was determined, diseases, including dysentery and smallpox, wreaked heavy tolls on European travellers crossing the isthmus.

At mid-century, travellers began to encounter a more virulent form of malaria: medical doctors called it ague or intermittent fever.[329] Naval surgeon James Lind warned of great mortality from ague, which stole some of the most useful inhabitants of the mother country. Malaria was classified as an intermittent fever on account of its beginning chill followed by fever and concluding with a sweat, subsiding fever and general sense of relief. Alternating hot and cold fits differentiated malaria from other fevers. Violent headaches, sickness of the stomach leading to vomiting, severe pains in all bones, and great thirst have been described symptoms. One paroxysm would subside, then another one would make its onslaught. Ague was dangerous to eyesight and could lead to blindness; it also caused enlargement of the spleen or liver. Quinine, from Peruvian bark, could protect against malaria. It was believed that Peruvian bark in wine, judiciously administered, could be a prophylactic and a remedy. We have the confirming saga of Joseph Despard Pemberton. En route to Vancouver Island, he crossed Panama shortly after Blanshard and recounted that the trip from the Old World to the New was perilous and fatiguing. No railway traversed the isthmus; travel was in open boats up the Chagres River, exposed to heat and malaria at all times. Pemberton contracted a fever and almost died, dispelling the fever by jumping from shipboard into the salt water. He reached Victoria and safety.[330]

The preferred palliative for sufferers from the ague was tincture of opium, or liquid laudanum, also known as the Thebaic tincture. It was prepared from a portion of caked opium, cinnamon and cloves, and white wine, the whole infused in alcohol then filtered.[331] It was effective in thirty minutes, bringing on a sense of ease, release from tension and pain, then welcome sleep, even lassitude. Laudanum was in every physician's medicine kit.

Governor Blanshard's state of health had not been the best since his arrival at Vancouver Island. Makeshift housing arrangements in unheated shelters until, at last, he occupied his cottage, what was then called the Governor's House, were surely contributing factors. The winter of 1849–1850 had been severe in Victoria, and the next was not much better—wet and windy with abundant snow on the ground. In damp housing a person might catch a cold and much worse. In returning to Victoria from his most recent call at Fort Rupert in October 1850, Blanshard had voyaged in an open canoe for seven wintry days, perhaps sleeping in damp and uncomfortable circumstances ashore. He reached Victoria in a critical state, suffering severely from continual attacks of ague and subsequent relapses. His governorship took a dark turn. In his words, his health had "completely given way…and shows no signs of amending."[332] A note of fatalism is revealed here. Without doubt, Blanshard was wracked by illness. And he wrote home to his father to tell him so, stating at the same time that he was requesting withdrawal from Vancouver Island. He knew himself that he desperately needed relief from his duties in order to recover and then resume official obligations.

In short, by mid-November 1850 his condition had deteriorated to an alarming state. He became very weak, with resulting lassitude approaching despair. Fort Victoria had no physician. Dr. Benson, formerly at Fort Victoria, had gone to Fort Vancouver. Helmcken was away on assignment. So perilous was the governor's health that on 19 November two servants of the Company were sent by canoe express to Nisqually to request that Dr. Tolmie hasten to Victoria to attend on the governor. Dr. and Mrs. Tolmie came immediately. The doctor's arrival and treatment would have been welcome relief to Blanshard, and Tolmie remained in consultation at Fort Victoria for several weeks. Toward mid-December the governor showed signs of recovering his health.[333]

By this time, Blanshard had taken matters into his own hands. On 18 November, the day before Tolmie was sent for, Blanshard described his condition to Earl Grey as "enfeebled to a degree which renders me incapable of the slightest exertion."[334] Here is what Dr. Helmcken recollected many years later: "Blanshard was troubled with tic douloureaux [a painful, grievous and sad twitch] of a bad kind—he had been in malarious countries—smoked a great deal and had to take morphine for his attacks and so being in bad health was a pessimist and blamed the condition of things, when in fact the drawback was in his own health... Under different conditions he would have been a very different man."[335]

The true state of medical matters is now revealed from professional medical opinion in London. Because Dr. Benson was away from Victoria, Blanshard could not obtain a medical certificate to present his case for relief at the Colonial Office. Meanwhile, as said, he had written privately to London to tell his father and other loved ones of his critical state of health. Henry Blanshard, ever solicitous of his son, sought written medical opinions. These he delivered personally to Herman Merivale, permanent under-secretary at the Colonial Office, in support of the governor's appeal for relief; they survive in the Colonial Office's Vancouver Island file, never previously attracting a historian's attention.[336]

The first letter, dated 28 March 1851, from John Spurgeon, MD, of Guilford Street, Russell Square, says: "Having read extracts by Mr. Blanshard from Vancouver's Island I have no hesitation in certifying to the necessity of his immediate removal from the Island and his returning to England." This is short, to the point. The second came from S.J. Goodfellow, MD, of 4 Russell Square; he was a licentiate of the Royal College of Physicians. Again, the letter is addressed to Henry Blanshard, this under date of 29 March 1851:

From the description which your son, Mr. Richard Blanshard, gives of his symptoms I can have no hesitation whatever in stating that his removal from Vancouver's Island is indispensably necessary for his recovery. It appears that he is labouring under the most severe form of intermittent fever, namely the daily or gastidian, & there is even good ground for assuming that it has merged into the remittent. He is also evidently suffering severely from internal congestions and other effects of ague, as frequent fainting, & breathlessness from slight exertions. Now as the ague has been brought on by living in a malarious climate there is not the most remote probability that he will recover while he continues to reside in that country, & it is on this account that I so strongly recommend his removal.

These corroborative medical opinions sufficed to identify Blanshard's illness and ways of getting relief.

By this time, Blanshard had decided to act as he thought best. (The biographer must ask: Did he make his move too soon? Did he compose his next letters in a fit of despair and desolation? We will never know.) His state of ill health, bordering on derangement and fear of death, in combination with the ruinous circumstances of his governorship, led him to write two letters to Earl Grey. These both bear the date 18 November 1850, a mere eight months and eight days since his arrival at Fort Victoria. These are worth quoting in full:

November 18, 1850
My Lord,
    As I shall have completed two years absence from England, before

your answer can reach me, may I take this liberty of requesting your Lordship to grant me leave to visit England, as I have urgent private affairs to attend to which require my presence there, and since my arrival here I have suffered so severely from continual attacks of ague and subsequent relapses that I am so enfeebled to a degree which renders me incapable of the slightest exertion. I am not able to enclose a medical certificate as the surgeon in the employment of the Hudson's Bay Company has been removed from this colony to one of their posts in Oregon.

Should your Lordship grant this application I trust you will direct a passage to be allowed me as far as Panama in one of HM Ships, as there are no direct means of communication, the indirect ones are very uncertain, enormously expensive and the heavy expenses which have been thrown on me by the Hudson's Bay Company, contrary to my expectation, for my passage out and during my residence here have greatly straightened my private finances.

The governor, we can see, addresses several interlocking matters of concern: his health, unavailability of medical help and certification of illness, broken promises by the Company and the exorbitant costs borne by himself. Anxiety and depression likely were accompanying symptoms.

He was clearly unable to continue in these desperate circumstances. His second letter of the same date took the matter further:

My Lord,

I regret to inform your Lordship that I find myself compelled to tender my resignation as governor, and solicit an immediate recall from this colony, as my private fortune is utterly insufficient for the mere costs of living here, so high have prices been run up by the Hudson's Bay Company, and as there are no independent settlers every requisite for existence must be obtained from them.

My health has completely given way under repeated attacks of ague, and shows no sign of amendment. Under these circumstances I trust your Lordship will at once recall me, and appoint some person as my successor whose larger fortune may enable him to defray charges which involve me in certain ruin. I trust that your Lordship will give directions that I may be furnished with a passage as far as Panama in one of HM Ships, as my state of health will not bear the long voyage round Cape Horn, and being compelled to defray the expenses of my passage out, by the Hudson's Bay Company who repudiated the bills their Chairman had authorized me to draw, has so straightened my present means, that I am unable to pay the heavy expenses of the route through California.

Blanshard's two letters reached 14 Downing Street in the same packet. In late March 1851, these letters circulated through the hands of the top men in the Colonial Office.

Meanwhile, courtesy of Henry Blanshard, the governor's father, the pair of letters from medical practitioners had reached the same in-letter box and were making their way across the desks of the four or five persons who made the recommendations for Lord Grey's ultimate decision and action.

The "official mind" now took the matter under review, with the usual cold logic that dominated that office. Merivale, permanent under-secretary, speculated that the letter of resignation was sent as a backup in case the first, for leave, was unacceptable. Some weeks before, Henry Blanshard had met with him to press this request. As to the unsavoury charge that the HBC was "repudiating their bills," a copy of the second letter must go to the Company for its answer. "I cannot help remarking on the inconvenience of Lieut. Blanshard's habit of indulging his hostility to the Company, whether well or ill founded, by throwing out these undefined and loose charges," grumbled Merivale. He lacked sympathy of the circumstances, or did not understand the true state of affairs. That was the view from Downing Street: the colony was half a world away. We also learn from Colonial Office minutes regarding Blanshard's pair of letters that Benjamin Hawes, the parliamentary under-secretary, held the novel view that inasmuch as there were no settlers, a governor might well be dispensed with.

Earl Grey brought the matter to an abrupt conclusion. On 3 April 1851, he laid Governor Blanshard's two letters before Queen Victoria. Late that same day he wrote Blanshard: "I am to inform you that Her

Majesty has been pleased to accept your resignation."[337] Blanshard would have received this with hints of regret or sorrow, or perhaps with sighs of relief for burdens happily cast aside. Already he would have been considering future options to counter fading prospects. Grey informed him, for he was still governor until replaced, that he would be able to take passage in one of Her Majesty's ships from Vancouver Island to Panama. Grey wrote to the Admiralty that on account of Blanshard's "state of health which will not admit of his making the long voyage round Cape Horn," his wishes should be met if it was in the power of the commander-in-chief Pacific to do so "without inconvenience to the public service."[338] All of this came to fruition; the government machinery turned easily.

Nearly ten months elapsed between Blanshard's letters of relief and resignation and his receipt of Grey's letter of acceptance dated 3 April 1851. Immediately upon acceptance of Blanshard's resignation, Grey asked the Company if "they have any other gentleman to recommend for the appointment."[339] Barclay, the Company secretary, wrote Douglas to outline what was afoot. The London Committee, he said, intended to recommend the chief factor at Fort Victoria, "as under the present circumstances it would be difficult to find a fit and proper person who would take the Office on the same terms as Mr. Blanshard did."[340] Such was Barclay's clumsy message; he had opposed the Company's colonization project in the first place. We get the feeling that, in Barclay's view at least, Douglas became governor by default. He was appointed in September 1851; his commission reached his hands in November of that year.

Blanshard continued his gubernatorial duties until Earl Grey's letter of acceptance arrived in Victoria. E.O.S. Schofield, one of British Columbia's earliest historians, archivists and librarians, makes the point (and it is a fair assessment) that Grey hardly realized Blanshard's unfortunate position. Little cordiality or sympathy were expressed by His Lordship; on the other hand, rewards were seldom forthcoming to governors. There were no distinctions in the offing either.

How inconsequential the Company thought Blanshard's role in the larger scheme of things is illustrated by a letter Peter Skene Ogden, at Fort Vancouver, wrote privately to Governor Simpson on 27 January

1851. Ogden said, in a bright turn of phrase, that Vancouver Island could "now boast of a Gov[ernor] six months of the year in his bed and ten colonists."[341] That was a grim reckoning of affairs. Another view comes from Helmcken, an unkind observation rather lacking in sympathy. Helmcken was a Company man through and through, married to the firm. He is disingenuous when he writes in his *Reminiscences* that it was the governor's illness, not the miscues of the HBC's colonization arrangements, that had produced the faltering colony. It is also a slur on Blanshard's character by one who was not in Fort Victoria when the governor suffered the severest effects of malaria.

The independent settlers—the syndicate of discontent—saw matters differently. They were those "on the spot" who had to contend with the Company's monopoly of land, trade, land prices, provisions and supply prices, export duties and more. They broiled at the Company's indifference to their issues. "The few settlers who were unconnected with the company," wrote a near-contemporary to the events, "expressed deep concern on the resignation of the first governor, that the aegis which had alone protected them from the apprehended despotism of the company should be withdrawn, and these defenceless colonists knew not how soon the lords of the soil might render their condition uncomfortable."[342] They objected to the colony's appalling prospects for development. They feared and opposed Douglas's appointment as governor, though dared not mention him by name. They knew of Governor Blanshard's woes and disappointment, of his disaffection and anger; these they shared. Without losing any time, they put together a Memorial (or as some would have it, incorrectly, a petition) and gathered as many signatures from independent settlers as they were able.

The Memorial is an appeal against monopolistic tyranny; it states that settlers had no control over their own destiny and, in fact, were being denied basic British legal rights. They feared Douglas's rule. That is why they urgently appealed to Blanshard to appoint an executive council before he departed the scene. The likely author of the Memorial was the Reverend Staines, the most highly educated among them. James Yates and James Cooper would have given advice upon consultation, and leading members of the Muir family at Sooke, all with grievances, make up the bulk of the fifteen signatories. It is, in brief, a sort of Magna Carta and deserves to be better known (the full text can be read in the Appendix). All the warnings that had been given in Parliament since 1846, and letters of prophecy by independent persons who feared corporate tyranny, seem to have come true.

The egregious suggestion that Blanshard orchestrated this document has no credibility. He was a servant of the Crown. He would certainly have been pleased to read it. He did not want it to find its way into hostile hands.

The Memorial holds an important place in the early state papers of the Colony of Vancouver Island.[343] Blanshard laid the document before the colonial secretary when he returned to England. Grey set it aside and did not have it circulated in the Colonial Office. The colonial administration did not want to release it, damaging as it was to their reputation. A conspiracy of silence continued. However, Blanshard brought it to the attention of the 1857 parliamentary inquiry, and a copy of it was requested for printing in its famous report of proceedings. So it came to be printed in full and thus made available for public consumption, a damning critique of the Company and of Douglas.

Upon receipt of Grey's letter accepting his resignation, Blanshard prepared for departure. Helped by his manservant, Robinson, he spent a month closing down the establishment, house and office.[344] Perhaps he shipped some of his personal effects in the annual Company ship homeward bound. One curious item he left behind was an HBC trade flintlock musket, its whereabouts now unknown.[345] Robinson also prepared to make his departure and return to England. He intended to return to Vancouver Island should Blanshard's arrangement for him of one hundred acres be confirmed by the Company; it was not. The *Daphne*, at Esquimalt, was soon to sail for southern waters. This was convenient. Blanshard's passage in a British man-of-war as far as Panama City had been authorized. And just as he had arrived in the colony under the White Ensign, so too would he make his departure.

We have little difficulty imagining Blanshard's fraught feelings at this late hour: likely he did not regret leaving. He had been eighteen months in Vancouver Island. Half that time had passed in the languid exchange of outward and inward mail concerning his resignation. He spent his time adjudicating minor cases and bringing Douglas to task. He had defended the rights of independent settlers, doing so against rising Company complaint. He had expended a fortune—£1,100— in maintaining himself and his servant in day-to-day living costs. In ill health, he had fulfilled the duties as set forth in his commission. Time had come to tidy up affairs. Always businesslike, and with sharp attention to detail, Blanshard took pains to ensure a succession of administration for the Colony of Vancouver Island.

He had instructions from his superior, Earl Grey, to establish a council of seven upon his arrival at Fort Victoria. This proved a vain hope: there were not enough settlers to make up that requirement. He did not want to leave with Douglas in complete charge, though Barclay in London had suggested that the governor nominate Douglas to the council so he had the authority to open mail in Blanshard's absence and administer the government.[346] Blanshard's coterie of friends and admirers, and the independent settlers, needed at least a modicum of shared executive power. Thus, in order to satisfy the plaintive appeal of the fifteen styling themselves "the whole body of independent settlers," in his stead he appointed on 27 August a provisional council (provisional because the Crown had to approve). This consisted of James Douglas, the senior member of the provisional council to preside at its future deliberations; John Tod; and James Cooper. Membership on this council was subject to the confirmation of the colonial secretary. Public affairs demand public notice and a degree of transparency. Thus, and in keeping with imperial practice, Blanshard issued a proclamation under the seal of the colony announcing the appointments of Douglas, Tod and Cooper. High expectation would have been in the air in these last days that Blanshard was in the colony. Those appointed to the council had their individual interests to guard. Public resentment against Douglas and Company rule was pervasive among the settlers, whom Company officers regarded as troublemakers. Douglas intended no changes: he would manage the corporate empire, sell lands to whom he wished and keep rivals at bay. The imperialism of monopoly would prevail.

We can imagine, too, the scene that took place in Blanshard's cottage, the Government House of the day, on 30 August, when, in his final acts as governor, Blanshard, fully dressed in the attire of his office, presided at this, the first Legislative Council of the Colony of Vancouver Island. Present were Douglas, the crafty master of business administration and trade strategy and a Company man to the core; old Chief Factor John Tod, Victoria's first retiree, a pleasant fellow of whom it was said in admiration of his pioneering feats that he had travelled overland from the continental interior, in 1814; and Captain James Cooper, staunch opponent of Douglas, a former seafarer in Company employ and thereafter independent trader (in ardent spirits and other). All were standing. A Bible lay at hand. Blanshard swore them in under oath of allegiance to the Crown. Blanshard authorized their appointments under the public seal of the Colony of Vancouver Island in the name of Her Majesty Queen Victoria. "The germ of colonial legislation was planted by Governor Blanshard in the formation of a legislative council, consisting of three members," wrote Matthew Macfie fourteen years after the event.[347]

A quorum having been duly constituted, all took their places. A new minute book, or journal, lay on the table. The entry for the inaugural meeting is written in Douglas's hand. Probably he acted as scribe for the initial entry proclaiming conciliar government. "Be it remembered" commences the report of proceedings, indicative of a time when those present understood that they stood at the gate of history, when change was in the wind, the old giving way to the new. Only two matters of business engaged the attention of the council that day. First, the governor announced his resignation. Until the arrival of a fresh commission, the senior member of council, Douglas, would fill the place according to the instructions, of which a printed copy was laid on the table. These were Blanshard's original instructions from July 1849. Second, members of the council resolved that they would meet at such times and in such places as would be hereafter appointed for the consideration of public affairs. The meeting ended. Polite goodbyes would have been said, with great hopes for future prosperity and health. Perhaps a farewell dinner was given Blanshard by the syndicate of discontent and their wives.

In retrospect, Governor Blanshard had concluded official duties in a perfunctory and correct manner, leaving nothing to chance. He left behind in the council's care the seal of the Colony of Vancouver's Island and its Dependencies. He also left behind the legal books acquired under the colonial account. (Douglas, apparently having no use for them, wondered what he should do with them.) Some of Blanshard's personal library came into Tod's possession. Blanshard left the relevant executive documents of his office in Douglas's safekeeping. These included Blanshard's correspondence with the Colonial Office, by no means a full file of in-letters and out-letters. Some went astray. As to those that remained in place, we might say that these were the beginning of the Archives of British Columbia, and among these papers was the council's minute book, previously mentioned. Blanshard bundled up his own papers for the trip home to Mother England. His commission with Queen Victoria's seal was his personal property. He sealed it, probably in oilcloth, for the trip to London.

On 1 September 1851 the *Daphne* put to sea with Blanshard as special passenger. He said goodbye to this land of sorrows and broken dreams, this place of personal ruination, this locale of medical debilities. As the day wore on, and as the man-of-war worked its way back and forth down the strait toward the open Pacific, the sight of Captain Grant's bold attempt at colonization at Sooke fell far astern—then disappeared beneath the horizon. Well might Blanshard ponder the Island's future.

"Our worthy friend Governor Blanshard lately sailed for England... and I am again appointed Governor pro temp[or]e, this is too much of a good thing. I am getting tired of Vancouver's Island."[348] So wrote Douglas to Simpson, two weeks after Blanshard's exit. As for the council, the next meeting did not occur until eight months later, 28 April 1852. The new governor, always preferring HBC faithful, appointed the reliable Roderick Finlayson to his own vacated place on the council. In a later meeting he took to obstructing any measure to have opposition favourite Edward E. Langford named to the council. A predictable scenario played itself out. The officers and servants of the Hudson's Bay

Company were left, just as they liked it, to their own devices, guardians of the northern frontier, watchful over the Indigenous nations and on the alert against American aggrandizement that was already harmful to their shipping and trade, and a manifest destiny that might overwhelm this distant toehold of the British Empire.

The *Daphne* arrived in San Francisco on 10 September, then sailed to Panama. There Blanshard, again indebted to the Navy for safe conveyance, disembarked with his baggage and his administrative and personal files. While crossing the Isthmus of Panama, he met with more misfortune. The vessel in which he was travelling sank, a tragedy for history, for many of his papers (likely in a steamer trunk) were underwater for several hours in the Chagres River and ruined. However, his commission and instructions survived with water damage, and are under lock and key in the Archives of the Province of British Columbia.[349] What else was lost is impossible to say. Once more the Isthmus of Panama had been, for him, a perilous passage between two seas. Malaria had claimed him outward bound; loss of documents, homeward bound. The Atlantic passage home by steam packet would have been a welcome change of scene. By the third week in November he was back in familiar London, his imperial tour to the far side of the world at an end.

For Blanshard a whirl of reunions and appointments ensued: a reunion with his aged father at 37 Great Ormond Street, appointments with physicians who knew his case, business matters to attend to and, not least, a call on the welcoming Miss Emily Hyde. These would be taken in turn. Also, he needed to see Earl Grey at the Colonial Office to present his case and explain his actions.

Part III:

Tides of Empire

Chapter 14:
Homecoming

Returned once more to the epicentre of empire, Blanshard wasted no time. The night had passed, and the new day brought fresh possibilities. "I have the honour to report to your Lordship that I have arrived in London from Vancouver's Island and shall be happy to receive any commands from your Lordship," he wrote Earl Grey on 27 November 1851. Pleasingly, he said that he had fully recovered his health. By return post the colonial secretary replied that he would be glad to see him at three in the afternoon the following Monday, 1 December.[350] Blanshard would have a chance to discuss colonial developments. Grey intended a reception of the man who had so promisingly gone away on imperial business and had come home again under a cloud after a mere two years' absence.

In high expectation and at the appointed hour, Blanshard arrived at Downing Street and attended on the colonial secretary. We do not know the nature of the discussion. Grey was always willing to talk about colonial affairs, though held his own strong opinions. Likely, Blanshard keenly defended himself and, as proof, laid before Grey the original copy of the Memorial (discussed in Chapter 13 and included as an appendix, page 280). We can imagine that Grey would have commented that he would consider the points raised. There was another matter, a bureaucratic one. Somehow Douglas had mislaid some of the colonial papers—that is, the official documents—and a malicious statement circulated that Blanshard was somehow to blame. Grey gave Blanshard permission to make abstracts of correspondence if the originals were not found. In the event, the problem solved itself when Douglas ordered copies from the Colonial Office. We have no idea what transpired further. Grey, as future office memoranda indicate, was noncommittal in response to Blanshard's request for further employment. Formality was the order of the day. Grey was managing a world empire; Vancouver Island was but a fragment of it. He had seen governors come and go. As a former governor, Blanshard could expect no praise or empathy from the disappointed secretary of state, whose Vancouver Island project of colonization had faltered. The interview closed, and a chapter in Vancouver Island's colonial administration ended. Blanshard never again made mention of the meeting.

Two months passed. Blanshard's next step was to write, on 31 January 1852, an extended letter to His Lordship about his life and career.[351] He reiterated that he had fully recovered his health and strength. More, he believed he should be found fully competent for a future assignment. He requested further employment in Her Majesty's service as a colonial secretary, consul or governor of any island territory, or as an attaché to an embassy. He never doubted his own capabilities. Blanshard enclosed copies of six certificates attesting to his valued service in India, for which he had been awarded a medal. He also noted receiving a letter—signed by forty-one persons, including James Douglas—of "unfeigned regret" at his imminent departure from the colony. This noted the loss of his valuable services and judged his administration as "upright, impartial and able."[352] This document does not survive, which is a pity.

"Melancholy as it is to reflect that I have borne H.M.'s commission for executing the affairs of Governor for a length of service during which some benefit might have been expected from my exertions," he wrote, "I am constrained to say that I have not accomplished the purposes for which sent out. There were not many materials to work with, scarcely an inhabitant except the Indian tribes and the Hudson's Bay Company servants, and no possibility of colonization being encouraged." Earl Grey's dusty reply to Blanshard was that he would consider every prospect but, alas, there were so many applicants and so few opportunities that nothing could be considered at present—but that he would keep it in mind for the future.[353] In short, employment was unlikely. Grey was always courteous, and all Blanshard could do was put the best face on His Lordship's letter and accept the reality that as to re-employment in colonial or diplomatic service, he must await developments. The drawbridge came up. Many a colonial governor found the empire project a graveyard of careers.

Blanshard also had urgent matters of a personal nature to attend to. In all the long months that Richard was on his ill-starred imperial mission, Emily was living with Henry and Miriam Blanshard in Brighton. Presumably, the original plan had been that after Richard became settled at Government House, with his promised thousand acres of agricultural land, rocks and forest in the colony assured, he would return to England to marry Emily, and they would proceed together to Vancouver Island. Or Emily would sail out at a later time, and they would marry in Victoria.

Instead, on 19 May 1852, Richard and Emily were married in the parish church at Aller. The marriage register states that he gave his "profession" as Gentleman and she gave her "condition" as Spinster. They were both aged thirty-five. Witnesses were her brother Charles Hyde, a solicitor, and his wife, Marianne Houghton Hyde. Richard and Emily took up residence in London.

On 28 March 1854 the patriarch Henry Blanshard died in London. This man of immense energy and vision, well connected in so many industrial and commercial circles, had also been a faithful protector of the interests of his three children—his daughter, Margaret, living with her husband, Richard Davis, in Barbados; our Richard Blanshard, the older son; and Henry "the Younger," working in Bloomsbury and residing in Brighton. By virtue of Henry's will, which followed the pattern of primogeniture, all estates, lands and properties of the deceased fell to Richard. Richard and Emily came into possession of 37 Great Ormond Street. We resume the story of their lives and estates in a later chapter. We note here, however, that two events had defined Richard Blanshard's future: his marriage to Emily and the death of his father, all within three years of his return from Vancouver Island. Here indeed were changes of fortune. New horizons beckoned.

There are hidden years in the unconstructed record of turbulent times, and for a few years Blanshard disappears from our sight and knowing. He would have seen the triumphal Great Exhibition of the Works of Industry of All Nations in the magnificent Crystal Palace, Hyde Park, London. He would have learned, as everyone did, of the audacious Great Gold Robbery on the South Eastern Railway in 1855. Britain drifted into war against Russia in the Crimea. Troubles were threatening in British India. Disturbances began near Kolkata (Calcutta) in January 1857, and revolts against the East India Company and the British Army became widespread; reprisals followed. In 1858 that corporation's affairs came under the control of the India Office, London.

Blanshard's concerns were of a different sort. There were family properties to visit and inspect, rents to collect, leases to be drawn up. In short, much private business of family and associates needed attending to, more particularly as on the death of his beloved father so much estate land had come into his possession. It could be that each January he wrote, as was the fashion in those days, a letter to the secretary of state for the colonies seeking further employment in Her Majesty's colonial service. No doubt he followed the affairs of Vancouver Island from afar. Then he received notice to give evidence and tell all to a select committee of the House of Commons.

Chapter 15:
Witness for the Prosecution

We retrace our steps to when Governor Blanshard departed Vancouver Island on 1 September 1851 in the *Daphne*. He did not leave behind the Memorial, or a copy of same, in whatever official papers he left in Government House. The Memorial had been addressed to him. In consequence, he kept it snug in his personal files. He did so with good reason: he feared the Memorial would find its way into the hands of Douglas and the principal officers of the Company in the field, and they, should they wish to cause mischief, might exact reprisals on the signatories. It went with him when he boarded the *Daphne*. He now acted with customary prudence. To guard against misfortune he made copies, perhaps at San Francisco, and had them sent home to his father's residence in London.

The Memorial was bound to have consequences. We are reminded that Blanshard provided Earl Grey with a copy. It steeled His Lordship's suspicions: the Company had made little if any progress in colonizing Vancouver Island, in spite of Colonial Office expectations. Furthermore, the Admiralty had forwarded to Grey Rear Admiral Moresby's visceral, damning reports. These were causes of additional anxiety. After all, the Colonial Office was answerable to the Ministry of the day, which was itself answerable to Parliament.

Unknown to Blanshard, on 20 December 1851, after his 2 December interview with the former governor, Grey confronted the Company on the accusations, calling for more efficient measures to be taken and urging greater Company zeal. Never at a loss for words, Pelly replied with the customary legerdemain he had perfected by long practice. He merely put the matter back into Grey's hands. He enquired what measures the Colonial Office had in mind and said that the directors would be pleased to entertain suggestions. That, as they say, was the last straw. The honeymoon between Grey and the Hudson's Bay Company was over.[354] Henceforth, successive governments, irrespective of party affiliation, would watch over these affairs with more narrow views and caustic appraisals.

In any event, political change was in the wind. Grey, under constant siege from many quarters as to his colonial administration in Vancouver Island, South Africa, South Australia, New Zealand and elsewhere, happily relinquished office at the change of government. The ministry of Lord Derby, formed February 1852, differed from its predecessor in its views about the Hudson's Bay Company.

Blanshard, sensing the opportunity presented by the new government, did not let the matter drop. Well might he have done so, but that was not the mettle of the fellow. His actions show that he had a moral obligation to defend the interests of the colony of which he had been inaugural governor. He welcomed the reaction from reform-minded Sir John Pakington, who succeeded Grey as colonial secretary. Blanshard, writing to Pakington on 30 August 1852, said this about the Memorial: "It was presented to me when on the immediate point of leaving the Island and I did not deposit any copy among the Colonial documents which I left there as the very nature of the memorial would draw down upon all who had signed it the ill will and oppression of the Hudson's Bay Company's servants, into whose hands the government of the Colony was passing."[355]

Once again, discussions occurred in the Colonial Office, for Pakington wanted to know how James Douglas had been made governor in succession to Blanshard. Arthur Blackwood, the legal advisor, put a stop to further inquiry: "The excuse for the employment of a gentleman belonging to the Hudson's Bay Company as Governor of a settlement where the interests of the Company are so predominant is to be found in the simple fact that as no funds are voted by Parliament for the payment of the Salary of an independent person as Governor, H.M. Government had no option but to employ one of the Hudson's Bay Company's officers, by which Company he is paid."[356] Pakington was not satisfied. He pressed Pelly's successor, Governor Eden Colvile, as to the number of settlers on Vancouver Island, also the number sent out. The answer disclosed the raw truth: only eleven persons had purchased land, and only 435 emigrants had been sent out.[357] Whereas Grey had been none too pleased at the slothful development of the colony but avoided casting aspersions on the very project he had helped create, Pakington was free of all that. From the moment Blanshard alerted him to the problems as reported in the Memorial, clear notice had arrived in the Colonial Office that the Company would come under fire, even if a select committee of Parliament had to be formed to make searching inquiries and recommend abolition of the monopoly.

Blanshard's written explanations alerted Pakington to Vancouver Island's difficulties. The former governor had pressed on Pakington the validity of the arguments of the dissatisfied who had written the Memorial. Now from Victoria came a new wind demanding change, and it disclosed growing dissent. A new document, a petition to the colonial secretary, had reached Pakington at the Colonial Office courtesy of the Honourable Charles Fitzwilliam, the member of Parliament for Malton (whose father, Earl Fitzwilliam, sat in the House of Lords). Charles Fitzwilliam—one of the "fancy travellers," as Douglas derisively called them—had been to Vancouver Island in 1852 and 1853, and his views aligned with Blanshard's and with Admiral Moresby's. The petitioners, writing from Victoria, called for the imperial government to take over the colony from the Company, as the five-year grant to the Company was about to expire. Particulars recited by the petitioners were the exorbitant price of land, the unsettled form of government, and the retarded progress of the colony. These reinforced Blanshard's charges. This document was signed by the usual settlers seeking reform. The Reverend Staines again had a hand in preparing the document. However, a new aspect had crept in, for two Company personnel had signed their names in support—Dr. William F. Tolmie and Roderick Finlayson, as owners of land and potential settlers.

Pakington took immediate action. On 9 March 1854 he brought

forth the petition in the House of Commons; on 12 June Earl Fitzwilliam did similarly in the House of Lords. Pakington was bent on change. Insurmountable odds stood in his way. Others, conversant with HBC intransigence, stated woefully that the connection with the Company was not about to terminate, and that the government had no power to remove the Company unless it could be shown that no settlement had been established on the Island. There the matter rested.[358] Nothing could be done to the Charter of Grant of 1849, which was due for renewal after five years; indeed, in 1854 it was renewed for a further five years. All the same, dark clouds hung over the affairs of the Hudson's Bay Company.

Behind the scenes were internal commotions. Simpson was furious that Tolmie and Finlayson had bolted from the Company's defence. He threatened vengeance: the recalcitrant duo must be moved east of the mountains or discharged, he railed. Douglas stepped in, appeasing the "Little Emperor" by explaining that Tolmie and Finlayson had added their signatures to those of the settlers out of fear of ridicule. In the event, Simpson demurred.[359]

The Vancouver Island agitators continued their struggle. They were tireless. The faction opposed to Douglas consisted of several prominent citizens, notably Captain James Cooper, the Reverend Staines and Robert Swanston. In 1854 Cooper complained to the Colonial Office of being squeezed out of commercial enterprise, a victim of Douglas's policies. Cooper had developed a trade in selling cranberries and had his own iron schooner to transport the cargo to consumers. Douglas shut him down. That year, too, Robert Swanston, an agent in trade to San Francisco, complained to the colonial secretary of how his shipping prospects to the west coast of the Island were barred by petty colonial bureaucracy. Similar battles were being fought elsewhere in the colony.

The names of these "troublemakers," as the Company regarded them, will not be found in the minute book of the Legislative Council, which was made up invariably of ex–Hudson's Bay Company personnel. Minority voices had scant credibility at the council table against the safe corporate hands familiar to Douglas. Cooper, who owed his membership on the council to Blanshard, received Douglas's censure: a resolution passed in council reflected negatively on him as a member

Formerly in Hudson's Bay Company employ as a mariner, James Cooper brought a schooner out from the United Kingdom and began trading in British waters. He ran afoul of James Douglas and became his strongest opponent, later testifying to Parliament against the HBC tyranny. *Image A–2100 courtesy of the Royal BC Museum*

of council and as a trader in spirits. Cooper was not to be cowed. As noted, he complained directly to the Colonial Office about Governor Douglas's overbearing action. Douglas refuted the complaints by this resident.[360] Indeed, Douglas, master of effective retorts, reported to the Colonial Office on the continued tranquility existing at Vancouver Island, the intelligence of the Indigenous peoples, the settlement of feuds, the legislation advanced, and the prosperity of the colonists. Douglas was always good at what nowadays is called damage control, putting the best face on matters of state; in his view, complaints against the HBC were unfounded. But this sort of messaging was wearing thin in the Colonial Office, and Moresby's strong critiques could not be set aside.

When James Douglas became governor of Vancouver Island, little changed in the way the Legislative Council transacted its affairs. It seldom met. When it did, discussion revolved around liquor licences, the only possible mode of taxation. The colonial affairs were run largely in ways other than by council fiat and regulation. So it came about, predictably we can now see, that a coterie of business associates and Company officers came to dominate the affairs of state. The Colonial Office took note of the Honourable Charles W. Fitzwilliam's charge that the government in Victoria was controlled by a tight little oligarchy. As the Opposition critic the Duke of Newcastle had said in Parliament at the time of Blanshard's appointment, the Company's benign influence on the colony would be even worse than the baleful influence of the Colonial Office; as he put it, "Of all colonizing companies, the Hudson's Bay Company is by far the worst. The very principles of the Hudson's Bay Company are not only like those of most other companies—commercial but monopolistic—not only absentee, but secret."[361]

On 1 March 1854 two documents were signed by James Cooper, a member of the Legislative Council, and sixty-nine other colonists. One was addressed to the Queen, the other, the Duke of Newcastle, now colonial secretary. These documents detailed the HBC's "overbearing and reckless assertion of a lawless and arbitrary power" and called for justice to provide relief against the "desperate retardation" at the critical point of the colony's history. Staines was appointed spokesperson for the group. He would sail for London and make representations on behalf of the memorialists to the Colonial Office on the paltry state of the settlement and the difficulties faced by Britons not connected to the Company. The grievances need not be recited here save that of the complaint against Douglas's appointment of his brother-in-law, David Cameron, to the Supreme Court of Justice. Staines was a champion against these injustices and a passionate representative. Douglas was furious at his "desertion" from the office as Company chaplain and schoolmaster; he terminated Staines's employment.[362]

Historian Hubert Howe Bancroft, who interviewed many of the participants who were opposed to the aptly named "Family-Company-Compact," relates how Staines missed the intended vessel of departure, for he had to gather up some stray pigs:

> *The vessel which he was to have taken, and which would have carried him safely to San Francisco, sailed from Sooke without him...A lumber-laden craft, however, left the same port shortly afterward, and on this Mr Staines embarked. But scarcely had the ship left the strait, when off Cape Flattery a storm struck her, throwing her on her beam ends. Instantly she was waterlogged and at the mercy of the waves. Most of the crew were at once swept overboard. Mr Staines, who was below, cut his way through the side of the ship. His cabin was flooded, and without was the wild waste of tumultuous waters. And there the poor man remained, between the lowering sky and the lowering sea; there he remained till he died. So the only survivor of the wreck reported when rescued by a passing ship, and then himself expired.*[363]

As for the unfortunate Mrs. Staines, who had suffered a dreadful shock and became very poorly, she arranged for the auction of the family possessions, farm and livestock, and returned to England on the next available Company ship, the *Princess Royal*.

The plight of the settlers continued. They prepared a further forceful document. In December 1854 what Governor Douglas called the "Remonstrance Memorial" of the inhabitants arrived on the desk in his office, Blanshard's former residence. These were "factious charges," the unhappy Douglas countered, and he laid the blame at the feet of the troublemaking trio, Messrs. Cooper; the now deceased Staines, whose influence lingered still; and Swanston.[364] The Remonstrance Memorial passed through the usual channels in London. The Company refuted Staines's charges; they backed up their man on the spot, Douglas.

As to land sales and jobbery by the Company, which was a concern of Governor Blanshard when in office, truth will out. If anyone doubted that the Hudson's Bay Company and the Puget's Sound Agricultural Company had Vancouver Island "locked up," so to speak, the statistics tell all. In 1853 there were 450 company personnel and settlers on the Island. Of the 19,807 acres taken possession of, 10,172 were held by the HBC, 2,374 by the PSAC, and the remainder by private individuals. The corporate land acquisitions continued in the next two years. In 1855, in the second report filed to government, the HBC had acquired a further 6,200 acres and the PSAC 2,575. There were an additional for-ty-three "settlers" by 1855, most of them with the HBC.[365]

Sir George Grey, the new colonial secretary, made the decision that foreshadowed the extinction of the Company's tenure on Vancouver Island under the Charter of Grant. He stood adamantly against the Company. By way of warning, in April 1855 he reminded the Company that the Charter of Grant could be voided at the pleasure of the Crown. Herman Merivale, the permanent under-secretary, taking the next step, asked the Company if it would voluntarily surrender it. Governor Colvile's reply to this proposal was that the governor and committee would have no objection provided the Company received reimbursement for its outlay in promoting settlement. In February 1856 the Colonial Office, on advice from the Law Officers of the Crown, instructed Douglas to call an assembly; this met on 12 August and consisted of seven men. Although this was the first step to ending Company rule, empires are not easily dissolved when shareholders' interests have to be taken into account, and the HBC was prepared to undergo searing inquiries rather than voluntarily relinquish its vast North American empire. Blanshard would have found this amusing, but he was barred from the confidential letters that passed between Colonial Office and Company. He had, in a way, always been an out-sider on this matter.

∽∽∽

Matters moved to a climax. The HBC licence of exclusive trade was due to expire 30 May 1859. The Company held Rupert's Land by royal charter, and it exercised rights over Vancouver's Island and its Dependencies by the Charter of Grant. These were well-entrenched positions. It was time for an investigation.

On 5 February 1857 the House of Commons ordered a select committee be appointed "to consider the State of those British Possessions in North America which are under the Administration of the Hudson's Bay Company, or over which they possess a License of Trade." Proceedings began immediately under the chairmanship of the Right Honourable Henry Labouchere, the latest secretary of state for the colonies. The committee consisted of nineteen members of Parliament and included such notables as Lord John Russell, Sir John Pakington, William Ewart Gladstone, J.A. Roebuck, Charles W. Fitzwilliam and Viscount Goderich. All were followers of the colonial progress of Britain in British North America. Only one of them, Fitzwilliam, had been to Vancouver Island, where he had formed hostile views against the Company's paltry colonization capabilities and progress. The already famous Gladstone, himself a former colonial secretary and one adamantly opposed to the Company being awarded the Charter of Grant in the first place, was an inveterate opponent of monopolies. So were most of the other members. Edward "Bear" Ellice, MP, was on the committee, an old hand of the HBC (sometime deputy governor of the HBC), who had been opposed to the Vancouver Island project from the outset. Earl Grey was nowhere present, but what he thought of unfolding events may be imagined, for the Vancouver Island colony was his experiment in empire-making.

These committee members were quintessential persons of the Victorian age. They respected the rights of property holders, for property was sacrosanct—and the HBC was a property holder of magnificent proportions. Besides, it had rights from the Crown and a licence that had been awarded or granted by previous governments. This was in a small way a trial of past administrations too. There was another factor: Indigenous affairs under the Company were generally understood by the politicians, public and the Colonial Office to be more beneficially arranged than if it were a wide-open and land-grabbing frontier, as in the American west. The Aborigines Protection Society and the Church Missionary Society, powerful in high places of government, kept watch. Not least, the British North American provinces, notably the Province of Canada, had an interest as well, imagining a transcontinental dominion that would keep Americans out of the mid-west, Prairie west and Pacific west, including Vancouver Island. Chief Justice the Honourable W.H. Draper, delegate from the Province of Canada, was there to testify to the need to define Canada's western boundaries and force the Hudson's Bay Company farther north. In all, twenty-four witnesses were called and examined.

On Monday, 15 June 1857, a fine and warm day, Blanshard made his way to the Houses of Parliament, an edifice in the richest neo-Gothic style on the London landscape. Fire had consumed its predecessor in 1834; the whole, Blanshard could see, had been rebuilt. Crossing New Palace Yard, he passed through the public entrance. He was shown to the Commons Committee Room. He waited in the anteroom until called in and examined. The Committee Room was richly panelled in oak, while the high leaded-glass windows admitted a natural light that animated all in the chamber.

Around the immense table sat fifteen sober-faced, stiff-necked members of Parliament, colonial experts all. These "frock coats," as they were dubbed, these mid-Victorian gentlemen, were dressed in starch collars, silk scarves, brocaded waistcoats and striped trousers. Each in his own way, at one time or another, had turned over the anguished prospects of the global British Empire in debate and discussions. At hand were piles of *Parliamentary Papers* or "Blue Books": these had been their customary reading, to say nothing of *Hansard*, official record of what was said in the Commons and in the House of Lords. Besides the Blue Books, committee members also knew of Vancouver Island by reputation as an unsavoury and unwelcoming place for settlers, where it seemed, on the face of it, that the Colonial Office and the Company worked hand in glove. The results had been disastrous in terms of settlement. Members were inquisitive about the local Indigenous peoples and threats posed to colonial security, trade and settlement. Recorders were present to take down all that was said in answer to any question posed.

All eyes turned to Blanshard, expert witness. The former governor took his seat. In the course of the day, 260 questions were put to him; he gave as many replies—in all, twenty-two pages of testimony. His answers reflected personal knowledge of affairs in that faraway quarter of the British Empire with which he had become acquainted in the course of nearly two years as first governor.

"By whom were you appointed?" was one of the first questions; "By Her Majesty" was Blanshard's response. When asked how he stood in relationship to the Hudson's Bay Company, he replied abruptly, "In none whatever." In short, he was the viceregal person, answerable to the Colonial Office. He was altogether independent of any control on the part of the Hudson's Bay Company.[366] He was asked about the geography, the potential for settlement, the cost and availability of arable land, about coal and harbours.

To what do you attribute the very limited resort of settlers to Vancouver's Island, which took place while you were there?
—I think, in a great measure, to the restrictions there were upon their obtaining land.
What was the nature of those restrictions?
—The high price.

He explained the price was £1 per acre, with a related condition that every purchaser of one hundred acres should bring out five labourers from England; he thought this an insuperable bar. He told of English persons from California, interested in acquiring land on Vancouver Island, being denied on their not being able to meet this qualification. In addition, the Company had surveyed ten square miles around Fort Victoria and embraced this as its own holdings.

I thought that all the island was conceded to them?
—True, but then it was on condition of selling the land; this they claimed as their own reserve.

When pressed on this point, Blanshard stated, "They refused to sell it."

Was that no obstruction to colonisation?
   —I should say that it was a very great one.

Questioning turned to the conditions of his appointment and his future prospects in the colonial service. The committee members were flabbergasted when they learned that he received no salary whatsoever, and that Governor Sir John Henry Pelly had reneged on the promise of a thousand acres that he himself might select upon his arrival in the colony. The point was pressed home.

So that you passed your two years there and got nothing by it?
   —Nothing whatever. All that I ever received from the Hudson's Bay Company was £175 for my passage out there, and it cost me about £300.

The inquisitiveness of Henry Labouchere, the colonial secretary and chairman, had now been raised to a high state.

Do you mean that you accepted the governorship of this colony, with the understanding that you were to get nothing whatever for your services in that respect?
   —Nothing at the first beginning. I was certainly led to believe that colonial settlers would flock out there; that all facilities would be given to them; and that of course as the colony increased a civil list would be formed; that the land sales and the royalties on the coal would produce a considerable colonial revenue.

Hearing this, some members of the committee surely thought Blanshard a downright fool, while others pondered his problems with sympathy. One member asked, to be reassured on this point, that the promised thousand acres was the inducement. "Just so," replied Blanshard, "and moreover: I also hoped that my services would be considered by Her Majesty's Government afterwards." Some members must have cast glances across the table at Sir John Pakington and Labouchere himself, both colonial secretaries since Earl Grey's time. Nevertheless, all knew that it was not the Colonial Office that was under scrutiny but the Company, its monopoly and licence, and its future.

Questions now turned to the matter of the day-to-day cost of provisions. Blanshard explained that he got no beneficial arrangement and painfully paid the cash price (three hundred percent above cost price), just like any other visitor. When asked if the California gold rush had a deleterious effect on colonization, he replied in the negative. He thought it was the terms and conditions of buying land, if indeed land could be purchased.

At this time J.A. Roebuck, possessing sharp insights into British colonization generally, posed a question about Blanshard's credentials and experience.

What previous knowledge had you of colonisation or colonial government?
—I had been in one or two of the West India islands; I had been in British Honduras, and I had been in India.
And upon the ground of the experience which you there gained, you thought that you could make a good Governor of Vancouver's Island?
—I saw no reason to believe the contrary.

In an age that valued the independence and self-sustaining capacities of the individual, Blanshard's comment would have passed without critique or censure, for the Colony of Vancouver Island was a business venture, unique in itself, and Blanshard was to the corporation born. He was a gentlemanly capitalist, firm and confident. Members of the committee would have been well aware of his wealth, legal qualifications and business capacities.

When asked about his gubernatorial duties, Blanshard replied that his main obligation consisted of settling disputes between the Company's officers and their servants. He explained that there was a great deal of dissatisfaction among the settlers and discontent among Company servants. There were a large number of cases, and when pressed on this he explained that the Company had promised a great many comforts and conveniences, and the disaffected were led to expect a far more comfortable life and higher wages than they received; "but still they were all there under agreement." This was not an inconsiderable matter, but it reflected the state of labour-management relations there. Most persons thought serfdom had been obliterated in the British Empire.

So that, in fact, as far as government was concerned, you had no duties to perform?
—None whatever, except as an ordinary magistrate...
So that, in fact, it was no colony at all?
—It was nothing more than a fur trading post, or very little more.

Questions turned to Blanshard's relationship with Chief Factor Douglas, and he was asked to describe the matter of the register of a ship. Blanshard explained that Douglas had encroached on the governor's authority and had to be corrected on the matter: indeed, as mentioned earlier, Douglas was held on his own recognizance pending further inquiries (which never occurred). Committee members understood that this had been a battle of wits and wills, and that the civil power was overruling the corporate power.

The matter of Edward Langford came up for discussion, for Langford had been making his own complaints known to the Colonial Office, hostile as he was to the Hudson's Bay Company and the Puget's Sound Agricultural Company. Langford had been appointed one of the new bailiffs, and his lands were close to or in Esquimalt. Blanshard stated that Langford had never heard of the PSAC until he arrived in the colony. (When asked about the difference between the Hudson's Bay Company and the Puget's Sound Agricultural Company, Blanshard, who was fully conversant on matters of corporate law, replied that he never could distinguish between the two. That was fair comment.)

Blanshard explained Langford's terms of employment as superintendent:

—He was engaged with them for a term of 15 years, which was terminable either at five or ten years upon due notice; he was to receive a salary of £60 a year, and he was to be supplied with everything which

243

he required in the way of labour, materials, and seed, and with those he was to form as large a farm as he pleased. I think it was restricted to 500 acres, if I remember rightly. His further remuneration, beyond this £60 a year, was to be half the profits of the farm when it was established.

Langford had been a landowner in Kent and was a former Army officer. He and his wife were raising a large family. The opportunities in the colony seemed promising, perhaps golden. He had been promised "every accommodation" by Sir John Pelly, but when Langford arrived on Vancouver Island, he was given a one-room log hut to live in, which Blanshard estimated to measure twenty feet by twelve.

So that a gentleman of position in England was expected, with his family, to live in a log hut, without any accommodation whatever?
—Exactly so.

He had been promised a house to live in upon his arrival, though Blanshard made the point that Langford hardly expected it to be complete. But he did expect better accommodation.

In the event, Blanshard had been alarmed at the situation Langford, his wife and family faced upon arrival, as the following reveals (and shows the governor's charitable nature):

How do you know all this?
—Because when he arrived there he had a large family, and his wife, who was a most lady-like woman, was within a day or two of her confinement, and I gave them rooms in my house, being extremely sorry to see an English lady reduced to such a state of inconvenience.

The child, George Langford, was born in Government House.[367]
Now the committee wanted to know how "Indian affairs" were dealt with during his tenure. Parliament and the powerful Aborigines Protection Society had kept a close watch on these matters since the searing inquiries of 1837, and they were a preoccupation of the parliamentary committee. Its inquiries about the Red River Settlement, in

present-day Manitoba, were intense, and ably defended by parties such as the bishop of Rupert's Land, the Right Reverend David Anderson, and the Church Missionary Society on behalf of its workers in the field.

Our interest is in Vancouver Island, and the parliamentary members demanded details of "the state of Indians on the island, and the mode of the Company in dealing with them." Blanshard had been impressed by the Company's treatment of Indigenous peoples. He had told the Colonial Office so in his first dispatch. To the query posed he replied, "The Indians were always very kindly treated by the Hudson's Bay Company." The committee asked if the Indigenous peoples were agriculturalists. They were fishing people, Blanshard explained; they traded exclusively with the Hudson's Bay Company out of necessity and because of the Company's exercise of monopoly.

He was asked about the three men who had run away from Fort Rupert and been murdered, and he described how HMS *Daphne* was called upon to assist in apprehending the murderers.

Is the character of the native tribes in Vancouver's Island warlike?

—In the north they are a very fierce and warlike set; about Fort Rupert.

He confirmed his personal knowledge of them from his travels to Fort Rupert, adding that the Company exercised no control over them.

But were those Indians any obstruction to colonisation?

—The northern part of the island, I think, they have never attempted to colonise; it is merely a fur-trading post, and they [the Company's servants and labourers] do not go very far from the walls [of the fort].

But would any settlers be afraid of the Indians?

—I should fancy not.

In fact, those Indians are no obstacle to the colonisation of the Island?

—No. In fact, down in the south, about Fort Victoria, they are very useful.

Have you had any experience of the red man on the continent of America?

—Not in North America.

You are not aware that he invariably disappears as the civilised man comes on?

—I cannot say so from my own knowledge, but I believe that it is a well-known fact, and it would be the case in Vancouver's Island.

Then if colonisation were to take place in Vancouver's Island, we should hear very little more of the Indian?

—Very little more.

In fact, though it may seem to be an inhuman statement to make, the sooner they get rid of the Indians the better?

—I believe it is what the United States' people call improving them.

Improving them off the face of the land?

—Exactly so.

The impression was left among committee members that the Indigenous peoples posed no obstacle to colonization, but then Blanshard was asked if the HBC provided "these Indians with arms and ammunition for the purpose of hunting."

—They sell them a large quantity of arms and ammunition…not only for the purposes of hunting, but for warlike purposes and purposes of self-defence. The Indians are very well supplied with fire-arms there, and of a very excellent quality.

Do you think that that conduces to the safety of a small white community?

—I do not think that it at all conduces to it.

Blanshard—who did not even have a corporal's guard as governor—had always been keen on having a mobile military force on Vancouver Island for purposes of defence and security. Half of it could be garrisoned at Work Point, Esquimalt; the other half, when required, at some northern post. This resembled a British regimental system of a battalion at home and another abroad. Fort Rupert had been his big worry, but he was concerned generally for colonial security against warlike nations. He knew of the then recent conflicts at and near Nisqually; true to his expectations, the Puget Sound War of 1855 turned the adjacent American frontier into a conflict zone. It brought US military and naval intervention, and the independent settlers were armed at government expense and engaged in operations against the local Indigenous peoples.[368] Blanshard had always been apprehensive of the prospect of a spillover into British territory.

But the committee did not press inquiries on that score, interested as members were in local administrative matters on British soil. Blanshard explained that the Indigenous people had no objection to hiring themselves out as labourers and were very useful in the building of trading posts, gathering coal or lumber work. He left no impression that the Indigenous peoples were a hindrance to colonization. When one committee member asked, "So that, so far from their being an obstruction to colonization, you think that they would be an assistance?" Blanshard replied simply, "Yes." If the committee were trying to get an exposé on HBC "Indian policy," they did not receive it from the former governor. In fact, there was no reason for him to change his views: he regarded the Indigenous peoples as kindly treated by the Hudson's Bay Company. Furthermore, as to the economic dependencies developed, he had noted that Indigenous labourers were hired and worked in the economic pursuits of the colony—in the Company's interests.

All during the inquiry, many strong opinions were expressed regarding the ill fortunes of Vancouver Island. And when, on 31 July 1857, the committee's report was published, it was no surprise to interested parties in Britain, Vancouver Island, Red River and Canada to read the following: "Your Committee are of opinion that it will be proper to terminate the connexion of the Hudson's Bay Company with Vancouver's Island as soon as it can conveniently be done, as the best means of favouring the development of the great natural advantages of that important colony. Means should also be provided for the ultimate extension of the colony over any portion of the adjoining continent, to the west of the Rocky Mountains, on which permanent settlement may be found practicable."[369]

In short, the report pointed the way to a possible colony of British Columbia and, further, if a link could come from the east, an expansion of Canada to Red River and beyond. The Company, for the time being, was allowed to maintain territorial rights to those parts of Rupert's Land and the "Indian Territories" that offered little prospect for permanent settlement. Change was in the air, and America's belief in its own manifest destiny arose again. In 1868 the Rupert's Land Act was passed by the Imperial Parliament, authorizing the acquisition by Canada of the North-West Territories, comprising Rupert's Land and the areas beyond. In consequence, in 1870 the whole of Rupert's Land was surrendered to the Canadian government for £300,000. This surely ranks among the most extraordinary real estate deals in history.

Without a doubt it was the problem of Vancouver Island that needed immediate attention, and the parliamentary committee was thorough in calling and interrogating witnesses in this regard—including Captain James Cooper. Richard Blanshard's evidence had been convincing and effective. At last he had been listened to in London.

Chapter 16:
The Bell Tolls: Retrospective

That Blanshard's ill health obliged him to offer his resignation cannot be denied. Nor can his impoverishment from maintaining himself at Vancouver Island totally on his own financial resources (which he estimated at an egregious £1,100 per annum) be excluded from his calculation to leave office. His situation was indeed pitiable. How close he came to death by illness or suicide is unknown. Given the character of the man, the likelihood of taking his own life seems slim, but who is to say? Loneliness and isolation invite despair, and using laudanum as an elixir presents a wretched and perilous combination for a critically ill person.

A touch of melancholy must have swept over him that last day at his so-called seat of power, when he bade farewell to Vancouver Island. He had said goodbye to many friends and admirers. Doubtless he said final words to the relieved Company officers, including Douglas, who were glad to see him go, for intruders were certainly unwelcome to them, and even visitors had spelled trouble. Wronged but not vindictive, he left the colony without regret but with scores to settle in the appropriate fashion when the time came, as surely it would. His resignation, we note, had not been requested by the Colonial Office. A cruel trick had been played on him. He was a casualty of empire. Empires are built on power, and as governor he had been without supreme power.

W. Colquhoun Grant, Vancouver Island's first settler, held strongly to the opinion that very bad health had obliged the governor to resign. This, he said, constituted a blow to the colony as a settlement project. "His loss," Grant stated to the Royal Geographical Society in his remarks of 1857, "was very much to be regretted, as he was a gentleman in every way qualified to fulfil the duties of his position, with credit to himself and with prosperous results to the country over which he was appointed to preside."[370] This was the first and, indeed, the only public defence of Blanshard that appeared in the contemporary media. Captain Grant, in his Royal Geographical Society articles, disclosed the problems that Governor Blanshard faced. Only on one specific matter was he in doubt. He estimated the Indigenous population of Vancouver Island at seventeen thousand. During the discussion of the paper at the society's Kensington headquarters on 22 June 1857, Blanshard, in attendance, made the following correction, as recorded by the secretary: "When he was there, he took great pains to make inquiries of the people who, he considered, were best qualified to judge, and they stated the numbers to be, at the outside, 10,000, and that the population was decreasing."[371] As to the colony's faltering progress, Grant reckoned that "of the four hundred men imported in the period of five years, about two-thirds had deserted, one-fifth had been sent elsewhere, and the remainder were employed on the Island." He estimated the population in 1853 at about 450, with 300 at Victoria, 125 at Nanaimo and the remaining few at Fort Rupert.[372] Blanshard had a great friend in Grant, who died too soon.

When in 1857 the parliamentary inquiry exposed the nature of the colony's difficulties and unprogressive ways (discouraging as they were to independent settlers), Grant's opinions rang true. His views carried weight in England. His presentation to the Royal Geographical Society occurred only a week after Blanshard's testimony, and his views may have influenced the conclusions of Parliament.[373] Grant held that Vancouver Island possessed several resources, which, if developed by free people, under free institutions, would make it a flourishing colony. "The position and natural advantages of Vancouver Island," he went further, "would appear eminently to adapt it for being the emporium of an extended commerce." Grant was pointing to the future. Events would prove the correctness of his assessment. He and Blanshard may have discussed these matters as opportunity arose. They had met first in 1850. Now they were reviewing the state of distant affairs. Both were fellows of the prestigious Royal Geographical Society. Grant's article and his subsequent and parallel contribution on Indigenous peoples and townsites of Vancouver Island, published 1861, was his last testament on the subject of the Island. He had a great fondness for the area and would have liked to have become governor of the Crown Colony of British Columbia, proclaimed 1858. In fact, he made a suggestion in that direction to the Colonial Office. But, like Blanshard, he was an outsider. And outsiders had little opportunity in a world still dominated by the Hudson's Bay Company and James Douglas.

"Blanshard's experience as governor was a tragedy. He was an Englishman with aspirations, learned in the law."[374] So concluded R.E. Gosnell, one of the earliest British Columbia historians and, moreover, a person of great insights into character and circumstance. Blanshard's appointment was truly unlucky for him. Historian H.H. Bancroft, writing a generation after the events, said the governor "seemed every way the son of misfortune," which certainly he was.[375] He had been lied to. Perhaps he was naive in taking up the official duties, but a fair field was offered by the chairman of the Hudson's Bay Company, Sir John Pelly, to establish a colonial administration in what was advertised as a most profitable location with a wondrous future. And such an appointment might lead to greater things in the imperial service. There is no need to recount here what has already been said about the obstructions and difficulties he faced in the field. Nor is there utility in remarking yet again on the disinterestedness of Earl Grey and the under-secretaries at the Colonial Office as to Blanshard's situation.

Who came to his support in the colony? Those who rallied to his aid in the last weeks of his governorship, all non-Company personnel, knew the mettle of the man. They understood his difficulties. They appreciated his circumstances. Above all, they knew first-hand that monopoly, as exercised by the Hudson's Bay Company, ruled all things, and that monopoly tends toward tyranny. To quote Mr. Gosnell again, what Sir John Pelly and others in the Company had not "reckoned on [were] the instincts of the free-born Britisher whom he proposed to transport to the virgin soil of the Far West, where the very air was redolent of freedom, and it was inevitable that some, if not all, of the colonists, knowing their rights, would demand them."[376]

The Colony of Vancouver Island was the runt of the British Empire, locked up in the control of two corporations. Blanshard's letters to the Colonial Office were regarded by the recipients as nothing more than a weary catalogue of forebodings and complaints and were treated as grumbles, incessant and even inconvenient attacks on the Hudson's Bay Company, but these reports had every right to exude that character. They described what he saw on the ground. Blanshard had come as close as any outsider to exposing the way the monopoly worked itself out—in land control, in denial of land to others, and in pushing newcomers to the margins. He also knew of (and exposed) price-fixing of provisions and supplies, and squeezing-out of any rivals.

Having an unauthorized grand inquisitor in their midst discomfited the Company officers. Surely they were happy to see him embark for the last time. Douglas saved his unbridled critique for a letter to Barclay at London headquarters. The former governor's communications to the Colonial Office, he wrote acidly, had been "marked by the same unaccountable animosity to the Company, which he entertained on his first arrival, and which has appeared in all his subsequent acts."[377] That Douglas held a grudge against Blanshard for the latter's complaints about homelessness on arrival was one source of the bother, but it was more than that. Douglas disliked intrusions. He balked at criticism of Company affairs. He did not like the governor examining, then correcting, his accounts that bore specifically on colonial expenditures. He railed at Blanshard's exposing the jobbery of the HBC and PSAC land development. He did not like Colonial Office oversight, always troublesome—and Blanshard was invariably the courier of troublesome news. Not least, Douglas guarded his own persona and his image with righteous zeal. So when Blanshard departed, Douglas was bound to write in defence of himself. Magnanimity was not in his personal arsenal.

As for Grey, it may be charged that he had failed to realize Blanshard's exposed position. He was prepared to sacrifice the governor to save his political skin. It was an unstated guiding principle of British colonial policy to preserve local law and custom as far as possible. Indigenous leaders and councils were to be maintained and not interfered with, except in cases of piracy or the murder of British subjects.

Grey's hands were tied in yet another way: systematic colonization was the order of the day and was not to be undertaken at government's expense. Did Grey jump in too soon in answer to Sir John Pelly's request to establish a colony to halt the course of American emigration northward after 1846? Certainly, but he was under ministerial pressure to establish a British bulwark against American expansionism. Did he overestimate the threat of that expansion? No. As for the governor's position, Blanshard's instructions were drawn up from the most recent information available in London; they contemplated a state of affairs exactly the reverse of what he found to prevail.

The broad policies were stated in London, but out on the margins, the colony and its governor were self-reliant. Former colonial secretary William Ewart Gladstone had forecast difficulties as early as 1848, when he had said let there be free colonization and let time elapse before taking other measures, such as the Hudson's Bay Company as colonizer: he urged the House of Commons not to forget "that there was now a great and worthy opportunity of planting a society of Englishmen, which if it did not afford a precise copy of our institutions, might still present a reflex of that truth, integrity, and independence, which constituted at this moment the ornament and glory of this country."[378] The practical Grey understood that the American settler frontier would turn north and cause unending problems on British soil. The HBC offered an inexpensive means of deterring that unwanted intrusion. In the circumstances, Blanshard had been appointed to fulfill the mandate. Government never wavered in its commitment to keeping the area in British hands. Here were the politics of expediency at work.

෴෴෴

Though no further imperial appointments were forthcoming, Blanshard was not at loose ends or in dire straits. He was, we are reminded, a man of property. As oldest son, the laws of primogeniture applied. When his father died in 1854, he inherited the real estate and such properties as were in his father's name, including his coal mine. Richard became owner of extensive lands in Essex, notably at Kirby-le-Soken. He sold the family residence, 37 Great Ormond Street. His father's railway stocks came to him as inheritance. Further, as trustee of the estate, all sorts of goods and chattels came his way, as well as considerable investment capital.

His marriage to Emily two years previous had brought another source of land and wealth. Blanshard's activities as a yachtsman, beneficial as they were to his health, likely played a part in the selection of land for tenant farming and a location to build a suitable residence. The pursuit of quiet country life underscored many a decision of people of their class and station.

Richard and Emily chose the southern part of the New Forest, Hampshire, to set down roots. Bound up in English history unlike any other part of England, so local historians tell us, it is near Southampton and within earshot of the gun sounded at Portsmouth at sunset. It is best known for its woodlands and for its moorlands. On a solitary ramble into Boldrewood, one discovers ancient oaks, twisted and braced up with ivy. A stream, if followed, will take you through greenest valleys and past the thickest woods. Here are joined, too, not only woodland but sea and moorland and river views. It has been said that there are more beautiful places in England, but none so characteristic. Boldre, two miles north of Lymington, lies in the valley of the Brockenhurst Water and is a place of meadows and wheatfields.

Fairfield, Lymington, in the Country of Southampton (Hampshire), is the address Richard Blanshard gives in his will as his residence. There, in a property of fifty-seven acres, with woodlands and fields giving a view of the Solent, Richard and Emily had constructed for themselves a handsome country house, Fairfield, though it was referred to locally as the Mansion. Photographs disclose a modern architectural piece for the Victorian heyday: two storeys, with shuttered windows above a verandah that stretched across the housefront and its entrance—a touch of Indian architecture. Photos taken from the lawn show trellised roses in profusion and a pebbled drive. Above the entrance is a balcony with roof and railings.

Their property lay convenient to Southampton and to the superb sailing of the Solent and Southampton Water. The property, with gross rental income of £408 10s., may have derived from her family wealth. They made many contributions to the well-being of St. John the Baptist Church, Boldre. Nearby was angling on the chalk streams—for salmon downstream and trout above. In 1871 Richard was appointed justice of the peace for Hampshire. Possibly he presided at the last of the old Forest law courts, held every forty days at Lyndhurst.[379] As late as mid-century, burglary, poaching and the smuggling of ardent spirits were pastimes of labourers and others.[380] Richard would have heard many a case in these criminal lines.

When not in residence, Richard and Emily maintained Fairfield with their servants, including housekeeper, groom and others. As was the convention of persons of their station, they always had a house "in town." The 1861 census shows the couple residing at 48 Devonshire Street in fashionable Marylebone, London, with a butler and lady's maid. They lived in comfortable circumstances, attended to their numerous properties, engaged in agricultural pursuits and husbanded the land. Richard maintained his business practice; he was a barrister in chambers at 53 Chancery Lane from as early as 1860 through to at least 1875. Passenger trains and steam vessels facilitated the couple's movements, and it may be imagined that they shifted from Hampshire to Essex as required, though their Hampshire property was their main residence. Richard had duties as justice of the peace and magistrate in both counties. He had estates to manage and oversee. He may also have made a journey to the West Indies to visit family and examine and inspect landholdings in estates and plantations. A man of property looks after his holdings as essential material foundations of family wealth and fortune, for the present as well as for the future. This was a tenet of success of the Victorians and their age, and Richard Blanshard was quintessentially Victorian.

Blanshard competed actively as a yachtsman. The mid-nineteenth century is known as the classic era of recreational sailing. Records of the Royal Thames Yacht Club indicate that he was elected to membership in December 1859. He owned two vessels concurrently from 1859 to 1862. One was a twelve-ton cutter (a single-masted vessel with two head sails and a main) named *Folly*. Could this be in reference to his

Vancouver Island misfortunes? This vessel, registered at Harwich, was ideal for coastal cruising and even sailing round the Essex foreland into the Thames Estuary to a moorage at the small riverine seaport Wivenhoe, south of Colchester, Essex. At Wivenhoe he owned a terrace house, a "bolt hole." At this town, ship repairs could be made, and crews arranged as required for the competitions of river and estuary sailing. This was vigorous and demanding sailing, for the Thames ebbs and flows twice daily, and the commercial river traffic can be frenetic.

At this sea gate to Colchester he kept his yacht, the large 112-ton schooner *Ione*.[381] The name is of interest, indicative of Blanshard's knowledge of the classics, which he would have studied at school and university. Ione is the name of a sea nymph, one of the Nereids. *Ione* would have required a hired crew, and Blanshard engaged as captain the faithful and competent William Ham, whom he names in his will. With Ham and the *Ione*, Blanshard likely went to Cowes, Isle of Wight, for the annual Royal Yacht Squadron Regatta. As sailors will attest, a sail via the Thames Estuary, then coastwise past the Goodwin Sands and the Cinque Ports all the way to the Isle of Wight would be an adventure in Dover Straits sailing. In 1851, as an added attraction to visitors taking in the jollities of the Great Exhibition, the Royal Yacht Squadron put up a Queen's Cup of 100 guineas. It was captured by the *America* of the New York Yacht Club. Before long, the likes of Lord Dunraven and other well-heeled yachtsman were contending for what is now called the America's Cup, the greatest prize of all.[382] Just as he wished, Blanshard could shift his residence for sailing purposes to Fairfield, Lymington.

It is pleasant to think that after all the anguish Richard Blanshard had experienced, all the disappointments, he gained some consolation in his later days of recreation on the River Thames and in the Solent. We have no idea if Emily shared in these sailing exploits. If not, she could rendezvous with him from the vantage point of Lymington. Cowes and the Isle of Wight were readily at hand. He maintained his membership in the Royal Thames Yacht Club until 1867.

Sadness came in 1866. On 4 February of that year, Emily died, in the fourteenth year of their marriage. She was forty-eight and had had previous illnesses. The cause of death is not known; the documents of the age did not require such details. We know Emily to have been of a charitable nature, kind and considerate of the needs of others. Richard was devoted to her.

"The decease of this truly excellent lady has thrown a gloom over the neighbourhood," remarked the *Lymington and Isle of Wight Chronicle*, 9 February 1866. "It is not only a large circle of friends that will deplore her loss, but that loss will be keenly felt by many of the poor of the town." We can imagine the cortege forming up at the Mansion at Fairfield, then moving out, the horses with their cockades drawing the hearse bearing the deceased's body. Then followed Richard Blanshard and family members, friends and servants, pallbearers and undertakers—all in the mournful black of the time. The solemn procession wound its way through the town and to the yard of the parish church of Boldre, St. John the Baptist. In advance of this event, man and wife had determined that they would share a common crypt or grave, and there, if you visit the location, you will see the pair of gravestones. Richard provided a memorial window to Emily at the Boldre Church. It does not survive.[383]

Richard and Emily had no children, though curiously Victorian families tended to be large. Is there an explanation? One alluring possibility is that the governor's prescribed opiates, duly administered in the form of laudanum during the time he was suffering grievously from the volatile ague at Victoria, brought on impotence, as medical opinion now holds on this matter generally. Diminished libido is another unwelcome effect of opiates, perhaps explaining his certain rise in despair and an urgent appeal for relief from duties on a short-term or permanent basis. The governor had written his two letters of resignation (one provisional, the other final) on a day of despair while still under treatment. Leadership, we know, functions poorly under illness or stress. Blanshard had been in a very bad way at the time. It may now be speculated that disease and medical treatment played a long-term role that explains why he and his wife had no children.

After his father's death in 1854, Richard spent a goodly time each year at his inherited Kirby-le-Soken, Essex. There, he was the respected lord of the manor. People knew him as the Squire of Kirby. His house was No. 2 The Terrace, Walton-on-Naze, and there, too, we can imagine extensive outbuildings. He had workable lands, 2,411 acres, and his properties grossed annually the extensive rental income of £2,256 11s. Among his properties was Horsey Island, with 929 acres of grazing land. In 1859 he became justice of the peace for Essex, and as such he could rule as magistrate on minor civil cases and keep the peace as required. We see him now, as he was in those days, well regarded, a country gentleman of means, and a fellow of benevolent actions. He was a major benefactor of the Kirby church, St. Michael's.[384]

After his return from Vancouver Island, he retained always a residence in London—and so it was to his last years. As a widower he lived for a time at No. 2 Albany Chambers, Piccadilly.[385] Albany, formerly a great house of nobility, had been subdivided into several large apartments, or "sets." Here, Blanshard's famed fellow resident Lord Macaulay said, one could lead a life peculiarly suited to their taste—"college life at the West End of London."[386] This famed address may still be found standing adjacent to the Royal Academy, Burlington Gardens, and opposite Fortnum & Mason. Striking objects in Blanshard's set were pictures, or portraits, of his late wife, Emily, and pictures of the memorial windows erected to her memory, presumably at Boldre church.[387]

Blanshard's club, the Conservative, was conveniently nearby, at 75 St. James's Street. London is famous for its celebratory dinners. He could easily attend gatherings of the Honourable Company of Goldsmiths, the Lord Mayor's Banquet, or Lincoln's Inn, the Royal Geographical Society and others if he so wished. But Blanshard was a private fellow, certainly no social butterfly. And he was a widower with no female pursuits in view. Perhaps he attended a reunion with Army officers he had campaigned with in the Second Sikh War. He might have taken an active interest in the affairs of the Royal Thames Yacht Club. More likely, he was content to continue the business obligations that devolved to him through the estate of his father. The mining and marketing of coal had been father Henry's preoccupation after East India shipping faded in value. This Richard took up. In 1874 we find reference to his being a principal in the Coxhoe Colliery, County Durham. He would also assist in legal and financial matters in regards to the business affairs of his sister, Margaret, and her husband, Richard Davis, in the West Indies.

A solitary cast pervades this Piccadilly studio portrait of the resolute barrister-at-law and former governor, a widower. *Image A-01113 courtesy of the Royal BC Museum*

A Piccadilly studio photographic portrait of Richard Blanshard survives, showing him in senior years, looking perhaps late sixties. He sits at a table. Advancing age since yachting days has made him well-ballasted but strong-looking nonetheless. He is dressed smartly but unostentatiously in town jacket and trousers. His right elbow rests on the table. And tellingly, at his right hand stands a one-foot-high statuette of a helmeted male in medieval attire, perhaps of the Norman period. Did Blanshard ask for it to be included in the photo? Is this a symbol, perhaps, of ancient lineage back to the Norman conquest, for "Blanshard" suggests a French origin? If Blanshard represented England eternal, it was surely modified by the progressive and energetic changes exhibited in the nineteenth century at home and abroad. This is the best photo of him in mature years. The world was swiftly changing around him. The sun of Pax Britannica was now low in the sky. The epoch that had begun with Waterloo was reaching its twilight hours, and Blanshard had lived through this same span of years.

The last photograph of him, again a studio portrait, perhaps aged seventy-six, shows a white-haired gentleman, full-bearded now, and still sporting a military moustache. He looks old before his years but appears as resolute and redoubtable as ever, one not to be crossed. There is no hint of humour or happiness, only the disclosure "Here I am, here I stand." He wears a double-breasted suit jacket, this one with a velvet collar insert. Shadows swiftly gathered around Richard Blanshard. In those advanced years he became an invalid, dependent on others. His eyesight failed, and eventually he became totally blind. He died at 29 Upper Berkeley Street, in elegant Marylebone, City of Westminster, on 5 June 1894, in his seventy-seventh year. It was a goodly age considering the adventures and hardships of an uncommon life.

According to plan, he was buried beside his wife in the churchyard at Boldre. Parishioners and others who knew him paid deepest respects. The *Lymington and South Hants Chronicle* for 14 June 1894 gives this tribute: "Since the death of his wife in 1866 he seldom spent much time at his Lymington residence, but his interest in the place was always kept up, and appeals to his charity for any local object always met with a generous response…in his death the poor have lost a generous benefactor. The procession left the Mansion at Fairfield about

Seemingly old before his time and blind in these sad later years, Richard Blanshard is here shown. *Image A-01114 courtesy of the Royal BC Museum*

11 o'clock, and as it passed through the town there was a very general mark of public mourning." The monument's inscription reads *Dominus dedit, Dominus abstulit, sit nomen Domini benedictum* ("The Lord has given, the Lord has taken away, let the name of God be praised" —Job 1:21).

It is unlikely that anyone of the town or parish knew that Richard Blanshard had ever been governor of Vancouver Island. He did not advertise his past experience there. Rather, he lived in the present, and there is no reason to believe, as some have suggested, that he was silent on Vancouver Island affairs because it was an experience he wished to blot out.[388] In fact, and this deserves emphasis, his last word and testament on the colony under the management of the Hudson's Bay Company was to be found in the evidence he gave to, and the report of, the parliamentary select committee, as detailed above.

Earl Grey died that same year of 1894. Heralded as an architect of the modern Commonwealth, his colonial policy embraced three essentials: maintain mutual dependence of colony and mother country; maintain free trade and extend it to the colonies; and maintain the colonies by good colonial administration and minimum expenditure where colonists could not manage or were not experienced. Grey was determined to repeal the Corn Laws; also, he was significant in the repeal of the Navigation Acts. In effect, Blanshard exemplifies his policies on Vancouver Island, and so we must turn to other causes for explanation of the governorship. Grey, Hawes and Merivale could only imagine what transpired in the HBC-dominated colony. Grey, we are told, was somewhat difficult to work with as a colleague. He had an independent spirit, which made him determined to take an independent, even crotchety, view of things. He was nonetheless open to argument and fond of discussion, though he stuck to his opinions. He wrote a long defence of his colonial administration in which the HBC, the Vancouver Island colony and Blanshard receive no notice: southern Africa, New Zealand and West Indian affairs were of more compelling concern to Grey.[389] There was no personal animus between Grey and Blanshard: both were hostages to fortune in Vancouver Island affairs.

With the passing of Blanshard and Grey, and James Douglas earlier, the old order was changing. British general and commissioner Charles Gordon was lost at Khartoum, and a frontier episode called the Jameson Raid brought a war in the Transvaal. An uprising was put down on the Upper Saskatchewan in 1885. Jingoism became the new creed of empire. When Blanshard passed from the scene, the addition of red or pink pieces on the British imperial map of the world continued unabated.

Colonel Richard Percival Davis, Richard's nephew, inherited Richard Blanshard's real estate and fixed assets. The probate of Blanshard's will dates to October 1894.[390] The "effects" of his estate are stated at £131,696 13s. 7d. and would be worth at least £14,250,000 today.

Colonel Davis's property, in the resort town of Walton-on-Naze, Essex, already exceeded 2,411 acres in 1875. Richard Blanshard's Essex property lay chiefly to the west of Walton and extended into Kirby-le-Soken. In short, Davis added further to these holdings, bringing in Richard's New House Farm. Thus, Walton and neighbouring Kirby-le-Soken became a considerable holding, ripe for agricultural development and, for the first time, tourist promotion. On the seashore, small-scale resort development, with connections by steamship and rail, and house construction were changing the character of the area. Many Londoners holidayed at Walton-on-Naze. The railway had come through in 1867, linking Walton with Colchester and Wivenhoe, regular haunts of Richard Blanshard.

His nephew, the Colonel, was of a different breed. He had spent his Army career in India, retiring from the Bengal Staff Corps in 1883. Back home in England, he turned to real estate development. He owned an early motor car. In a special waterfowl hunting boat, he made his way through marshy waters close to the thousand-acre Horsey Island, which Richard Blanshard's father had bought early in the century for the purposes of developing its agricultural potential. We last hear of Colonel Richard Percival Davis as one of the prominent figures of Essex County, a county councillor and high sheriff of Essex.[391]

No biography of Richard Blanshard would be complete without a closing reference to his nemesis, James Douglas. The latter had been the Company's first choice as governor, we recall. Politics then intervened and Blanshard was duly appointed. When Blanshard's resignation was accepted, Douglas's name was again brought forward. He reluctantly accepted, for to him obedience was the very first and most important of duties. He was already running the Company's far western empire. He faced immense problems and was masterful in management. He weathered many a storm. Sometimes he had to deal with a fractious council or legislative assembly. Political reform seemed always on the agenda, and he did not easily warm to innovations. Sharing power did not come to him naturally—except with those close to him, mainly family. Furthermore, there were problems of colonial defence, and in this matter he guarded Company independence as he had always done. Growth of the settlement was slow but steady, and he operated as circumstances required and as his Company superiors demanded. He was serving two masters, the Colonial Office (and the Crown) and the Hudson's Bay Company. Trade and empire seemed virtually synonymous.

Douglas, as governor, recognized the loss of his private life. Being a slave to the Colonial Office had its shortcomings. Evidence of this is disclosed in his private correspondence, when he told his son-in-law A.G. Dallas that he (Dallas) was probably better out of the lieutenant-governorship of Rupert's Land (which in 1869 became Canadian territory):

> *The Crown appointment of Rupert's Land would have given you, socially, a fine position and also provided what your mental & physical nature so much requires—a sphere of active usefulness. On the other hand, there are many objections—it is often a thankless and always a profitless office—the salary never pays one's expenses—so that one has to barter liberty, freedom and independence, to become at once the slave of the public, and a puppet in the hands of the Colonial Office, for a mere name, for a fleeting shadow. On the whole the appointment would not have promoted your happiness therefore you have no cause to regret this [loss].*[392]

Here is a fascinating reflective perception of the problems of governorship.

The Colony of Vancouver Island's progress under Douglas was one of fits and starts. Its growth was slow, its stature stunted. Take, for instance, the size of the incomer population that managed and developed the new economies of the colony. In the first census taken, to year-end 1854, the European or settler population of Vancouver Island numbered 774, of whom 265 were white women.[393] "Our colony is not increasing in population," Chief Factor Work confided to a friend. "I have already told you of the advantages of soil, climate, etc., which experience fully realizes. The home Government...leaves us to get on as best we may."[394]

With personal reluctance but at the demand of the Colonial Office, Douglas constituted a Legislative Assembly. He put the best face on it; duty called.[395] Douglas was proud of his achievement, even vain, and as such he was quite capable of high-sounding phrases that differed from the actual conditions in the colony.[396] Evidence of this is demonstrated in His Excellency's speech on 12 August 1856 at the inaugural meeting of the General Assembly of Vancouver Island.

The history and actual position of this colony are marked by many remarkable circumstances. Called into existence by an Act of the Supreme Government immediately after the discovery of gold in California, it has maintained an arduous and incessant struggle with the disorganizing effects on labour of that discovery. Remote from every other British settlement, with its commerce trammeled, and met with restrictive duties on every side, its trade and resources undeveloped.

Self-supporting and defraying all the expenses of its own government, it presents a striking contrast to every other colony in the British Empire, and like the native pines of its storm-beaten promontories, it has acquired a slow but hardy growth.

Its future progress must, under Providence, in a great measure depend on the intelligence, industry and enterprise of its inhabitants and upon the legislative wisdom of this assembly.[397]

Douglas had always feared American expansionist tendencies and squatters. The Haida Gwaii gold rush of 1850 foreshadowed the future. It disclosed Douglas's worst fears. He shared Blanshard's views. He warned the Colonial Office, on the basis of his discussions with American adventurers, that if their gold-seeking proved successful, Americans would "establish an independent government until by force or fraud they became annexed to the United States."[398] He had seen a variant of this in Oregon. And when gold was discovered in the bars of the Thompson and Fraser rivers, and miners and adventurers arrived in number, Douglas sent the colonial secretary this dire warning, dated 8 May 1858:

If the country be thrown open to indiscriminate immigration, the interests of the Empire may suffer from the introduction of a foreign population, whose sympathies may be decidedly anti-British. Taking that view of the question it assumes an alarming aspect, and suggests a doubt as to the policy of permitting the free entrance of foreigners into the British territory for residence without, in the first place, requiring them to take the oath of allegiance, and otherwise to give such security for their conduct as the Government of the country may deem it proper and necessary to require at their hands.[399]

Patriotism ran deep in Douglas, reflecting above all his Oregon rearguard actions and necessary retreat to Vancouver Island. In 1858, as governor, Douglas refused to allow a salute to be fired or a procession to be conducted in Victoria on the Fourth of July.[400]

London acted quickly. The Colonial Office, also fearful of American expansion, appointed the governor of Vancouver Island to be, in addition, governor of a new Colony of British Columbia, created by act of Parliament on 2 August 1858. It was proclaimed at Fort Langley, Fraser River, on 19 November that same year. This was "the natal day of British Columbia," Judge F.W. Howay remarked famously. Even so, the groundwork had been laid in Fort Victoria on 11 March 1850, when Blanshard read himself in under his Queen's commission.

The new mainland colony was born in crisis. It was a dreary, rainy day at Fort Langley. The procession landed from the veteran steamer *Beaver* and made its way on soggy ground to and through the gate. The Union Jack was run up. The party was accompanied by a guard of honour. A salute of eighteen guns was fired. In the teeming rain, the key persons took refuge in the principal building within the palisades. The governor read a proclamation dated 3 November stating that the Hudson's Bay Company's licence of exclusive trade with Indigenous peoples in the colony was revoked. The civil and criminal laws of England were acknowledged.

With all the pomp and circumstance that could be mustered, as suited such occasions, yet another formal dependency of the British Empire overseas had been proclaimed. This was Douglas's achievement, but it was fully manifested by the power and certitude of the secretary of state for the colonies, Sir Edward Bulwer-Lytton. With

Justly acclaimed lion of the British trading frontier, Sir James Douglas, KCB, knighted in 1863, was a master of business expansion, paranoid of American takeovers, and guardian of the realms of Vancouver Island and British Columbia. He succeeded Blanshard as governor of Vancouver Island. The Beaver, *September 1934*

a handful of officials, the rule of law was maintained, though not without complications.

Sir James Douglas, KCB, knighted in 1863 in recognition of twelve years' service, would retire from office in 1864, battle-worn and not a little scarred. In 1871 the United Colony of British Columbia joined the Dominion of Canada, becoming the sixth province of a transcontinental nation that had been forged into existence. Douglas may be pardoned for this self-serving reflection: "I cannot express the interest I feel in the welfare of these colonies [Vancouver Island and British Columbia]," he wrote to an associate on 10 December 1863. "They have for years been the objects of my tenderest care. Every step in the process of construction has been anxiously studied."[401]

Douglas lived his retirement years in Victoria, as did many of the commissioned field officers of the Company. The most senior Company officers of the Western Department acquired spacious acreages in greater Victoria. It may be roughly gauged that as of 1858 the HBC owned as much as did the private owners already listed. In short, the lands were owned by the Company or by persons connected to the Company. Their holdings dominate the official district map of 1858. First on the scene, and meeting qualifications for ownership, these persons had the advantage of being insiders, well placed to benefit themselves

A painting of Fort Victoria, circa 1860. *Image e000756686 courtesy of Library and Archives Canada*

and their corporate friends: Douglas had Fairfield (ironically, the same name as Blanshard's Hampshire estate); William Henry McNeill, south Oak Bay; John Work, Hillside and Gordon Head; John Tod, Estevan, Willows; William Fraser Tolmie, Mayfair and Burnside; Isabella Ross, widow of Charles Ross, Ross Bay. It was all in the family too. John Sebastian Helmcken and George Blenkinsop had holdings. Advantaged by his profession, colonial surveyor J.D. Pemberton obtained prime properties at going rates. Here was a gentry class, self-serving of course and ready to dispose of property to colonial newcomers who managed to arrive by sea from the distant British Isles. Unpleasant memories of frigid winters in isolated northern posts faded with the liveliness and the conviviality of young Victoria. These fur barons retired to comfortable circumstances. Some of them took up civic duties as managers of the new regime. Helmcken, in many ways an outsider to the old corporate breed, rose to exalted positions, becoming first Speaker of the Legislative Assembly, then leading the delegation to Ottawa that secured beneficial terms for British Columbia's union with Canada in 1871. It comes as no surprise to learn that when, in 1858, the town lots of Victoria had been at last laid out, they collectively approximated the lands owned by James Douglas.[402]

The life of Richard Blanshard provides fascinating insight into the experiences, toils, disasters and successes of a Victorian gentleman. A gentlemanly capitalist of the age that stood between the end of the Napoleonic Wars and the high tide of British imperial endeavour, he entered the field of colonial administration when the so-called Colonial Reformers were powerful and the "little Englanders" wanted to get rid of the Empire altogether. The governorship appealed to his ambition, and he was attracted to its prospects. He possessed the best of higher education and legal training; he was born to enterprise. His father and grandfather were self-made men who, by their willingness to take risk and their abilities to invest both wisely and in profitable speculations, broadened the fortunes of their families. The biographer is struck by the unity of the Blanshard family as a self-made unit of resilience within the larger field of industry, banking, shipping, plantations and other means of enterprise. They owed their lives and successes to no company. Rather, they were the originators of wealth and the promoters of commerce. Doubtless they represent thousands of their kind.

As to Richard Blanshard, he was a young man when he arrived at Vancouver Island. Handsome, articulate, intelligent and prepossessing, it is not surprising that he stood in wonder at the wilds that were presented to him. The whole vast domain was unsettled by Europeans, though heavily populated by Indigenous peoples. Much of it was unexplored. He became accustomed to the frontier life, though his stay was short. He had much to do, contrary to what many historical commentators have said. But in everything except spirituous liquor regulation, he was confined to dealing with matters related to solving troublesome problems between the Hudson's Bay Company and its employees. He oversaw the colony's accounts, including the financial terms of the deeds of conveyance, or "treaties," with various Indigenous groups. He fought back against US Army pressures to recover deserters who had escaped to Fort Victoria with ultimate intention of reaching the California goldfields by ship. Further, he sought to solve matters related to seized British shipping in Puget Sound waters. He feared for the security of the colony, as all his successors did. London was half a world away, and the Colonial Office was out of touch with realities on the frontier. The Navy was his guardian and the colony's too. The commanders-in-chief on the Pacific Station, and the officers and men of British warships, backed by the Admiralty and the Foreign Office, gave Blanshard every support, his only institutional aid.

The Fort Rupert coal speculation was a quagmire—Blanshard could see this clearly. The murder of Britons by the Nahwitti necessitated his intervention, and James Douglas agreed with the direction of this policy. Blanshard's rule was not to shoot first. All the same, one of Queen Victoria's little wars had occurred. Douglas called it the Nahwitti war. The Company always had the last word, outflanking the young governor. The machinery of justice, investigation and retaliation never ran smoothly, and Blanshard will likely never be free of charges that he made mistakes in bringing the matter to a close. A soiled reputation, even though inspired by the malicious intent of opponents, is hard to cleanse. Humankind seeks out the victims.

Blanshard faced dire illness in consequence of his travels to Vancouver Island and his life when there. This surely hampered his ability to carry out his duties. Perhaps, too, it clouded his vision. The tone of his letters to the Colonial Office discloses his razor-sharp mind but also his melancholic perspectives on a dismal and unproductive scene. He thought the system of colonization a dud, a folly. He correctly thought the Hudson's Bay Company and Puget's Sound Agricultural Company inseparable and conniving partners in a scheme to dominate all agricultural land in and near Fort Victoria—and thereby squeeze out the individual seekers of land. Both Douglas and the HBC in London balked at these charges. The Company imposed its will on the Colonial Office, for it was powerful in London and Westminster, just as it was powerful in Victoria and Vancouver's Island and its Dependencies. The Colonial Office was helpless and unhelpful. As demonstrated, the Company's importation of labourers and bailiffs was an artful scheme designed to keep the resources of the colony in its own hands. Settlers were not encouraged to stay; emigration schemes from the British Isles got little attention; and prospective Britons in California wanting to settle in Vancouver Island were discouraged. In regards to the latter, in 1865 Matthew Macfie, the Congregational Church minister of Victoria, wrote that "the system of petty despotism and caprice exercised by the heads of the company, together with the attempted monopoly of the available land convenient to the town, filled those intending settlers with disgust, and repelled them from the Colony."[403]

Blanshard, feeling the impotence of his position, had thrown away the reins of office. Resignation was a relief. From the outset the scheme held little promise. When James Douglas became governor of Vancouver Island in November 1851, he recommended to the London Committee several ameliorative changes, a liberalization of the rules, if you wish.[404] This coincided with the survey of the town of Victoria and the sale of city lots, as well as the laying out of a townsite at Esquimalt, as suggested by Blanshard. The reduction of the price of an acre of land from one pound to four shillings and two pence was but one of the changes. Another was that alien persons, taking an oath of allegiance, could pre-empt land. A land office was set up in Victoria. These and

A charming view of the entrance to the port of Victoria, showing Indigenous persons and canoes in the foreground while in the busy waterway sailing ships carry on the flourishing trade for which James Douglas had selected this locale. *Image c114507k courtesy of Library and Archives Canada*

other measures instituted by Governor Douglas and aided by Surveyor Pemberton sped the settling of Vancouver Island.[405]

Blanshard and Douglas were opposites, one the servant of the Crown, the other of the Company. They were irreconcilable in experience and character too. Blanshard was the intruder as far as Douglas was concerned. Douglas never understood the role of governor until he was vested with the attendant responsibilities—and even then he took them on reluctantly. He employed the position to the advantage of the Company until the Colonial Office demanded his dedication to the service of the Crown. A reluctant governor at first, he came to enjoy and exercise the power of the office. In all things, the Company's interests were to be protected as the shield of empire, even if its monopoly diminished. The character of European imperialism was largely determined not from the metropolis but on the spot. The remnant of the Oregon country that became, in time, British Columbia is an example of the multiplication of British responsibilities at the ends of the earth. The difficulties always arose on the border, the place of the turbulent frontier. So it was in Haida Gwaii and in the British Columbia gold rush.

British Columbia archivist Willard Ireland wrote tellingly of Governor Blanshard, "It is easy to belittle the significance of his work. The fact remains, however, that with his coming the rule of the fur trader gave way to the rule of the Crown. His was the distinction of being the first governor of that part of our province that was first brought under imperial rule. It was he who laid the constitutional foundations of our province."[406] British Columbia's colonial history is full of quizzical governors. Ridicule has been heaped on Blanshard's brief and uncomfortable tenure in the office, and it is usual to assume that Blanshard was insignificant. Times and circumstances did not favour him. As said, American Hubert Howe Bancroft's moniker for Blanshard was "son of misfortune." But Blanshard established civil government: he built the framework for subsequent administrators acting for the Crown. This was accomplished against the driving force of the largest corporate monopoly ever seen in northern and western Canada.

Blanshard found solace in the years after his time in what Douglas had called "the perfect Eden." As we have seen, he married Emily Hyde, lived a rich country life in Hampshire and Essex. He oversaw the family's extensive land and business holdings. He served as justice of the peace in both counties. He was an ardent and accomplished yachtsman. He and his wife were beneficent citizens and landowners in an age of self-help and extensive poverty. They had no issue. Their married life was cut short by her early death. Years of solitude followed for Richard Blanshard, but facing difficult circumstances on his own was nothing new to him. He never wrote of his experiences on the

Pacific margins of North America. He had said all he wanted to the inquiring committee of Parliament. The darkening shadows gathered. His life closed in a state of blindness and ill health. As governor of Vancouver Island, His Excellency Richard Blanshard left a legacy that bespeaks greatness: the establishment of government at Vancouver Island was preliminary to what is now British Columbia, Canada. That is his epitaph.

Author's Note and Acknowledgements

History's gold—the rich nuggets of fact that lead to historical understanding through analytical interpretation—are like the fabled treasures of the Sierra Madre. Finding nuggets is like moiling for tracings on some remote creek. But, aye, it's the search that's the thing! For most of my life as a historian I have chased after the treasures that form this book. My rule of thumb has been to consult documents in their original form. I examined Admiralty, Colonial Office and Hudson's Bay Company records in the late 1960s, all in London.

I recall winter days in Beaver House, Great Trinity Lane, City of London, then the headquarters of the Hudson's Bay Company. The portico above the main entrance boasted a bas-relief of the ship *Nonsuch*, with text declaring that Captain Zachary Gilliam had sailed from Gravesend to Hudson Bay on 3 June 1668, and beneath it again there's a beaver, carved into the stone. I was guided through corporate records by the archivist, Miss Alice Johnson. Pleasant interruptions came at eleven o'clock and then again at three, when the tinkling bell announced the arrival of the tea trolley and a lovely cuppa and a biscuit. From below through the floorboards arose the pungent aroma of skins of fur-bearing animals soon to be auctioned off. Come closing hour I was obliged by Company rules to leave my notes for inspection overnight, presumably so that the archivist could see what nuggets of history's gold had been unearthed in those papers—and to keep an eye on an errant snoop. The Company, conscious of its role in history, wanted no stains on its corporate memory. I was breaking ground on an unexplored subject, so I was an object of curiosity. No bar of access to documents was raised. I posed no difficulty to the guardian archivist, and overnight the Company learned more about Fort Victoria and its letters (a volume they later published in the Hudson's Bay Record Society series). I was happy to be the light that lit that trail.

To return to those days of sharper eyesight, using pencil only to make notes on four-by-six-inch cards, without access to a photocopier or the use of a camera, reminds me how advantaged the scholar is today. All the same, there is no substitute for seeing the original and mining its jewelled treasures. In later years I researched in the same files, in microfilms held in Library and Archives Canada, Ottawa, and in the British Columbia Archives, Royal British Columbia Museum, Victoria. Digitalization has allowed me to catch up: Colonial Office correspondence for Vancouver Island and British Columbia can now be traced on BC Genesis Project (bcgenesis.uvic.ca), University of Victoria.

It is always hard to put ourselves in other people's shoes. From my early days as a working historian, the name Richard Blanshard, first governor of the Colony of Vancouver Island, caught my attention. Why, I wondered, was a young British barrister-at-law administering an infant British colony on the Northwest Coast, one run by fur traders? One looks longingly for answers. Seldom is he mentioned in the annals of British Columbia. *Miraculous* is the word best used when Blanshard's name appears in a Canadian history book, even one devoted to British Columbia! His arrival commenced formal British rule, law and practice in western North America. Writers nowadays prefer to start with that heroic titan James (later Sir James) Douglas, Blanshard's successor. Indeed, there is a tendency to favour the Hudson's Bay Company as the prototype of colonization and development, disregarding at the same time its detractors, challengers and opponents. That the Hudson's Bay Company was "a Good Thing," to use the judgment of the author of *1066 and All That*—just as the North-West Mounted Police (later the Royal Canadian Mounted Police) was "a Good Thing" for establishing law and order in the Canadian Prairies and later the Northwest Territories and Yukon—is a matter not at issue. It is beneath the scenes where historical reality lies, the cut and thrust of people and movement, of character and circumstance. The inquisitive reader yearns to learn more about struggles for authority, motivations of participants, and roots of power and influence, all the while keeping in mind the rivals, the ardent contenders and even those consigned to the shadows. Indigenous peoples of the far west knew of coal, gold and copper deposits before Europeans arrived; indeed, they guided newcomers to the surest locations. The area, as said, was natural space in which Indigenous peoples had lived for perhaps ten thousand years—a space, too, of diverse languages and dialects, polities, village sites, histories and legend. These peoples were swept along in rapidly changing, irreversible circumstances. Pestilence made terrible inroads. Much would be modified and, in cases, irrevocably changed by tides of empire sweeping these shores. Change was rapid as European influences advanced. The story is rife with turmoil and dislocation: I have written about these matters elsewhere, notably in *Gunboat Frontier*, a study of areas or zones of conflict in British Columbia, Washington State and Alaska, 1846 to 1890. There I examined the problems and effects of Indigenous consumption of spirituous liquor and the eradication of slavery. In the present work, I do not aim to provide a general appreciation of these matters, only to deal with them in the context of Governor Blanshard's period in office. Here, different themes and subthemes command attention, notably executive action and warnings given to London about local conditions—and London's reaction.

Blanshard's diaries do not survive. Nor do his private papers. The fetid waters of the Chagres River in Panama claimed them all during his homeward passage. Correspondence with family and friends cannot be traced either. Fortunately, there are many contemporary first-hand witnesses. Online research in British files has unearthed material that gives insights into his personal wealth, rank and station; residences, education, legal training and soldiering; and marriage, yachting pursuits and country properties in Durham, Hampshire and Essex. Marriage records, wills and probate records provide amazing detail. Pertinent records are held in the British Columbia Archives (notably papers of Sir James Douglas and Dr. John Sebastian Helmcken); the National Archives, Kew, England (where Colonial Office papers are housed); and the National Maritime Museum, Greenwich (where insights are to be uncovered about Blanshard's reliance on the Royal Navy). Hudson's Bay Company Archives (now in the Archives of Manitoba, Winnipeg) are rich in detail. New material continues to come to light, such as W.S. Tolmie letters, digital copies of post journals, and notes by Blanshard's manservant. Of the above, the only complete file is the Colonial Office series on Vancouver Island (CO

305/1-3); this is in the National Archives, Kew. Among those moul-
dering files, in elegant longhand or awkward scribble, is to be found
the cut and thrust of history; the researcher can recreate the "official
mind" of British imperial activities at work in Whitehall and in the
wilderness, at home and in the colony. Blanshard's despatches and HBC
records form the bedrock of this book. Quotations that pepper my
text are taken from manuscript and printed sources of the age rather
than from secondary works. I hope in this way to have retained something of the raw feelings and the tortuous outlook of that bygone age.
I have benefited from certain texts prepared for H.H. Bancroft, in the
Bancroft Library, University of California, Berkeley; also papers on the
seizure of the *Albion* in the Beinecke Library, Yale University. Details of
Royal Navy ships derive from the P.W. Brock files, Maritime Museum
of British Columbia, Victoria.

This is not a study in Indigenous treaties and land claims; rather
it is a biography of Blanshard. As governor, he did not address matters related to Indigenous peoples except in regards to the security of
the colony, its settlers and HBC trading. The colonial project was only
just beginning. The reader is reminded that in this work we are at the
entry point of colonization and formal empire. Matters of gender fall
beyond the compass of this work, as do sexually transmitted diseases.
By contrast, liquor consumption and Blanshard's executive action of
prohibition are examined here. Indigenous slavery was coerced out of
existence by the civil power backed by the Royal Navy, and that was the
work of decades.

Place names, more contentious now than ever, are based on the
works of Robert Galois, Andrew Scott and John Walbran (see bibliography). Indigenous names, places and populations for the 1850s are
difficult to state with certainty. For populations, I have been guided
by James Mooney, Wilson Duff, and Randy Bouchard and Dorothy
Kennedy (see bibliography). Abraham P. Nasatir's rare compilation
of documents (including Admirals' papers) on British activities in
California and Oregon has been of immense value.

The historian toils alone but cannot complete the writing of a
book without help. Vancouver Island's colonial history is complex;
even the chronology seems disjointed. For guidance, I have many to

thank. Willard Ireland, W. Kaye Lamb and Margaret Ormsby encouraged my naval and colonial studies in dark days when, in the face of rising social history, demography and statistical analysis, my choices for research had gone out of fashion. I have been guided by recent works on Vancouver Island by Richard Somerset Mackie, Stephen Royle, David Rossiter and Daniel Clayton. John S. Galbraith's knowledge of the Hudson's Bay Company's expansion, consolidation and contraction in western North America in the nineteenth century is demonstrated in his magisterial book. Gloria Griffen Cline's life of Peter Skene Ogden brought insights into critical events in western America during the mid-nineteenth century. I thank John Motherwell for sources and Andrew Loudon for biographical materials, census and probate records. I also thank Steve Anderson, Jack Bryden, Britta Bryden, John Clifford, John Dewhirst, Jan Drent, Caroline Duncan, Helen Edwards, Joe Fama, James Hendrickson, Arifin Graham, Rear Admiral C.H. Layman, Wilfred Lund, John Lutz, Charles Maier, David Thornton McNab, Gary Mitchell, Denton Pendergast, Fern Perkins, Lincoln Rutter, Anna Sander, Geoffrey Stevenson, Kenton Storey, Judy Thompson, Neville Thompson, Camilla Turner, Frances Welwood, Ron Welwood, John Whittaker and Patrick S. Wolfe. Once again, abundant thanks to Marilyn and the eternal flame of wisdom.

I thank my esteemed editor, Audrey McClellan, and the publisher and staff at Harbour Publishing. I alone am responsible for opinions expressed and errors committed.

Barry Gough
Victoria, BC, Canada

Appendix:
"Memorial to His Excellency
Richard Blanshard"

The document printed here was signed by nearly all the independent settlers of the Colony of Vancouver's Island and its Dependencies, and by the Reverend Robert John Staines, the Hudson's Bay Company's chaplain at Fort Victoria. It does not bear a date, but was likely drawn up on 29 August 1851. This document was prepared without loss of time when it was learned that the governor's resignation had been accepted by Earl Grey, secretary of state for the colonies, and that Blanshard was on the eve of his departure.

The Memorial states succinctly the position of the colonists, and it sets forth so plainly their idea of the Hudson's Bay Company that it earns a place among the few early state papers of the Colony of Vancouver Island. The settlers were reform-minded. The Company saw them as troublemakers. All the same, this is a statement advocating political reform and the protection of rights and liberties, and for these reasons alone takes its place in Canadian constitutional history.

Sometime after his return to London, Blanshard sent a copy to the Colonial Office. On 15 June 1857 Blanshard, as a witness, and asked about the grievances listed in the Memorial, produced a copy of the document for the parliamentary committee on the Hudson's Bay Company. It was printed in full in the Report from the Select Committee on the Hudson's Bay Company; together with the Proceedings of the Committee, Minutes of Evidence, Appendix and Index *(p. 293). It is reprinted here in full:*

To His Excellency RICHARD BLANSHARD, Esquire, Governor of Vancouver Island

May it please Your Excellency,
We, the undersigned, inhabitants of Vancouver's Island, having

learned with regret that your Excellency has resigned the government of this colony, and understanding that the government has been committed to a chief factor of the Hudson's Bay Company, cannot but express our unfeigned surprise and deep concern at such an appointment.

The Hudson's Bay Company being, as it is, a great trading body, must necessarily have interests clashing with those of independent colonists. Most matters of a political nature will cause a contest between the agents of the Company and the colonists. Many matters of a judicial nature also, will, undoubtedly, arise in which the colonists and the Company (or its servants) will be contending parties, or the upper servants and the lower servants of the Company will be arrayed against each other. We beg to express in the most emphatical and plainest manner, our assurance that impartial decisions cannot be expected from a Governor, who is not only a member of the Company, sharing its profits, his share of such profits rising and falling as they rise and fall, but is also charged as their chief agent with the sole representation of their trading interests in this island and the adjacent coast.

Furthermore, thus situated, the colony will have no security that its public funds will be duly disposed of solely for the benefit of the colony in general, and not turned aside in any degree to be applied to the private purposes of the Company, by disproportionate sums being devoted to the improvement of that tract of land held by them, or otherwise unduly employed.

Under these circumstances, we beg to acquaint your Excellency with our deep sense of the absolute necessity there is, for the real good and welfare of the colony, that a council should be immediately appointed, in order to provide some security that the interests of the Hudson's Bay Company shall not be allowed to outweigh and ruin those of the colony in general.

We, who join in expressing these sentiments to your Excellency are unfortunately but a very small number, but we respectfully beg your Excellency to consider that we, and we alone, represent the interests of the island as a free and independent British colony, for we constitute the whole body of the independent settlers, all the other inhabitants being in some way or other so connected with and controlled by the

Hudson's Bay Company, as to be deprived of freedom of action in all matters relating to the public affairs of the colony, some indeed by their own confession, as may be proved if necessary. And we further allege our firm persuasion, that the untoward influences to which we have adverted above are likely, if entirely unguarded against, not only to prevent any increase of free and independent colonists in the island, but positively to diminish their present numbers.

We therefore humbly request your Excellency to take into your gracious consideration the propriety of appointing a Council before your Excellency's departure, such being the most anxious and earnest desire of your Excellency's most obedient and humble servants, and Her Majesty's most devoted and loyal subjects.

(Signed)
James Yates, Landowner
Robert John Staines, Trinity Hall, Cambridge,
    Chaplain to the Honourable Hudson's Bay Company
James Cooper, Merchant and Landowner
Thomas Monroe, Lessee of Captain Grant's Land at Sooke
William M'Donald, Carpenter and Householder
James Sangster, Settler
John Muir, sen., Settler, Sooke
William Fraser, Settler, Sooke
Andrew Muir, Settler, Sooke
John M'Gregor, Settler, Sooke
John Muir, jnr., Settler, Sooke
Michael Muir, Settler, Sooke
Robert Muir, Settler, Sooke
Archibald Muir, Settler, Sooke
Thomas Blinkhorn, Settler, Michousan

Endnotes

Chapter 1: "Faraway World"

1 *Splendor sine occasu*—"Splendour without ceasing"—is the motto of the Province of British Columbia.

2 Robert Galois, "Measles, 1847–1850: The First Modern Epidemic in British Columbia," BC *Studies* 109 (Spring 1996): 43.

3 Never in a political sense were the Songhees a single tribe, according to Wilson Duff. The total population of these groups in 1850 was 700 (J. Douglas census). James Mooney, *The Aboriginal Population of America North of Mexico* (Washington: Smithsonian, 1928), 28. In regards to the Straits Salish (of which the Songhees and Esquimalt Nations are part), Wilson Duff lists all the tribes and bands as of the year 1850, their names listed by Reserve Commissioner in 1916, and the individual band names and population in 1963. Wilson Duff, *The Indian History of British Columbia: Volume 1, The Impact of the White Man* (Victoria: Provincial Museum of British Columbia, 1964), 28.

4 Quoted in James G. Swan, *The Northwest Coast or, Three Years' Residence in Washington Territory* (1857; Seattle: University of Washington Press, 1972), 67. The 1972 printing contains an introduction by Norman H. Clark that is highly critical of us policy toward Indigenous peoples. Doubtless, Richard Blanshard was familiar with Captain Vancouver's perspective, published in *Voyage to the North Pacific*, 3 volumes (London, 1798). Blanshard would also have been familiar with the *Atlas* that accompanied Vancouver's account, containing the famed (but then incomplete) chart of Vancouver Island. Preliminary surveys of Esquimalt and Victoria, respectively, were undertaken by Her Majesty's brig *Pandora*, Commander James Wood, and HMS *Herald*, Captain Henry Kellett. Master W.W. Dillon's surveys of Shushartie Bay and the western entrance to Beaver Harbour were published by the Hydrographer to the Admiralty in 1851. Systematic surveying of these waters to high standard was not commenced until Captain G.H. Richards's prodigious work in the late 1850s and early 1860s. The Admiralty's *Sailing Directions* for Vancouver Island and the southern coast were first published in 1864.

5 Historic site plaque of the Victoria Historical Society and Oak Bay Municipality, 1994, corner of Beach Drive and Oliver Street in Oak Bay, BC. In July 1842, Douglas and six men proceeded from Nisqually in the *Cadboro* to the south end of Vancouver Island. They made a careful survey of its several ports and harbours, and Douglas chose a site for the proposed establishment in what he called "the port of Camosack." He thought this decidedly the most advantageous situation for the limited measures and means required for a marine depot. (He was not thinking of it as an urban cluster and the capital of a province within the Canadian federation!) The prospect of open lands with agricultural potential ranked high in his calculations. Fresh water would probably, he concluded, be found sufficient for the establishment in very dry seasons.

6 By the treaty between Russia and the United Kingdom, the 141st degree of west longitude to the Arctic Ocean established Alaska's eastern boundary and British North America's northwestern boundary in these latitudes. The United States was not party to this designation. The United States purchased Russian America in 1867.

7 In the House of Lords, 29 June 1849, re the Hudson's Bay Company being granted Vancouver Island for colonization, the Earl of Aberdeen, foreign secretary in 1846 at the time terms of the Oregon Treaty were being agreed, "applauded the arrangement with the Company, the settlement of Vancouver's Island having been the only subject that occasioned him, when in office, any anxiety for the preservation of peace." From *Annual Register 1849* (London, 1849), 131. For the view that this was a "sell-out" of British interests, see James R. Gibson, *Farming*

the *Frontier: The Agricultural Opening of the Oregon Country, 1786–1846* (Vancouver: UBC Press, 1985), 202–5.

8 It may be argued that Fort Vancouver was doomed from the outset, though we know that only from hindsight. The entrance to the Columbia River was hazardous to shipping and often a graveyard of ships, and Nisqually and Victoria assumed enhanced positions in corporate plans. In 1845 the Company began to shift its marine department headquarters to Victoria. Fort Vancouver had outlived its usefulness as the hub of Company trade in the Pacific. The student of these affairs needs to ask if the Company's withdrawal from the lower Columbia weakened the British diplomatic posture leading up to the treaty. British travellers to Fort Vancouver expressed no sympathy for backing the Company under pressure of American settlers (in 1846 numbering a formidable five thousand).

9 Rear Admiral Phipps Hornby to Sec. of the Admiralty J. Parker, 14 November 1849, PHI/2/1, 207–8, National Maritime Museum (hereafter NMM).

10 C.R. Johnson, Service Record, Admiralty Papers (hereafter Adm) 3/39; W.R. O'Byrne, *Naval Biographical Dictionary* (London, 1849), 585. Also, Rear Admiral P.W. Brock, dossier of the *Driver*, copy, Maritime Museum of British Columbia (hereafter MMBC). Extensive particulars about the *Driver* are in David Lyon and Rif Winfield, *The Sail and Steam Navy List: All the Ships of the Royal Navy, 1815–1889* (London: Chatham, 2004), 160.

11 Earl Grey, minute of 24 June 1848, Colonial Office Papers (hereafter CO) 305/1; Grey to Sir J. Pelly, 20 June 1849, CO 305/2.

12 Stephen Royle, *Company, Crown and Colony: The Hudson's Bay Company and Territorial Endeavour in Western Canada* (London: I.B. Tauris, 2011), 151.

13 Details based on observations and experience of Peter Skene Ogden, early 1852. See Gloria Griffen Cline, *Peter Skene Ogden and the Hudson's Bay Company* (Norman: University of Oklahoma Press, 1974), 203.

14 This dates from 1859. See Matthew Macfie, *Vancouver Island and British Columbia: Their History, Resources and Prospects* (London: Longman, Green, 1865), 8.

15 Instructions to Cdr. C.R. Johnson from Phipps Hornby, 16 January 1850, Adm 50/253.

16 Captain John Shepherd, for one, had sent the C-in-C a glowing report on the provisions (vegetables and beef, principally) that the HBC could always provide the Navy, but that was before the California gold rush, when all sorts of foreign and British merchant vessels called at Fort Victoria and Esquimalt looking for food. First come, first served. Rear Admiral Fairfax Moresby was highly critical of the HBC's boastfulness of always being able to supply Royal Navy ships with provisions, but to this and other charges, James Douglas always had an explanation in defence to give to London headquarters so as to deflect or counter accusations. Douglas was a master of politics, the great prototype of British Columbia premiers, who knew the unique particulars of the political economy of this far-flung realm of imperial power, this strange foothold of empire.

17 Thomas Robinson, journal entry for 8 March 1850, Add MSS 1007, BC Archives (hereafter BCA).

18 Although James Douglas spelled it *Camosack*, and the pertinent two treaties of 13 April 1850, with the Kosampson and Swengwhung, give it as *Camoson*, Roderick Finlayson, in charge of the post and in regular contact with the local Indigenous peoples, spelled it *Camosun*. This last has become the customary spelling and is best relied on, given Finlayson's familiarity with the matter.

19 Fern Perkins, "Graveyard Gleanings: The Building of Fort Victoria with the French Canadian and Metis Construction Crew," *Stories in Stone* (Old Cemeteries Society, special number, Fort Victoria 170 Years) 23, no. 1 (Spring 2013): 27.

Endnotes

20 Penelope Edmonds, *Urbanizing Frontiers: Indigenous Peoples and Settlers in 19th-Century Pacific Rim Cities* (Vancouver: UBC Press, 2010), 26–28. The author examines, in comparative perspective, Victoria on Vancouver Island and Port Phillip/Melbourne, Australia.

21 Captain John T. Walbran, *British Columbia Coast Names, 1592–1906* (Vancouver: Douglas & McIntyre, 1977), 512 (hereafter Walbran).

22 On this point, see Jean Barman, "Race, Greed, and Something More," in *On the Cusp of Contact: Gender, Space and Race in the Colonization of British Columbia*, ed. Margery Fee (Madeira Park: Harbour Publishing, 2020), 6.

23 On labour and economic contributions of the local Nations, see extensive treatment by John Sutton Lutz, *Makúk: A New History of Aboriginal-White Relations* (Vancouver: UBC Press, 2008), esp. ch. 4. Also, Kenton Storey, *Settler Anxiety at the Outposts of Empire: Colonial Relations, Humanitarian Discourses, and the Imperial Press* (Vancouver: UBC Press, 2016). These matters bear on larger issues of world history. A school of historiography argues that local Indigenous persons and agencies were collaborators in the processes of empire and not, retrospectively, victims of them. This is significant. As in "missionary studies," the question arises as to the role subjects contribute to their own conversion to Christianity or, indeed, to colonization by outsiders. The key term, to my way of thinking, is *collaboration* or *accommodation*. Old ideas of empire formation have been demolished. The champion of this line of reasoning, Ronald Robinson, led the way in his widely accepted "Non-European Foundations of European Imperialism: Sketch for a Theory of Collaboration," in *Studies in the Theory of Imperialism*, eds. Roger Owen and Bob Sutcliffe (London: Longmans, 1972).

24 All fourteen Fort Victoria, or Douglas, or Vancouver Island treaties are printed in British Columbia, *Papers Connected with the Indian Land Question, 1850–1875* (Victoria: Queen's Printer, 1875), 5–11. The Lekwungen document was signed on 13 April 1850 by Snaw-nuck and twenty-nine others. Dr. Alfred Robson Benson and Joseph William McKay signed for the Company.

25 The recent review of this is Peter Cook et al., *To Share, Not Surrender: Indigenous and Settler Visions of Treaty-Making in the Colonies of Vancouver Island and British Columbia* (Vancouver: UBC Press, 2021).

26 See Lutz, *Makúk*, 48–49. See also, among other studies, Edmonds, *Urbanizing Frontiers*.

27 James Swan reports this in *The Northwest Coast or, Three Years' Residence in Washington Territory*.

28 We sense here the social instincts of correction and improvement that would come to dominate the Victorian age, though locally confined to few persons (clergy, police, governor). Sources used include Bishop of Columbia to Governor A. Kennedy, 6 February 1866; Rev. Garrett to Kennedy, 5 February 1866; and P. Hankin to Kennedy, 8 February 1866; also Kennedy to Colonial Office, 1 March 1866; all printed, and published in a Confidential Print, in CO 880/5.

29 Franz Boas, *The Kwakiutl of Vancouver Island* (New York: G.E. Stechert, 1909), 444–45.

30 Quoted in E.O.S. Scholefield and F.W. Howay, *History of British Columbia* (Vancouver: Clark, 1914), 3:786, 789. Henceforth cited as Scholefield and Howay, *British Columbia*.

31 Proceedings at Fort Victoria are based on entries for 1 January to 9 March 1850, Fort Victoria Post Journal, B 226/b/3, Hudson's Bay Company Archives (hereafter HBCA).

32 Dr. John S. Helmcken, quoted in Walbran, 40–41.

33 A description of the steamer *Beaver* from the 1850s, published in the *Victoria Gazette* in December 1859.

34 John Work and Josette were married under the rites of the Church of England in Victoria on 9 November 1849. They had eleven children.

35 Walbran, 41.

36 Presumably, Blanshard settled his manservant's mess account.

37 Patricia Meyer, ed., *Honoré-Timothée Lempfrit, OMI, His Oregon Trail Journal and Letters from the Pacific Northwest, 1848–1853* (Fairfield, WA: Ye Galleon Press, 1985), 210.

38 Blanshard to Douglas, 26 June 1850, Vancouver Island Correspondence Outward, C/AA/10.4/1, BCA.

39 Cdr. R. Johnson to Phipps Hornby, 21 June 1850, PHI/3/5, NMM. The ship's proceedings may be followed in log Adm 53/3837.

40 Dorothy Blakey Smith, ed., *The Reminiscences of John Sebastian Helmcken* (Vancouver: UBC Press, 1975), 83 and n. 1. Henceforth cited as Helmcken, *Reminiscences*.

41 In September 1843, Captain Allan Scarborough of the *Cadboro* spent nearly a week marking this difficult channel (laying buoys and other markers) into Victoria's Inner Harbour. See Journal of the Schooner *Cadboro*, July to December 1843, BCA.

42 See sources cited in Dorothy O. Johansen and Charles M. Gates, *Empire of the Columbia: A History of the Pacific Northwest*, 2nd ed. (New York: Harper & Row, 1967), 207, n. 1.

43 Quoted in G. Hollis Slater, "Reverend Robert John Staines: Pioneer Priest, Pedagogue, and Political Agitator," *British Columbia Historical Quarterly* 14, no. 4 (October 1950): 196.

44 Eden Colvile to George Simpson, 15 October 1849, in E.E. Rich, ed., *London Correspondence Inward from Eden Colvile 1849–1852* (London: Hudson's Bay Record Society, 1956), 182. Henceforth *Eden Colvile*.

45 Quoted in Slater, "Reverend Robert John Staines," 199.

Chapter 2: "The Rivals"

46 *Daily News* (London), 17 February 1849. Also, CO 305/2, 137–39.

47 "Vancouver's Island: Copy of Correspondence between the Chairman of the Hudson's Bay Company and the Secretary of State for the Colonies, Relative to the Colonization of Vancouver Island, ordered by the House of Commons to be Printed, 10 August 1848," *Parliamentary Papers*, 619. This was the first of many such; the next was in March 1849. Public accountability was the order of the day, as was transparency. The conduct of colonial affairs lay under great suspicion: not on whether there should be colonial expansion, but on how it should be done and by whom.

48 It has often been suggested that the post was first called Fort Albert and Fort Camosun, but in HBC files it is always referred to as Fort Victoria.

49 This point, based on George Simpson's views, is cogently advanced by Gibson, *Farming the Frontier*, 61.

50 G. Simpson to Governor and Committee, 1 March 1842, in Glyndwr Williams, ed., *London Correspondence Inward from Sir George Simpson* (London: Hudson's Bay Record Society, 1973), 107.

51 From Berthold Seeman, *The Voyage of H.M.S. Herald, 1845–51*, 2 volumes (London: Reeve, 1853), ch. 8; quoted in Scholefield and Howay, *British Columbia*, 1:483–84.

52 Great Britain, Parliament, *Report from the Select Committee on the Hudson's Bay Company*, 1857, 335.

53 This was 1853, when Captain J. Alden of the US revenue and surveying vessel *Active* paid a courtesy visit. James S. Lawson, "Autobiography," manuscript, 1879, p. 72, P-A 44, Hubert Howe Bancroft Collection, Bancroft Library, University of California, Berkeley (hereafter HHB).

54 Although see "The Rent Ceremony" on the Hudson's Bay Company History Foundation website for descriptions of the four rent ceremonies that occurred in the twentieth century: www.hbcheritage.ca/history/fur-trade/the-rent-ceremony.

Endnotes

55 J. Staines to Edward Cridge, 10 October 1849, in Slater, "Reverend Robert John Staines," appendix, 237.

56 "An Act for regulating the Fur Trade, and establishing a Criminal and Civil Jurisdiction within certain Parts of North America," United Kingdom, Statutes of the Realm, 1&2 Geo. IV, c.66.

57 W.S. Wallace, ed., *John McLean's Notes of a Twenty-Five Years' Service in the Hudson's Bay Territory* (Toronto: Champlain Society, 1932), 5. This work was first published in 1849 by the reputable London publisher Richard Bentley, "Publisher in Ordinary to Her Majesty," and it may be suggested that Blanshard was familiar with what was then a recently published book. For McLean's "character assassination" of Sir George Simpson, see Champlain Society edition, 383–90.

58 John S. Galbraith, *The Little Emperor: Governor Sir George Simpson of the Hudson's Bay Company* (Toronto: Macmillan of Canada, 1976), 62.

59 Robert Michael Ballantyne, *Snowflakes and Sunbeams; or The Young Fur-Traders* (London: Ward, Lock, 1856), 33.

60 Wallace, ed., *John McLean's Notes of a Twenty-Five Years' Service in the Hudson's Bay Territory*, 333.

61 Quoted in Donald W. Meinig, *The Great Columbia Plain: A Historical Geography, 1808–1910* (Seattle: University of Washington Press, 1968), 100.

62 G. Simpson to P.S. Ogden, 14 March 1825, D 4/5, fols.16d-17d, HBCA.

63 John S. Galbraith, *The Hudson's Bay Company as an Imperial Factor, 1821–1869* (Berkeley and Los Angeles: University of California Press, 1957), 12.

64 Ibid.

65 Ibid.

66 Fern Perkins, "Tombstone Tourist: A Journey back to the Early Years of Charles and Isabella Ross," *Stories in Stone* (Old Cemeteries Society, special number, Fort Victoria 170 Years) 23, no. 1 (Spring 2013): 23–26. Widow Ross was buried in her own land. For Ross and other important examples, see, superbly illustrated with maps, Sylvia Van Kirk, "Colonised Lives: The Native Wives and Daughters of Five Founding Families of Victoria," in *Pacific Empires: Essays in Honour of Glyndwr Williams*, Alan Frost and Jane Samson, eds. (Carlton South: Melbourne University Press, 1999), 215–33.

67 To review: Charles Ross had been placed in charge at Fort Victoria, with Roderick Finlayson second-in-command. In 1844 Ross died and Finlayson succeeded to the post. When Douglas was sent to Fort Victoria from Fort Vancouver, Finlayson was relieved of his duties to a certain extent. He was made head accountant and remained in that capacity until 1862. He was made chief trader in 1850, and in 1859 received his commission as chief factor.

68 Perkins, "Graveyard Gleanings," 28–29.

69 Captain Courtney to Phipps Hornby, 15 November 1848, PHI 2/1.86-87, NMM.

70 Ballantyne, *Snowflakes and Sunbeams*, 20.

71 Helmcken, *Reminiscences*, 281.

72 Edgar Fawcett, *Some Reminiscences of Old Victoria* (Toronto: William Briggs, 1912), 26–27.

73 Fort Victoria journal, 11 March 1850.

74 Authoritative studies are Robert H. Ruby and John A. Brown, *Indian Slavery in the Pacific Northwest* (Spokane: Arthur H. Clark, 1993), and Leland Donald, *Aboriginal Slavery on the Northwest Coast of North America* (Berkeley and Los Angeles: University of California Press, 1997).

75 Blanshard to Grey, 8 April 1850, CO 308/2. Blanshard answered directly to the Colonial Office, not the Company, though copies of Blanshard's letters were routinely sent to the Company for information (in this case, the letter is to be found in A 8/6, ff. 104–6, HBCA).

76 Douglas to A.C. Anderson, 18 March 1850, quoted in Walter N. Sage, *Sir James Douglas and British Columbia* (Toronto: University of Toronto Press, 1930), 157–58.

77 Quoted, Sage, *Sir James Douglas and British Columbia*, 157–58.

78 W.K. Lamb, "Some Notes on the Douglas Family," *British Columbia Historical Quarterly* 17 (January–April 1953): 42–43.

79 Quoted in Glyndwr Williams, ed., *Hudson's Bay Miscellany, 1670–1870* (Winnipeg: Hudson's Bay Record Society, 1975), 205.

80 William Connolly to Simpson, 27 February 1829, D 4/122, fols. 27-30d, HBCA.

81 Margaret A. Ormsby, "Sir James Douglas," *Dictionary of Canadian Biography*, vol. 10, www.biographi.ca/en/bio/douglas_james_10E.html.

82 General Joel Palmer's and Joseph Watt's recollections of Douglas, 1844, are in General Palmer's Narratives, 14 June 1878, pp. 14–16, P-A 58, HHB. For related views, see Barry M. Gough, ed., "Sir James Douglas as Seen by His Contemporaries: A Preliminary List," BC *Studies* 44 (Winter 1979/1980): 32–40.

83 Adapted from quote in Jean Friesen, "George Hills," *Dictionary of Canadian Biography*, vol. 12, www.biographi.ca/en/bio/hills_george_12E.html.

84 In addition to Sage's *Sir James Douglas*, cited above, attention is drawn to M. Ormsby's entry on Douglas in *Dictionary of Canadian Biography* cited previously. It contains a comprehensive list of primary sources. See also biographies by Dorothy Blakey Smith, Derek Pethick, John Adams and others. Quotations are from William Joseph Trimble, *The Mining Advance into the Inland Empire* (1909; Fairfield, WA: Ye Galleon Press, 1986), 193. G.M. Sproat was an ethnologist, entrepreneur and devoted contributor/advisor to the Archivist of British Columbia; the second observation about Douglas being well liked by "the boys" is by one William Stout, a steamer captain who visited Fort Victoria in the 1840s.

85 Sage, *Sir James Douglas*, 112.

86 Douglas to P.S. Ogden, 14 August 1850, Fort Victoria, B 226/b/3, f.5d, HBCA.

87 William R. Kennedy, *Sporting Adventures in the Pacific whilst in Command of the "Reindeer"* (London: Sampson Low, 1876), 189.

88 See Barry Gough, *Britannia's Navy on the West Coast of North America, 1812–1914* (Victoria: Heritage House, 2016), ch. 5.

89 See "Five Letters of Charles Ross, 1842–44," *British Columbia Historical Quarterly* 7, no. 2 (April 1943): 103–18.

90 For discussion, see Barry Gough, *Gunboat Frontier: British Maritime Authority and Northwest Coast Indians, 1846–1890* (Vancouver: UBC Press, 1984), ch. 1; also illustrations (and captions) plates 1, 2 and 3 show 250 seamen and marines of HMS *Constance*, 1848, in a display of force. See also Helmcken, *Reminiscences*, 26–27.

Chapter 3: "Frontier Frictions"

91 Blanshard to Johnson, 15 March 1850, Fort Victoria, encl. 1 in Johnson to Phipps Hornby, 21 June 1850, PHI 3/5, NMM.

92 George Dickey, ed., *The Journal of Occurrences at Fort Nisqually, 1833–1859* (Tacoma: Metropolitan Park District, 1988), entry for 26 September 1849.

93 Paul Kane, who painted his portrait in oils in 1847, calls him Che-a-Clack, Chief of the Sangeys.

94 Galbraith, *Hudson's Bay Company as an Imperial Factor*, ch. 10. See also Brian Coyle, "The Puget's Sound Agricultural Company on Vancouver Island, 1847–1857," MA thesis, Simon Fraser University, 1977. Coyle explains that the development of early British Columbia was not all the result of the search for furs and gold. See also Barry Gough, "Corporate Farming on

Endnotes

Vancouver Island: The Puget's Sound Agricultural Company, 1846–1857," in *Canadian Papers in Rural History*, vol. 4, ed. Donald H. Akenson (Gananoque, ON: Langdale, 1984), 72–82.

95 When he and his family moved to southern Vancouver Island, Tolmie turned his attention to farming. He was the first person to introduce thoroughbred stock on the island: Durham cattle, Berkshire pigs and Leicester sheep were bred on his Cloverdale Farm.

96 American population figures for 1849 and 1853 are from Dennis Noble, *The Coast Guard in the Pacific Northwest* (Washington DC: US Coast Guard, 1988), 1.

97 Galbraith, *Hudson's Bay Company as an Imperial Factor*, 265–67.

98 In 1861 the belligerent Victor Smith, collector of customs and a Treasury Department spy, intrigued to make Port Angeles a military district (fearing war with the British), as well as headquarters for customs collection. Raw politics expressed themselves: bringing in the steam revenue cutter *Shubrick* with its shotted 12-pounders, Smith forced Port Townsend to surrender the customs books, and the customs office was moved to Port Angeles in 1862. In the winter of 1863 came a catastrophe: the earth dam above the town gave way, the customs house was carried out into the harbour and the town lay in ruins. In 1866, Port Townsend regained the headquarters. Hubert Howe Bancroft, *History of Washington, Idaho and Montana, 1845–1889* (San Francisco: History Publishing, 1890), 219–26.

99 The HBC resorted to using US–flagged vessels for cross-border trade; it employed canoes to freight smaller cargoes.

100 By 1854 this "customs warfare" resulted in the San Juan archipelago dispute, which ultimately became the "Pig War" that began with a fight over who had the rights of property and taxation of same. I.N. Ebey, justice of the peace and US collector of customs, encamped on San Juan Island. The HBC steamer *Otter*, skippered by Captain Sangster, collector of customs for the port of Victoria, arrived to investigate. He told Ebey that he would arrest all foreign persons and seize all foreign vessels found navigating the waters west of Rosario Strait and north of the middle of the Strait of Juan de Fuca. This was preliminary to intensification of the double issue of who owned the archipelago and who could sail its waters. Sangster demonstrates the HBC monopoly position (as backed by Chief Factor Douglas). See Bancroft, *History of Washington, Idaho and Montana*, 86–88.

101 Ogden's famous speech to the Cayuse has been reprinted several times. One reliable reproduction is Douglas Mackay, "Men of the Old Fur Trade [Peter Skene Ogden]," *The Beaver* 269 (June 1939): 7–9.

102 On Ogden's role, and a sound history of this episode, its causes, eventualities and results, see Cline, *Peter Skene Ogden and the Hudson's Bay Company*, 181–95. For new insights see Cassandra Tate, *Unsettled Ground: The Whitman Massacre and Its Shifting Legacy in the American West* (Seattle: Sasquatch, 2020); George W. Fuller, *A History of the Pacific Northwest, With Special Emphasis on the Inland Empire,* 2nd ed. rev. (New York: Knopf, 1966), 142–69.

103 Simpson to Governor and Committee, 24 August 1848, in *Report of the Provincial Archives Department 1913* (Victoria, 1913), V51.

104 See Bancroft, *Washington, Idaho and Montana*, 121, n.21, where the post sites are listed.

105 Richard Kluger, *The Bitter Waters of Medicine Creek: A Tragic Clash between White and Native America* (New York: Knopf, 2011), 30. On Patkanim's plot and reprisals against, see Fuller, *A History of the Pacific Northwest*, 166–69. On Patkanim's attempt to exterminate settlers and his accommodations to the fast-changing political situation, see Bancroft, *History of Washington, Oregon and Montana*, 11–14.

106 Material for this discussion of Oregon wars and politics is based on Johansen and Gates, *Empire of the Columbia*, 221–27. Also, for "Indian wars," see Fuller, *History of the Pacific Northwest,* chs. 9, 13, 14 and 15.

107 Further details may be found in Bancroft, *Washington, Idaho and Montana*, ch. 1.

108 Fuller, *History of the Pacific Northwest*, 166–67.

109 On this theme, see Roxanne Dunbar-Ortiz, *An Indigenous Peoples' History of the United States* (Boston: Beacon Press, 2014), 226-28.

110 W. Colquhoun Grant, "Description of Vancouver Island," *Journal of the Royal Geographical Society* 27 (1857): 316. Read at the Royal Geographical Society, London, 22 June 1857.

Chapter 4: "Seagoing Governor"

111 W.F. Tolmie to Simpson, 25 March 1850, D 5/27, f.563d., HBCA.

112 Hill was in the class of 1837, USMA. A summary of his service is given in *Seventeenth Annual Reunion Association of the Graduates of the United States Military Academy* (1886), 101–4.

113 Now a national wildlife refuge.

114 Fort Victoria post journal, B 226/b/3, 11 March 1850, HBCA.

115 Blanshard to Grey, 8 April 1850, Fort Victoria, no. 2, CO 305/2, 27v.

116 Blanshard to Hinderwell, 15 June 1850; also Blanshard to W. Brotchie, 24 July 1851, F160 2, BCA.

117 Murray Morgan, *The Last Wilderness* (Seattle: University of Washington Press, 1976), 30–34. See also US Senate Exec. Doc. 30, 31st Cong., 2nd sess., 15 February 1851. Also, *Report of Decisions of the Commission for Settlement of Claims under the Convention of February 1853* (Washington, DC: A.O.P. Nicholson, 1856), 376 ff.

118 W.F. Tolmie to Captain Bennett H. Hill, 17 April 1850, in Steve A. Anderson, ed., *William Fraser Tolmie at Fort Nisqually: Letters, 1850–1853* (Pullman: WSU Press, 2019).

119 Roy Harvey Pearce, *The Savages of America: A Study of the Indian and the Idea of Civilization*, rev. ed. (Baltimore: Johns Hopkins University Press, 1965), 240.

Chapter 5: "Heart of Darkness"

120 Respectively, from shore to inland, Kwakiutl proper, Komkiutis, and Walas Kwakiutl. Here I follow Robert Galois, *Kwakwa̱ka'wakw Settlements, 1775–1920: A Geographical Analysis and Gazetteer* (Vancouver: UBC Press, 2012), 214.

121 The three chapters on these people in Wayne Suttles, ed., *Northwest Coast: Handbook of North American Indians*, vol. 7 (Washington: Smithsonian Institution, 1990), 359–90, are foundations of my work here.

122 Ruth Benedict, *Patterns of Culture*, new ed. (Boston: Houghton Mifflin, 1959), 173–222, 283–84.

123 Helen Codere, *Fighting with Property: A Study of Kwakiutl Potlatching and Warfare, 1792–1930* (New York: American Ethnological Society, 1950).

124 See Galois, *Kwakwa̱ka'wakw Settlements,* for village sites and territories. Randy Bouchard and Dorothy Kennedy also give details of Nahwitti territories in the translation of Franz Boas's *Indian Myths and Legends from the North Pacific Coast of America*, trans. Dietrich Bertz (Vancouver: Talonbooks, 2006), 377 n. 1. James Douglas, at Hope Island in 1840, called Bull Harbour Port Bull. Douglas diary 1840, in James Gibson, ed. *"Opposition on the Coast": The Hudson's Bay Company, American Coasters, the Russian-American Company, and Native Traders on the Northwest Coast, 1825–1846* (Toronto: Champlain Society, 2019), 225.

125 Galois, *Kwakwa̱ka'wakw Settlements,* 200. Captain G.W.C. Courtney of HMS *Constance* found similarly; Courtney to Phipps Hornby, 15 November 1848, Adm 1/5589.

126 *Cormorant* was in the same class as *Driver*. See Lyon and Winfield, *Sail and Steam Navy List,* 160.

Endnotes

127 G.T. Gordon to Captain J.A. Duntze, 7 October 1846, from Nisqually; this and related correspondence, including Rear Admiral Sir George Seymour's commendatory appreciation of Gordon for advancing the search and production of coal from Vancouver Island, is printed in "Vancouver's Island: Returns to Three Addresses the House of Commons, 16 August 1848, 6 February & 1 March 1849," *Parliamentary Papers*, House of Commons, 103, 1849, pp. 3–12.

128 John Haskell Kemble, *The Panama Route 1848–1869* (1943; New York: Da Capo, 1972), 137–38.

129 John Haskell Kemble, ed., "Coal from the Northwest Coast, 1848–1850," *British Columbia Historical Quarterly* 2, no. 2 (April 1938): 123–30.

130 Simpson to Messrs. Chief Factors P.S. Ogden, J. Douglas, J. Work, Board of Management, 25 June 1850, D 4/42, fol., 12, HBCA. Simpson's reference to what he called "the Indian title to the lands at the coal mine" is noteworthy.

131 Register of Land Purchases from Indians, MS-0772, BCA. These first appeared in print in *British Columbia, Papers Connected with the Indian Land Question, 1850–1875* (Victoria: Queen's Printer, 1875), 11.

132 [J.S. Helmcken], "Fort Victoria in 1850," *Victoria Daily Colonist*, 1 January 1890.

133 *Eden Colvile*, 191.

134 Fort Rupert Post Journal, 13 April 1850, B 185/a/1, HBCA.

135 P.S. Ogden and J. Douglas to Captain J.A. Duntze, 7 September 1846, "Vancouver's Island: Returns to Three Addresses," 5–6.

136 Douglas to Capt. J. Shepherd, 28 May 1849, in *Report of the Provincial Archives Department, 1913*, p. V 75.

137 Blanshard obtained, by his inquiries, "List of Passengers from England on the barque *Harpooner*." See MS-0611.1.8.2, Richard Blanshard fonds, BCA.

138 For further details on the Muirs, see Derek Pethick, *Men of British Columbia* (Saanichton: Hancock House, 1975), 60–63. The story is told, in the imagined voice of John Muir, in Daryl Ashby, *John Muir: West Coast Pioneer* (Vancouver: Ronsdale, 2005).

139 Report of failure to find coal in the deep shaft at Fort Rupert, the miners' despair and the decision to shift to Suquash is given by Douglas in his letter to Barclay, 18 March 1852. See Bruce McKelvie, "The Founding of Nanaimo," *British Columbia Historical Quarterly* 8 (July 1944): 171.

140 Fort Rupert Post Journal, 23, 24, 26 April 1850, B 185/a/1, HBCA.

141 Andrew Muir diary, BCA.

142 Fort Rupert Post Journal, 30 March 1850, B 185/a/1, HBCA.

143 Blanshard to Grey, 8 April 1850, CO 305/2, 27v.

144 Blanshard to Grey, 8 April 1850, CO 305/2.

145 Lynne Bowen, "Independent Colliers at Fort Rupert: Labour Unrest on the West Coast, 1849," *The Beaver* 69, no. 2 (April/May 1989): 30.

146 Fort Rupert Post Journal, 4 September 1849, B 185/a/1, HBCA.

147 Quoted in Walbran, 522–23.

148 Fort Rupert Post Journal, 30 March 1850, B 185/a/1, HBCA; see also W. Kaye Lamb, "The Governorship of Richard Blanshard," *British Columbia Historical Quarterly* 14 (January–April 1950): 9.

149 Blanshard to Grey, 10 July 1850, CO 305/2.

150 Blanshard to Moresby, 17 June 1851, copy, A 8/6. f/192, HBCA.

151 He continued to promote this policy. See Blanshard to Phipps Hornby, [?] October 1850, PHI/3/5, NMM.

152 Minute by H. Merivale, 3 July 1850, on Blanshard to Grey, 8 April 1850, CO 305/2, fols. 27 and 28.

153 Workers made a start on the house project on 14 March, but soon halted construction. Fort Victoria Post Journal, 14 March 1850, B 226/b/3, HBCA.

154 Phipps Hornby to Johnson, 21 January 1851, PHI 2/2, p. 222, NMM.

155 For the Royal Navy's previous visits to San Francisco Bay near the outset of the California gold rush, the Admiralty files contain reports from the commanding officers of HM vessels *Pandora*, *Constance* and *Inconstant*, respectively. See also Phipps Hornby papers, NMM. An extensive account of these proceedings is given by Abraham P. Nasatir, "The Gold Rush and the British Navy, San Francisco, 1849," *Brand Book No. 6* (San Diego: San Diego Corral of the Westerners, 1979): 93–103.

156 "[From our own Correspondent] State of California, San Francisco, 1 May 1850," *Times*, issue 20532, 4 July 1850, 5. The priest mentioned is Honoré-Timothée Lempfrit, OMI.

157 Blanshard to Grey, 8 April 1850, CO 305/2.

158 *Report from the Select Committee on the Hudson's Bay Company*, 290.

Chapter 6: "English Gentleman"

159 This is Lord Brougham's description. An evaluation of this new entrepreneurial class is given in Douglas Pike, *Paradise of Dissent: South Australia, 1829–1857*, 2nd ed. (Carleton: Melbourne University Press, 1967), 4–5.

160 Margarette Lincoln, *Trading in War: London's Maritime World in the Age of Cook and Nelson* (New Haven and London: Yale University Press, 2018), 51–54. Basil Lubbock, *Merchantmen under Sail, 1815–1932* (Greenwich: Society for Nautical Research, 1974) provides an excellent précis regarding Indiamen.

161 In the Bodleian Library, Oxford.

162 In 1833, when the East India Company monopoly ended, the *Thames* was sold for £10,700, a very high price. This vessel is immortalized in a painting by E.W. Cooke, RA, in Lubbock, *Merchantmen under Sail*, 4.

163 P.J. Cain and A.G. Hopkins, *British Imperialism, 1688–2000*, 2nd ed. (London: Longman, 2002).

164 This may be traced in the University College London slavery databases. The claims paid to Henry Blanshard date to 1814.

165 *The Bankers' Magazine*, 1846 (extract). Information from Andrew Loudon.

166 *Bradshaw's Descriptive Railway Hand-Book*, pt. 4, 1863, 80.

167 By a codicil to his will, dated 27 March 1854, those shares in Clarence Railway became shares in the West Hartlepool Harbour and Railway following amalgamation.

168 The remarkable establishment, the Foundling Hospital, was started by Captain Thomas Coram in 1739 for "deserted children." In Richard Blanshard's time the hospital housed "illegitimate" children whose mothers were known.

169 Quoted in John Morley, *Life of Gladstone* (London: Macmillan, 1905), 1:26.

170 Entry on Richard Blanshard in Joseph Foster, *Alumni Oxoniensis, 1715–1886*, 4 volumes (London, 1888).

171 Included in his letter to Earl Grey, [?] January 1852, CO 305/3, 44–49, are testimonials from Lord Gough, Major General Sir W.S. Whish, Lieutenant Colonel Franks, Major Edwardes and Captain Price; these provide incidental detail of Blanshard's services of a voluntary nature in India during the Second Sikh War. As Blanshard was not "carried on the books" of military units, he has no official military record that can be traced. But the testimonials and certificates make for fascinating reading, all in support of Blanshard, who by this time had returned from Vancouver Island and was seeking further employment, colonial or diplomatic.

Endnotes

172 Cain and Hopkins, *British Imperialism*, 291.

173 Charles Allen, *Raj: A Scrapbook of British India, 1877–1947* (Harmondsworth: Penguin, 1979), 16–17, 19, 129, 140.

Chapter 7: "Earl Grey Disposes"

174 Pelly to Douglas, 4 August 1849, Fort Victoria Corresp. Inward, 1849–1859, BCA.

175 Minutes, Lord Carnarvon, 27 October 1858, and Sir Edward Bulwer-Lytton (Colonial Secretary), 29 October 1858, CO 323/252, 414–20.

176 This is drawn from John W. Cell, *British Colonial Administration in the Mid-Nineteenth Century: The Policy-Making Process* (New Haven, CT: Yale University Press, 1970).

177 H.G. Grey, 3rd Earl, *Colonial Policy of Lord John Russell's Administration*, 2 volumes, 2nd ed. (London; R. Bentley, 1853); W.P. Morrell, *British Colonial Policy in the Age of Peel and Russell* (Oxford: Oxford University Press, 1930), chs. 19 and 20; and Kenneth Bell and W.P. Morrell, eds., *Select Documents of British Colonial Policy, 1830–1860* (Oxford: Clarendon Press, 1928), introduction.

178 Willard E. Ireland, "The Appointment of Governor Richard Blanshard," *British Columbia Historical Quarterly* 8, no. 3 (July 1944): 213–26. Also, Minutes, Hudson's Bay Company, A 1/66, HBCA.

179 Hubert Howe Bancroft, *History of British Columbia 1792–1887* (1887; reprint, New York: Arno, 1970), 264–65.

180 Blanshard took pains to make sure Colonial Secretary Sir J. Pakington knew about the HBC's maladministration on Vancouver Island. See Blanshard to Pakington, 30 August 1852, CO 305/3, 56–56v.

181 Ireland, "Appointment of Governor Richard Blanshard," 186–87.

182 Blanshard's Commission and Instructions, 16 July 1849, CO 381/77, 23–74. Printed in James E. Hendrickson, ed., *Journals of the Colonial Legislatures of the Colonies of Vancouver Island and British Columbia 1851–1871*; Volume 1: *Journals of the Council, Executive Council, and Legislative Council of Vancouver Island, 1851–1866* (Victoria: Provincial Archives of British Columbia, 1980), 379–91. The Commission is at pp. 379–83. Also, Pelly to Grey, 15 June 1849, A 8/4, HBCA. The matter may be followed in MS-0611, fol.1, BCA.

183 In Hendrickson, *Journals of the Colonial Legislatures*, 1:383–91.

184 Draft of Warrant to Blanshard re: Seal of Vancouver Island, 28 June 1850, typescript, MS-601.2, BCA. Original to Governor Blanshard, 28 June 1850, no. 3, CO 305/2/195756. Warrant to prepare Letters Patent appointing Blanshard governor and commander-in-chief in and over the Island of Vancouver and its Dependencies, 9 July 1849, printed and draft, MS-0611, fol. 3, BCA.

185 Barclay to Douglas, 3 August 1849, A 6/28, fol. 49d, HBCA.

186 Pelly to Simpson, 7 September 1849, D 5/26, HBCA.

187 Eden Colvile to Simpson, 7 December 1849, D 5/26, HBCA.

188 *Report from the Select Committee on the Hudson's Bay Company*, 288.

189 Minute by Grey, 16 September 1846, on Pelly to Grey, 7 September 1846, CO 305/1.

190 Between 1848 and 1877, a period of so-called "indifference," the following were added: Orange Free State (1848), Vancouver Island (1849), Rangoon and Pegu (1852), Oudh (1856), British Columbia (1858), Queensland (1859), Lagos (1861), Basutoland (1868), Griqualand West (1871), Perak and other Straits Settlements (1874), Transvaal (1877). There were others of lesser importance.

191 George R. Mellor, *British Imperial Trusteeship, 1783–1850* (London: Faber and Faber, 1951), esp. ch. 8; Eugene Stock, *History of the Church Missionary Society* (London: Church Mission-

ary Society, 1899), 2:313–32. Bishop Anderson of Rupert's Land provided powerful testimony to the 1857 parliamentary inquiry in support of HBC relations with the Indigenous peoples.

192 Reported by Grey, minute of 7 December 1846, CO 305/1, 23–23v.

193 Quoted in Scholefield and Howay, *British Columbia*, 1:498.

194 Gladstone, with prodigious memory, reverted to this matter in 1858 during debates on New Caledonia, HBC rights and the projected Colony of British Columbia, 20 July 1858, *Hansard*, 3rd ser., vol. 151, 1858, cols. 1806–1808.

195 Draft of Grant, enclosed in order-in-council, 4 September 1848, BT 1/470/2506, National Archives, Kew. Privy Council modifications to, and discussion of, this and other provisions are in Privy Council report, 31 October 1848, CO 305/1, 185–87v.

196 [Herman Merivale], Memorandum on the Position of the Hudson's Bay Company in Vancouver's Island, confidential, late 1848, Confidential Print, CO 880/2, vol. 44, 1848, 3–4.

197 See Barry Gough, "Crown, Company, and Charter: Founding Vancouver Island Colony—A Chapter in Victorian Empire Making," *BC Studies* 176 (Winter 2012/13): 44–45.

198 Royal Grant, Letters Patent, 13 January 1849, A 37/1, HBCA. First printed version is in CO 880/2, vol. 45, 1849, 9 pp.; see also, Hendrickson, *Journals of the Colonial Legislature*, 1:374–78.

199 Ibid.

200 For explanation of the Wakefield theory/system, see Richard Somerset Mackie, "The Colonization of Vancouver Island, 1849–1858," *BC Studies* 96 (Winter 1992–93): 8–12. Theory does not translate into administrative form: specific application is a different matter. Vancouver Island terms were a modification, or variant, of the idealistic Wakefieldian scheme, which was based on land set at a specific price. Imperial variants abounded. Under colonial surveyor Joseph Despard Pemberton, the land prices and holding requirements were eased, but the general idea did not disappear until civic government came to Victoria as a city (est. 1864). By this time, HBC formal dominion had been relinquished by the corporation.

201 Earl Grey's speech in the House of Lords, reported in *Annual Register 1849*, 131.

202 The Act empowered the colonial legislature to provide for the administration of justice. In the absence of a legislature the power devolved to the governor.

Chapter 8: "Vice-Regalities"

203 When Blanshard departed the colony, the purchase price of the horse was put on the books of the Puget's Sound Agricultural Company. Siskyo is referred to in Tolmie to Douglas, 2 May 1851, quoted in Anderson, *William F. Tolmie at Fort Nisqually*, 107. The editor errs in his comments on Blanshard: "the fool's pair" refers to the two nags.

204 Fort Victoria had a lockup, or jail, at the lowest floor, or basement, in one of its bastions.

205 *Report from the Select Committee on the Hudson's Bay Company*, 290.

206 Blanshard to Grey, 15 June 1850, CO 305/2.

207 Pelly to Grey, 7 September 1846, CO 305/1.

208 Pelly to Grey, 4 October 1850, CO 305/2, 168–69.

209 A. Colvile to Grey, 18 December 1850, CO 305/2, 175 (recto and verso). The Colonial Office minutes are on p. 175 v. They reveal the Colonial Office's helpless state. For a similar reply, see Pelly to Grey, 4 October 1850, CO 305/2.

210 Blanshard's despatch to Grey, no. 3, is dated 15 June 1850, CO 305/2, 31–32 (received 5 September 1850). A copy was sent to the HBC on 21 September 1850.

211 Roderick Finlayson, Biography, 1891, 21.

212 Thomas A. Rickard, *Historic Backgrounds of British Columbia* (Vancouver: Wrigley for the Author, 1848), 289.

Endnotes

213 No better demonstration of this exists in historical science than William Joseph Trimble, *The Mining Advance into the Inland Empire* (1914; reprint, Fairfield, WA: Ye Galleon Press, 1986). See chs. 1–4 for Fort Colvile and developments to the northward; see ch. 11 for Trimble's appreciation, in comparative perspective, of the establishment of British law, order and management.

214 This and other details are from Barry Gough, "Walter Colquhoun Grant," in *Dictionary of Canadian Biography*, vol. 9, www.biographi.ca/en/bio/grant_walter_colquhoun_9E.html.

215 James E. Hendrickson, ed., "Two Letters from Walter Colquhoun Grant," BC *Studies* 26 (Summer 1975): 9.

216 W. Colquhoun Grant, "Description of Vancouver Island," *Journal of the Royal Geographical Society* 27 (1857): 273.

217 Information from J.S. Whittaker and Oak Bay Archives. For Grant's survey sheet for "Mr. Tod's Allotment," see "Map of the Victoria District Vancouvers Island 1850 Part 04" in the collection of Hudson's Bay Company maps in the University of Victoria Libraries Vault: vault.library.uvic.ca/concern/generic_works/f28548ff-5572-434e-affe-158d34ce0036?locale=en.

218 *Eden Colvile*, 187, where Colvile's letter to Simpson, 7 December 1849, is printed.

219 W.C. Grant to Dr. Norton Shaw (Royal Geographical Society), 16 December 1857, Royal Geographical Society Archives, London; also quoted in Gough, "Walter Colquhoun Grant."

220 Grant, "Description of Vancouver Island," 320.

221 Helmcken, *Reminiscences*, 84.

222 Helmcken, *Reminiscences*, 285.

223 Dorothy Blakey Smith, "Blinkhorn, Thomas," in *Dictionary of Canadian Biography*, vol. 8, www.biographi.ca/en/bio/blinkhorn_thomas_8E.html.

224 The witness was the Honourable Charles Fitzwilliam, whom we shall meet in Chapter 15.

225 All figures above concerning Colvile's counting of settlers and land sales, and Company press advertisements, are drawn from Galbraith, *Hudson's Bay Company as an Imperial Factor*, 296–99.

226 Attributed to Lord Acton.

227 Bancroft, *Washington, Idaho and Montana*, 69.

228 Simpson to Douglas, 20 February 1850, private, D 4/71, HBCA. For analysis see Galbraith, *Hudson's Bay Company as an Imperial Factor*, 295, where Simpson's letter is printed in part.

Chapter 9: "Haida Gwaii Gold in the Balance"

229 P. Hankin, Memoirs of, EBH 19A, p. 39. BCA. Hankin was in HMS *Hecate*, Captain Richards.

230 John Scouler, "Observations on the Indigenous Tribes of the N.W. Coast of America," *Royal Geographical Society Journal* 11 (1841): 215–51, esp. 218.

231 Blanshard to Grey, 18 August 1850, CO 305/2.

232 See Frederic W. Howay, ed., *Voyages of the* Columbia *to the Northwest Coast, 1787–1790 & 1790–1793* (1941; Portland: Oregon Historical Society, 1990), 200, 204, 240–41, 298, 379.

233 For more extensive treatment, see Gough, *Gunboat Frontier*, ch. 7; see also Gough, "The Haida-European Encounter, 1774–1900: The Queen Charlotte Islands [Haida Gwaii] in Transition," in G.G.E. Scudder and N. Gessler, eds., *The Outer Shores: Based on the Proceedings of the Queen Charlotte Islands First International Symposium* (Vancouver: University of British Columbia, 1984), 249–60.

234 The six HBC expeditions are listed in Robert Galois, "Gold on Haida Gwaii: The First Prospects, 1849–53," BC *Studies* 196 (Winter 2017/18): 16–18. Nine American vessels visited Haida Gwaii between November 1851 and September 1852; two made more than one expedition (Galois, "Gold on Haida Gwaii," 18–20). See also Bancroft, *Washington, Idaho and Montana*, 55–57.

235 Earl Stanley to H. Merivale, 2 June 1852, copy, A 8/7, ff. 13–14, HBCA.

236 Gough, *Gunboat Frontier*, ch. 7; see also, G.P.V. Akrigg and Helen B. Akrigg, *H.M.S.* Virago *in the Pacific, 1851–1855: To the Queen Charlottes and Beyond* (Victoria: Sono Nis, 1992), 118–21, 130–34.

237 Governor Douglas to Duke of Newcastle, 8 June 1853, CO 305/4. Commander Prevost of the *Virago* (same class as *Driver* and *Cormorant*) made inquiries of the event but did not take punitive action. See his report to Moresby encl. in Moresby's to Admiralty, 13 October 1853, Adm 1/5630, Y73. The Admiralty approved Prevost's judicious report.

238 Howay's account in Scholefield and Howay, *British Columbia*, 2:3. The quest of Blanshard and Douglas to secure Haida Gwaii in order to keep Americans out can be followed in "Correspondence relative to the Discovery of Gold at Queen Charlotte's Island," *Parliamentary Papers*, 1853 (778), and "Further Correspondence relative to the Discovery of Gold at Queen Charlotte's Island," *Parliamentary Papers*, 1853 (778-1).

239 By this time James Douglas was governor of Vancouver Island, and he was commissioned lieutenant-governor of the Queen Charlotte Islands on 29 July 1852.

240 Summary report by Douglas, Fort Victoria, to Barclay, 3 January 1852, printed in *Report of the Provincial Archives Department, 1913* , p. V 111.

241 Douglas to Grey, 29 January 1852. CO 305/3, no. 3742, 42. Douglas states that the *Susan Sturgis* had come to the rescue (later he says the *Demaris Cove*), but the evidence points to the *Susanna*. I have not been able to trace details of the Makah response or recompense paid. Compare Bancroft, *Washington, Idaho and Montana*, 57, n. 32.

242 Art Downs, *Wagon Road North* (Quesnel: Northwest Digest, 1960), 6–7.

Chapter 10: "The Track of the Storm"

243 [J.S. Helmcken], "Fort Victoria in 1850," *Victoria Daily Colonist*, 1 January 1890.

244 As noted in Chapter 5, Captain G.T. Gordon, on the *Cormorant*, keenly believed in the promise of Suquash and reported such to his superiors in 1846. His report shows authenticity, but if results are any indication, he proved wildly bullish in his expectations and sadly misleading.

245 Hartwell Bowsfield, ed., *Fort Victoria Letters 1846–1851* (Winnipeg: Hudson's Bay Record Society, 1979), lx–lxi.

246 Blanshard to Grey, 10 June 1851, no. 16, in *Vancouver Island Despatches: Governor Blanshard to the Secretary of State: 26 December 1849 to 30 August 1851* (New Westminster, Government Printing Office, 1863), 11–12.

247 Blanshard to G. Blenkinsop, 22 June 1850, Vancouver Island Correspondence Outward, C /AA/10.4/1, BCA.

248 Walbran, 237. The passages on either side are Race (adjacent to Vancouver Island) and Current (Hardwicke Island).

249 Blanshard's arrangements with Helmcken, notably his private letter to Helmcken, 6 August 1850, can be followed in C/AA/10.4/1, BCA.

250 Helmcken to Blanshard, 2 July 1850, C/AA/40.3/R2, BCA.

251 Blanshard to Grey, 10 July 1850, CO 305/2, 37.

252 Helmcken, *Reminiscences*, 138.

253 Blanshard to Grey, 10 July 1850, CO 305/2, 36v.

254 Grey to Blanshard, 20 November 1850, CO 305/2, 39 and 39v.

255 Re: liquor proclamations and legislation, see Gough, *Gunboat Frontier*, appendix II, "Statutory Provisions on Liquor Relating to British Columbia Indians, 1850–1876," 219–23; see also ch. 6 of the same book, "Of Slaves and Liquor," 85–94 and sources 240–42.

256 Act Regulating the Importation of Spirituous Liquors, 13 May 1850, GR-0771, BCA. This legal instrument was issued by executive power, not legislated authority.

257 Douglas to Sir John Pakington, 11 November 1852, CO 305/3. The matter was reviewed by the Colonial Council on 28 April 1852, but found "free from any material defect." *Minutes of the Council of Vancouver Island* (Victoria: BC Archives Memoir No. II), 16.

258 Under the *License Act*, HBC vendors paid £100 per year for a vending licence; private vendors, such as James Yates, £120. Yates was not particularly pleased, but Douglas was overjoyed at the revenue.

259 Pelly to Grey, 14 January 1852, A 8/6, fol. 224, HBCA.

Chapter 11: "The Nahwitti War"

260 Grant, "Description of Vancouver Island," 294.

261 Walbran, 356. Walbran's information came from George Hunt of Alert Bay. See also Walbran entries for Sutil Point (477–78) and Mexicana Point (337). It must always be remembered that in the 1840s through 1860s these were largely uncharted waters; place names frequently changed and local knowledge did not always find its way into nineteenth-century charts and the first BC *Coast Pilot*. Advice to readers: Walbran was not faultless, nor were his informants. Galiano became Nigei Island in 1900, by designation of the Geographic Board of Canada.

262 Douglas to Barclay, 5 October 1850, A 8/6, fol. 148, HBCA. Forty years later the events still resonated in memory. Blenkinsop to Helmcken, 21 September 1887, AE H3, B61, BCA; also, Helmcken, "Fort Rupert in 1850," *Victoria Daily Colonist*, 1 January 1890, 4.

263 Andrew Muir's diary, BCA.

264 This and the next quote are from Blanshard to Grey, 18 August 1850, CO 305/2, 41–42.

265 Later this structure was covered with clapboard siding, and today, as Helmcken House, a sometime museum, it stands on its original site near the Royal British Columbia Museum. Helmcken's later contributions to the history of British Columbia are of inestimable value, as can be seen in his Reminiscences written in 1892.

266 Blanshard to Helmcken, 6 August 1850, C/AA/10.4A/1, BCA.

267 Here I follow the analysis in my *Gunboat Frontier*, ch. 3, to which the reader is directed for additional citations and sources.

268 Douglas to Blenkinsop, 20 September 1850, B 226/6/3, fols. 12d-13d, HBCA.

269 Douglas to Blenkinsop, 27 September 1850, B 226/b/3, fols. 12d-13d, HBCA.

270 Lieutenant Burton's report suffers from brevity, and he hints at two camps of the quarry. Enclosed in J. Parker to Benjamin Hawes, 27 February 1851, WO 1/549, no. 1801, 545.

271 Phipps Hornby to Blanshard, 10 January 1851, Valparaiso, MS-0611.8, BCA.

272 Phipps Hornby to J. Parker, 29 August 1849, encl. in Adm to CO, 5 November 1849, and B. Hawes to Pelly, 16 November 1849, A 8/6, fol. 4, HBCA. This was the view at precisely the time when Blanshard was making his way to Vancouver Island. As stated earlier, he met Sir Phipps Hornby in Lima, or Callao, and may have been briefed on the matter then.

273 See Bowsfield, *Fort Victoria Letters*, 197–99.

274 Bowsfield, *Fort Victoria Letters*, 199.

275 This is according to Helmcken. See Gough, *Gunboat Frontier*, 45.

276 Captain E. Fanshawe to Blanshard, 21 July 1851, HM Sloop *Daphne*, Beaver Harbour, encl. no. 1, in Blanshard to Grey, 4 August 1851, included in *Vancouver Island Despatches*, 13.

277 G. Blenkinsop's account of events was quoted in Douglas to Barclay, 4 August 1851, A 11/72, fols. 150–52, HBCA; printed in Bowsfield, *Fort Victoria Letters*, 202–5.

278 Lieutenant Lacy's report of proceedings to Fanshawe, 21 July 1851, copy, in Blanshard to Grey, 4 August 1851, *Vancouver Island Despatches*, 13.

279 For further particulars see Gough, *Gunboat Frontier*, 44–45.

280 Douglas to Grey, 31 October 1851, CO 305/3, 66–67. For discussion, see Derek Pethick, *James Douglas: Servant of Two Empires* (Vancouver: Mitchell Press, 1969), 97.

281 Douglas to Blenkinsop, 15 August 1851, B 226/b/3, 119–120, HBCA.

282 John Moresby, *Two Admirals: Sir Fairfax Moresby, John Moresby: A Record of a Hundred Years* (London: Methuen, 1913), 107–14.

283 Moresby's report of 21 November 1851, encl. in F. Peel to Pelly, 13 January 1852, A 8/6, fols. 238–39; also, Pelly to Grey, 2 February 1852 (recounting Douglas's approval of measures), A 8/6, 239, HBCA.

284 Grey to Blanshard, 20 March 1851, RG7: G8C/1, 15, LAC. See also Scholefield and Howay, *British Columbia*, 1:523–24.

285 Blanshard to Grey, 11 August 1851, (no. 18), CO 305/3, 4.

286 Law Officers of the Crown, Report to Earl of Clarendon (Foreign Office), 28 July 1853, FO 83/2314, 188–89. Subsequently sent to all commanders-in-chief. Many extraordinary cases of intervention facing British cruiser commanders existed in the South Pacific. Throughout the islands, invariably *before* formal sovereign possession was taken (or not taken at all), the British wove a net or web of legal influence in Polynesia and Melanesia. See Barry Gough, *Pax Britannica: Ruling the Waves and Keeping the Peace before Armageddon* (London: Palgrave Macmillan), ch. 8 "The Imperial Web in the South Pacific." The case law can be followed in the much-neglected John M. Ward, *British Policy in the South Pacific (1786–1893): A Study of British Policy in the South Pacific Islands prior to the Establishment of Governments by the Great Powers* (Sydney: Australian Publishing, 1948). Also, John Bach, *The Australia Station: A History of the Royal Navy in the South West Pacific, 1821–1913* (Kensington: New South Wales University Press, 1986).

287 Barclay to Douglas, 1 January 1851, A 6/29, fol.28–29, HBCA. Revelation that Douglas was under London's close watch is evidenced in Barclay to Douglas, 6 December 1850, A 6/29, fol. 24, HBCA. What alerted the London Committee to Douglas's non-engagement was the fact that the Colonial Office had received Blanshard's report of 18 August 1850, reporting deserters murdered by Indigenous persons. And since this news came via the same post as Douglas's letter of 17 August, they asked why he hadn't reported it. Every time the Colonial Office was in doubt about proceedings in the colony as reported by Blanshard, they referred the matter to the HBC for further information and explanation. Lack of trust is patent. HBC's doubts about Douglas continued, as did their watchful oversight. See Barclay to Douglas, 1 March 1851, A 6/29, fol. 44d, HBCA.

288 Douglas to Grey, 15 April 1852, CO 305/3, 103–108.

289 Admiralty minute, 30 July 1869, Adm.1/6092.

290 See Gough, *Gunboat Frontier*, chs. 11–13.

291 See Gough, *Gunboat Frontier*.

292 [Frederick Dally] "Memoranda of a trip round Vancouver Island…" 1866, 8, EBD16m, BCA.

293 Captain James Douglas Warren provides extensive details of murders, noting other encounters (one victim was the *Royal Charley*) in his account "Among the Indians of the North West Coast," 1882, HHB.

294 This item is reprinted in Helmcken, *Reminiscences*, 297–331.

295 Helmcken, *Reminiscences*, 107.

296 Helmcken, *Reminiscences*, 107.

297 Blanshard to Helmcken, 5 August 1850, private, in Lamb, "Governorship of Richard Blanshard," 13.

298 A. Barclay to P.S. Ogden, 1 January 1851, A 6/29, p. 26, 26v, HBCA.

299 Douglas's reports to Barclay, 24 November 1851 and 18 March 1852, provide a comprehensive factum on the search for subsurface coal near Fort Rupert and at Suquash. Douglas Letters to Hudson's Bay Company on Vancouver Island Colony, 1850–55, typescript, 24–26 and 47–55 respectively, BCA.

300 Walbran, 348–49. There are various nineteenth-century Indigenous names and spellings for this location.

301 Douglas to Barclay, 10 August 1852, Douglas Letters to Hudson's Bay Company on Vancouver Island Colony, 1850–55, typescript, pp. 89–93, BCA.

302 Douglas wrote to the Colonial Office about the Nanaimo coal discoveries on 22 and 27 August 1852. Excerpts of the latter appeared as "Report of a Canoe Expedition along the East Coast of Vancouver Island," *Journal of the Royal Geographical Society* 24 (1854): 245–49.

303 Legal and court challenges and decisions, beginning in 1963, led to judicial recognition of Indigenous title and especially rights of hunting and fishing as laid down in the Royal Proclamation of 1763. See Paul Tennant, *Aboriginal Peoples and Politics: The Indian Land Question in British Columbia, 1849–1989* (Vancouver: UBC Press, 1990), 218–19.

304 A detailed history of Nanaimo coal mining under McKay is included in Greg N. Fraser, *Joseph William McKay: A Métis Business Leader in Colonial British Columbia* (Victoria: Heritage House, 2021), 48–66.

Chapter 12: "Blighted Prospects"

305 Blanshard to Douglas, 5 August 1850 (in succession to his earlier missive of 26 June 1850), BCA.

306 The above correspondence, including Blanshard to Douglas, 26 June and 5 August 1850, also Douglas to Barclay, 10 September 1850, is in BCA. Lamb, "Governorship of Richard Blanshard," 2–3, reprints essential items. Similar arguments are in Sage, *Sir James Douglas*, 164–65. Douglas to Barclay, 3 April 1850, A 11/72, HBCA.

307 Dorothy Blakey Smith, *James Douglas, Father of British Columbia* (Toronto: Oxford University Press, 1971), 38.

308 H.H. Berens to Duke of Newcastle, 26 June 1860, printed in *Papers in Connection with Crown Lands in British Columbia and the Title of the Hudson's Bay Company* (Victoria: Queen's Printer, 1881), 11.

309 Barclay to Blanshard, 1 January 1851, *Papers in Connection with Crown Lands*, 9–10.

310 Douglas to Newcastle, 28 March 1860, *Papers in Connection with Crown Lands*, 8.

311 Further details and site plans are in Peter Neive Cotton, *Vice Regal Mansions of British Columbia* (Vancouver: British Columbia Heritage Trust, 1981), 11–17.

312 Blanshard to Grey, 12 February 1851, CO 305/3, 6.

313 Edwin Ernest Rich, *History of the Hudson's Bay Company, 1670–1870* (London: Hudson's Bay Record Society, 1958–1959), 2:778.

314 *Report from the Select Committee on the Hudson's Bay Company*, 288.

315 Barclay to Douglas, 3 August 1849, BCA; Lamb, "Governorship of Richard Blanshard," 4.

316 *Report from the Select Committee on the Hudson's Bay Company*, 288.

317 Lamb, "Governorship of Richard Blanshard," 5.

318 Scholefield and Howay, *British Columbia*, 1:528.

319 Douglas to Barclay, 21 March 1851, Douglas Letterbook to Barclay, 1850–1855, p. 10, BCA. This is printed in Sage, *Sir James Douglas*, 166–67.

320 Later admiral of the fleet, Sir Fairfax Moresby, GCB, 1786–1877, was born in Kolkata, India, of English parents. He entered the Navy in 1799 and as a young officer fought in various capacities during the French and Napoleonic Wars. His anti-slavery and anti-piracy activities, also supporting the Albany settlement, were conducted to his credit. He had various commands before rising on *The Navy List*, to rear admiral, 20 December 1849. The Pacific command constituted a coveted appointment on account of the benefits conferred by the conveyance of Mexican bullion, or specie, from west-coast ports (undertaken by HM ships on Pacific Station near the completion of their commission). The Navy was the Wells Fargo for the safe shipping of specie from this young and turbulent republic.

321 Rear Admiral Fairfax Moresby to Admiralty, 7 July 1851, copy, encl. in Peel to Pelly, 20 December 1851, A 8/6, fols. 203–211, HBCA. Moresby's movements may be followed in his letter book Adm 50/260, entries for 27 June to 3 July 1851.

322 Ibid.

323 A. Kuper to Rear Admiral Moresby, 4 February 1853, in W. Kaye Lamb, "Four Letters relating to the Cruise of the *Thetis*," *British Columbia Historical Quarterly* 6, no. 3 (July 1942): 202.

324 Pelly to Grey, 14 January 1852, copy, A 8/6, fol. 219, HBCA.

325 Douglas to Simpson, 20 March 1854, B 226/b/11, fols. 38–38d, HBCA.

326 Alice E.J. Fanshawe, *Admiral Sir Edward Gennys Fanshawe G.C.B.: A Record* (London: Spottiswoode and Co., for private circulation, 1904), 269–75.

327 Richard Blanshard, Inquest on the Body of Wm. Gillespie, 13 May 1850, F160 1, BCA.

328 One of Douglas's biographers, Walter Sage, found no fault with Blanshard's actions (*Sir James Douglas*, 166). Douglas never complained about it, in correspondence at least. See further, *Report of the Select Committee on the Hudson's Bay Company*, 290–91.

Chapter 13: "At Death's Door"

329 For medical appreciations of malaria, see Kevin Brown, *The Seasick Admiral: Nelson and the Health of the Navy* (Barnsley: Seaforth, 2015), 27–30.

330 For a preliminary view on Pemberton, see Scholefield and Howay, *British Columbia*, 4:37. He did magnificent work as a surveyor and compiled a well-informed *Facts and Figures Relating to Vancouver Island and British Columbia Showing What to Expect and How to Get There* (London: Longman, Green, Longman, and Roberts, 1860).

331 *Encyclopedia Britannica* (Edinburgh, 1771), 3:416.

332 Blanshard to Grey, 18 November 1850, no. 2 of this date, CO 305/2.

333 Victor J. Farrar, ed., "Nisqually Journal," *Washington Historical Quarterly* 12 (1921): 146–220; also, Lamb, "Governorship of Richard Blanshard," 25.

334 Blanshard to Grey, 18 November 1850, CO 305/2.

335 Helmcken, *Reminiscences*, 118.

336 J. Spurgeon to Henry Blanshard, 28 March 1851, and S.J. Goodfellow to Henry Blanshard, 29 March 1851, CO 305/2, 89–90 and 91–93, respectively.

337 Grey to Blanshard, 3 April 1851, CO 305/2, 55–55v.

338 Grey to Blanshard, 3 April 1851, and Colonial Office to Admiralty, 7 April 1851, CO 305/2, 56–56v.

339 Blanshard to Grey, two letters, 18 November 1850, and minutes thereon by Blackwood, Merivale, Hawes and Grey of 29–31 March 1851, CO 305/2, 48–51.

340 Barclay to Douglas, 16 April 1851, B 226/b/5a, fol. 3d, HBCA.

341 P.S. Ogden to G. Simpson, 27 January 1851, private, D 5/30, HBCA.

342 Macfie, *Vancouver Island and British Columbia*, 312–13.

343 Scholefield and Howay, *British Columbia*, 1:524. The Memorial is printed at 524–26.

344 Blanshard left behind some furniture, and he was reimbursed £3 2s. 6d. cash for it. The total cost of running Government House, including this furniture reimbursement, to 1 June 1853, was £457 15s. d. (every item detailed—turpentine, nails, Indigenous labour in the garden, garrets, etc.). See Vancouver Island Colony Journal, 1848–60, E 22/2, p. 16, HBCA.

345 See photo of James K. Nesbitt holding the HBC trade musket: HP97525, BCA.

346 Barclay to Blanshard, 1 May 1851, A 6/29, fols. 10d-11, HBCA.

347 Macfie, *Vancouver Island and British Columbia*, 312.

348 Douglas to Simpson, 15 September 1851, private, D 5/31, HBCA.

349 *Report from the Select Committee on the Hudson's Bay Company*, 287–88. In 1922 Sir Leicester Harmsworth, the publisher, presented Blanshard's commission and instructions to the British Columbia Archives. Filed at ZZ-97441, BCA. See also Lamb, "Governorship of Richard Blanshard," 37, n. 132.

Chapter 14: "Homecoming"

350 Blanshard to Grey, 27 November 1851, CO 305/3, 45v; Grey's minute, 29 November 1851, ibid.

351 Blanshard to Grey, 31 January 1852, CO 305/3, 44–48.

352 Blanshard cites and quotes from this letter in his correspondence to Grey of 31 January 1852, CO 305/3. I have been unable to trace this remarkable goodbye letter of thanks and appreciation. This letter is not to be confused with the Memorial.

353 Grey's minute of 4 February on Blanshard's letter to him of 31 January 1852, CO 305/3, 53–53v. Grey's letter to Blanshard was dated 9 February 1852.

Chapter 15: "Witness for the Prosecution"

354 Galbraith, *Hudson's Bay Company as an Imperial Factor*, 300–301.

355 Blanshard to J. Pakington (Colonial Office), 30 August 1852, from 37 Great Ormond St., London, CO 305/3, 56–56v.

356 Minute by A. Blackwood, 1 September 1852, CO 305/3, 56v.

357 E. Colvile to Pakington, 24 November 1852, *Parliamentary Papers*, 1852–53, lxv, House of Commons 83.

358 Bancroft, *History of British Columbia*, 261–62.

359 Galbraith, *Hudson's Bay Company as an Imperial Factor*, 299–300.

360 J. Cooper to Colonial Office, 8 October 1852, CO 714/161 (IND 18627), 14.

361 *Hansard*, 3rd ser., vol. 106, 553–54. Printed in part in Sage, *Sir James Douglas*, 144–45. Newcastle was the Earl of Lincoln when he gave his four-and-a-half-hour assault on the HBC's tyranny of monopoly on 19 June 1849. He subsequently, as the Duke of Newcastle, became colonial secretary. He engaged trenchantly with Douglas regarding Colony of British Columbia affairs.

362 Extensive details are given in G. Hollis Slater, "Rev. Robert John Staines: Pioneer Priest, Pedagogue, and Political Agitator," *British Columbia Historical Quarterly* 14, 4 (October 1950): 187–240.

363 Bancroft, *History of British Columbia*, 242–43.

364 Douglas to Colonial Office, 11 December 1852, no. 42, CO 714/161 (IND 18627), 25.

365 Alexander Begg, *History of British Columbia from Its Earliest Discovery to the Present Time* (1894; Toronto: McGraw-Hill Ryerson, 1972), 201; Rich, *The History of the Hudson's Bay Company*, 2: 770.

366 Blanshard's testimony appears in *Report from the Select Committee on the Hudson's Bay Company*, 285–97.

367 Flora Hamilton Burns, "Victoria in the 1850s," *The Beaver*, 280 (December 1949): 37. This article prints the recollections of William John Macdonald (later mayor of Victoria, colonial politician and Canadian senator).

368 The first treaty Governor Stevens arranged (as superintendent of Indian affairs for the Washington Territory) was with the Nisqually, Puyallup, Muckleshoot and Squaxin; it is known as the Medicine Creek Treaty. By the end of 1855 he had completed treaties with the major Indigenous groups west of the Cascades; other treaties were signed soon thereafter elsewhere in the territory. See Richard Kluger, *The Bitter Waters of Medicine Creek: A Tragic Clash Between White and Native America* (New York: Alfred A. Knopf, 2011), ch. 5. These treaties differ from all deeds of conveyance or agreement signed with Vancouver Island or British Columbia tribes.

369 *Report from the Select Committee on the Hudson's Bay Company*, p. iv.

Chapter 16: "The Bell Tolls: Retrospective"

370 Grant, "Description of Vancouver Island," 320.

371 *Proceedings of the Royal Geographical Society* 1 (1855–57): 489.

372 James Audain, *From Coalmine to Castle: The Story of the Dunsmuirs of Vancouver Island* (New York: Pageant Press, 1955), 31.

373 Surveyor Joseph Pemberton stated that Grant got no farther inland than the watershed of the Sooke River and generally misrepresented the country. Pemberton, *Facts and Figures Relating to Vancouver Island and British Columbia*, 3–5.

374 R.E. Gosnell, "Colonial History 1849–1871," in *The Pacific Province*, vol. 21 of *Canada and Its Provinces*, ed. Adam Shortt and Arthur G. Doughty (Toronto: Publishers Association, 1914), 89.

375 Bancroft devotes a chapter to Blanshard's administration and misfortune. See his admirable, well-informed but delightfully contentious *History of British Columbia*, ch. 7, pp. 263–84; quote at 275.

376 Gosnell, "Colonial History," 86.

377 Douglas to Barclay, 15 September 1851, printed in Bowsfield, *Fort Victoria Letters*, 215–16. Douglas refers to earlier correspondence, specifically to Blanshard's critique of him re Government House. See Douglas to Barclay, 10 September 1850, also in Bowsfield, 118–19.

378 W.E. Gladstone, House of Commons, 18 August 1848, *Hansard* 3rd ser., vol. 101, 289.

379 John R. Wise, *The New Forest: Its History and Scenery*, introduction by John Lavender (1883; Wakefield, Yorkshire: S.R. Publishers, 1971), 79–80. "The people of Lyndhurst ought, I always think, to be the happiest and most contented in England, for they possess a wider park and nobler trees than even Royalty" (89).

380 Wise, *The New Forest*, 169–71.

381 Membership records and registry, Royal Thames Yacht Club, Knightsbridge, courtesy archivist Celine Fernandez. The club's history is recounted in Douglas Phillips-Birt, *The Cumberland Fleet: Two Hundred Years of Yachting* (London: Royal Thames Yacht Club, 1978).

382 Peter Kemp, *Racing for the America's Cup* (London: Hutchinson, 1937), 13–19.

383 I am grateful to Rear Admiral C.H. Layman for this information. As Blanshard's will indicates there were two such memorial windows, the other may have been installed in the parish church, St. Michael's, near their Essex residence.

384 Details from Victoria County History, University of London, Texts in Progress, Landownership, Kirby-le-Soken; also Richard Blanshard death notice, *Essex Review*, 3–4 (1894): 163.

385 *Return of Owners of Land in England and Wales 1873*, entry on Richard Blanshard, County Durham, that gives the London address of owner as 2 Albany Chambers; W. Lord Byron had been a previous occupant of the same set.

Endnotes

386 George Otto Trevelyan, ed., *Life and Letters of Lord Macaulay* (New York and London: Harper & Brothers, 1876), 2:85. It was "that luxurious cloister, whose inviolable tranquility affords so agreeable a relief from the roar and flood of the Piccadilly traffic" (2:90).

387 The pictures or paintings of Emily Blanshard were willed to Miss Annie H. Norris, daughter of his late friend Henry Norris. Blanshard's will, January–February 1894, MS-0611.7, BCA.

388 *Victoria Times Colonist*, 2 January 2008, p. B15.

389 Obituary, *Annual Register for 1894* (London: Longmans Green, 1895), 187–95.

390 Copy, MS-0611.1.7, BCA. Richard Blanshard entry in *National Probate Calendar for 1894* shows executors of the will as Colonel R.P Davis, Indian Army; George T. Woodruffe, Esq.; and William Legh Cahussac, ret'd Major General H.M. Army.

391 Alan Thacker and Elizabeth Williamson, eds., *A History of the County of Essex*, vol. 11: *Clacton, Walton and Friton*, The Victoria History of the Counties of England (London: Institute of Historical Research, London University, 2012). Information on R. Blanshard's property and Colonel R.P. Davis's inheritance is on p. 26; railways, p. 29; silhouette portrait of Colonel Davis, p. 43. This volume contains many maps. The map at pp. 2–3 shows how lands and waters were overcome by holidaymakers, roads, piers, railways and seaside resorts. Henry and later Richard Blanshard's Horsey Island, with its duck pond and decoy blind, can be seen; also the small hamlet of Kirby, where the Blanshard terrace house stood. The Naze, on the northeast of the Essex coastline, had a series of sandy beaches overlooked by gentle cliffs. The parish name was Kirby-le-Soken; parish church in Kirby. Walton Tower stands at the northernmost headland.

392 Douglas to A.G. Dallas, 3 June 1869, James Douglas Private Letter Book, Correspondence Outward, March 22, 1867–October 11, 1870 (transcript of same: B/40/2a, pp.142ff), BCA. I owe this reference to Dr. Dorothy Blakey Smith; letter to author, 17 May 1974, in author's archive.

393 For analysis, see W. Kaye Lamb, "The Census of Vancouver Island, 1855," *British Columbia Historical Quarterly* 4, no. 1 (January 1940): 51–58. This discusses W.C. Grant's estimate for the year 1853 of about "450 souls...of these 300 at Victoria and between it and Sooke...about 125 at Nanaimo and the remainder [25] at Fort Rupert." See also Begg, *History of British Columbia*, 201; and Peter Johnson, *Voyages of Hope: The Saga of the Bride Ships* (Victoria: TouchWood, 2002), 41.

394 J. Work to Edward Ermatinger, 8 August 1856, in Scholefield and Howay, *British Columbia*, 1:555.

395 Sources for Douglas's objections: his diary, 1 May 1865, Archives MS B/20/1864, BCA. Also, Blakey Smith, *James Douglas, Father of British Columbia*, 57–58, and Sage, *Sir James Douglas*, 189–90. The latter prints in full Douglas to Henry Labouchere, 22 May 1856.

396 This is the observation of Sage, *Sir James Douglas*, 192.

397 *Minutes of the House of Assembly of Vancouver Island, 1856–1858*, Archives Memoir No. 3 (Victoria, 1918), 13–15.

398 Douglas to Grey, 29 January 1852, CO 305/3.

399 "Gold Discovery Papers," 13, quoted in Scholefield and Howay, *British Columbia*, 2:25–26.

400 Scholefield and Howay, *British Columbia*, 2:174.

401 Douglas to Mr. Good, 10 December 1863, Douglas Correspondence Book, BCA; quoted in Trimble, *Mining Advance into the Inland Empire*, 194.

402 Van Kirk, "Colonized Lives," 217.

403 Macfie, *Vancouver Island and British Columbia*, 62.

404 Douglas to Barclay, 9 December 1851, titled "On the affairs of Vancouver's Island," in Douglas, Letters to Hudson's Bay Company on Vancouver Island Colony, 1850–55, typescript, 35–40, BCA. This reveals Douglas's ameliorative solutions.

405 Douglas's land proclamations, printed in Macfie, *Vancouver Island and British Columbia*, 527–31.

406 Quoted in *Victoria Times Colonist*, 2 January 2008, B15.

Sources

Abbreviations

Adm   Admiralty Papers, TNA

BCA   British Columbia Archives, Royal British Columbia Museum, Victoria

BT   Board of Trade Papers, TNA

DCB   *Dictionary of Canadian Biography / Dictionnaire bibliographique du Canada*

CO   Colonial Office Papers, TNA

FO   Foreign Office Papers, TNA

HBC   Hudson's Bay Company

HBCA   Hudson's Bay Company Archives, Archives of Manitoba, Winnipeg

HHB   Hubert Howe Bancroft Collection, Bancroft Library, University of California, Berkeley

LAC   Library and Archives Canada, Ottawa

MMBC   Maritime Museum of British Columbia, Victoria

NMM   National Maritime Museum, Greenwich, England

TNA   The National Archives, Kew, Surrey, England

Walbran   John Walbran, *British Columbia Coast Names* (1909)

Manuscripts, by Repository

British Columbia Archives and Records Service, Victoria

Government Papers GR-0771: Act of 13 May 1850 Regulating the Importation of Spirituous Liquor, issued by Richard Blanshard.

Blanshard, Richard. Papers

ZZ-97441, Commission with Great Seal, photo (partial) of.

MS-0611.9, Commission and Great Seal (original), dated 16 July 1849.

MS-0611, Commission and instructions, initialled by Queen Victoria.

MS-0611.4, Warrant and Letters Patent Vice Admiralty.

MS-0611, Official papers and correspondence of R. Blanshard.

MS-0611.7, R. Blanshard, will of and codicil January–February 1894, typescript.

MS-0611.8, Instructions, original, dated 16 July 1849 (initialled VR), also Warrant, original, dated 28 June 1849, to use Public Seal of Vancouver Island (signed Earl Grey), also List kept by Blanshard of Settlers from England on barque *Harpooner 1849,* barque *Cowlitz* 1850, *Norman Morrison* [sic] 1850, barque *Tory* 1851. Also, autograph letters. Also letters from Admiralty, Rear Admiral Phipps Hornby, Rear Admiral Fairfax Moresby, Bound Letterbook.

Instructions to, and correspondence with, J.S. Helmcken re: Fort Rupert, C/AA/10.4A/1.

MS-0611.10 Blanshard, Richard. First known photograph of.

A-01113, Blanshard, Richard. Later photograph of.

[Dally, Frederick] Memoranda of a trip round Vancouver Island... 1866. EBD16m.

Douglas, James, Papers

Various but mainly Letters to Hudson's Bay Company on Vancouver Island Colony, 1850–55, typescript. Originals in HBCA.

Register of Land Purchases from Indians. MS-0772. Now known as Vancouver Island treaties.

Great Britain. Colonial Office. Despatches to Vancouver Island, 21 July 1849–16 August 1858, C/AA/10.2/1A-3A.

Muir, Andrew. Private Journal or Diary.

Add MSS 1007 Robinson, Thomas. Journal.

C/AA/10.4/1, Vancouver Island—Governor's Correspondence Outward, June 22, 1850–March 5, 1859. Blanshard & Douglas.

Hudson's Bay Company Archives, Archives of Manitoba, Winnipeg

Fort Nisqually Journal. See Dickey, George, ed., entry below.

A 6 series: correspondence [available on microfilm LAC].

B 185/a/1: Fort Rupert Post Journal.

B 226/a: Fort Victoria Post Journal.

B 226/b: Fort Victoria Correspondence Books.

B 226/c: Fort Victoria Correspondence Inward.

National Maritime Museum, Greenwich

Phipps Hornby Papers, various items re: Royal Navy and Vancouver Island when Rear Admiral Sir Phipps Hornby was C-in-C Pacific, 1847–1850; see also Abraham P. Nasatir and Gary Elwin Monell, eds., *British Activities in California and the Pacific Coast of North America to 1860.* See Bibliography for full citation.

National Archives, Kew, Surrey

Adm 1 and 2. Respectively In-and Out- letters from Board of Admiralty to flag and other officers commanding HM Ships; also copies to other departments of state.

Adm 3/39. Service record, C.R. Johnson.

Adm 53/3837. HMSS *Driver*, ship's log, 3 January to 17 April 1850.

BT Board of Trade papers re: Vancouver Island.

CO 60. British Columbia. Original correspondence (with Home authorities), 1858–71. (Note: Entry Books, 1858–71, are listed under CO 338.). Correspondence with HBC, Law Officers of the Crown, Governors, and other departments of state.

CO 61. British Columbia. Acts, 1858–67.

CO 305. Vancouver Island. Original correspondence (with Home authorities), 1846–67 (Entry Books, 1849–77), listed under CO 410. Correspondence with HBC, Law Officers of the Crown, Governors, and other Departments, including Admiralty.

CO 306. Vancouver Island. Acts, 1852–66.

CO 307. Vancouver Island. Sessional Papers, 1864–66.

CO 308. Vancouver Island Government Gazettes, 1864–66.

University of California, Berkeley, Bancroft Library

Cooper, James. *Maritime Matters on the Northwest Coast and Other Affairs of the Hudson's Bay Company in Early Times*. 1878. P-C 6.

Finlayson, Roderick. *History of Vancouver Island and the Northwest Coast*. 1878. P-C 15.

Lawson, James S. *Autobiography*. 1879. P-A 44.

Palmer, General Joel. *Narratives*. 1878. P-C 58.

Warren, James Douglas. *Among the Indians of the Northwest Coast*. 1882. P-C 32.

Yale University Library, Beinecke Library, New Haven, CT

Western Americana, item 3. Docs. re: seizure British ship *Albion*, Puget Sound, 22 April 1850, for cutting spars on US side of the Strait of Juan de Fuca in violation of revenue laws 1849–1850.

Great Britain (arranged chronologically)

"Hudson's Bay Company. Return to an Address of the Hon. House of Commons, 26 May 1842. For: Copy of the Existing charter or grant by the Crown to the Hudson's Bay Company, together with copies or extracts of correspondence which took place at the last renewal of the charter…" House of Commons *Sessional Papers*, 1842, no. 547.

"Treaty between Her Majesty and the United States of America for the Settlement of the Oregon Boundary, signed at Washington, 15 June 1846." *Parliamentary Papers*. Cmd. papers (722). The Treaty of Washington, so designated; also known as the Oregon Boundary Treaty.

"Papers relating to the Colonization of Vancouver's Island," *Parliamentary Papers*, 1848.

[Foreign Office] *Warrant to prepare letters patent under the great seal for appointing Richard Blanshard, Esq., to be governor and commander-in-chief in and over the island of Vancouver and its dependencies.* London: printed at Foreign Office, 1849.

"Papers re: Vancouver's Island." *Parliamentary Papers, 1849,"* xxxv (House of Commons 103). Contains the Privy Council Report on Vancouver's Island, 31 October 1848, also reports of Royal Navy officers, the Charter of Grant in full, and corresp. with HBC.

"Vancouver's Island: Returns to Three Addresses the House of Commons, 16 August 1848, 6 February & 1 March 1849," *Parliamentary Papers,* House of Commons 103, 1849, 3–12.

"Vancouver's Island. Correspondence between the Chairman of the Hudson's Bay Company and the Secretary of State for the Colonies, Relative to the Colonization of Vancouver's Island" 1848, *Parliamentary Papers,* House of Commons, 1847–1848, House of Commons *Sessional Papers,* 619. Contains thirteen letters, some with enclosures, including J. Douglas's report on the Island in 1842 and the authorization for the Company to colonize it.

"Vancouver's Island. Return made since 1849 by the Hudson's Bay Company to the Secretary of State for the Colonies, relating to Vancouver's Island." *Parliamentary Papers,* House of Commons, 83.

"Correspondence Relative to the Discovery of Gold at Queen Charlotte Islands," 1853. *Parliamentary Papers,* House of Commons, 788.

"Further Correspondence Relative to the Discovery of Gold at Queen Charlotte's Island," 1853, *Parliamentary Papers,* House of Commons.

"Correspondence relative to the establishment of a representative Assembly at Vancouver's Island," *Parliamentary Papers,* 1857.

"Report from the Select Committee on the Hudson's Bay Company; together with the Proceedings of the Committee, Minutes of Evidence, Appendix, and Index [also map 1857]," *Parliamentary Papers,* House of Commons, 31 July and 11 August 1857 (Session II), xv, 224, 260. Also printed as *House of Lords Papers,* 197.

"Return to an Address of the Hon. House of Commons," dated 17 February 1859. Contains materials on E.E. Langford's charges.

Charters, Statutes, Orders-in-Council, etc. relating to the Hudson's Bay Company. London: for the Company, 1931.

Books and Articles

Akrigg, G.P.V., and Helen B. Akrigg. *H.M.S.* Virago *in the Pacific, 1851–1855: To the Queen Charlottes and Beyond.* Victoria: Sono Nis Press, 1992.

Allen, Charles. *Raj: A Scrapbook of British India, 1877–1947.* Harmondsworth: Penguin, 1979.

Sources

Anderson, Steve A., ed. *William Fraser Tolmie at Fort Nisqually: Letters, 1850–1853.* Pullman: Washington State University Press, 2019.

Annual Register 1849. London, 1849. Critique and defence of colonial policy re colonies generally, also Vancouver Island colonization (124–129).

Archives of British Columbia. *Report of Provincial Archives Department of the Province of British Columbia for the Year ending December 31, 1913.* Victoria, 1914. Contains colonization proposals.

Archives of British Columbia. *Memoir No. II: Minutes of the Council of Vancouver Island, 1851–1861,* edited by E.O.S. Scholefield. Victoria, 1918.

Ashby, Daryl. *John Muir: West Coast Pioneer.* Vancouver: Ronsdale, 2005.

Audain, James. *From Coalmine to Castle: The Story of the Dunsmuirs of Vancouver Island.* New York: Pageant Press, 1955.

Bach, John. *The Australia Station: A History of the Royal Navy in the South West Pacific, 1821–1913.* Kensington: New South Wales University Press, 1986.

Ballantyne, Robert Michael. *Snowflakes and Sunbeams; or The Young Fur-Traders.* London: Ward, Lock, 1856.

Bancroft, Hubert Howe. *History of British Columbia, 1792–1887.* 1887; reprint, New York: Arno, 1970.

Bancroft, Hubert Howe. *History of the Northwest Coast.* 2 volumes. San Francisco: History Company, 1884.

Bancroft, Hubert Howe. *History of Washington, Idaho, and Montana, 1845–1889.* San Francisco: History Company, 1890.

Barman, Jean. "Race, Greed, and Something More." In *On the Cusp of Contact: Gender, Space and Race in the Colonization of British Columbia,* edited by Margery Fee. Madeira Park: Harbour Publishing, 2020.

Begg, Alexander. *History of British Columbia from Its Earliest Discovery to the Present Time.* 1894; reprint, Toronto: McGraw-Hill Ryerson, 1972.

Bell, Kenneth, and W.P. Morrell, eds. *Select Documents of British Colonial Policy, 1830–1860.* Oxford: Clarendon Press, 1928.

Benedict, Ruth. *Patterns of Culture,* new ed. Boston: Houghton Mifflin, 1959.

Blakey Smith, Dorothy. "Thomas Blinkhorn." In *DCB,* vol. 8. University of Toronto/ Université Laval, 2003–. www.biographi.ca/en/bio/blinkhorn_thomas_8E.html.

Blakey Smith, Dorothy. *James Douglas, Father of British Columbia.* Toronto: Oxford University Press, 1971.

Blakey Smith, Dorothy, ed. *The Reminiscences of Doctor John Sebastian Helmcken.* Vancouver: UBC Press, 1975.

Boas, Franz. *Indian Myths and Legends from the North Pacific Coast of America,* translated by Dietrich Bertz; edited by Randy Bouchard and Dorothy Kennedy. Vancouver: Talonbooks, 2006.

Boas, Franz. *The Kwakiutl of Vancouver Island*. New York: G.E. Stechert, 1909.

Bowen, Lynne. "Independent Colliers at Fort Rupert: Labour Unrest on the West Coast, 1849." *The Beaver* 69, no. 2 (April/May 1989): 25–31.

Bowsfield, Hartwell, ed. *Fort Victoria Letters 1846–1851*. Winnipeg: Hudson's Bay Record Society, 1979.

Bridge, Kathryn. *Henry & Self: The Private Life of Sarah Crease 1826–1922*. Victoria: Sono Nis Press, 1996.

British Columbia. *Papers Connected with the Indian Land Question, 1850–1875*. Victoria: Queen's Printer, 1875.

Brown, Jennifer. *Strangers in Blood: Fur Trade Company Families in the Indian Country*. Vancouver: UBC Press, 1980.

Brown, Kevin. *The Seasick Admiral: Nelson and the Health of the Navy*. Barnsley: Seaforth, 2015.

Burns, Flora Hamilton. "Victoria in the 1850s." *The Beaver* 280 (December 1949): 36-39.

Cain, P.J., and A.G. Hopkins. *British Imperialism, 1688–2000*, 2nd ed. London: Longman, 2002.

Cell, John W. *British Colonial Administration in the Mid-Nineteenth Century: The Policy-Making Process*. New Haven, CT: Yale University Press, 1970.

Clayton, Daniel. "The Creation of Imperial Space in the Pacific Northwest." *Journal of Historical Geography* 26 (2000): 327–50. Reprinted in Samson.

Clayton, Daniel. *Islands of Truth: The Imperial Fashioning of Vancouver Island*. Vancouver: UBC Press, 2000.

Cline, Gloria Griffen. *Peter Skene Ogden and the Hudson's Bay Company*. Norman: University of Oklahoma Press, 1974.

Codere, Helen. *Fighting with Property: A Study of Kwakiutl Potlatching and Warfare, 1792–1930*. New York: American Ethnological Society, 1950.

Cook, Peter, Neil Vallance, John Lutz, Graham Brazier and Hamar Foster, eds. *To Share, Not Surrender: Indigenous and Settler Visions of Treaty-Making in the Colonies of Vancouver Island and British Columbia*. Vancouver: UBC Press, 2021.

Cotton, Peter Neive. *Vice Regal Mansions of British Columbia*. Vancouver: British Columbia Heritage Trust, 1981.

Coyle, Brian. "The Puget's Sound Agricultural Company on Vancouver Island, 1847–1857." Master's thesis, Simon Fraser University, 1977.

D'Arcy, Paul, general ed. *The Cambridge History of the Pacific Ocean*. 2 volumes. Cambridge: Cambridge University Press, 2023.

De Lorme, Roland L. "Policing the Pacific Frontier: The United States Bureau of Customs in the North Pacific, 1849–1899." Typescript of paper presented at the Pacific Northwest History Conference, Ellensburg, WA, 1977.

Sources

Dickey, George, ed. *The Journal of Occurrences at Fort Nisqually: Commencing May 30, 1833, Ending September 27, 1859.* Tacoma: Metropolitan Park District, 1988.

Donald, Leland. *Aboriginal Slavery on the Northwest Coast of North America.* Berkeley and Los Angeles: University of California Press, 1997.

Douglas, James. "Report of a Canoe Expedition along the East Coast of Vancouver Island [27 August 1852]." *Journal of the Royal Geographical Society* 24 (1854): 245–49.

Duff, Wilson. "The Fort Victoria Treaties." BC *Studies* 3 (Fall 1969): 3–57.

Dunbar-Ortiz, Roxanne. *An Indigenous Peoples' History of the United States.* Boston: Beacon Press, 2014.

Edmonds, Penelope. *Urbanizing Frontiers: Indigenous Peoples and Settlers in 19th-Century Pacific Rim Cities.* Vancouver: UBC Press, 2010.

Farrar, Victor J., ed. "Nisqually Journal." *Washington Historical Quarterly* 12 (1921): 146–220.

Finlayson, Roderick. *Biography.* Privately printed, 1891. Available online at University of British Columbia Library, open.library.ubc.ca/collections/bcbooks/items/1.0222287

Fisher, Robin. *Contact and Conflict: Indian-European Relations in British Columbia, 1774–1890,* 2nd ed. Vancouver: UBC Press, 1992.

Fitzgerald, James Edward. *Charter and Proceedings of Hudson Bay Company, with Reference to Vancouver's Island.* London: Simmons, 1849.

"Five Letters of Charles Ross, 1842–44." *British Columbia Historical Quarterly* 7, no. 2 (April 1943): 103–18.

Foster, Joseph. *Alumni Oxoniensis, 1715–1886.* 4 volumes. London, 1888.

Fraser, Greg N. *Joseph William McKay: A Metis Business Leader in Colonial British Columbia.* Victoria: Heritage House, 2021.

Friesen, Jean. "George Hills." In *DCB,* vol. 12. University of Toronto/Université Laval, 2003– . www.biographi.ca/en/bio/hills_george_12E.html.

Fuller, George W. *A History of the Pacific Northwest, With Special Emphasis on the Inland Empire,* 2nd ed. rev. New York: Knopf, 1966.

Galbraith, John S. "Conflict on Puget Sound." *The Beaver* 281 (March 1951): 18–22.

Galbraith, John S. *The Hudson's Bay Company as an Imperial Factor, 1821–1869.* Berkeley and Los Angeles: University of California Press, 1957.

Galbraith, John S. *The Little Emperor: Governor Sir George Simpson of the Hudson's Bay Company.* Toronto: Macmillan of Canada, 1976.

Galois, Robert. "Gold on Haida Gwaii: The First Prospects, 1849–53." *BC Studies* 196 (Winter 2017/18): 15–42.

Galois, Robert. *Kwakwa̱ka̱'wakw Settlements, 1775–1920: A Geographical Analysis and Gazetteer.* Vancouver: UBC Press, 2012.

Galois, Robert. "Measles, 1847–1850: The First Modern Epidemic in British Columbia." *BC Studies* 109 (Spring 1996): 31–43.

Gibson, James R. *Farming the Frontier: The Agricultural Opening of the Oregon Country, 1786–1846*. Vancouver: UBC Press, 1985.

Gibson, James, ed. *"Opposition on the Coast": The Hudson's Bay Company, American Coasters, the Russian American Company, and Native Traders on the Northwest Coast, 1825–1846*. Toronto: Champlain Society, 2019.

Gosnell, R.E. "Colonial History 1849–1871." In *The Pacific Province*. Volume 21 of *Canada and Its Provinces*, edited by Adam Shortt and Arthur G. Doughty. Toronto: Publishers Association, 1914.

Gough, Barry M. *Britannia's Navy on the West Coast of North America, 1812–1914*. Victoria: Heritage House, 2016. Revised, expanded and updated edition of *The Royal Navy and the Northwest Coast*.

Gough, Barry M. "Corporate Farming on Vancouver Island: The Puget's Sound Agricultural Company, 1846–1857." In *Canadian Papers in Rural History*, Volume 4, edited by Donald H. Akenson, 72–82. Gananoque, ON: Langdale, 1984.

Gough, Barry M. "Crown, Company, and Charter: Founding Vancouver Island Colony—A Chapter in Victorian Empire Making." *BC Studies* 176 (Winter 2012/13): 9–54.

Gough, Barry M. "Forests and Sea Power: A Vancouver Island Economy, 1778–1875." *Journal of Forest History* 12, no. 3 (July 1988): 117–24.

Gough, Barry M. *Gunboat Frontier: British Maritime Authority and Northwest Coast Indians, 1846–90*. Vancouver: UBC Press, 1984.

Gough, Barry M. "The Haida-European Encounter, 1774–1900: The Queen Charlotte Islands [Haida Gwaii] in Transition." In *The Outer Shores: Based on the Proceedings of the Queen Charlotte Islands First International Symposium*, edited by G.G.E. Scudder and N. Gessler. Vancouver: University of British Columbia, 1984.

Gough, Barry M. "The Imperial Web in the South Pacific." In *Pax Britannica: Ruling the Waves and Keeping the Peace before Armageddon*. London: Palgrave Macmillan, 2014.

Gough, Barry M. "Law and Empire: The Extension of Law to Vancouver Island and New Caledonia." *Western Legal History* 6, no. 2 (Summer 1993): 217–28.

Gough, Barry M. *The Northwest Coast: British Navigation, Trade, and Discoveries to 1812*. Vancouver: UBC Press, 1992.

Gough, Barry M. *The Royal Navy and the Northwest Coast of North America, 1810–1914: A Study of British Maritime Ascendancy*. Vancouver: UBC Press, 1971. New edition (2016), *Britannia's Navy*, cited above.

Gough, Barry M., ed. "Sir James Douglas as Seen by His Contemporaries: A Preliminary List." *BC Studies* 44 (Winter 1979–80): 32–40.

Sources

Gough, Barry M. "Walter Colquhoun Grant." In *DCB*, vol. 9. University of Toronto/ Université Laval, 2003– , www.biographi.ca/en/bio/grant_walter_colquhoun_9E. html.

Grant, Walter Colquhoun. "Description of Vancouver Island." *Journal of the Royal Geographical Society* 27 (1857): 268–320.

Grant, Walter Colquhoun. "Remarks on Vancouver Island, Principally Concerning Townsites and Native Population." *Journal of the Royal Geographical Society* 31 (1861): 208–13.

Grey, H.G., 3rd Earl. *The Colonial Policy of Lord John Russell's Administration.* 2 volumes. London: R. Bentley, 1853.

Harris, Cole. "The Native Land Policies of Governor James Douglas." *BC Studies* 174 (Summer 2012): 101–22.

Hazlitt, William Carew. *British Columbia and Vancouver's Island.* London: G. Routledge, 1858.

Helmcken, John Sebastian. "Fort Rupert in 1850." *Victoria Daily Colonist*, 1 January 1890.

Hendrickson, James E., ed. *Journals of the Council, Executive Council, and Legislative Council of Vancouver Island, 1851–1866. Volume 1 of Journals of the Colonial Legislatures of the Colonies of Vancouver Island and British Columbia, 1851–1871.* 5 volumes. Victoria: Provincial Archives of British Columbia, 1980.

Hendrickson, James E. "Richard Blanshard." In *DCB*, vol. 12. University of Toronto/ Université Laval, 2003– . www.biographi.ca/en/bio/blanshard_richard_12E.html.

Hendrickson, James E., ed. "Two Letters from Walter Colquhoun Grant." *BC Studies* 26 (Summer 1975): 3–15.

Howay, Frederic W., ed. *Voyages of the Columbia to the Northwest Coast, 1787–1790 & 1790–1793.* 1941; Portland: Oregon Historical Society, 1990.

Ireland, Willard E. "The Appointment of Governor Blanshard." *British Columbia Historical Quarterly* 8, no. 3 (1944): 213–26.

Ireland, Willard E. "Pre-Confederation Defence Problems of the Pacific Colonies." *Canadian Historical Association Report* (1941): 41–54.

Johansen, Dorothy O., and Charles M. Gates. *Empire of the Columbia: A History of the Pacific Northwest*, 2nd ed. New York: Harper & Row, 1967.

Johnson, Peter. *Voyages of Hope: The Saga of the Bride Ships.* Victoria: TouchWood, 2002.

Keddie, Grant. *Songhees Pictorial: A History of the Songhees People as Seen by Outsiders, 1790–1912.* Victoria: Royal British Columbia Museum, 2003.

Kemble, John Haskell, ed. "Coal from the Northwest Coast, 1848–1850." *British Columbia Historical Quarterly* 2, no. 2 (April 1938): 123–30.

Kemble, John Haskell. *The Panama Route, 1848–1869.* 1943; New York: Da Capo, 1972.

Kennedy, William R. *Sporting Adventures in the Pacific whilst in Command of the "Reindeer."* London: Sampson Low, 1876.

Kluger, Richard. *The Bitter Waters of Medicine Creek: A Tragic Clash between White and Native America.* New York: Knopf, 2011.

Lamb, W. Kaye. "The Census of Vancouver Island, 1855." *British Columbia Historical Quarterly* 4, no. 1 (January 1949): 51–58.

Lamb, W. Kaye. "The Governorship of Richard Blanshard." *British Columbia Historical Quarterly* 14 (January–April 1950): 1–40.

Lamb, W. Kaye, ed. "Four Letters Relating to the Cruise of the '*Thetis*' 1852–53." *British Columbia Historical Quarterly* 6, no. 3 (July 1942): 189–206.

Lamb, W. Kaye. "Some Notes on the Douglas Family." *British Columbia Historical Quarterly* 17 (January–April 1953): 42–43.

Layland, Michael. *The Land of Heart's Delight: Early Maps and Charts of Vancouver Island.* Victoria: TouchWood, 2013.

Layland, Michael. *A Perfect Eden: Encounters by Early Explorers of Vancouver Island.* Victoria: TouchWood, 2016.

Lincoln, Margarette. *Trading in War: London's Maritime World in the Age of Cook and Nelson.* New Haven, CT: Yale University Press, 2018.

Lowther, Barbara J., comp. *A Bibliography of British Columbia: Laying the Foundations, 1849–1899.* Victoria: Social Sciences Research Centre, University of Victoria, 1968. Continuation of Strathern (below).

Luard, H.R. *Graduati Cantabrigienses.* Cambridge: Alma Matris Academiae, 1934.

Lyon, David, and Rif Winfield. *The Sail and Steam Navy List: All the Ships of the Royal Navy, 1815–1889.* London: Chatham, 2004.

Lubbock, Basil. *Merchantmen under Sail, 1815–1932.* Greenwich: Society for Nautical Research, 1974.

Lutz, John. *Makúk: A New History of Aboriginal-White Relations.* Vancouver: UBC Press, 2008.

Macfie, Matthew. *Vancouver Island and British Columbia: Their History, Resources and Prospects.* London: Longman, Green, 1865.

Mackay, Douglas. "Men of the Old Fur Trade [Peter Skene Ogden]." *The Beaver* 269 (June 1939): 7–9.

Mackie, Richard. "Colonial Land, Indian Labour, and Company Capital: The Economy of Vancouver Island, 1849–1858." Master's thesis, University of Victoria, 1984.

Mackie, Richard Somerset. "The Colonization of Vancouver Island, 1849–1858." *BC Studies* 96 (1992–1993): 3–40. Reprinted in Samson.

Marshall, Daniel. Articles in *The Orca* on Fort Rupert, Suquash and treaties.

Martin, Robert M. *The Hudson's Bay Territories and Vancouver's Island with an Exposition of the Chartered Rights, Conduct, and Policy of the Honourable Hudson's Bay Corporation.* London: T. and W. Boone, 1848.

Sources

Mayne, Richard Charles. *Four Years in British Columbia and Vancouver Island: An Account of Their Forests, Rivers, Coasts, Gold Fields, and Resources for Colonization*. London: John Murray, 1862.

McKelvie, Bruce. "The Founding of Nanaimo." *British Columbia Historical Quarterly* 8 (July 1944): 169–88.

Meinig, Donald W. *The Great Columbia Plain: A Historical Geography, 1808–1910*. Seattle: University of Washington Press, 1968.

Mellor, George R. *British Imperial Trusteeship, 1783–1850*. London: Faber and Faber, 1951.

Merivale, Herman. *Lectures on Colonization and Colonies*, 2nd ed. London: Longman, 1861.

Meyer, Patricia, ed. *Honoré-Timothée Lempfrit, OMI, His Oregon Trail Journal and Letters from the Pacific Northwest, 1848–1853*. Fairfield, WA: Ye Galleon Press, 1985.

Mooney, James. *The Aboriginal Population of America North of Mexico*. Washington: Smithsonian, 1928.

Moresby, John. *Two Admirals: Sir Fairfax Moresby, John Moresby: A Record of a Hundred Years*. London: Methuen, 1913.

Morgan, Murray. *The Last Wilderness*. Seattle: University of Washington Press, 1976.

Morley, John. *Life of Gladstone*. 3 volumes. London: Macmillan, 1905.

Morrell, W.P. *British Colonial Policy in the Age of Peel and Russell*. Oxford: Oxford University Press, 1930.

Morris, James. *Heaven's Command: An Imperial Progress*. New York: Harcourt, 1973.

Morton, Arthur S. *History of the Canadian West to 1870–71*, ed. Lewis G. Thomas, 2nd ed. Toronto: University of Toronto Press, 1973.

Mouat, Jeremy. "Situating Vancouver Island in the British World, 1846–49." *BC Studies*, no. 145 (2005): 224–32.

Nasatir, Abraham P. "The Gold Rush and the British Navy, San Francisco, 1849." *Brand Book No. 6* (San Diego: San Diego Corral of the Westerners, 1979): 93–103.

Nasatir, Abraham P., and Gary Elwyn Monell, comps. *British Activities in California and the Pacific Coast of North America to 1860: An Archival Calendar Guide*. San Diego: San Diego State University Press, 1990.

Newsome, Eric. *The Coal Coast: The History of Coal Mining in B.C. 1835–1900*. Victoria: Orca, 1999.

Noble, Dennis. *The Coast Guard in the Pacific Northwest*. Washington DC: US Coast Guard, 1988.

Norcross, E. Blanche, ed. *Nanaimo Retrospective: The First Century*. Nanaimo Historical Society, 1979.

O'Byrne, W.R. *Naval Biographical Dictionary*. London, 1849.

Ormsby, Margaret A. *British Columbia: A History*. Toronto: Macmillan of Canada, 1958.

Ormsby, Margaret A. "Sir James Douglas." In *DCB*, vol. 10. University of Toronto/ Université Laval, 2003– . www.biographi.ca/en/bio/douglas_james_10E.html.

Papers in Connection with Crown Lands in British Columbia and the Title of the Hudson's Bay Company. Victoria: Queen's Printer, 1881.

Pearce, Roy Harvey. *The Savages of America: A Study of the Indian and the Idea of Civilization*, rev. ed. Baltimore: Johns Hopkins University Press, 1965.

Pemberton, Joseph Despard. *Facts and Figures Relating to Vancouver Island and British Columbia Showing What to Expect and How to Get There*. London: Longman, Green, Longman, and Roberts, 1860.

Perkins, Fern. "Graveyard Gleanings: The Building of Fort Victoria with the French Canadian and Metis Construction Crew." *Stories in Stone* (Old Cemeteries Society special number Fort Victoria 170 Years) 23, no. 1 (Spring 2013): 27.

Perkins, Fern. "Tombstone Tourist: A Journey back to the Early Years of Charles and Isabella Ross." *Stories in Stone* (Old Cemeteries Society, special number, Fort Victoria 170 Years) 23, no. 1 (Spring 2013): 23–26.

Perry, Adele. *On the Edge of Empire: Gender, Race and the Making of British Columbia*. Toronto: University of Toronto Press, 2001.

Pethick, Derek. *James Douglas: Servant of Two Empires*. Vancouver: Mitchell Press, 1969.

Pethick, Derek. *Men of British Columbia*. Saanichton: Hancock House, 1975.

Phillips, James W. *Washington State Place Names*. Seattle: University of Washington Press, 1971.

Phillips-Birt, Douglas. *The Cumberland Fleet: Two Hundred Years of Yachting*. London: Royal Thames Yacht Club, 1978.

Pike, Douglas. *Paradise of Dissent: South Australia, 1829–1857*, 2nd ed. Carleton: Melbourne University Press, 1967.

Poole, Francis. *Queen Charlotte Islands: A Narrative of Discovery and Adventure in the North Pacific*. London: Hurst and Blackett, 1872.

Ralston, Keith. "Miners and Managers: The Organization of Coal Production on Vancouver Island by the Hudson's Bay Company." In *The Company on the Coast*, ed. E. Blanche Norcross. Nanaimo: Nanaimo Historical Society, 1953.

Rich, Edwin Ernest. *The Fur Trade and the Northwest to 1857*. Toronto: McClelland and Stewart, 1867.

Rich, Edwin Ernest. *The History of the Hudson's Bay Company, 1670–1870*. 2 volumes. London: Hudson's Bay Record Society, 1958–59; also, 3 volumes. Toronto: McClelland and Stewart, 1960. I have used the London edition.

Sources

Rich, Edwin Ernest, ed. *London Correspondence Inward from Eden Colvile, 1849–1852*. London: Hudson's Bay Record Society, 1956.

Rickard, Thomas A. *Historic Backgrounds of British Columbia*. Vancouver: Wrigley for the Author, 1848.

Robinson, Leigh Burpee. *Esquimalt: "Place of Shoaling Waters."* Victoria: Quality Press, 1948.

Robinson, Ronald. "Non-European Foundations of European Imperialism: Sketch for a Theory of Collaboration." In *Studies in the Theory of Imperialism,* ed. Roger Owen and Bob Sutcliffe. London: Longmans, 1972.

Royle, Stephen. *Company, Crown and Colony: The Hudson's Bay Company and Territorial Endeavour in Western Canada*. London: I.B. Tauris, 2011.

Ruby, Robert H., and John A. Brown. *Indian Slavery in the Pacific Northwest*. Spokane: Arthur H. Clark, 1993.

Sage, Walter N. *Sir James Douglas and British Columbia*. Toronto: University of Toronto Press, 1930.

Samson, Jane, ed. *British Imperial Strategies in the Pacific, 1750–1900*. Volume 8 of *The Pacific World*. Aldershot: Ashgate Variorum, 2003.

Saw, Reginald. "Sir John H. Pelly, Bart." *British Columbia Historical Quarterly* 31, no. 1 (January 1949): 23–32.

Scholefield, E.O.S., and F.W. Howay. *British Columbia from the Earliest Times to the Present Day*. 4 volumes. Vancouver: S.J. Clarke, 1914. (Volume 1 by Scholefield; Volume 2, Howay; spines of bound edition say Howay and Scholefield).

Scott, Andrew. *The Encyclopedia of Raincoast Place Names: A Complete Reference to Coastal British Columbia*. Madeira Park: Harbour Publishing, 2009.

Scouler, John. "Observations on the Indigenous Tribes of the N.W. Coast of America." *Royal Geographical Society Journal* 11 (1841): 215–51.

Slater, G. Hollis. "Reverend Robert John Staines: Pioneer Priest, Pedagogue, and Political Agitator." *British Columbia Historical Quarterly* 14, no. 4 (October 1950): 187–240.

Stock, Eugene. *History of the Church Missionary Society*. 4 volumes. London: Church Missionary Society, 1889. Volume 2 contains relevant material.

Storey, Kenton. *Settler Anxiety at the Outposts of Empire: Colonial Relations, Humanitarian Discourses and the Imperial Press*. Vancouver: UBC Press, 2016.

Strathern, Gloria M., comp. *Navigations, Traffiques and Discoveries 1778–1848: A Guide to Publications Relating to the Area Now British Columbia*. Victoria: Social Sciences Research Centre, University of Victoria, 1970.

Suttles, Wayne, ed. *Northwest Coast: Handbook of North American Indians*, Volume 7. Washington: Smithsonian Institution, 1990.

Swan, James G. *The Northwest Coast or, Three Years' Residence in Washington Territory*. 1857; Seattle: University of Washington Press, 1972.

Tate, Cassandra. *Unsettled Ground: The Whitman Massacre and Its Shifting Legacy in the American West*. Seattle: Sasquatch, 2020.

Tennant, Paul. *Aboriginal Peoples and Politics: The Indian Land Question in British Columbia, 1849–1989*. Vancouver: UBC Press, 1990.

Thacker, Alan, and Elizabeth Williamson, eds. *A History of the County of Essex*, Volume 11: *Clacton, Walton and Friton*. London; Victoria History of the Counties of England, Institute of Historical Research, London University, 2012.

Tolmie, William Fraser. *The Journals of William Fraser Tolmie Physician and Fur Trader*. Vancouver: Mitchell, 1963.

Trevelyan, George Otto, ed. *Life and Letters of Lord Macaulay*. 2 volumes in one. New York and London: Harper & Brothers, 1876.

Trimble, William Joseph. *The Mining Advance into the Inland Empire*. 1914; Fairfield, WA: Ye Galleon Press, 1986.

Van Kirk, Sylvia. "Colonised Lives: The Native Wives and Daughters of Five Founding Families." In *Pacific Empires: Essays in Honour of Glyndwr Williams*, Alan Frost and Jane Samson, eds., 215–33, 313–16 (notes). Carlton South: Melbourne University Press, 1999.

Van Kirk, Sylvia. *Many Tender Ties: Women in Fur-Trade Society, 1670–1870*. Norman: University of Oklahoma Press, 1980.

Vancouver Island Despatches: Governor Blanshard to the Secretary of State, 26 December 1849 to 30 August 1851. New Westminster: Government Printing Office, 1863. Copy in Rare Books and Special Collections, UBC. Available online. Microfilm in BCA.

Wakefield, Edward Gibbon. *A View of the Art of Colonization, with Present Reference to the British Empire*. London: John Parker, 1849.

Wallace, W.S., ed. *John McLean's Notes of a Twenty-Five Years' Service in the Hudson's Bay Territory*. Toronto: Champlain Society, 1932.

Walbran, John T. *British Columbia Coast Names, 1592–1906: to Which Are Added a Few Names in Adjacent United States Territory, Their Origin and History*. 1909; Vancouver: J.J. Douglas, 1971.

Ward, John M. *British Policy in the South Pacific (1786–1893): A Study of British Policy in the South Pacific Islands prior to the Establishment of Governments by the Great Powers*. Sydney: Australian Publishing, 1948.

Williams, Glyndwr, ed. *Hudson's Bay Miscellany, 1670–1870*. Winnipeg: Hudson's Bay Record Society, 1975.

Williams, Glyndwr, ed. *London Correspondence Inward from Sir George Simpson*. London: Hudson's Bay Record Society, 1973.

Wise, John R. *The New Forest: Its History and Scenery*, introduction by John Lavender, 1883; Wakefield, Yorkshire: S.R. Publishers, 1971.

Index

Note: Page numbers in **bold** refer to photographs or illustrations.

Index

Index

Index